ROUTLEDGE LIBRARY EDITIONS: JEWISH HISTORY AND IDENTITY

Volume 1

THE JEWISH PRESENCE IN LATIN AMERICA

THE JEWISH PRESENCE IN LATIN AMERICA

Edited by
JUDITH LAIKIN ELKIN AND
GILBERT W. MERKX

Taylor & Francis Group

LONDON AND NEW YORK

First published in 1987 by Allen & Unwin Inc.

This edition first published in 2020
by Routledge
2 Park Square, Milton Park, Abingdon, Oxon OX14 4RN

and by Routledge
52 Vanderbilt Avenue, New York, NY 10017

Routledge is an imprint of the Taylor & Francis Group, an informa business

© 1987 Allen & Unwin Inc.

All rights reserved. No part of this book may be reprinted or reproduced or utilised in any form or by any electronic, mechanical, or other means, now known or hereafter invented, including photocopying and recording, or in any information storage or retrieval system, without permission in writing from the publishers.

Trademark notice: Product or corporate names may be trademarks or registered trademarks, and are used only for identification and explanation without intent to infringe.

British Library Cataloguing in Publication Data
A catalogue record for this book is available from the British Library

ISBN: 978-0-367-44247-7 (Set)
ISBN: 978-1-00-300850-7 (Set) (ebk)
ISBN: 978-0-367-90038-0 (Volume 1) (hbk)
ISBN: 978-0-367-90040-3 (Volume 1) (pbk)
ISBN: 978-1-00-302205-3 (Volume 1) (ebk)

Publisher's Note
The publisher has gone to great lengths to ensure the quality of this reprint but points out that some imperfections in the original copies may be apparent.

Disclaimer
The publisher has made every effort to trace copyright holders and would welcome correspondence from those they have been unable to trace.

The Jewish Presence in Latin America

Edited by

Judith Laikin Elkin

Gilbert W. Merkx

Boston
Allen & Unwin
London   Sydney   Wellington

Copyright © 1987 by Allen & Unwin, Inc.
All rights reserved.

Allen & Unwin, Inc.
8 Winchester Place, Winchester, MA 01890, USA

The U.S. Company of
Unwin Hyman, Ltd

P.O. Box 18, Park Lane, Hemel Hempstead, Herts HP2 4TE, UK
40 Museum Street, London WC1A 1LU, UK
37/39 Queen Elizabeth Street, London SE1 2QB, UK

Allen & Unwin Australia Pty Ltd
8 Napier Street, North Sydney, NSW 2060, Australia

Allen & Unwin (New Zealand) Ltd, in association with
Port Nicholson Press, Ltd
Private Bag, Wellington, New Zealand

Library of Congress Cataloging-in-Publication Data

The Jewish presence in Latin America.

(Thematic studies in Latin America)
Bibliography: p.
Includes index.
1. Jews—Latin America—Congresses. 2. Latin America—
Ethnic relations—Congresses. I. Elkin, Judith Laikin,
(Date)   II. Merkx, Gilbert W. III. Series.
F1419.J4J49   1987   305.8'924'08   86-26531
ISBN 0-04-497012-9 (alk. paper)

British Library Cataloguing in Publication Data

The Jewish presence in Latin America.
1. Jews—Latin America
I. Elkin, Judith Laikin   II. Merkx, Gilbert W.
980'.04924   F1419.J4

ISBN 0-04-497012-9

MANUFACTURED IN THE UNITED STATES OF AMERICA

Contents

Preface	**ix**
Acknowledgments	**xi**

I   INTRODUCTION

1
Jewish Studies as a Subject of
Latin American Studies   3
Gilbert W. Merkx

II   HISTORICAL ISSUES

2
Sephardic Immigration to Argentina
Prior to the Nazi Period   13
Victor A. Mirelman

3
Jewish Roots of Brazil   33
Anita Novinsky

4
**Latin America and the Jewish Refugees:
Two Encounters, 1935 and 1938**   45
Haim Avni

III   COMPARATIVE DIMENSIONS

5
Adaptive Strategies of Jews in Latin America   71
Robert M. Levine

6
Demographic Trends of Latin American Jewry   85
Sergio DellaPergola

7
The Origins of Zionism in Latin America   135
Haim Avni

8
Jewish Education in Latin America   157
Daniel C. Levy

IV   ADAPTATION AND EVOLUTION

9
Economic and Social Mobility of Jews in Brazil   187
Henrique Rattner

10
**Jews and the Argentine Center:
A Middleman Minority**   201
Bernard Segal

11
**Costa Rican Jewry:
An Economic and Political Outline**   219
Lowell Gudmundson

12
Capitalism, Socialism, and the Jews:
***The View from* Cabildo**   *233*
Carlos H. Waisman

V   *DEFINING A NEW IDENTITY*

13
Argentine Culture and Jewish Identity   *255*
Leonardo Senkman

14
Informal Jewish Education in Argentina   *271*
Israel Even-Shoshan

15
Culture, Identity, and Community   *285*
David Schers

16
Latin American–Jewish Writers:
Protecting the Hyphen   *297*
Saúl Sosnowski

17
The Evolution of the Latin American–Jewish Communities:
Retrospect and Prospect   *309*
Judith Laikin Elkin

List of Contributors   *325*

Index   *329*

Preface

The pioneering studies of Latin American Jewry presented in this volume have been selected from among papers presented at the Research Conference on the Jewish Experience in Latin America, held in Albuquerque, New Mexico on March 12–14, 1984. The conference was cosponsored by the Latin American Jewish Studies Association (LAJSA) and the University of New Mexico Latin American Institute, with the assistance of the National Endowment for the Humanities, the Mellon Foundation, the American Jewish Committee, the World Jewish Congress, and the Jewish community of Albuquerque.

Twenty-seven scholars from the United States, Israel, Argentina, Mexico, Brazil, and Peru participated in the conference. Three dozen other interested persons also attended, including members of LAJSA (whose annual meeting took place during the conference), representatives of Jewish organizations and of the Albuquerque Jewish community, and students, faculty, and staff of the University of New Mexico. Intense discussion and critical exchanges as well as camaraderie marked the sessions, reflecting the personal involvement of those present and the broad implications of the issues they addressed.

Scholarly research on Latin American Jewry has only recently come of age. In the fall of 1981 Meyer Bass, a retired Jewish community organizer, visited the Latin American Institute to suggest that a conference be organized on the subject of Latin America's Jews. His suggestion met with a favorable response from Gilbert W. Merkx, director of the Institute, given the Institute's interest in furthering knowledge of Latin America through the study of its ethnic minorities. Scholarly support came quickly from the newly-founded LAJSA through its president, Judith Laikin Elkin, as well as from Haim Avni, then Head of the Institute of Contemporary Jewry at Hebrew University in Jerusalem. Together, Merkx, Elkin, and Theo R. Crevenna, deputy director of the Institute, then began efforts to raise the necessary funds.

It soon became clear that the scholarly value of such a conference was not at all obvious to potential sponsors. Traditional funders of research on Latin America viewed the subject as a "Jewish" issue, while traditional funders of Jewish research viewed it as a "Latin American" issue. Thus, the search for financial support became an educational process in itself.

While the scholarly nature of the conference was never doubted by its planners, it soon became evident that more than scholarly issues were involved. Jewish communities in Latin America face fundamental questions regarding strategies for survival in the context of environments that frequently are hostile. While American Jewish organizations have been relatively outspoken in publicizing human rights violations affecting Jewish populations in Latin America, the leadership of local Jewish communities in the region have sometimes opted for a low-profile strategy in dealing with their own governing regimes. Moreover, the implications of the situation of ethnic minorities in Latin America have often been purposely ignored or denied by governments and overlooked by intellectuals concerned with matters salient to the dominant populations. Clarification of the relevance to Latin America of the status of its Jewish citizens was a primary outcome of the conference.

In the event, the high quality of the papers presented more than justified the scholarly expectations of its planners and sponsors, while the political ramifications drew the attention of the national press. We regret that space limitations prevent the inclusion of all the papers presented, but those appearing in this volume, all of which have undergone revision since the conference, may be regarded as representative. We hope that these studies will enrich our understanding of Latin America's societies and of its Jewish communities, while demonstrating the evolution and the maturity of current research on Latin American Jewry.

Judith Laikin Elkin
Ann Arbor

Gilbert W. Merkx
Albuquerque

Acknowledgments

This book has been made possible by the support and cooperation of many people. We would like in particular to thank the American Jewish Committee and its director for Latin American Affairs, Jacobo Kovadloff, for subvention of the editing of this volume. We are also most grateful to John L. Michel, former executive vice president, and Lisa Freeman-Miller, editor, of Allen and Unwin, Inc., for their encouragement of this project. Russell H. Till provided design and production services, and the staff of the University of New Mexico Latin American Institute helped with typing. Our special thanks go to the contributors to this volume, who, despite the problems of communicating across three continents and several languages, were understanding and always cooperative.

I
Introduction

1
Jewish Studies as a Subject of Latin American Studies

Gilbert W. Merkx

Introduction

The consideration of Latin America's Jewish communities as a subject of intellectual significance began with the 1972 Experts Conference on Latin America and the Future of Its Jewish Communities, held in New York under the auspices of the Institute of Jewish Affairs.[1] The conference was held at the end of the decade of rapid Latin American growth that preceded a sharp rise in petroleum prices. The Vietnam War was drawing to a close, and the preoccupations generated by that conflict were very much in evidence during the conference.

Although the experts at the conference decried the lack of basic research, assertions about the nature of the critical issues confronting Latin American Jewry were not lacking. Among the opinions expressed were that Jewish communities of Latin America were growing and numbered nearly one million people; that U.S. power in the region was shriveling in both relative and absolute terms; that Latin American nationalism was a growing and impressive force; and that the plight of Latin American Jewry was essentially the plight of Latin America's middle classes, threatened as national bourgeoisies were replaced by multinational corporations. Some participants argued that Latin American Jewry was a powerful and influential force, whereas others were concerned that the emergence of revolutionary vio-

---

1. *Proceedings of the Experts Conference on Latin America and the Future of Its Jewish Communities* (London: Institute of Jewish Affairs, 1973).

lence posed a threat to Jewish communities and proposed that those communities should identify with the forces of revolutionary change or be left behind by history. The only participant who took strong issue with the dominant views expressed at the conference was Natan Lerner, who argued that the marginality of Latin American Jewry had increased considerably over the previous decade.[2]

By the mid-1980s it had become evident that the dominant views expressed by the experts in 1972 were symptomatic of the period rather than predictive of the future. With the advantage of hindsight, it can be said that the minority viewpoint of Natan Lerner was essentially accurate. Latin American Jews are far less numerous than was previously believed, and the survival of most Jewish communities in the region can be considered problematic. Latin America in the decade after 1972 was dominated not by the forces of revolution, but by the institutionalization of repression and reaction. The power of the United States did not fade, but was increasingly exercised. Nationalism as a determinant of public policy was replaced by neo-orthodox economic liberalism. Multinational corporations faded as the villains of underdevelopment, to be replaced by the international banking system. The challenge to the survival of Jewish communities during the decade came not from social upheaval and nationalism, except in the case of Nicaragua, but rather from the larger conditions of life in Latin American societies.

The studies presented in this volume, which are revisions of works originally presented at the 1984 Research Conference on the Jewish Experience in Latin America, reflect both the growth of basic research on Latin American Jewry in the years since the Experts Conference and the newer preoccupations that concern students of Latin America.[3] As do all ethnic studies movements, research on Latin American Jewry represents in considerable measure a means to self-knowledge; therefore, a major proportion of the scholars contributing to this new field are themselves of Latin American Jewish origin. Other researchers, particularly those from Israel, approach the field from the perspective of comparative studies of world Jewry.[4] A third group of scholars view research on Latin American Jewry as

---

2. See the comments by Natan Lerner on pp. 125–131 of *Proceedings of the Experts Conference*.

3. This field of research has been greatly stimulated by the Latin American Jewish Studies Association, which was founded in March 1982, during the Washington meetings of the Latin American Studies Association. LAJSA held its first research conference in October 1982, the proceedings of which are reported in Judith Laikin Elkin, ed., *Resources for Latin American Jewish Studies* (Ann Arbor: LAJSA, 1984).

4. The work of Professor Haim Avni and his associates at the Institute for Contemporary Jewry of the Hebrew University in Jerusalem has been particularly noteworthy in this regard.

offering a fresh perspective on Latin America itself. All three views are represented in the present volume.

From the third perspective just mentioned, that of the Latin Americanist, two questions naturally emerge: What has been the role of Jews as actors in the ongoing processes of Latin American economic, social, and political change? What does the experience of Jewish minorities in Latin America reveal about the character of Latin American society?

The Jewish Role in Latin America

Although Jews were certainly present as *Marranos* or *Conversos* (converts to Christianity) among the Iberian colonists of the New World, they were not significant as communities in colonial Latin America except in Curaçao, Brazil, and (for a brief time) Peru. These early communities were largely absorbed by their host societies, as were the individual Jews scattered throughout the rest of colonial Latin America. When the larger waves of Mediterranean and Eastern European Jews arrived in Latin America at the end of the nineteenth century, they numbered far fewer than other migrant populations. Only in Argentina and Uruguay did the Jewish populations approach or slightly surpass 1% of the total population. In the rest of Latin America, Jews never constituted as much as 0.1% of the population.[5]

Where Jews were able to penetrate the higher social classes, as in the case of Portuguese Jews in Venezuela and the Dominican Republic or of the Alsatian Jews in Mexico, they were eventually assimilated by those upper classes and they lost their identity as Jews. In those countries such as Argentina and Uruguay where Jewish communities were sufficiently numerous to sustain organized community life, such cultural manifestations as Jewish theater and literature had little impact on the national culture. The contrast with the broad influence and popular acceptance of Jewish literature in the United States is noteworthy.

Nor have Jews been a significant political force in Latin America, either collectively or as individuals. Despite the concentration of Jews in the professions such as law and medicine from which many Latin American politicians have been drawn, Jewish politicians have been more notable by their absence than by their presence. Only in Argentina, Uruguay, and Brazil have some Jews had political careers. Although Jews have at various times

---

5. The author is greatly indebted to information provided in Judith Laikin Elkin, *Jews of the Latin American Republics* (Chapel Hill: University of North Carolina Press, 1980), and in the papers presented at the 1983 Research Conference on the Jewish Experience in Latin America.

and in various countries occupied important ministerial positions, they have been appointed for their technical skills rather than their political influence.

In economic terms, the Jewish experience in Latin America has been more successful, compared with that of native populations. The individual and collective social mobility of Jews has been high, leading to impressive proportions of professionals and entrepreneurs in the Jewish community. In this respect Jews have played a useful role in the economic development and modernization of Latin America. Yet the larger significance of this Jewish role should be qualified by noting that in no important sector of economic activity have Jews been dominant. Moreover, other immigrant populations have also provided entrepreneurial and professional talent to Latin America. Whether Jewish social mobility in Latin America has been any more spectacular than that of the Japanese, German, or Lebanese communities is an open question. It would be difficult to argue that the overall course of Latin American economic development would have been markedly different in the absence of Jewish migration.

The most visible aspect of the Jewish presence in Latin America has been as the symbolic target of national animosities. The anti-Semitism of medieval Catholic imagery continues to permeate popular culture in Latin America. Anti-Semitism remains a major theme in the nationalist diatribes of the extreme right and its military allies. Ironically, the extreme left in Latin America has also become increasingly anti-Semitic, because of links between guerrillas in Latin America and terrorist groups in Europe and the Middle East.

The most interesting aspects of the Jewish role in Latin America are therefore not related to the importance of that role in shaping modern history. Instead, two paradoxes command attention. The first reflects the discrepancy between the relative success of Jews in climbing the social ladder and their continuing political and ideological marginality. The second concerns the contrast between the relatively minor historical role of Jews and their exaggerated importance in the contemporary myths of popular Latin American culture. The causes and consequences of these two paradoxes offer new insight into the nature of Latin American societies.

Latin America from the Perspective of the Jewish Experience

It was once commonplace to observe that history tends to reflect the views of the victors, political science the study of the powerful, and economics the study of the successful. More recently the previously accepted visions of North American history and society have been redefined by the advent of ethnic, women's, and labor studies and the rise of minority perspectives in the social sciences. Yet for Latin America, as for much of the Third World, such a reconceptualization exists as potential rather than as actuality, pushed aside by the conflict over national destinies, the search for national identities, and the accumulation of national resentments. The Jewish experience, that of a quintessential minority, gives a view of Latin American social reality that is missing from the perspectives of either the dominant classes or the majority populations.

The Jewish experience in Latin America is particularly interesting when compared with Jewish experiences in the United States and Israel, cases with differing relationships between Jewish identity and national identity. In the United States, Jewish identity and national identity are discrete and unrelated. One is no less an American and no more an American for being Jewish, and no more or less Jewish for being an American. In Israel, Jewish identity and national identity are coterminous; being Jewish confers citizenship. In the Latin American republics, national identity and Jewish identity have been antithetical, contradictory, or problematically related, at least in the eyes of the majority populations. Precisely because Jewishness is problematic in Latin America but not in the other two cases, that problematic nature is attributable not to the character of Jewry or Jewish communities but to the character of Latin American societies.

The features that characterize Latin American Jewish communities present a profile that differs in several respects from those in the United States and Israel. Prior national origin and culture have retained their saliency for Latin American Jewish communities, whether they be Sephardic, Alsatian, German, Eastern European, Moroccan, or Turkish, although some observers report a blurring of lines in the younger generation.[6] The relatively hostile environment of Latin America has not produced the cooperation among these groups that might have been expected. Greater separation and social distance appear to mark ethnic boundaries within the Jewish communities of Latin America than in those of North America, with less social, religious, or marital crossing of community lines.

Latin American Jewish communities are also marked by a far more conservative religious tradition than are their counterparts in the United States or Israel. Assimilation to the host culture is more likely to result in the severing of ties to the Jewish community, and intermarriage with non-Jews has a similar result. Outmigration of Jews from Latin America is far higher than in the U.S. case. Jewish social mobility upward in the class structure and horizontally toward major population centers has led to less social integration of Jews in national society, except for those who abandon Jewish identity.

One hypothesis that can be advanced to explain the Latin American

6. I am indebted to Professor Elkin for this observation.

outcome is that it reflects the greater significance of social class distinctions in Latin America. Latin American economies are marked not only by a lower level of aggregate income than those of the developed nations, but also by more sharply skewed income distributions, by monopolistic and clientelistic domination of certain sectors of economic activity, and by more particularistic avenues for social mobility. These factors tend to increase the social distance between classes, the value attached to higher status, and the importance of insider community networks. The significance of the economic and class distinctions that cultural differences among Jewish communities of different national origins have produced in the process of adapting to Latin America may therefore override the influence of a common religious inheritance.

The greater salience of class distinctions in the Latin American context, in combination with the monopolistic and clientelistic features of the economy, can also be advanced as factors contributing to the conservatism and inner-directedness of Latin American Jewish communities. As outsiders in social contexts marked by family and patronage networks, Latin American Jews are forced to a greater extent than are Jews in the United States to rely on the contacts and networks of their own communities. The substitution of intragroup for intergroup networks also contributes to the lack of cooperation among Jewish communities.

The isolation of Latin American Jewish communities may also reflect those features of Latin American politics that have precluded the emergence of Jews as politicians. If ethnic communities are to be a factor in national politics, either as collectivities or through the advancement of their representatives, incentives for political participation must exist. In stark contrast to the United States and Israel, where ethnically based appeals and alliances characterize politics, Latin America is marked by the absence of ethnic politics. Jewish communities generally remain apolitical with respect to the larger society, failing to generate political leaders who serve a broker function in delivering the ethnic vote in return for trade-offs. When Jews do take up political careers, which has happened occasionally in Brazil, Uruguay, and Argentina, they do so not as Jews representing an ethnic constituency but as nationals appealing to the non-Jewish vote.

The risks of political involvement by minority communities are high in societies in which democratic regimes are fragile and subject to replacement by authoritarian regimes. Achievements obtained according to rules of competitive democracy are only as lasting as the democratic regime itself. Almost as fragile are the protections afforded by legal systems and their rights and procedures, which are liable to suspension by authoritarian regimes. The instability of democratic regimes in Latin America has been a continuing disincentive to minority political participation and a factor contributing to the climate of uncertainty that hangs over Jewish communities and reinforces their political marginalization.[7]

Political instability is nevertheless an insufficient explanation for the lack of Jewish political activity in Latin America. Although Jews are a numerically tiny proportion of the Latin American population, one might expect their visibility in the middle-class professions of some republics to suggest a concomitant visibility in public affairs. The absence of such visibility reflects at least two factors: (1) prejudice specifically directed against Jews and (2) the culture of Latin American political discourse, in which minority concerns are generally missing from political agendas.

The persistence of anti-Semitism in contemporary popular Latin American culture contrasts remarkably with the decline of such prejudice in Europe and the United States. The roots of anti-Semitism in the medieval Christian tradition are clear, but far less apparent are the reasons for the survival of such stereotypes in countries and among groups in which Catholicism is actively practiced by only a small proportion of the populace. Analogous to anti-Semitism, but without similar religious origins, is the persistence of other ethnic stereotypes hostile to supposedly foreign elements, as expressed in the extensive lexicon of terms such as *turco, chino, gachupín, indio,* and *gringo.* The pervasive hostility and suspicion with which minorities are characterized in Latin American popular culture and the reluctance to extend national identity to minority group members appear to reflect more than inherited prejudice and Catholic tradition.

The Latin American suspicion of outsiders has been attributed by anthropologists to the weakness of national institutions that treat citizens universalistically; dependence on familistic and clientelistic in-group networks comes to be relied on as the only safe resource.[8] The weakness of national institutions also contributes to a more modern aspect of Latin American culture: the increased access to knowledge about the developed world. This so-called demonstration effect leads to a widespread sense of national inferiority with respect to the developed nations, not only among Latin Americans but throughout the underdeveloped world. In Latin American popular culture, Jews are associated with international capital, with high levels of achievement in the developed countries, and with the success of Israel as an outpost of capitalism in the Middle East. Hence Latin Ameri-

---

7. For an eloquent statement of these issues, see Leonardo Senkman, "Latin American Jewry between Revolution and Reaction," *Jewish Frontier* (March 1981), 10–13.

8. Eric R. Wolf and Edward C. Hansen, *The Human Condition in Latin America* (New York: Oxford University Press, 1972). See especially pp. 200–204 and 350–358. A more recent analysis will be available in L. Roniger, *Hierarchy and Trust in Modern Mexico and Brazil* (Albuquerque: University of New Mexico Press, in press).

can Jews, implicitly stripped of their citizenship in the Latin American republics, become surrogates for nationalistic resentments.

If the link between anti-Semitism and resentment born of underdevelopment is correct, one would expect the persistence of discrimination to be inversely correlated with the extent of economic development. This appears in fact to describe the Jewish experience in Latin America. Jews fare better in the great metropolitan cities than in the provinces and better in countries with successful growth records than in those whose economies have stagnated or remained underdeveloped. Particularly interesting in this regard is the contrast between the deteriorating situation of the large Jewish community in Argentina and the contemporaneous improvement in the situation of Jews in Brazil.

The impressive development of the Brazilian economy from 1964 to 1980 and Brazil's emergence as an important regional power seem to have coincided with a growth in national self-esteem and a reduction in anti-Semitism. The situation of Mexican Jews seems to have improved for similar reasons. Yet in one of those ironic twists of fate that so often have affected Latin America, the Brazilian and Mexican economies are now suffering major setbacks that might undermine the self-confidence of the citizenry and hence increase xenophobia.

Conclusion

The future of Latin America's Jewish communities appears problematic at best. The highly stratified and particularistic nature of Latin American society has sustained national cultures that tend to be hostile toward all minority groups, with a particular animosity to those with foreign linkages. This context has in turn contributed to the conservatism and insularity of Jewish communities in the region. Maintaining both Jewish and national identity in such a context is a major problem for Latin American Jewry.

Necessary preconditions for the improvement of civic life in Latin America and a concomitant lessening of prejudice against outsiders include the resumption of economic growth and the consolidation of pluralistic democracy. Although progress toward democracy is evident, the short-run prospects for economic growth in Latin America are bleak, given low commodity prices and the size of the region's external debt. The remainder of the 1980s will be a period of little economic growth for Latin America, and democratic institutions will remain fragile. National resentments are more likely to increase than to abate. Thus the factors that have led to the decline of Jewish communities will remain in place. The dilemma of Latin American Jewry remains inextricably tied to the dilemma of Latin American development.

II
Historical Issues

2
Sephardic Immigration to Argentina Prior to the Nazi Period

Victor A. Mirelman

Moroccan Jews in Argentina

On April 2, 1888, Elías J. Abejdid was born in Buenos Aires. His parents, Isaac Elías Abejdid and Sol Abejdid, had his name inscribed in the register of births of Congregación Israelita de Buenos Aires a year later. The father had been in Buenos Aires only a short time. Born in Tetuán, Morocco, in 1857, he lived for some time in Gibraltar and in Portugal. At the age of twenty, he obtained a Portuguese passport and left for Rio de Janeiro, where in 1884 he was naturalized as a Brazilian. A year later, still in Rio, he started a commercial partnership with Manoel Antonio Osorio. At the beginning of 1887 he traveled to Santos, an important port further south.[1]

The story of Isaac Elías Abejdid could well be that of many other Moroccan Jews who left their hometowns and native lands during the nineteenth century to seek their fortunes in the New World. A majority of those who finally settled in Buenos Aires or in cities and towns of the Argentine interior followed a pattern similar to that just described. Most came from the Moroccan coastal cities, especially Tetuán, but also from Tangier and Larache. Most were young men—some in their teens—who later returned home to marry. Many then returned to South America, where they prospered in commerce. As they left Morocco, some settled in Oran, Algeria, and

---

1. Congregación Israelita de la República Argentina (hereafter CIRA), *Registro de Nacimientos*, 168; Egon and Frieda Wolff, *Os Judeos no Brasil imperial* (São Paulo: 1975), 263–264.

others in Gibraltar or in various Spanish or Portuguese cities. The wave of immigration to South America went first to Brazil, including cities in the north such as Belém but mainly to Rio, then the capital. Later, some of these Jews continued on to other areas of the continent, including the Amazonian towns of Belém and Manáos in Brazil and Iquitos in Peru. Others moved to Caracas, or south to Montevideo or Buenos Aires. Thus, many of the Moroccan Jews to be found in Buenos Aires in the 1880s had previously tried their fortunes in Brazil for varying periods of time. Only after 1880 was there a direct migratory current of Jews from Tetuán and Tangier to Argentina.

During the last three decades of the nineteenth century, a considerable number of Moroccan Jews, unsettled by the Spanish–Moroccan wars of 1859–1860, made their way to Argentina. Local Jews, who had suffered pillage and massacre at the hands of their Muslim neighbors on the eve of the Spanish conquest of Tetuán, welcomed the Spaniards as saviors. The Spanish occupation was relatively benign for the Jews, but it lasted just two years. With the departure of the Spanish on May 2, 1862, the Moroccan reaction provoked the departure of many Jews from Tetuán. During the 1860s the majority left for Algiers, especially to the city of Oran, but a growing number migrated to other areas of Spanish Morocco, including Tangier, Ceuta, and Melilla, and others settled in Gibraltar, Spain, and Portugal. Latin America, and especially Brazil at this early stage, attracted the most venturesome.[2]

Jewish emigration from the coastal communities of Morocco was more pronounced than immigration from the interior. In cities such as Meknes and Fez, contact with European culture and commerce was limited, whereas in Tangier and Tetuán there was constant interchange with Europe. This induced many, especially the young, to try their fortunes abroad.[3]

There were differences between the two larger coastal cities, Tangier and Tetuán, that explain why most emigrants came from the latter. The Jews of Tangier, as Michael Laskier wrote, "were not as economically impoverished as their counterparts in Tetuán. Even among the poorer segments of the Tangier community, one could engage in commercial activities of this strategic commercial port. . . . In Tetuán, on the other hand, there was [sic] hardly any important industries or commercial activities, and local Jews were in fact leaving town."[4] Poverty—lack of jobs and opportunity—

2. Sarah Leibovici, "Tétouan: une communauté éclatée," *Les Nouveaux Cahiers* 59 (Winter, 1979–80): 13–14; Isaac Benchimol, "La langue espagnole au Maroc," *Revue des Ecoles de l'Alliance Israélite*, (Paris) 2 (July–Sept., 1901): 127.

3. Michael Laskier, *The Alliance Israélite Universelle and the Jewish Communities of Morocco: 1862–1912* (New York: 1983), 86.

4. Laskier, *Alliance*, 64.

proved to be the most compelling motivation to seek amelioration of their condition abroad.

The creation of the Alliance Israélite Universelle (AIU) schools in Tetuán (1862) and Tangier (1864) contributed enormously to the development of a new generation of Jews imbued with the spirit of progress. These schools played a central role in the modernization of Jewish communities in the coastal cities, more so than in the interior where religious traditionalism was more deeply rooted and opposition from rabbis and leaders more intense. The graduates of AIU spoke Spanish, French, and some English; they had been exposed to European mores, customs, and dress; and they were motivated to reap the benefits of modern civilization. The AIU schools also taught students modern crafts and skills in the hope of changing the occupational structure of the Jewish communities. However, in the period up to World War I no significant change took place in this area. Most young Moroccan Jews opted for either commerce or emigration as the best alternatives to escape poverty. Those who emigrated were "mainly from Tetuán, Larache and Elksar; some were from Tangier and fewer from Fez and Marrakesh. Many emigrants were in their teens."[5]

Even the graduates of AIU schools opted to emigrate because of the sparse economic opportunities in their hometowns. According to AIU reports, of the 417 boys who graduated from the Tetuán school between 1862 and 1869, 182 (43.6%) emigrated; 104 of these opted for Algeria, 41 for Spain (including Ceuta, Melilla, and the Canary Islands), and 11 went to Brazil.[6] Those settling in Brazil tended to remain several years, returning with fortunes to Tetuán or moving to other South American countries, principally because of the suffocating heat, yellow fever epidemics, insects, and so on.[7] Figures for Tangier for the period 1875–1879 show a trend of emigration to Algeria, Spain, Portugal, and Brazil.[8]

Studies by Robert Ricard, Sara Leibovici, and Laskier indicate that during the 1880s and after, "the emigration trends from the north, particularly from Tetuán, apparently gained additional momentum.... Whereas before 1880 more emigrants from Tetuán went to Algeria and Spain, the trend during the 1880s was more towards Latin America."[9] In his report on the AIU schools for 1884–1885, David Cazès wrote:

---

5. Laskier, *Alliance,* 133.
6. Laskier, *Alliance,* 134; see also Leibovici, "Tétouan," 16.
7. Robert Ricard, "Notes sur l'emigration des Israélites marocaines en Amérique espagnole et au Bresil," *Revue Africaine* (Algiers) 88, Nos. 1–2 (1944): 84–85.
8. Laskier, *Alliance,* 135.
9. Laskier, *Alliance,* 135–136.

The school of Tetuán has only worked for export.... 95% of the students emigrate.... Today Algeria is not enough for this activity, and they go to Spanish America. There is a large number in Caracas, in Colon, in Panama, in Paramaribo, in Buenos Aires; some established themselves in the United States, they are in New York, Baltimore, Philadelphia, etc.[10]

The emigrants were Spanish-speaking Jews who were naturally attracted by countries where their mother tongue, or a similar one such as Portuguese, was spoken. Most were young, between twelve and thirty years of age, and fleeing the oppressive and sterile atmosphere of the *mellah*, or Jewish neighborhood, hoping to improve their condition in new and free countries.[11]

The first Moroccan Jews to arrive in Buenos Aires were most likely to be young men traveling by themselves or with a relative or friend, seeking to establish themselves in commerce there. Historical documents in Argentina testify to their presence in the early 1870s. However, documentation concerning the emigration of Jews from the Moroccan communities reflects the intention of emigrants to settle in Brazil, whereas no mention is made of Argentina until well into the 1880s.[12] Thus, it can be inferred that Jews found Argentina an alternative only after a sojourn in Brazil. Marcos Esnaty, for example, had moved with his parents from Gibraltar to Pernambuco (present-day Recife) in the mid–1860s. Around 1870 he migrated to Buenos Aires, where he prospered in the stock market, real estate, and ranching. Though Esnaty married a Christian woman, he maintained contact with other Jews in Buenos Aires. Probably owing to his intermarriage, he was not active in the Jewish life of the city, then in its formative stage.[13]

Isaac Benchetrit (also Benjetrit), a native of Tetuán, was in Buenos Aires early in 1880. He had probably moved there after a few years' sojourn in Montevideo, because his son, born in the latter city in mid–1878, was circumcised on January 11, 1880, in Buenos Aires. Dr. Aquiles Modena, an Italian Jewish physician who had been performing the rite in Buenos Aires since 1874, also circumcised Benchetrit's second son (to our knowledge the first Sephardic Jew born in Buenos Aires) on June 12, 1881, ten days

10. David Cazès, "Rapport sur les écoles de l'alliance de Tanger et de Tetuán," *Bulletin de l'AIU* (hereafter *BAIU*) (1884–1885): 52.
11. *Association des anciens élèves de l'Alliance Israelite Universelle, Bulletin Annuél* (Tangier) 8 (1900): 13–17; Ricard, *Notes,* 84. For Larache, see Eugene Aubin, *Le Maroc d'aujourd'hui,* 6th. ed. (Paris: 1910), 91, where he asserts: "Parmi les juifs, quelques negociants et beaucoup d'artisans; un movement d'emigration vers l'Amérique du Sud commence a se dessiner dans la communauté qui est pauvre et peu organisée."
12. Leibovici, "Tétouan," 20.
13. Bernard Ansel, "The Beginnings of the Modern Jewish Community in Argentina 1852–1891," Ph.D. dissertation, University of Kansas, 1969, 145–146.

after his birth.¹⁴ By 1882 a J. Benchetrit, either a relative of the aforementioned Isaac or someone else of Moroccan origin, advertised his Turkish cigar shop, centrally located at 205 Maipú Street in Buenos Aires.¹⁵

At the time the only Jewish organization in Buenos Aires was the incipient Congregación Israelita, a synagogue founded in 1862 by Western and Central European Jewish merchants. Its purpose was to hold religious services, especially for the high holy days; to provide assistance to coreligionists who were either sick or in need; and to care for burial arrangements. During the 1870s and 1880s some Moroccan Jews established links with these Europeans, becoming members of the Congregación and taking leadership positions.¹⁶

The presence of the Eljarrat family of Morocco is documented in the minute books of the Congregación. Both Isaac and Abraham Eljarrat were among officials of the synagogue in 1873. Fifteen years later Lazaro Eljarrat, age thirty-two, married a Moroccan compatriot, Sultana Bensimon, age fifteen, at the Congregación Israelita.¹⁷

During the late 1880s a few more Moroccan Jews joined: José Benzaquén in 1885; Samuel Sotto on January 25, 1886; Alberto Cohen and Luis Bernal on June 15, 1886; and A. Amsalem and a someone known only as Laluche attended the General Assembly of September 20, 1888.¹⁸ Some of these men attained prominence in the small circle of the Congregación and were asked to join its board of directors. Sotto was voted in as a board member on July 29, 1886, and again on March 3, 1889; Benzaquén was elected secretary of the board at the annual assembly in 1890.¹⁹

Most of the Moroccans, however, did not join the Congregación Israelita. Preferring to socialize among their own, they gathered for religious services at private homes. To register a birth or to perform a Jewish wedding, they approached Rabbi Henry Joseph of the Congregación Israelita. Joseph, an English businessman, had been accredited by the Chief Rabbi of France, and was recognized by the Argentine government in 1883 as the

---

14. A. Modena, "La Circoncisioni a Buenos Aires," *Vessillo Israelitico* (Casale–Monferrato: 1883), 352. Dr. Modena spelled the name Benjetrit, probably phonetically in his native Italian. Ansel, "Beginnings," 147, registered Samuel Levy (born in Dec. 1886) as the first recorded Sephardi born in Argentina. There may have been a few other Sephardic births between 1881 and 1886.

15. See the advertisement in *The Standard* (Buenos Aires), 4 Feb. 1882, 2. The ad appeared daily from February through September 1882.

16. Victor A. Mirelman, "Jewish Life in Buenos Aires before the East European Immigration," *American Jewish Historical Quarterly* 67 (March 1978): 195–207.

17. CIRA, *Asambleas*, 1873; CIRA, *Registro de Casamientos*, 8.

18. CIRA, *Minutes*, 25 January 1886, 15 June 1886, and 30 September 1888.

19. CIRA, *Minutes*, 29 July 1886, 3 March 1889, and 7 September 1890.

official registrar of births, marriages, and deaths among Jews. Thus Abraham Levy, who after living in Gibraltar and Brazil settled in Buenos Aires around 1883 with his wife Tamar, registered the birth of their son Samuel on December 10, 1886, at the Congregación Israelita. One of the witnesses was Abraham's brother Haim, who had also settled in Buenos Aires.[20] Two other births to Moroccan families were registered by Rabbi Joseph. One was the aforementioned Elías Abejdid, witnessed by José Benzecri,[21] a Moroccan, and Luis Ullman, a European Jew who performed the circumcision. The other was Solomón Benzaquén, son of Isaac and Mesody Benzaquén, born February 4, 1888, witnessed by José Elías Mamán and Jacob Mesod Benshimol, all Moroccan immigrants. Moreover, four weddings among Moroccan Jews took place at the Congregación between October 1886 and September 1891. The families involved and the families of the witnesses indicate the presence of a substantial number of Moroccans in Buenos Aires.

By the end of the 1880s, Moroccan Jews were numerous enough in the Argentine capital to warrant organizing their own communal institutions. In 1888, León Serfaty, a Tetuánese residing in Buenos Aires, was charged by Abraham Ribbi, the director of AIU schools in Tetuán, to propagandize the work of the AIU among his fellow immigrants. A branch of the AIU was constituted in 1892, led by conspicuous members of the Congregación Israelita, and correspondence between Ribbi and Serfaty indicates that a Tetuánese group was taking shape in Argentina.[22]

On January 15, 1889, José Elías Mamán, one of those involved in promoting Jewish causes, petitioned the Ministry of Justice and Religion for authorization to establish a synagogue of the Spanish and Portuguese rite. Mamán, who styled himself in the petition as "rabbi," evidently was requesting the right to perform marriages according to the traditions of his community. Up to November 2 of the preceding year, when the Law of Civil Marriage was passed, all marriages had been in the hands of the Catholic church. Religious authorities of non-Catholic creeds required special authorization from the ministry to perform marriages among their coreligionists. Apparently it took some time for the civil registers to start complying with

---

20. Interview with Samuel de A. Levy, March 1972. Samuel was active in most Sephardic institutions in the city, and by means of his journal *Israel*, founded in 1917, kept in contact with the communities in the interior of Argentina and other South American countries, as well as with the Jewish communities in Morocco itself. His birth was registered at CIRA, *Registro de Nacimientos*, 167.

21. Most probably the same José Benzecri living in Rio de Janeiro in 1886, where he had established a commercial partnership with David Amram and Samuel Nahon, selling clothes and fabrics. Wolff and Wolff, *Judeos*, 246.

22. Leibovici, "Tétouan," 20.

the new legislation, prompting the Moroccan Jews to obtain a special permit.[23]

At the same time, efforts were made to reach an understanding with the leadership of the Congregación Israelita that would take note of the specific ritual needs of the Moroccan Sephardim. In 1889 Isaac Benchetrit wrote to the Congregación Israelita as representative of a group of Sephardim, attempting to establish whether it would be agreeable to hold separate services for the two groups and also asking for separate representation.[24] From sparse documentation, we infer that compromise between the two groups was not feasible because of their differences in ritual practice. The Moroccans continued celebrating their services in private homes. By 1891 the important daily *La Prensa* reported the celebration of the high holy days and the festival of Sukkot at a private home at 810 Moreno Street. The services were led by the aforementioned Haim (Jaime) Levy.[25] The following month, on November 15, 1891, they formally founded their own synagogue, Congregación Israelita Latina. The board was formed of Moisés Benzaquén, president; Abraham Benchetrit, vice president; Samuel Cohen, secretary; Samuel Sotto, treasurer; and Salvador Levy, Abraham Levy, Solomón Benmuyal, Isaac Benchetrit, Lazaro Eljarrat, and David Benyanes, members-at-large. Most of the members of this first board had previously been associated with the Congregación Israelita.[26]

Ritual differences and the growth in numbers of Moroccan Jews were the main reasons for founding separate congregations. Indeed, there was no major personal rift; the leaders of both congregations maintained cordial relations and collaborated on various projects. In 1894 Achille Levy, the president of the Congregación Israelita as well as of the Committee of Friends of the AIU, noted with satisfaction the involvement of Samuel Sotto, Salvador Levy, and Salomón Benmuyal, respectively president, vice president, and acting rabbi of the Congregación Israelita Latina, in the work of the AIU. Achille Levy considered them an influential element and arranged to have Sotto and Benmuyal appointed as officers of the Alliance Committee. He stated that "I wanted very dearly that Mr. Sotto become part of the Committee for I know that before long he will bring a contingent of 100 adherents as active members."[27] Sotto continued leading the Moroccan

23. *Informes de los consejeros legales del poder ejecutivo,* vol. 8 (Buenos Aires: 1900), 224. For the marriage question in Argentina and how it affected the Jews, see Mirelman, "Jewish Life," 200–203.
24. CIRA, *Minutes,* 14 April 1889.
25. *La Prensa,* 16 November 1891, 6.
26. CIRA, *Cartas Recibidas,* 1 (1891): 12; CIRA, *Minutes,* 25 November 1891.
27. Leibovici, "Tétouan," 20.

congregation for many years, and also contributed to the work of the AIU, especially with respect to his native community of Tetuán.[28]

At the same time these developments were occurring, the Jews of Buenos Aires were at work on a common need: the acquisition of land for a Jewish cemetery. Delegates from the three main groups—the Congregación Israelita of Western European Jews, the Congregación Israelita Latina of Moroccan Jews, and Poale Zedek, a society of recently arrived Russian Jews—began meeting together in September 1893, and constituted a Jewish Burial Society. The Moroccans were represented by Sotto, Benmuyal, Salvador Levy, and Leon Serfaty. Benmuyal, as acting rabbi, assisted at the burial rites of members of his community; he was elected vice president of the new society. Once more, some controversies ensued because of conflicting burial customs. Notwithstanding the continued good relations between the groups, the Moroccans founded a separate burial society, Guemilut Hasadim, in 1897, acquiring a lot in Avellaneda, just outside the city limits.[29]

During the 1890s and up until World War I the flow of Jews from Morocco to Argentina continued unabated. With the founding of the Jewish Colonization Association (JCA) and the launching of its agricultural colonies, another type of emigration of Moroccan Jews, more systematic but less numerous, was promoted by the AIU: that of teachers for the colonies' Jewish schools. In April of 1895, four graduates of the École Normal of Paris left for Argentina.[30] In 1899, the Association des Anciens Élèves de l'Alliance à Tanger reported with elation that the subsidies for emigration to Latin America, usually limited to two people, had been considerably augmented. That year they were able to send twelve young candidates: five to Buenos Aires, two to Caracas, two to Belém, and one each to Maracaibo, Valparaiso, and Iquitos. Similar efforts were made in Smyrna (Turkey) by an analogous association, which, at its own cost, sent young people who had been educated at the AIU school there and "who do not always find a remunerable job in their own town."[31] By the end of the century there were twenty schools in the JCA colonies, all directed by graduates of the AIU schools in European Turkey, Smyrna, and Morocco. The advantage they had over teachers trained in other countries was their knowledge of Ladino and

---

28. In 1895 Sotto, as president of the Congregación Latina, sent £20 sterling for the Jewish victims of cholera in Tetuán through the AIU; see Leibovici, "Tetouan," 20. In 1894, 80 new adherents from Buenos Aires were registered at the AIU, among them several Moroccans; see *BAIU* (1894): 141, 153–154.

29. Sociedad de Entierros, *Minutes,* 26 Sept. 1893, 3 Oct. 1893, 10 July 1894, 16 Sept. 1894; Chevra Keduscha, *Minutes,* 11 Feb. 1894 and 18 Feb. 1897.

30. *BAIU* (1894): 66.

31. As quoted in *BAIU* (1899): 118–119.

Spanish, which enabled them to teach the program required by the Argentine education authorities.

The leadership of the AIU actually stimulated emigration from the poverty-stricken communities of Morocco. In their eyes the *oeuvre d'emigration* was justified by both its material and its educational values. Moroccan Jewry, with enormous pockets of misery and deficient education, benefited from the prosperity that many emigrants attained in Latin America. The AIU therefore sought to impart to its students the skills they needed for success abroad. A movement to encourage some alumni to emigrate to Senegal and Sudan, then under French domination, had little success. Evidently Latin American societies, modeled after those of Spain and Portugal, were more attractive than those of Black Africa.[32] Encouragement, moreover, was forthcoming from those already in Argentina. Isaac Benchimol, who had been teaching for a number of years at the Mauricio colony of JCA, wrote in 1901 that Jewish emigration to South America was proving to be beneficial to the Jewish population of Tetuán. Letters describing economic success or visits to the city of birth after success has been attained had an impact on those who had not yet moved. They "did away with poverty, lifted morale . . . and developed individual initiative." Benchimol urged the school authorities of AIU to introduce the teaching of Spanish at schools in the interior of Morocco, where Jews spoke Arabic. This would provide students with an additional tool in case they contemplated migrating to Latin America, for "Latin America needs hands."[33]

Several of the Tetuánese Jews who resided for considerable periods in Argentina attained distinction in world affairs. David Cazès (1851–1913) was a historian and educator who held positions of prominence in several Alliance schools in the Middle East, Smyrna, and North Africa. He was also director of the JCA in Buenos Aires for a decade (1893–1904).[34] Samuel D. Levy was born in the *mellah* of Tetuán in 1874; he attended the AIU school there and later the École Normale of the AIU in Paris. In 1891 he was sent to Tangier as assistant director. He directed the AIU schools in Tunisia and in Casablanca until he joined the JCA, when he spent a decade in Mauricio in the Province of Buenos Aires as teacher, manager, and social worker. Upon his return to Casablanca prior to World War I, Levy dedicated his efforts to Jewish affairs there. A leading Zionist, he repeatedly represented Moroccan Jewry in international and Zionist congresses.[35]

32. *BAIU* (1898): 102; (1899): 118–119; and (1901): 98–99.
33. Benchimol, "Langue espagnole," 133.
34. *The Jewish Encyclopedia*, s.v. "Cazès, David"; H. Avni, *Argentina, "Ha-Aretz ha-Yeuda* (Argentina, "The Promised Land") (Jerusalem: 1973), index (in Hebrew).
35. Laskier, *Alliance,* 219–222.

In 1905, according to the calculations of Samuel D. Levy, reporting from Mauricio, there were 3000 Sephardim in Argentina; 750 of these were in Buenos Aires. Almost all were Moroccan, for "85 percent are Tetuánese, and the rest from Gibraltar, from Tangier of the Moroccan coast, and Turks."[36]

Within a few years, most Moroccan Jews created good economic situations for themselves in Argentina. Far from trying to restrict the immigration of more of their fellow countrymen, they made every effort to bring to the new latitudes their families, relatives, and friends. Usually these relatives stayed with those who had first arrived until they became acquainted with conditions in the new country. After that they would go to a city or town in the interior and establish a branch of the main house in Buenos Aires. An eyewitness reported at the turn of the century that he knew "some Moroccan merchants established in Buenos Aires and having up to five, six, and even eight branches of their commerce disseminated in the main centers of the Republic."[37]

A census conducted by Rabbi Samuel Halphon in 1909 confirms this. In the town of Villaguay, Province of Entre Ríos, there were only twelve Jews: a Russian family of six, five young men from Tetuán, and a widow who was also from Tetuán. The five Tetuánese men were managers of branches of stores owned by compatriots in Buenos Aires. The owners had become rich selling fabrics, linens, and clothing and were now wholesale dealers. In the town of Gualeguaychu, in the same province, Halphon noted the presence of three Russian Jewish families, one French family, and five single Moroccan Jews. A decade earlier there had been other Moroccan Jews there, but they had left for Buenos Aires. Others came later, and in turn left their places to more recent arrivals from Morocco: "It's a chain without end."[38]

Halphon's study also shows that the Moroccans were the first Jewish settlers in many cities of the interior; some established themselves as early as the 1880s, though the majority arrived later.[39] The first Moroccan Jews arrived in the city of Santa Fe in the 1880s. Although they remained a small community (11 families of 79 people in 1909), they had acquired a cemetery by 1895. Moroccan Jews also established themselves in rural towns along the railroad tracks west of Santa Fe, from La Sabana to Calchaqui. Halphon counted 62 families and 96 single persons for a total of 358 Moroc-

---

36. Pulido Fernández, *Españoles sin patria y la raza sefardi* (Madrid: 1905), 643–644.
37. *Benchimol*, "Langue espagnole," 128; M. L. Ortega, *Los Hebreos en Marruecos* (Madrid: 1919), 301–302 quotes the same.
38. Samuel Halphon, "Enquête sur la population israélite en Argentine," *Jewish Colonization Association* (1909): 285.
39. Halphon, "Enquête," 303–304.

can Jews in these country towns. They ran general stores selling fabrics, haberdashery, shoes, and the like. Their knowledge of Spanish contributed to their commercial success, but Halphon noted that in spite of the fact that almost all were graduates of the AIU schools, they lived in close contact with their Argentine countrymen and ended up abandoning many religious practices. For circumcisions and for Passover needs, however, they resorted to the Jewish community of Santa Fe. They also buried their dead in that city. In the towns of Villa Maria and Rio Cuarto (both in the Province of Córdoba) and Villa Mercedes and San Luis (in the Province of San Luis), as well as further west in Mendoza, Moroccan Jews settled in the final decades of the nineteenth century.[40]

In Buenos Aires the Moroccan Jews preferred to settle to the south of the city, in Barrio Sur. By 1905 they had established two additional small congregations: Hes Hayim at 738 Venezuela Street, just two blocks away from the Congregación Latina at 594, and Chaar Achamayim at 420 Junín Street in the Once neighborhood. In 1905 members of Hes Hayim formed their separate burial society, Hesed Ve'emet, acquiring a portion of the cemetery previously bought by Guemilut Hasadim.[41] From the sources cited, as well as from documentation available at the archives of the Congregación Israelita Latina and Ets Ajaim in Rosario (also Moroccan), we infer that the Moroccans wandered into the interior of Argentina in larger proportions than did other Jewish immigrants.

In the interbellum period there was constant immigration of Jews from Tetuán and other areas of Morocco, though in more limited numbers than Eastern European Jews.[42] An indication that the absolute numbers of Jews arriving from Morocco were dwindling is given by the 1936 census of the city of Buenos Aires. It showed just 420 persons born in Morocco, Spain, Tangier, Algeria, Gibraltar, Portugal, and Tunis who declared themselves to be Jewish. All the rest of the Moroccan community, numbering in the thousands, had been born in Argentina, some to Argentine parents. That the immigration of families with small children was almost nil is indicated by the fact that only 5 of the foreign-born Moroccan Jews were under the age of fifteen.[43]

For a few Moroccan Jews, emigration to Argentina was only tempo-

40. Halphon, "Enquête," 251–310.
41. Pulido Fernández, "Españoles," 644; see also the *Minutes* of Hesed Veemet, which start in 1905 upon its inception.
42. See Ricard, "Notes," 86, where, based on data obtained from the French consulate in 1929, the following numbers for emigrants from Morocco to Argentina are given: 1924: 50; 1925: 43; 1926: 36; 1927: 45, indicating that most of them were Jewish.
43. *Municipalidad de la Ciudad de Buenos Aires, Cuarto Censo General (Oct. 22, 1936)*, vol. 3 (Buenos Aires: 1939), 310–323.

rary. They came back home after achieving economic stability, in some cases after ten years but sometimes even after thirty. Many among the returnees had adopted Argentine citizenship because an Argentine passport provided some protection in unstable Morocco. Thus, in 1927, out of 95 Argentines who depended on the consul general of Argentina in Rabat, 79 (83%) were naturalized citizens who had been born in Morocco.[44] Such was the case of Jacobo Bibas, vice consul of Argentina in the Spanish protectorate of Morocco in 1935, who was born in Tangier and then lived in Rosario in the Province of Santa Fe, where he was active in local Jewish organizations.[45]

Jews from the Ottoman Empire

In addition to the Moroccan emigration, a second Sephardic migration developed from the Ottoman Empire toward the end of the nineteenth century. The financial debacle of the Empire left a strong imprint on the population as a whole, Jews included, as a result of the impoverishment of communities with little mineral wealth and no industrial development that were constantly threatened with overpopulation.[46] Christians and Muslims were the first to leave, followed by the Jews. People from Beirut, Aleppo, and Damascus, as well as from Istanbul and Smyrna, left for Egypt, Western Europe, the United States, and several of the Latin American republics.

Christians and Muslims from the Ottoman Empire preceded Jews into Argentina by more than a decade. By 1887 an English Jew living in Córdoba remarked that the country was suitable for Jewish settlement; this suitability was strictly limited to members of the agricultural class "because itinerant vendors have no chance here on account of the many Arabs who are to be

44. Ricard, "Notes," 87.
45. Isaac Laredo, *Memorias de un viejo tangerino* (Madrid: 1935), 434. Other cases of Jews from Tangier who moved to Buenos Aires are found on pp. 279 and 461. Bibas had been on the board of the Banco Comercial Israelita in Rosario and president of the Bene Kedem, a Sephardic Zionist organization founded by the Keren Hayesod delegate, Ariel Bension, in 1927.
46. Abraham Galante, *Histoire des Juifs de Rhodes, Chio, Cos, etc.*, (Istanbul: 1935), 81; A. Galante, *Histoire des Juifs d'Anatolie. Les Juifs d'Izmir (Smyrne)*, vol. 1 (Istanbul: 1937), 161–162; A. Galante, *Histoire des Juifs d'Istanbul*, vol. 2 (Istanbul: 1942), 119; David de Sola Pool, "The Levantine Jews in the United States," *American Jewish Yearbook* (1913–1914): 209; Walter Paul Zenner, *Syrian Jewish Identification in Israel*. Ph.D. dissertation, Columbia University, New York, 1965, 1–98, describes the economic, social, political and religious situation of the Jews in Aleppo and Damascus during the later decades of the nineteenth century and the first of the twentieth; see also Philip K. Hitti, *The Syrians in America* (New York: 1924), 48–52.

Table 2.1
Syrian Immigration to Argentina, 1890–1908

Years	Syrian immigrants to Argentina	Average per year
1890–1895	1,485	247
1896–1900	8,394	1,678
1901–1905	15,591	3,118
1906–1908	23,669	7,889

Source: Compiled from data found in *Guía Assalam, Edicion Arabe-Castellano*, Buenos Aires, vol. 3 (1909), 4, based on official immigration reports.

seen (Mohametans) selling Christian beads and crosses and every other article that is saleable."[47]

Catholics of the Maronite rite started fleeing Syria and Lebanon during the 1880s because of the persecutions they were subject to at the hands of Muslims and other sects. The liberal immigration laws of Argentina attracted a substantial number of these. According to official reports, what started as a limited migration rapidly developed into an impressive flow (see Table 2.1). The actual number of Syrian immigrants in 1908 was 9056. Some eyebrows were raised at this influx. The otherwise liberal and open-minded daily *Buenos Aires Herald* wrote in 1898 that "ethnographists would do well to watch the immigration returns. Are we becoming a Semitic republic? The immigration of Russian Jews is now the third largest on the list, whilst Syrian Arabs (Turcos) and Arabians are also flocking to these shores. The last two races are, however, Christians."[48]

The vast majority of Syrian immigrants became peddlers, a fact that soon came to concern the Ministry of Agriculture and Department of Immigration. The latter considered that "the Syrian immigrants do not represent an efficient economic and social factor. . . . their role as consumers is minimal; and as producers their role is null."[49] Moreover, their commerce as peddlers, far from being beneficial, implied excessive competition to small businessmen. In 1889 the Department of Immigration urged the govern-

47. *Jewish Chronicle* 13 May 1887, 6. Juan Bialet-Masse, *El estado de las clases obreras argentinas a comienzos del siglo* (1904; reprint, Córdoba: 1968), mentioned *turcos* and Jews as peddlers in the Chaco (p. 135) and *turcos* in La Rioja (p. 178), Mendoza (p. 562), and San Juan (p. 595) also as peddlers and petty merchants.

48. *Buenos Aires Herald*, 5 July 1898, 2.

ment to take measures to attract the Syrians to occupations more compatible with the needs of the country, such as agriculture. Maronite Reverend Kassab attempted unsuccessfully to influence his parishioners in this direction.[50] In 1906 Wadi and Alejandro Schamun, editors of the Arabic-language journal *Assalam*, published in Buenos Aires, alerted their Syrian fellow immigrants to the danger implied in dedicating themselves exclusively to small commerce and peddling. In cooperation with the Department of Immigration, some Syrians were placed in agricultural colonies, especially in the Province of Santa Fe. But most Syrians, Christians and Jews alike, remained small merchants and peddlers.[51]

Prejudice against Syrians is clear in the above-mentioned report. It is quoted here because it also reflects the attitude toward Jewish Syrians and Turks who followed the Maronites to Argentina and who also began as peddlers and petty merchants. In the eyes of the general population, there was little difference between a Maronite and a Jewish Syrian: All were called *turcos*.

Jews started to emigrate from all areas of the Ottoman Empire at the end of the nineteenth century. At first they went to Egypt; although a small number moved on from there to Palestine, most then opted for the New World. Economic factors were the main impulse. The small communities in southeastern Turkey, as well as the large centers of Damascus and Aleppo in Syria, suffered from the diversion of international trade to the newly opened Suez Canal and the subsequent demise of the caravan trade through their own communities.[52] Jews from Aleppo and Damascus in particular, who had previously represented English companies trading in cotton and woolen cloth, went to Manchester starting in the nineteenth century and remained there as merchants dealing in these wares. The new center of Syrian Jews in Manchester stayed in touch with the numerous new communities of compatriots mushrooming in America, especially in New York (Brooklyn) and Buenos Aires.[53]

Most Ottoman Jewish immigrants to Argentina settled in Buenos Aires. Those who originated in the same city tended to stay together, forming

---

49. *República Argentina, Ministerio de Agricultura, Memoria Presentada al Honorable Congreso por el Ministro de Agricultura Dr. Wenceslao Escalante, Enero 1899–Octubre 1900* (Buenos Aires: 1900), 137–138.

50. *República Argentina, Ministerio de Agricultura Dr. Wenceslao Escalante, Enero 1899–Octubre 1900* (Buenos Aires: 1900), 133–141.

51. *La Prensa*, 10 May 1907; *La Nación*, 7 May 1907.

52. Hayyim J. Cohen, *The Jews of the Middle East, 1860–1972* (Jerusalem: 1973), 76, 99–100.

53. Joseph A. D. Sutton, *Magic Carpet: Aleppo-in-Flatbush* (New York: 1979), 5.

nuclei resembling their home communities. At the turn of the century, Ladino-speaking Jews from Smyrna, Constantinople, and other areas settled along the streets 25 de Mayo and Reconquista, not far from the port. By 1904 they were numerous enough to found their first charitable society, the Hermandad.[54] The same year, a recently arrived Jew from Aleppo wrote to his family that he had found many acquaintances from his home town. They took rooms in the Once district, still a center of Aleppine Jewish life.[55] Damascene Jews arriving in Buenos Aires during the same period settled in the area of Boca and Barracas, a populous zone of predominantly Italian (especially Genoese) immigrants.[56] Old World ties thus proved important in determining patterns of settlement among Sephardic Jews, as they were for other immigrant groups.

Jews left Ottoman territories in larger numbers during the first decades of the twentieth century. Two factors weighed heavily with them: letters enthusiastically describing peaceful Argentina, with its liberal laws and economic possibilities, and the 1908 revolution of the Young Turks. Aimed at securing constitutional government, the revolution paradoxically worked hardship on Jews and Christians by introducing compulsory military service. Until that time, Jews and Christians had paid a special exemption tax to avoid conscription into the army. Because serving in the army meant added difficulty in supporting a family and interfered with strict religious observance, escaping the draft became a force propelling Jews out of the empire.[57] Nevertheless, many Jews did serve during the Balkan wars and World War I. Though some served with distinction and many died, following the collapse of the empire many more deserted and sought to migrate. These wars affected some Jewish communities more directly than others. The city of Adrianople, on the border of Turkey, Greece, and Bulgaria, suffered especially from the hostilities. The resulting political instability there and the rule of the Greeks in many other cities of western Tur-

---

54. *Habima Haivrit* 1(6) (1921): 11–12; B. Issaey, "La colectividad sefardí bonaerense en el quinquenio 1958–1962," in *Pinkas fun der Kehila* (Buenos Aires: 1963), Spanish section, 46; minutes from Hessed Shel Emet (an organization formed around the synagogue Es Ajaim at 25 de Mayo 696), 19 August 1917.

55. Nissim Teubal, *El inmigrante, de Alepo a Buenos Aires* (Buenos Aires: 1953), 68–69, 79–80.

56. Alberto Massri, president of Asociación Unión Israelita Sefaradí "Luz Eterna," in a speech commemorating the fiftieth anniversary of the institution, 1970.

57. De Sola Pool, *Levantine Jews*, 209; Zenner, *Syrian Jewish*, 53–54; Hitti, *Syrians*, 51. During World War I many Jews served in the Turkish army. At the end of the war some of them deserted and fled. Zenner, p. 54 tells of a Syrian Jew who fled to Jebl-el-Druze and later to Argentina.

key—Smyrna in particular—led to the flight of thousands of Jews, many of whom migrated to Argentina.[58]

Not all the Jews who arrived in Argentina from the Ottoman Empire had chosen South America as their final destination. Take the case of three Aleppine Jews who left for the United States in 1904. Barred because of trachoma from entering the United States, they changed their route to Argentina, where they could disembark without documentation.[59] On the other hand, some emigrants preferred Argentina from the start. Such was the case of a family that migrated at the beginning of the century from Aleppo to Cairo. The head of the family left for the United States just prior to World War I, but finally resolved, on the instigation of friends in Buenos Aires, to settle in that city.[60] Others came to Argentina after several years elsewhere. For example, Syrian Jews who had migrated to Haiti at the turn of the century left Port-au-Prince because of rising anti-Semitism. A group of these proceeded directly to Buenos Aires.[61] For different reasons, Syrian Jews who had lived in Manchester moved to Buenos Aires in the course of their trade in woolen and cotton cloth between the two cities.[62] Argentina, especially its capital city, was always considered to be a major possibility when choosing a country to which a Jew could emigrate. Ezra Garazi, who settled in New York in 1911, confirmed this when he reminisced, "I chose New York because it was reported that to peddle in Argentina one had to carry a heavier satchel than in New York."[63]

The first young men to arrive from Ottoman territories clearly intended to return home once they had earned enough money to live comfortably. The desire to reintegrate themselves into the closely knit family and community life of their early years weighed heavily on them. They were not *golondrinas*—those southern European (mostly Italian) farm workers who came annually to Argentina to harvest the crops and then returned to their homes in Europe.[64] Turkish and Syrian Jews had in mind other ways of making a living: in commerce. But the process of capital accumulation took years because they started from the bottom, peddling in the streets of Buenos Aires or towns in the interior. With heavy loads of cloth and other types of merchandise they made their rounds all day long. A few could not

---

58. Cohen, *Jews*, 76, 97.
59. Teubal, *Inmigrante*, 68; Sutton, *Magic Carpet*, writes that most of those rejected because of trachoma went to Buenos Aires (p. 8).
60. Interview with Jacques Mizrahi, Buenos Aires, 7 April 1972.
61. *Jewish Chronicle*, 12 August 1904, 19; Teubal, *Inmigrante*, 84.
62. Teubal, *Inmigrante*, 83–84.
63. Sutton, *Magic Carpet*, 13.
64. R. Foerster, *The Italian Migration of our Times* (Cambridge, Mass.: 1924), 261–262.

endure the effort and their longing for family and friends impelled them to sail home.⁶⁵ But the majority stayed. Nissim Teubal, who left Aleppo in 1906 at the age of fifteen to join his brother Ezra in Buenos Aires, wrote in his memoirs:

> In the proximities of Buenos Aires, I made a type of covenant with myself. When I shall have earned, I said to myself, the first 300 pounds, I shall return to Aleppo, and in Aleppo I will be considered a Croesus. . . . But when Buenos Aires was in sight, I increased the sum. Three hundred pounds was too little; I would wait until I had five hundred. That sum continued growing. I needed more and more. Mad with enthusiasm and ambition, I said to myself that I would not return to Aleppo other than with a real fortune.⁶⁶

But Nissim and his brother never returned to Aleppo. In 1910 they brought their parents, brothers, and sisters to Buenos Aires. So it was with most of the Ottoman Jews. The revolt of the Young Turks, the Balkan wars, and finally World War I, with the disruption of trans-Atlantic travel and the dismemberment of the Ottoman Empire, produced a radical change in the mentality of the Jewish emigrant. Jews now left for the Americas with the intent of making their permanent homes there. Those who went to Argentina had ample knowledge of conditions in the country. Many already had relatives and friends there; they were assured of jobs until they could start their own businesses.

Ashkenazic Jews who had arrived from the various areas of Eastern Europe as well as Sephardim from Morocco and the Ottoman Empire all organized communal institutions. The decision on the part of each group to buy cemetery lots indicated a final break with the communities of their youth. Argentina was to be their home. Parallel to these acquisitions came the consolidation of religious, educational, cultural, and mutual aid centers for all these communities, each along independent lines.

The old world ties of Buenos Aires Sephardim still constituted a paramount factor in determining their patterns of settlement, and they continued to live in clusters based on cities or areas of origin. When they moved, they did so in chain migrations: Turkish Jews moved from Centro near the port to Villa Crespo; Damascene Jews moved in clusters from Boca–Barracas to Flores and Belgrano; Aleppine Jews settled in Ciudadela.⁶⁷

By organizing separate mutual aid societies, the Damascene, Aleppine, Turkish, and Moroccan Jews accentuated their separateness. The Turkish

---

65. Teubal, *Inmigrante*, 83.
66. Teubal, *Inmigrante*, 75.
67. On the chain migration of Italians to Argentina, see S. L. Bailey, "The Adjustment of Italian Immigrants in Buenos Aires and New York, 1870–1914," *The American Historical Review* 88(2) (April, 1983): 291.

Jews organized a *kehilla*, or community, in March 1919, which centralized all their educational, religious, and welfare activities.[68] Two years later, they expanded their charitable activities to provide the poor with the essentials for the Jewish holidays and medical services.[69]

Typically, burial societies were independent of synagogues and schools, though the members and even officials of these institutions overlapped. The burial societies had a mutual aid character, providing widows and orphans with a fixed stipend on the death of the head of family. In addition, many friendship circles were created in specific neighborhoods to provide for poor members in need.[70]

Although the distance between Ashkenazic and Sephardic immigrants in Buenos Aires is easily explained by their differing backgrounds, languages, traditions, and attitudes, the factors that caused the various Sephardic groups to remain apart from one another are more subtle. There were, for one thing, language differences among them. Traditions also differed. The two Syrian communities were estranged before coming to Argentina.[71] Attachment to religion varied from one community to the other, Syrians being the most fervent believers, the Moroccans the most liberal. Further, each group settled in different neighborhoods and most of their members worked nearby; their societies, quite understandably, were based in these neighborhoods, thus limiting the possibilities for socializing with members of other Sephardic groups. Finally, their strong emotional ties to their native communities prevented them from considering the benefits of stronger all-Sephardic societies.[72]

---

68. Both original groups had their own burial societies called Hesed Shel Emeth (HSE, with variants in spelling) and synagogues. The basic and most important achievement of their unification was the union of these burial societies; the synagogues continued to exist afterward. HSE of Centro, founded in 1916, met at the Es Ajaim synagogue at 25 de Mayo 696; HSE of Villa Crespo was part of Kahal Kadosh and Talmud Torah La Hermandad Sefaradí, founded in 1914. See Hermandad Sefaradí, *Minutes*, 9 Feb., 2, 13, and 16 March, 1919; and HSE (Centro), *Minutes*, 9 March 1919.

69. Comunidad Israelita Sefaradí, *Memoria*, 17 Oct. 1920. See also M. Bejarano, "El cementerio y la unidad comunitaria en la historia de los Sefaradim de Buenos Aires," *Michael*, Tel Aviv 8 (1983), 24–31.

70. See *Estatutos* of Bene Emeth (Damascene burial society, founded on Oct. 17, 1913) of 1922, article 67, *Estatutos* of Hesed Schel Emeth Sefaradit (Aleppine burial society, founded Aug. 5, 1923) of 1925, article 3, and *Reglamento General* of the same year, articles 3–6. Among Moroccan Jews—besides Gemilut Hassadim, their burial society—there were other aid institutions such as Hessed Laalafim, Kisse Eliyahu, Hesed Veemet. Among Aleppine there was Ahaba Vehajaba, and Ahavat Sedek.

71. Zenner, *Syrians*, 17; and Cohen, *Jews*, passim.

72. In 1905 the only group with a cemetery of its own was the Moroccan. However, they would not admit other Jews. Their burial society decided that "all members who are not descendants of South European [i.e., Spain and especially Gibraltar] or North African parents shall enjoy all rights . . . except that of burial." Hesed Veemet, *Minutes*, 31 July 1905.

The Sephardic societies bear some resemblance to the *landsmanschaften* founded by Ashkenazim on the basis of common origin in the same town or area. However, their differences outweigh their similarities. The *landsmanschaften*, which arose by the dozen in Buenos Aires during the World War I period and the 1920s, built a social atmosphere for the immigrants from a specific area of origin in Poland, Galicia, Rumania, or Bessarabia. But their main object was to facilitate the economic absorption of the immigrants. Members could borrow from the *landsmanschaft*, and because of its mutual aid feature, their families had support in case of sickness, death, or unemployment. These funds, as well as others established in many Jewish neighborhoods, paved the way for the formation of hundreds of credit cooperatives, which began during the 1920s and survived for four decades. The Ashkenazic *landsmanschaften* had a secular orientation, aiding members in establishing themselves firmly; in contrast, the Sephardic organizations were charitable in their approach.[73]

The Jewish press played an enormous role among Ashkenazic immigrants to Argentina, but it played a weaker role among Sephardim. A number of Yiddish-language daily newspapers, as well as dozens of weeklies and monthlies, advocated every social, political, or cultural viewpoint, inundating the neighborhoods where East European Jews lived. The local Yiddish press had more readers than there were members of the Ashkenazic mutual aid societies. Tens of thousands of immigrants in Buenos Aires and the interior used the Yiddish papers to search for job opportunities, social news, advice on how to survive in Argentina, guidance in understanding and adjusting to the wider community, information on Argentine politics, economics, and social conditions, and news about the Old World Jewish communities. The Yiddish press was a helpful tool in the search for "missing" husbands and fathers who had migrated to Argentina and had, for one reason or another, severed contact with their families in Europe. Moreover, Yiddish newspapers launched crusades for or against specific issues. There were diatribes concerning the local Yiddish theater and the involvement in it of Jewish white slave dealers, the *kehilla* form of community organization versus an *alianza* or federation, the support or boycott of Jewish colonization in Birobidzhan or in Palestine, and so forth.

Sephardim in Argentina before the Nazi era did not participate in these controversies. Their concerns centered on earning a living and abiding as much as possible within traditional religious and cultural values, with little or no involvement in politics. In general terms, they were lukewarm to

---

73. On *Landsmanschaften* in Argentina, see L. Zitnitsky, "Landsmanschaften in Argentine," *Argentiner IWO Shriftn* 3 (1945), 155–161; P. Katz, *Yiddn in Argentina* (Buenos Aires: 1946), *Poilishe Yiddn in Dorem Amerika* (Buenos Aires: 1941); *Galitziener Yiddn, Yoblbuch, 1925–1965* (Buenos Aires: 1966).

Zionism but very solicitous about helping their Jewish compatriots. In the absence of specifically Sephardic newspapers, they read the general Argentine press. Only in 1917 was a Sephardic newspaper, *Israel,* founded. It carried articles and notes about Sephardim, mainly about the Moroccan Jews of Buenos Aires. Correspondents in the interior of Argentina and neighboring countries contributed additional information. The pro-Zionist leanings of *Israel* were atypical of Sephardim in Buenos Aires until 1930, when a new journal, *La Luz,* was initiated, raising the level of Sephardic journalism in Buenos Aires.[74]

---

74. V. A. Mirelman, "Early Zionist Activities among Sephardim in Argentina," *American Jewish Archives* 34(2) (Nov., 1982): 190–205.

3
Jewish Roots of Brazil

Anita Novinsky

Introduction

Masters of *nouvelle histoire*—Georges Duby, Robert Mandrou, Jacques LeGoff, and others—have shown that the collective mind has a relative autonomy and that change in the mentality of groups is a very slow process. Despite the drastic change that Western society has experienced, much of its old mental structure persists. Thus, the topics discussed in this book have their roots in the distant past. Economic structures have changed, but archaic forms of thinking continue to dominate and interfere with the political and religious thought of our time. There are surprising similarities between the situation of converted Jews at the time of the Inquisition and their situation in the twentieth century. The weight of ancient prejudice can still be felt in everyday life.

In a break with tradition, this chapter is not concerned with the question of whether or not the New Christians (Portuguese converted Jews) secretly practiced the Jewish religion. This has been the central preoccupation of many scholars, and I have expressed my own opinion on the matter in other writings.[1] Here the concern is with a segment of the Jewish

---

1. Benzion Netanyahu, "On the Meaning of the Hebrew Sources Related to the Marranos (A Reply to Critics)," *Hispania Judaica* (1980): 79–102; "Some Theoretical Considerations about the New Christian Problem," in *The Sephardi and Oriental Jewish Heritage*, Jerusalem, The First International Congress on Sephardi and Oriental Jewry, 1982, Edited by Issachar Ben Ami, The Magnes Press, The Hebrew University of Jerusalem pp. 3–12. See also Novinsky, *Cristãos Novos na Bahia*, Editora Perspectiva, São Paulo, Brazil, 1970. Chapter I: A Problem of Historiography.

people that, several generations after conversion to Catholicism, was still considered Jewish by the society in which it lived. If conversion was not an exceptional phenomenon in the history of the Jews of the Diaspora, in Iberian countries it assumed specific paradoxical features. No matter what the dimensions of their Jewish faith, the descendants of the New Christians wrote a chapter of Jewish history that had repercussions at the national and international levels.

Traditional historiography lacks a strong scientific basis for describing the evolution of the conversion problem in Portugal and its colonies. The behavior of the so-called *Marranos* has been treated as coherent and homogeneous, as though it were detached from Iberian reality. Only with access to the Portuguese and Spanish archives has scholarly research begun in earnest. But although considerable headway has been made into the history of the Jews and *conversos* of Spain, the historiography of the Jews and New Christians in the Portuguese empire has progressed slowly. Most of the Portuguese sources are still unpublished, and the documents concerning the Jewish question are being carefully catalogued only now.

Recent historians, moreover, notably the Spanish and French, have tended to minimize the importance of the Inquisition, criticizing traditional historiography for what they claim is an exaggerated view of the cruelty of that tribunal. A lack of familiarity with Portuguese sources and an uncritical treatment of Portuguese documents have allowed many authors, both Jews and non-Jews, to offer opinions that have led to confusion. The term *New Christian,* for example, is infrequently used by Jewish authors, who seem to prefer *Marrano,* a word that never appears in Portuguese documents. The attempt to transcend this terminological confusion by using *Marrano* for those who maintained a commitment to the Judaic faith and *New Christian* for Catholics of Jewish origin is equally inconvenient, as many New Christians, faithful followers of the Jewish religion, were condemned without ever having considered themselves *Marranos* (a pejorative term at the time). Some New Christians were committed to Judaism and some were not; all of those whose roots were Jewish, however, considered themselves New Christians. I am concerned here only with New Christians accused of being crypto-Jews.

The Inquisition and Jews in Brazil

Studies of the Inquisition are opening new fields and generating new approaches to the history of Jews in the Brazilian Diaspora. It is, to begin with, impossible to speak of Jews in Latin America during the colonial period without mentioning the influence of the Inquisition. It was the reality of the Inquisition that oriented the destiny of the Jews in Brazil, and the study of this institution opens new perspectives on the history of Jews and of Latin America.

Modern students of the Inquisition emphasize the tribunal's interest in heresy, witchcraft, sodomy, bigamy, and the like. But it was the Jewish question that came to preoccupy church and state, becoming for both institutions the crucial issue. In spite of all the effort put into a solution by state functionaries, however, their suggestions were never accepted by the tribunal. For example, in 1683 the so-called Law of Extermination, proposing the expulsion of convicted Jews (or their offspring) from the kingdom of Portugal, was put forth for consideration. Discussed among the different power factions during the reign of Don Pedro II, it was opposed, not surprisingly, by the Inquisition, for it would have undermined a principal source of revenue: the confiscation of Jewish convicts' property.[2]

For centuries the Jews of Portugal were considered foreigners and were held responsible for the misery of the nation. In large part, the Catholic clergy were responsible for anti-Semitic propaganda as well as for the disastrous consequences of the resultant policies.[3] The sermons preached at autos-da-fé were directed not against the New Christians who had sinned, but against the entire Jewish people. Heresies other than Judaism were not even mentioned in these sermons.[4] The target was always the Jews. The Catholic church used religion in this manner to legitimate an arbitrary order upon which the politics of domination were founded. The existence in Portuguese society of a group that could be held out as "foreign" and "heretical" allowed for the control of an important faction of the middle class made up of New Christians; it reinforced the old regime and contributed to the defense of the interests of the dominant class.

From the time of its discovery, Brazil was a favorite refuge for Jews converted to Catholicism. Voluntary immigrants, exiles or fugitives, they arrived during the colonial centuries already converted to Catholicism; only in the nineteenth century did they arrive as Jews. Throughout this extended

---

2. The Law of Extermination was proclaimed on September 1, 1683, by King D. Pedro II. All the New Christians condemned in auto-da-fé for the crime of Judaizing were forced to leave Portugal in the maximum period of two months. All their goods were to be confiscated. They could not take with themselves children under seven years. The children under three years would be put in the *roda dos engeitados* or foundling hospital. The older ones, if they had no relatives, were to be put in the homes of *catechumenos* until their parents could prove (from abroad) that they were living in the law of Christ, or until the children would be grown up enough to be sent to the Portuguese conquered territories. See the opinion of the Inquisitors against this law: *Fundo Geral* (Codice 1587, National Library, Lisbon, manuscript), 1.

3. Among the anti-Jewish books published in the Iberian Peninsula in the seventeenth and eighteenth century, at least seventeen were written by Catholic clergymen.

4. Howard Norton, "Os sermoes anti-judaicos nos autos da fe (seculo XVIII)" (Ph.D. diss., department of history, University of São Paulo, 1981, tape).

period, they were present in all sectors of Brazilian life. Never in the history of Brazil was there a period without Jews.

Examining this long trajectory, two concurrent phenomena stand out: New Christians enjoyed an opportunity to accumulate wealth and ascend the social scale, but they were forced to face a long and uninterrupted insecurity. Never in the colonial period were Jews able to feel secure in Brazil, regardless of the prestige they acquired. In this sense it is possible to say that they were simultaneously integrated and marginalized, living paradoxically as both masters and outcasts. In spite of three centuries of Christianization and the power that came with wealth, nothing served as a guarantee; in Brazil, New Christians were exposed to the same dangers and humiliations experienced by Jews in other regions. Baptism and assimilation did not free them from harassments that included sentences of life imprisonment, the confiscation of possessions, and not infrequently the death penalty.[5]

The New Christians who arrived in Brazil during the colonial centuries were faced with an anti-Judaism that had been transferred from the Iberian peninsula to the New World and from Jews to Catholic converts. They also confronted two situations, however, that distinguished their experience from that of their coreligionists who had fled to other European countries or the Middle East: an economy based on agriculture and the institution of the Inquisition.

During the first two centuries of Portuguese colonization, the greater number of crypto-Jews resided in rural areas on sugar plantations. By the first half of the seventeenth century, Brazil was the largest sugar producer in the world. And about 60% of the sugar mills in the state of Bahia were owned by Jews, who were recognized by local authorities as experts in sugar production.[6]

The Jews involved in agriculture can be divided into three social categories: wealthy plantation owners who purchased as many as ninety slaves to work in their mills; small-scale farmers who grew sugar on rented land and owned from ten to twenty slaves; and poor farmers who grew corn, manioc, and fruit on their own or with the help of their wives and children. In certain cases, members of this last group came to own one to four slaves.

---

5. See Anita Novinsky, *Cristãos novos na Bahia* (Edit. Perspectiva e Edit. Universidade de São Paulo, São Paulo, 1970).
6. Eduardo de Oliveira França, "Engenhos, Colonização e Cristãos Novos na Bahia Colonial," in *Colonização e migração, Anais do IV Simposio nacional dos professores universitarios de historia* (Editora Universidade de São Paulo, São Paulo, 1969), 181–241. About Diogo Fernandes, New Christian and expert in sugar fabrication, the governor of Pernambuco, Jeronimo de Albuquerque, wrote to King D. Joao III (August 1556): "outro mais suficiente na terra que ele nao se achara." In *Revista do Instituto histórico e geográfico Brasilero* XLIX (Part I, 1886): 584–586.

Sources of the period show that Jews were living in the south of Brazil in the first half of the sixteenth century. Various Judaic rituals were being practiced in the home of the captain major of São Vicente.[7] The richest information on Jewish life in the colony, however, dates from the seventeenth century, from the jungles of Matoim in the state of Bahia.[8]

It is very strange that, with the exception of the period of Dutch occupation, no chroniclers, travelers, or local residents mention either New Christians or Jews, despite a presence that spanned several centuries. All the information available leads to the conclusion that fear of the tribunal of the Inquisition was responsible for this silence and those who participated in or witnessed heresies took care to keep them undiscovered.

The seventeenth century is characterized by two events that, to a certain extent, changed the course of Jewish life in Brazil: increased activity on the part of the Inquisition and the Dutch invasion of the Northeast. The functionaries of the church tribunal increased the rigor of their Brazilian "visits." From 1605 through the second half of the eighteenth century, New Christians suspected or accused of following the Jewish faith were registered in the "book of the guilty."[9] Many of them were well known in Bahian social circles: people of status such as writers, state functionaries, and wealthy plantation owners. They made up an important fraction of the local bourgeoisie, and many were well acclimated to their new habitat. The insecurity that marked their lives, however, frequently led them to develop a cloak of conformity, which was used to cover a deep inquietude, perceptible in the writings of the period.

As free men in key positions, the New Christians occupied an important place between the dominant classes and the servile masses. Some, because of personal wealth and services rendered the king, gained the status of blood aristocrats. As such, they were able to come to the aid of coreligionists who, fleeing Portugal, arrived in Brazil in a deplorable state.

Although Jews in colonial Brazil intermarried with Old Christians, they continued to resist the Catholic religion. Not that New Christian businessmen and intellectuals consciously practiced Judaism. More frequently, their resistance took the form of continued identification with the Jewish people and their proscribed faith and of refusal to accept Catholic dogma or to obey ecclesiastical authorities.

---

7. Jeronimo Leitão, Captain Major of São Vicente, was married to a Jewish woman, Ines Castelão (or Mendes). See *Primeira visitação do santo offício ás partes do Brasil, Pelo Licenciado Heitor Furtado de Mendonça. Denunciações de Pernambuco 1593–1595* (São Paulo, Série Eduardo Prado, 1929), 99–103.

8. See W. Pinho, *História de um Engenho no reconcavo* (Rio de Janeiro, 1946).

9. *Livro dos culpados* (Arquivo Nacional da Torre do Tombo, Lisbon, Portugal manuscript). See also A. Novinsky, "Uma fonte inédita para a história do Brasil," *Revista de História* 94 (Universidade de São Paulo, 1973): 563–572.

In spite of the continual threat of the church, most Jews did not leave the colony. There were several reasons for this: Many had mixed with Old Christian families and, having been in Brazil for several generations, were tied to the land both economically and culturally. It is interesting to note, moreover, that whereas Amsterdam was considered the "Jerusalem in exile" by Portuguese Jews, Brazil was the promised land of the New Christians. The notion that Jewish suffering was tied to the lack of a national territory was set out clearly by the Portuguese humanist and chronicler Damião de Góes in the sixteenth century; this level of consciousness is not seen, however, in the Brazilian writings of the period.[10]

Massacres of New Christians accused of practicing Judaism did not take place in colonial Brazil. Geographical and human conditions created new types of action and the absence of an officially established Inquisition tribunal probably allowed for greater flexibility at the local level. At the same time, anti-Judaism can be observed in the adoption of old concepts and stereotypes, most clearly at the level of official entities and institutions.

One such anti-Jewish prejudice was expressed in political terms: Jews were constantly accused of being traitors who had turned over Brazilian territory to Dutch heretics. During the entire period of the Dutch occupation of northeastern Brazil (1524–1525 and 1630–1654), the Jews were held responsible for this Portuguese political disaster.[11] Some Jews suffered imprisonment and the confiscation of their possessions as well as the humiliation of being accused of treason. It is known now that the history of this period has been skewed by both Jewish and non-Jewish historians drawing on partisan documentation. The generalizations one encounters equating Jewish life in Brazil with Jewish life outside the country demonstrate the need for historical revision. If there were Sephardic Jews in Holland or Aleppo—or any other place, for that matter—with an economic interest in the Dutch occupation of Brazil, such evidence is insufficient proof that Brazilian New Christians shared the same sentiments. Charles Boxer has already pointed out the error and prejudice of this affirmation. Nor is there one word on New Christian treason in the texts of the Jesuits, the most reliable chroniclers of the period.[12] To the contrary, in the manuscript

---

10. Damiao de Góes, "Cronica do Felicissimo D. Manuel," in *Clássicos portugueses* (Lisboa: Livraria Clássica Editora, 1944). Also cited in Novinsky, *Cristãos novos*, 31 n. 27.

11. See Anita Novinsky, "A Historical Bias: The Participation of the New Christians in the Dutch Invaders of Brasil" (XVII century) Reprint from the V World Congress of Jewish Studies, Volume II (Jerusalem: 1972) pp. 141–154.

12. Charles R. Boxer, *Os holandeses no Brasil*, Coleção Brasiliana, Vol. 312 (São Paulo: Companhia Editora Nacional, 1961), 31. Boxer showed that Dutch navigators were perfectly familiar with Brazilian harbors and had no need of the Jews for guides on their expeditions of 1624 and 1630 (*Os holandeses*, 29). See also C. R. Boxer, *Salvador Correa de Sa e a luta pelo Brasil e Angola (1602–1686)*, Coleção Brasiliana, Vol. 353 (São Paulo: Companhia Editora Nacional e Universidade de São Paulo, 1973), 56–57, n. 5.

sources of the time, one encounters New Christians actively defending Brazilian territory with their money, projects, and lives.[13]

In regard to the Dutch invasion, neither New Christians nor Old Christians behaved homogeneously. The investigation commissioned by Bishop D. Pedro da Silva of Bahia in 1636, for example, revealed intimate collaboration with the enemy by some members of the Catholic clergy.[14]

It is very difficult to be precise about the demographic density of New Christians or Jews in Brazil in the seventeenth and eighteenth centuries. By means of the "list of names" and other documents, one can identify as Jewish 20% of the free white population of Salvador, capital of Brazil in the eighteenth century. The Catholic clergy left valuable and suggestive information about this question. In one document sent to the Inquisition by the vicar of the city of Salvador, there is a reference to the *gente da nação* (Portuguese of Jewish origin) who had populated the area in great quantity because they considered it the best place in the world to live and do business.[15] The same document goes on to say that "the majority of inhabitants in this land are Jews."[16] In confidential correspondence with the Inquisition in Brazil, the Jesuits likewise complained of the Jews' influence, pointing out the threat posed by their laws and customs and asking the king to expel them from the country.[17]

From 1624 to 1654, with the Dutch in control of the Brazilian northeast, New Christians lived in a different climate, one presumably permeated with Judaism. The communal character of their life-style is insufficiently known, and more research is necessary. Little is known about New Christian social organization, about the style of their religious life, or about sociability in synagogues and schools, and just as little is known of mixed marriages and New Christian mentality. Contrary to the historians' contention, not all these Jews left Brazil when the Dutch were expelled. Some sought refuge in the distant backlands of Rio Grande do Norte, emerging a generation later as well-established cattle ranchers. Others located in the state of Paraíba where nearly 100 years later a secret community was found and accused of Judaism. Visiting the *sertão* (jungle) region of Seridó, I myself encountered strange reminiscences of this Jewish past. Along these same lines, it is interesting to

13. Novinsky, "A Historical Bias."
14. See Novinsky, "Uma Devassa do Bispo Dom Pedro da Silva" 1635–1637. Introdução de Anita Novinsky, (separata do Tomo XXII dos *Anais do Museu Paulista*, São Paulo, 1968), pp. 217–285.
15. Novinsky, *Cristãos novos,* 68.
16. *Cadernos do promotor da Inquisição de Lisboa,* No. 15 ANTT (Arquivo Nacional da Torre do Tombo, Lisboa) (manuscript) in National Archive in Portugal (XVII century) and Novinsky, *Cristãos novos,* 68 n. 21. Diogo Correa, "familiar" of the Holy Office, wrote to the Inquisition in the seventeenth century that a third of the people in Brazil were Jews (68 n. 22).
17. *Inquisição de Lisboa,* No. 13852 (Arquivo Nacional da Torre do Tombo, Lisboa, manuscript). Also cited in Novinsky, *Cristãos novos,* 72 n. 35.

remember that forty of the most traditional families of the state of Rio Grande do Norte voluntarily reconverted to Judaism after having lived as ostensible Christians for nearly three centuries. Indeed, they created a Jewish school where the Bible, ancient history, and the Hebrew language are taught.

In south central Brazil the Jews led a much different life. The Jewish interest in that region was the same as that of the rest of the population: gold. The gold rush led to an increase in immigration and a high rate of mobility. In the eighteenth century, the greatest number of New Christians registered in the Inquisition archives were concentrated in the two states most directly affected by the gold rush, Rio de Janeiro and Minas Gerais.

Lisbon, at this point, established a more rigorous economic policy followed up with strong religious repression, but the consequences of this change in policy are only now beginning to emerge from Inquisition records. The greatest number of imprisonments for Judaism in all of colonial history date from the first third of the eighteenth century. The Inquisition, most notably from 1710 to 1720 and from 1726 to 1735, fell furiously upon traditional New Christian families, decimating entire communities. In the first half of the eighteen century, 1811 people of Jewish origin (804 women and 1007 men) were denounced to the Inquisition as suspected of Judaism.[18] Of these, approximately 500 were sentenced to life imprisonment in Portugal. Analysis of the trial records of 444 Brazilian New Christians (226 men, 218 women)—including 21 cases of capital punishment—permits certain conclusions. The majority of the accused were born in Brazil; some of them were grandchildren and great-grandchildren of Brazilians.

The occupations of the 226 male prisoners were as follows:

Agriculture and ranching	59	(26%)
Businessmen (international and regional commerce)	54	(24%)
Professionals (doctors, lawyers, pharmacists, apothecaries, musicians, etc.)	27	(12%)
Free laborers (including the unskilled and unemployed)	22	(10%)
Children at home	13	(6%)
Miners	16	(7%)
Government employees (including soldiers)	22	(10%)
Students	7	(3%)
Religious occupation (priests, seminarians, etc.)	6	(2%)

Nearly half of the New Christians imprisoned in this period were women, and they played an important role in colonial society, in the transmission of Judaism.

18. See Novinsky, "Uma fonte inédita."

It should be pointed out that during the gold cycle in Brazil the middle class was made up in large part of Jews. For this reason, in most cases when the inquisitors dispatched an order of imprisonment for a New Christian, they included instructions "to confiscate all possessions"; when the suspect was not a New Christian, imprisonment was ordered "without the confiscation of possessions." Given their professional stature and position in society, the New Christians can be considered an important nucleus of the incipient national bourgeoisie. Because they were born in the colony their interests were tied to it; for this reason they were considered a threat by Portugal, concerned as it was with the subjugation of Brazil. Of all the different groups in the colony, the New Christians had the greatest interest in battling imperial domination; their conflicts with Portugal constitute one of the most interesting dimensions of Jewish activity in Brazil. The period in which Jews were most intensely persecuted by the Inquisition coincides with a period of increased social tension and conflicts, one in which the representatives of the crown became alarmed at the rebelliousness of the colony's inhabitants. New Christians were present in all of the period's principal social conflicts, taking leadership roles in some of them.[19]

It is interesting to consider the cultural level of certain New Christians in Brazil. There were poets, writers, professionals, and some who had considerable libraries.[20] A branch of the family of the famous Portuguese humanist Antonio Nunes Ribeiro Sanches (phisitiam of Catarina II of Russia) lived in Brazil; two of its members, Jose Henriques Ferreira and Manuel Henriques de Paiva, founded the first scientific Society for Natural History in the city of Rio de Janeiro.[21] In the field of ideas, the New Christians left profound marks on Brazilian culture, even influencing the Catholic clergy. Many members of Jewish families entered the church despite legislation barring them; it was in the heart of the church that the most enlightened ideas of the time bloomed. It is interesting to compare the heretical clerical

---

19. The leader of the 1684 revolution in Maranhão, Manoel Bekmann, was denounced by the local Governor to the king as a Jew and a traitor, and to the Inquisition as a New Christian and a heretic. Hanged as a traitor, he can be considered a precursor of Brazilian nationalism. See Maria Liberman, *O levante do Maranhão "Judeu cabeça do Motim"* (São Paulo: Editora Universidade de São Paulo e Centro de Estudos Judaicos, 1983).

20. Antonio Ferreira Dourado, who lived in the eighteenth century, is considered the first poet of Goias (Brazil). Condemned by the Inquisition, his confiscated goods were found to include hundreds of pages of poems and memoires. See A. Novinsky, *Inventarios de bens confiscados a Cristãos novos do Brasil, seculo XVIII* (Lisbon: Imprensa Nacional—Casa da Moeda, 1978), 36–44.

21. The Academia Fluviense, Médica, Botânica e Farmaceutica was inaugurated January 18, 1772, in the palace of the viceroy of Brazil Marques do Lavradio. See Jose Lopez Dias article, "Duas cartas do físico-mór e médico do Vice-Rei do Brasil a Ribeiro Sanches," *Imprensa Médica* (Lisboa, Ano XXIII: February–March 1959): 1–13.

thought of the colony (or of Portugal, where the clergy's ideas originated) with the critical thought of Catholic exegetes of the 1980s or with the much more modest ideas of the representatives of liberation theology in Brazil. It is possible, in fact, to speak of a heretical tradition in the Brazilian clergy, influenced by the ideas of Catholics of Jewish origin and by intimate association with New Christians. Recent theological critiques of Catholic dogma and doubts about the divinity of Jesus, the coming of the Messiah, the virginity of Mary, the resurrection, and miracles of Christ all appear in the Brazilian clergy's texts of more than three centuries ago.

Insofar as the persistence of Judaism is concerned, it is curious to note that in this same eighteenth century a secret Jewish community was discovered on the banks of the Paraíba do Norte river and was accused of heresy. Nearly all of the New Christians in this community were peasants who made a living off the land, planting subsistence crops such as sugar cane, rice, corn, manioc, and the like. Having lived in the region over several generations, they maintained Jewish customs and tended to marry endogamously. They were denounced by someone from outside the group who had penetrated, through marriage, into the core of the community. Between 1729 and 1736, forty-eight members of the community, both men and women, suffered life imprisonment and the confiscation of their possessions.[22] One woman, Guiomar Nunes, was burned at the stake. She became the inspiration for a play by Dias Gomes, one of Brazil's greatest writers.[23]

At the end of the eighteenth century, the situation of Jews in Brazil changed drastically. Now New Christians were persecuted not for Judaizing, but for endorsing the ideas of the Freemasons and the French Enlightenment. The ideological orientation of the inquisitors had changed, but prejudice against Jews continued to exist.

Summary

It can be said that the Jews who lived in Brazil during the colonial period enjoyed, on the one hand, a prosperity that made them equals of the most privileged and dominant class and suffered, on the other, a prejudice that differentiated them from all others. Many, perhaps the majority, melted into the mass of the population; but some, by way of family structure, remained identified as Jews. They played a fundamental role in the con-

---

22. The story of this village is part of a forthcoming book by A. Novinsky, about the Inquisition and the New Christians in Brazil of the eighteenth century.
23. Dias Gomes, *O santo inquerito* (Editora Civilisação, Coleção Teatro de Hoje).

struction and development of Brazil, but under conditions that did not allow for their survival as Jews. Through extermination and assimilation, the numerous Jewish population of Brazil disappeared.

It is impossible to speak of the Jewish experience in colonial Brazil without mentioning racism. Contrary to the opinion of many authors, racial democracy has never existed in Brazil. Jews were not permitted to live in the Portuguese empire. Every step taken by New Christians was observed and their speech analyzed for heretical opinion. Portuguese legislation was unambiguous: Regardless of the number of generations since Catholic conversion, descendants of Jews were not to enjoy equality with other citizens. Prestigious positions such as official state posts, university education, entrance into military and religious orders were all denied them.[24] Of course, in the exceptional context of the recently discovered continent, anti–New Christian laws were not always obeyed; but they were there to be used when it was in the interest of those applying them. Little, almost nothing, was to be permitted the descendants of the Jews converted by force in 1497. This anti-Judaism was not religious, but eminently economic and political. Religion certainly played a part, but in Brazil, as in Portugal, the real reason for persecution of New Christians was political.

Certain twentieth century forms of anti-Semitism can be said to present strange similarities to Iberian anti-Judaism. The *blutschande* (blood shame) of Nazi Germany does not differ from the theory of purity of blood that developed in earlier centuries in Iberian countries. Through discriminatory legislation, church and state stipulated the limits to the economic and social participation of descendants of Jews living in the vast Portuguese empire. Racism as it became known in modern times was practiced three centuries earlier by Portuguese church and state. If there were New Christians who remained attached to Judaism and identified with the Jewish people, there were others who adopted Catholicism for reasons of belief or in order to survive. But renunciation of Judaism was impossible because the registers of the Inquisition kept track of Jewish ancestry.[25] The farcical nature of the persecution launched against persons who could not cease being Jewish was recognized by various Portuguese politicians and churchmen, and its political character did not go unnoticed by contemporaries.[26] Understood in this manner, the reality of Jews in this period renders the old debate over whether or not New Christians were followers of the Judaic religion of secondary importance.

24. See Maria Luiza Carneiro Tucci, *Racismo e preconceito no Brasil colonial* (São Paulo: Editora Brasiliense, 1983).
25. See Novinsky, "Uma fonte inédita"; A. Novinsky, "Sistema de poder e repressão religiosa," *Anais do Museu Paulista* XXIX (São Paulo, 1979), 5–12.
26. D. Luiz Cunha, *Testamento político* (São Paulo: Editora Alfa-Omega, 1976), 76, 85.

The Jewish experience in this enormous country was different from that encountered by Jews who emigrated to other regions. And an understanding of the life led by Jews in Brazil, their economic and cultural role and their mentality and conflicts, is greatly facilitated by the existence of an excellent source, the secret registers of the Holy Office of the Portuguese Inquisition. Hebrew sources are unenlightening because New Christians in Brazil lived an entirely Brazilian reality.

Twenty years ago, the reader who opened a book on the history of Brazil would rarely encounter information about New Christians and their role in the construction of the country, nor even about their persecution by the church. Today, history books used in the school system refer to the Jewish presence, even if they are not well focused. In the Portuguese language version of the *Encyclopedia Britannica* (*Mirador*), there are entries for *New Christians* and *Inquisition* that recount the Jewish experience in Brazil.

In the history department at the University of São Paulo, a group of students are preparing doctoral dissertations on Jewish history in the colonial and national periods. Some of this work has been published, and has been referred to in this chapter; other contributions are forthcoming. New approaches augur new directions in Brazilian historiography and a new chapter in Jewish history.

4
*Latin America and the Jewish Refugees: Two Encounters, 1935 and 1938**

Haim Avni

Introduction

In the last days of March 1933, less than two months after Adolf Hitler's ascent to power, the first signs were evidenced of the global onslaught that Nazi Germany was to launch on the Jewish people. Preparations were made for a total boycott of Jewish businesses and professional services in Germany, which was to start on Saturday, April 1, 1933, and to last until the National Socialist party's leadership ordered its cessation. The preparations were much publicized, alarming German Jewry as well as Jewish communities abroad. In Germany, thousands of Jews became convinced that sooner or later they would have to seek safety through emigration. Latin American Jewry was alerted and protest assemblies were organized, such as the one held in Buenos Aires on March 27, 1933.

Two days later, the members of the Board of the Sociedad de Protección a los Inmigrantes Israelitas (SOPROTIMIS) in Buenos Aires were summoned urgently to an extraordinary meeting. The only item on the agenda was a cable received from HIAS-ICA-Emigdirekt (HICEM), the international Jewish emigration society. According to minutes of that meeting, HICEM

*This research was made possible by the support of the Memorial Foundation for Jewish Culture, New York, and by a research grant from the Tauber Institute, Brandeis University, Waltham. This is the sixth publication of the project "Latin America and the Jewish People during the Holocaust," which is being carried out at the Division for Latin America, Spain and Portugal of The Institute of Contemporary Jewry, The Hebrew University of Jerusalem.

requested they "take steps [to obtain] . . . permits of entry for Jewish refugees from Germany."[1]

From that time on, the main contribution of the Latin American countries toward the rescue of Jews during the Holocaust era was their grant of entry permits to *refugiados*.

This chapter examines in detail two specific cases in which these countries were collectively called upon to take a major part in the solution of the refugees' problem, looking particularly at their willingness to receive Jewish refugees.

The Situation in Germany in 1935

The first case under discussion took place in the spring of 1935, two years after Hitler's ascent to power. It consisted of an intensive campaign of persuasion to accept refugees, launched by the High Commissioner for Refugees. The final aim of the Nazi policy at this stage, not always explicitly declared, was to force the Jews to leave Germany. "Liberation" of the Reich from the Jewish presence assumed the form of a variety of persecutory laws and decrees, which were applied with changing rhythm and severity from the first day of the boycott. In 1933, German Jewry numbered 525,000 and in 1935, despite the objective need for emigration caused by the Nazi final aims, 450,000 Jews remained.[2]

This situation was not readily grasped by the Jews. The first panic in April 1933 led to the emigration of 37,000 Jews that year, of 23,000 in 1934, and of only 21,000 throughout 1935.[3] Even those who regarded emigration as the principal solution still thought in terms of an orderly transfer of occupational activity and living conditions from one country to another. Preparations to this end, according to them, ought to be long and thorough.[4] Latin America, like other havens of refuge, was only considered in "normal" concepts and, therefore, attracted comparatively little attention.

---

1. SOPROTIMIS Archives, *Actas,* 29.3.1933: 53, The Central Archives for the History of the Jewish People, Jerusalem.

2. Herbert A. Strauss, "Jewish Emigration from Germany, Nazi Policies and Jewish Responses," *Leo Baeck Institute Yearbook* 25 (1980): 317, Table I. The estimate for mid-1935 was arrived at by deducting the figures of emigration from the estimate for January 1933. The number of those affected by Nazi "racial measures," including mixed marriages and "Jewish descent," reached about 867,000; see p. 318.

3. Werner Rosenstock, "Exodus 1933–1939, A Survey of Jewish Emigration from Germany," *Leo Baeck Institute Yearbook* 1 (1956): 377.

4. Abraham Margaliot, "The Problem of Rescue of German Jewry during the Years 1933–1945," in Y. Gutman and E. Zuroff (Editors), *Rescue Attempts during the Holocaust, Proceedings of the Second Yad Vashem International Historical Conference—April 1974,* Yad Vashem (Jerusalem: 1977), 247.

Demand for immigration facilities to Latin America of a considerably higher level was presented by James G. McDonald, High Commissioner for Refugees (Jewish and Other) Coming from Germany. This agency was created by the League of Nations on October 26, 1933. Out of fear of Germany's reaction, however, it was not established as a direct dependent of the League but rather as an independent office, with a permanent governing committee of its own. In 1934–5 the high commissioner's budget amounted to $138,000, most of which was provided by Jewish organizations: the American Joint Distribution Committee (JDC), the Jewish Colonization Association (JCA), and others. Some governments, the United States among them, supported the high commissioner's activities, but their contribution consisted of no more than token payments.[5]

At the end of 1934, McDonald believed that the problem was limited to those refugees who had until then escaped from Germany and who, according to his estimate, numbered 70,000–80,000 Jews and non-Jews.[6] Out of this number, 30,000 people still had to find new homes, which had to be sought beyond the limits of the European countries or Palestine where other, luckier refugees had settled. McDonald's belief that the time was ripe for "the liquidation of the problem" figured at the top of the items for discussion on the agenda of the meeting of the Permanent Committee set for February 12, 1935. He referred to this belief in some of his correspondence and it was in this connection that the high commissioner planned an extensive trip to South America.

"It is proposed that our visit should include the following countries: Brazil, Uruguay, Argentina, Chile, Ecuador, Peru and Colombia," wrote McDonald to Dr. Samuel Guy Inman, who accompanied him on this trip. "In each of these [countries], we would undertake to secure by direct negotiations with the governmental authorities permission for the admission of a limited number of Jewish and Christian refugees from Germany." McDonald believed this number would encompass the residue of the refugee problem; the Latin American countries were thus called upon by him to fulfill a decisive role.[7]

In preparation for the trip, McDonald endeavored to secure as many letters of recommendation as possible. When he visited Rome in November

---

5. Yehuda Bauer, *My Brother's Keeper, The History of the American Joint Distribution Committee, 1929–1939*, The Jewish Publication Society of America (Philadelphia, 1974), 142 fn. 10. McDonald to d'Avigdor Goldsmid, 10 January 1935, H 14, James G. McDonald Papers, Rare Book and Manuscript Library, Columbia University Libraries.

6. Séance du Conseil d'Administration, 26 October 1935, vol. 3: 179, memorandum to the Argentine government, Jewish Colonization Association, archives in London. 80,000 are mentioned in another of his letters.

7. McDonald to Inman, 31 December 1934, H 12 and H 15, McDonald Papers.

1934 and again in January 1935, he met for that purpose with Cardinal Pacelli, secretary of the Vatican state; and, while in Washington early in 1935, he saw the ambassadors of eight Latin American countries "from all of whom . . . except Honduras and Uruguay, I received definitely encouraging responses." The Brazilian representative, who, according to McDonald, was an intimate of the president of Brazil, seemed particularly optimistic regarding the mission. The Argentine ambassador was also most reassuring. As McDonald's preparations proceeded, he heard that Louis Oungre, the powerful director general of the JCA, was also going to South America to inspect the Jewish agricultural colonies in Argentina and Brazil. McDonald took care to coordinate their plans so that any positive results of his negotiations could be followed up by the leaders of that rich and influential organization.

In addition to attempting to solve what seemed to be left of the general refugee question, McDonald also intended to find a solution to the special problem of several hundreds of Jewish and non-Jewish university professors, scientists, and intellectuals who had fled Germany and could not find employment in their professions in Europe. McDonald equipped himself with detailed biographical information on each case, intending to present these individuals as candidates for employment by institutions of higher learning, research centers, and industry. For that purpose, and because of his need for adequate orientation, consultation, and guidance, he required a suitable companion for his trip, which he found in the person of Dr. Samuel Guy Inman.[8]

Equipped with prestigious recommendations and accompanied by his knowledgeable colleague, McDonald set out on his mission late in February 1935. It was to be the only time in the entire Holocaust era that direct negotiations on the immigration of Jewish (and other) refugees were conducted with heads of states and other leaders of the Latin American nations in their own capitals. In each of these countries (except Argentina), McDonald and Inman were received by the president of the state, had long discussions with the ministers of foreign affairs, economy, interior, and labor, and met with other political, cultural, and academic personalities.

---

8. McDonald to Bentwich, 11 January 1935, H 12, McDonald Papers. "He is an old friend of mine, with whom I was associated years ago in a very hard struggle against oil interests and to forestall armed intervention in Mexico," McDonald described Inman, and added: "He has made more than twenty trips through South America, speaks and writes Spanish perfectly, has an extraordinary acquaintanceship in academic and political circles." At that time Inman was, inter alia, the executive secretary of the Committee on Cooperation in Latin America, an interdenominational Protestant organization that was coordinating many evangelical and other religious, educational, and welfare services in Latin America. Further, he was the author of several scholarly studies on Latin America and a prolific journalist who covered many aspects of Latin American life.

McDonald and Inman in Euro-America

The first target of McDonald's and Inman's endeavors were the countries where a tradition of benevolent immigration policy already existed: Brazil, Argentina, Uruguay, and Chile. The waves of European immigration commencing at the end of the nineteenth century had contributed a very large proportion of the population of Argentina and Uruguay. The impact of European immigrants on the southern states of Brazil—from São Paolo to Rio Grande do Sul—was also considerable, as was the case in the southern provinces of Chile. The largest Jewish communities were located in this region. Large Jewish agricultural settlement projects had developed there, particularly in Argentina and Brazil. At the beginning of the Holocaust era, the JCA owned large reserves of land in these countries, which could eventually be used for the settlement of refugees.[9]

McDonald and Inman arrived in Brazil in March 1935. The possibilities of that immense Federal Republic to absorb immigrants seemed to them enormous; contrary to the pessimistic views of almost everyone they consulted, they felt confident of the ultimate success of their mission because their request for the absorption of refugees seemed to them utterly modest. In the memorandum they submitted to President Getulio Vargas and his ministers, they asked for "an exceptional arrangement for the admission of approximately 500 individuals or 125 families a month," representing only 6000 immigrants per year or 12,000 over two years. Their hope that Vargas would support their petition and instruct his aides accordingly was, however, disappointed. In his reply, the minister of labor, industry and commerce referred McDonald to the Brazilian constitution, promulgated less than a year earlier, which fixed a quota of 2% of the total number of the respective nationals "permanently settled in Brazil during the last fifty years." The annual immigration quota from Germany amounted to 3080 individuals, most of whom were supposed to be farmers. The minister was ready to allocate 10% of this figure to Jewish immigration but, even in that case, the 308 "chosen" immigrants were supposed to be agriculturists.[10]

---

9. 216,395 hectares (534,495 acres) out of the 617,468 hectares (1,525,145 acres) that JCA owned in Argentina were in 1932 still available for settlement. The Quatro Irmaos colony in Rio Grande do Sul, Brazil, was inhabited in 1936 by 101 Jewish and 488 non-Jewish families. JCA's land there exceeded 100,000 hectares (250,000 acres). Jewish Colonization Association, *Rapport de la Direction Generale* (1932): 2 (1937): 56–69.

10. *Draft of an Interim Report of the Mission to South and Central America of Dr. Samuel Guy Inman and the High Commissioner, by James G. McDonald, March–June 1935,* Jewish Colonization Association, archives in London, Séance du Conseil d'Administration, 26 October 1935, vol. 3, 142–161 (36–55 of the report; subsequently referred to as JCA–McDonald Report). The document was given only a very limited circulation (see McDonald Papers, H 17). A copy of Inman's part reached Dr. Arthur Ruppin, A 107/231, Central Zionist Archives, Jerusalem.

This attitude typified the nationalistic atmosphere McDonald and Inman encountered in Brazil and that was mirrored by the constitution. Fascist organizations—the Integralista party most prominently—kept watch to ensure that the xenophobic measures were applied; their pressure frightened even those officials who might have been inclined to take a more humanitarian attitude. "In these circumstances," wrote McDonald, "I was led gradually and reluctantly to resort finally to the search for a technical—and, I confess it, a legalistic—formula."[11]

There was a glimmer of light at the Brazilian foreign office, where Dr. Vaz de Mello, head of the passport division, seemed to have found a legalistic solution. If McDonald would emphasize in a new memorandum that he was pleading for stateless refugees, he could argue that such a category of *apatrides* was not included in the quota system as defined by the constitution; those immigrants could then be treated as an ex-quota group. Vaz de Mello agreed, in the name of the Foreign Office, to support a special agreement to be drawn up between the high commissioner and the Ministry of Labor. He even volunteered to formulate the memorandum in such a way as to make it acceptable to the other ministry. At the very last moment, however, he put forward two conditions: that all the *apatrides* be farmers and that the JCA submit a detailed plan for the establishment of agricultural colonies for them. Louis Oungre, the general director of the JCA, who was then in Brazil, stated that he could not draw up such a plan without laying it before the JCA Council in Paris. McDonald decided, therefore, to leave Brazil and return after several weeks, when the Brazilian conditions could be met. Five weeks later, upon his return to Rio de Janeiro, McDonald was completely disillusioned. No plan had been received from the JCA, the memorandum to the Ministry of Labor had yet to be authorized by the foreign minister (who was on a trip abroad), and even McDonald's request to see the draft of the memorandum was refused. Frustrated and desperate, he left Brazil.

He found a similar situation in Argentina. Soon after his arrival in Buenos Aires, McDonald realized that it would be worse than futile to ask the government to make a formal change in its immigration regulations. He therefore resigned himself, in his meeting with the minister of agriculture, Engineer Luis P. Duhau, to pleading "for some modifications in the interpretation of the immigration regulations." McDonald presented the refugee issue not as an immigration matter, but as a problem "of common humanity, comparable to an earthquake or flood that had rendered homeless tens of thousands of men and women." He requested "the admission of approx-

11. This and extensive quotations that follow are to be found in JCA–McDonald Report, 128–29.

imately 50 families or not more than 250 individuals a month during a period of one or two years." The administrative procedure that would enable the Argentine government to respond to that request without infringing its own regulations was indicated to him by the director general of immigration, Dr. Guillermo Zalazar Altamira. In order to apply it in practice, the plan needed the support of the minister and the under secretary of agriculture. Both were opposed to it but, as McDonald reported, "it was not until I explained the possibility of there being a large number of Catholics among the refugees . . . that they showed real concern." Even then they did not agree to adopt Dr. Zalazar Altamira's suggestion. "My last interview with the Under Secretary was most friendly but far from satisfactory. Warm in his expressions . . . he, nonetheless, would not say definitely that he approved Dr. Zalazar Altamira's programme." McDonald concludes his report concerning Argentina gloomily: "No reader of this report will be more conscious than I am that this indefinite result of more than three weeks' intensive efforts is highly unsatisfactory."

In Uruguay (whose minister in Paris, Alberto Guami, served as vice chairman of the executive committee supporting the high commissioner), McDonald found that the immigration laws were "reasonably satisfactory." Entrance into the country was open to those individuals who had either obtained a contract to work there or possessed a sum equal to $400. "On the whole, it appears that the government is friendly to Jewish immigration," wrote McDonald, raising the possibility that if an institution were to be set up "with considerable capital, it would be possible to secure from the government an exemption from the requirement of [U.S. $400] . . . per person." This true willingness to accept refugees was overshadowed by the fact that the economic crisis, already ebbing in Argentina, was at a critical stage in Uruguay.

In Chile, where Inman arrived alone, the economic situation was considerably different. "Economically and politically, Chile has largely recovered from the depth into which it fell in 1930–33," he reported; but he added that "poverty is still dreadfully evident and no one knows when it might lose its patience."

During the four days of his visit, Inman met with President Arturo Alessandri, the ministers of foreign affairs and finance, and various leading academic personalities. From the foreign affairs minister he heard that there were no restrictions on Jewish or other immigration but that immigrants were requested to prove that they would not become a public charge. When Inman referred the foreign affairs minister and later the president himself to a document that a Jewish refugee had given him in confidence and in which it was alleged that immigration to Chile had been stopped, both denied the veracity of that information. Alessandri added that if Inman knew of any individual who had experienced difficulty in obtaining a visa, he should immediately cable him and he would order the visa issued at once.

This agreeable attitude toward Jewish immigration was confirmed by the activists of the Chilean Jewish organizations. But these added that the government would not want "to disturb the political balance by bringing in any large number of Jews." They were all in agreement that whenever lower officials or consuls caused special difficulties to immigrants, the local Jews could count on the support of higher ranking officials, especially when it was proved that the immigrants would be supported financially by Jewish organizations.

The four Euro-American countries were thus divided into two uneven groups: the large federal republics of Argentina and Brazil, on the one hand, and the smaller Chile and Uruguay, on the other. Although the potential of the first two countries to absorb newcomers was much greater than that of the other two, they evinced extreme reluctance to accept refugees. The fact that in Brazil as well as in Argentina the Jewish communities were well established and that in both these countries a large number of Jews were already agriculturists and could offer their co-religionists diversified facilities of absorption did not modify the basically negative attitude of those governments toward Jewish immigration. Chile and Uruguay, on the other hand, demonstrated a more favorable attitude, and it can be assumed that if sufficient funds had been found, a considerable number of the refugees for whom McDonald was seeking a new home would have been accepted there.

Attempts in Indo-America

In contrast to the nations of the "southern cone," which for long or short periods of their modern history had tried to attract masses of European immigrants, the other Latin American countries did not have liberal immigration policies. Peru, Paraguay, and Mexico, as well as some of the other countries, had at one moment or another absorbed some extracontinental immigration, but they had neither encouraged it consistently nor made the newcomers welcome. The ruling classes of these nations were largely of Iberian descent, but the large majority of the populations were of Indian or *mestizo* origin. The general scarcity of European immigrants in these Indo-American countries also implied a paucity of Jews; only in a few cities were there incipient Jewish communities.

Inman pursued the high commissioner's mission in the Indo-American countries alone, because McDonald had returned to Rio de Janeiro. In April 1935, Paraguay was still investing all its efforts in war with Bolivia over the

Chaco territory. International mediation, however, appeared to make a settlement and peace possible. The president received Inman cordially and informed him "that there are no restrictions upon immigration in Paraguay; . . . that they would be glad to receive as many of the Jewish immigrants as it seemed could be absorbed." Following McDonald's instructions, Inman suggested that Paraguay accept 15 families per month and up to 900 individuals per year. "The Minister of Economy said that this number . . . would be absorbed without difficulty."

Impoverished Bolivia, which was on the verge of losing the war against Paraguay, was not visited. Inman proceeded to Peru after concluding his visit to Chile. He found the country divided by internal strife: The universities were closed for long periods, the leaders of the opposition were in hiding, and riots were impending. The cordiality with which he was received by the ministers of foreign affairs and of development was in clear contrast to the prevailing gloomy atmosphere. From the president of the republic, Inman learned that Peru was interested in absorbing immigrants "and could take the whole 15,000 refugees, if they would go on the land." The president also agreed that technicians who could assist in the development of infant industries would be accepted. Dr. Inman, paraphrasing the president, concluded that "there are no restrictions on the Jewish refugees coming to Peru and no race prejudice."

A warm welcome also awaited Inman and his mission in Colombia. The ministers of education and of finance gave him all the time he required. In their view immigration did not constitute a problem, as was proved by a decree signed by the president three weeks before Inman's arrival. Its purpose was to facilitate the immigration of individuals who did not possess passports because they had been denied them by their own countries. The decree authorized the Colombian consul general in Paris to issue entry permits to "individuals of good antecedents who dispose of enough resources for subsistence during the first month of their residence [in Colombia] and who intend to bring into the country useful activities." On receiving this information from President Alfonso Lopez Pumarejo, Inman concluded: "Colombia being a great country of open spaces with many opportunities—this should mean considerable [sic] in meeting our immigration problem."

The climax of Inman's trip to the Indo-American countries was his visit to Ecuador. Half a year prior to his arrival there, the government, headed by President Jose María Velasco Ibarra, had taken a major step in connection with immigration. On January 31, 1935, several months after the election of the president, the government signed a preliminary agreement with a group of Jewish activists who had formed a "Comité pour l'étude de l'agriculture, de l'industrie et de l'immigration en Equateur." In this agreement, the government offered the group a concession of 485,000 hectares (1,200,000 acres) in order to develop a large-scale colonization project. "The Government of the Republic of Ecuador, inspired by its traditional altruistic and humanistic ideology and animated by the desire to offer a new homeland to people who have become apatride as the result of the Great War and of the later political perturbations, has given its agreement to the present contract of immigration." So read the introduction to this agreement, which was ratified by the Ecuadorian Congress. In its first article, the government undertook to grant "free entry into the country to immigrants of the white race, coming from Europe and America, without distinction of nationality or religion." The other articles enumerated the guarantees and economic advantages the government intended granting to the immigrants.[12] According to their declarations, the initiators of the project intended bringing into Ecuador tens of thousands of settlers, and the figure of 50,000 was mentioned in this connection.

Upon his arrival, Inman found it necessary to moderate some of the enthusiasm shown by the authorities regarding this project instead of pleading with them to encourage immigration. In an interview with the minister of public works and agriculture, he raised "several questions about the international society." When he met with the minister of finance, he expressed reservations and emphasized the fact that the high commissioner was not involved in this particular project. In a summary of his concluding report, Inman expressed the opinion that "such a vast plan would be exceedingly unwise and have fatal results, since neither would most of the refugees be able to adapt themselves to the very difficult and rough tropical country life of Ecuador, nor would such a great number of one race be able to enter a country without creating enormous prejudices which would react against them."[13] Nevertheless, the agreement was not abrogated and in November 1935 it was confirmed.[14]

The hurried trip to the small countries of Central America—Panama, Nicaragua, El Salvador, and Honduras—made by Inman revealed that "each government is willing to make special concessions to Jewish refugees from Germany without passports." But Inman also added that the "opportunities for making any kind of a decent living are exceedingly scarce. So I have only opened up the matter of immigration believing that few would choose to come."[15]

12. Michael C. Astour, *History of the Freeland League and of the Territorialist Idea* (in Yiddish) The Freeland League (Buenos Aires and New York: 1967), vol. I, 110–115; *Extrait du Contrat,* A 107/232, Central Zionist Archives.
13. JCA–McDonald Report, 171–173 (65–67), *Extracts from Dr. Inman's Report and Letters,* Confidential Document #1/136, A 107/231, Central Zionist Archives.
14. L. M. Fruchtbaum, "Latin America—Land of Colonization, Ecuador (part II)," *Freeland* (New York) (June–July 1955): 2–4.
15. JCA–McDonald Report, 174–175 (68–69), 233–234.

The largest country of Central America, Mexico, constituted an exception in that general situation. At the very north of Latin America, Inman found an attitude similar to the one characterizing the extreme south of the subcontinent. Severe immigration regulations were in force, combined here with anti-Semitic feelings caused by economic rivalries. All he succeeded in achieving was "that the Mexican government, at our request, is carefully considering the admission of a few hundreds of refugees during the next year."[16]

An extraordinary case of willingness to accept Jewish immigrants was provided by the Dominican Republic. On his way to South America, in February 1935, Inman had spent a week in that country and found that "President Trujillo was very much interested in colonization and that ... the government is ready to give some of the best land to these colonies." In April of that year, two Jewish activists from Cuba negotiated with the Dominican government the possibility of establishing colonies of German Jews. Their proposals gained a favorable response from the secretary of agriculture and commerce. In a memorandum issued by that minister, the advantages of absorbing skilled workers and technicians as well as intellectuals were weighed against the handicap of settling "a foreign element with so well-defined racial and psychological characteristics," and he concluded that the benefits to be derived overruled the disadvantages. This willingness to develop a project of settlement for immigrants led Inman to believe that Santo Domingo could be seriously considered as a haven for refugees.[17]

Ecuador and the Dominican Republic, two countries with almost no Jewish presence, emerged from Inman's report as those most willing to accept refugees. Their capacity to do so was, however, much more restricted than their willingness. Other Indo-American countries also showed openness to immigrants and, in the case of Colombia, legal expression was even given to that trend. All these states, however, conditioned the actual reception of refugees upon the investment of large funds, mainly in agriculture.

Results of the Efforts

To what extent had the aims of McDonald and Inman been achieved? After a month of intensive activity in Brazil, McDonald wrote, "The victory has been in securing opportunities here for some of the intellectual refugees ... but in our major task, the securing of special permission to admit refu-

16. *Extracts,* A 107/231, Central Zionist Archives, 7.
17. Cesar Tolendino, Secretary of State for Agriculture and Commerce, 9 April 1935 to the Secretario de Estado de la Presidencia, Santo Domingo, 9 April 1935, JCA–McDonald Report, 175–176 (69–70), Annex M, 235–236.

gees . . . the results of our efforts are still uncertain."[18] A similar conclusion can be arrived at by analyzing McDonald's and Inman's final reports.

In almost every country, their contacts with the ministers of education, the rectors of universities, and even the presidents of the nations on the matter of the placement of scientists and professors produced some concrete proposals or, at least, detailed promises to invite some of the individuals to immigrate.[19] Ultimate success on this front still depended on a thorough follow-up and on intensive administrative dealings with the governments or with the employing institutions directly. Success seemed tangible enough to McDonald and his staff, however, for them to insist that Inman's report should not be published lest some North American or European institutions use this information and offer candidates of their own for the available positions to the interested Latin American governments, thus competing with the refugees.

The results on the main front were less evident. Success in this depended on the objective ability of each country to receive Central European, mainly middle-class immigrants, either in their own professions or in new ones, and on the willingness of the government and people of each nation to absorb them. McDonald and Inman reported that in most countries, potentiality and willingness were clearly disproportionate. When comparing the larger Euro-American countries, which had immense potential to absorb newcomers, with the smaller nations of that group, more willingness was found precisely where less objective possibility existed. Comparing the underdeveloped Indo-American states with the more developed Euro-American ones shows that an even larger gap existed between potential and willingness. If a scale were drawn, small, underdeveloped Ecuador would be at one end, with the rich United States of Brazil at the other. Absorption of refugees in Latin America depended, therefore, upon increasing the will to receive such immigrants.

McDonald presented his report to his board members, who were the unofficial representatives of the democratic nations, on the one hand, and to the major Jewish organizations, on the other. McDonald thus indicated that these two parties could, by their intervention and activity, change the situation in Latin America regarding the immigration of refugees.

In the eyes of McDonald the unofficial status of the high commissioner's office constituted a major impediment to his success. He strove to change this situation and to have his office become an official agency of the

18. McDonald to d'Avigdor Goldsmid, 6 April 1935, H 14, McDonald Papers.
19. "Summary of Report on Placing of German Refugee Scholars in Hispanic America, Prepared by Samuel Guy Inman," High Commission for Refugees, Document A/134, A 107/230, Central Zionist Archives.

League of Nations. His failure in this respect and the aggravation of the refugee problem late in 1935 induced him, at the end of that year, to tender his resignation publicly.[20] No official support for his work was offered by the individual democratic governments. McDonald managed, late in December 1934, while dining at the White House, to elicit a promise by President Roosevelt to contribute to the budget of his commission. The United States government and its Ambassadors to Latin America, however, were not involved in any direct way in McDonald's efforts to secure favorable decisions from the respective Latin American governments. The same also applied to other democratic governments. "Usually the foreign diplomats had been authorized merely to express the interest of their countries in the success of our mission—not to offer support through formal diplomatic representations," wrote McDonald in his final report.[21]

This official apathy on the part of the democratic powers was counterbalanced by an apparent similar attitude on the part of the Nazi ambassadors. Only in Bogotá, Colombia, did Inman report some official German reaction to his visit; even that was merely in the form of an apologetic statement made by the German ambassador in a personal conversation to the effect that the situation of the Jews in Germany was not as tragic as described by Inman. Neither the democratic powers nor the Nazi regime apparently attempted to influence the willingness of the Latin American governments to accept or reject refugees.

The Jewish organizations constituted the second party more explicitly alluded to in the high commissioner's reports as being capable of increasing the willingness of the Latin American nations to receive refugees. In McDonald's view, the local Jewish communities assumed an essential importance in this respect. He therefore deplored the exiguous Jewish leadership he found in Brazil, and he felt that the local communal leaders should have been helped and supported by the world Jewish organizations. "The long range possibilities of this country should be studied with the closest attention by all those Jewish leaders who do not have some other single formula to solve the problem of a future home for the Jews of Central Europe," he wrote to Sir Osmond E. d'Avigdor Goldsmid, then one of the leading personalities of the JCA and later its president. In McDonald's opinion, expressed two weeks after his arrival in Brazil, that country offered a possibility for the establishment of "a Jewish community comparable to that

---

20. Confidential report on conversations on centralization plans, H 4, *JGM Papers*, Letter of resignation of James G. McDonald, High Commissioner for Refugees (Jewish and Other) Coming from Germany, addressed to the Secretary General of the League of Nations, Printed in Great Britain, London, December 27th, 1935.

21. McDonald to Bentwich, 11 January 1935, H 12, McDonald Papers; JCA–McDonald Report, 4 June 1935, 111 (5).

in the United States . . . or . . . at least several times larger than the community in Argentina."[22]

The issue of the extent to which the Jewish organizations shared McDonald's alertness to the potential of Latin American countries for absorbing refugees on a large scale remains to be investigated. Considerable material on the attitudes of such organizations as the JDC and the JCA—both of major importance in that connection—has been published, but requires more comprehensive analysis.[23]

A positive response on the part of the Jewish organizations to the challenge presented by the high commissioner would have necessitated a radical change in their budgetary schemes and priorities. In the actual circumstances of an apparent lull in the brutal Nazi persecutions in Germany, as it was felt in the first half of 1935, such a change would have been extremely difficult to conceive.

Changes in 1938

Three years later, in July 1938, when an intergovernmental conference met in France at Evian-les-Bains to discuss the refugee problem, things had changed radically. At this conference the willingness of the Latin American nations to receive refugees was put to a second test. The conference was convened by President Roosevelt in direct connection with the dramatic increase in the need for immigration following the *Anschluss* of Austria on March 12, 1938. Some 185,000 Austrian Jews were now subject to the same policy that had been enforced on German Jews. A short while after the annexation of Austria, Adolf Eichmann arrived in Vienna, opened there the Zentralstelle für Jüdische Auswanderung (Central Bureau for Jewish Emigration), and almost immediately made it known to Austrian Jews that there was no future for them in that country. His brutal dealings with Viennese Jewry brought Eichmann his first distinction. The geographic extension of the persecution rendered the number of Jews exposed to forced emigration in excess of the 1933 level, despite five years of mass emigration from Germany. As the measures applied against the Jews of Germany also became harsher at this time, all signs pointed to the urgent need for immigration.[24]

The demand for immigration did increase dramatically as the hope of survival under the Nazi regime waned. Some of the Jews remaining in

22. Letter of 21 March 1935, H 14, McDonald Papers.
23. Yehuda Bauer, *My Brother's Keeper,* Chap. 4; Haim Avni, *Argentina y la historia de la immigracion judia 1810–1950* (Jerusalem and Buenos Aires: Maynes Press, 1983), 408–426.
24. Bauer, *My Brother's Keeper,* 223–226; Strauss, "Jewish Emigration," 326 (Table VII).

Germany had no hope, because of their advanced age, of finding a haven in any new country. Many of the wealthier Jews who were still in Germany and who had managed to preserve their wealth and even increase it were now seeking means to emigrate.[25] Nevertheless, in July 1938, German Jewry had not as yet experienced the *Kristallnacht* of November 10, 1938, or the expulsion of some 15,000–17,000 Polish Jews into the no-man's-land between the German and Polish borders that occurred on October 28. The increased demand for immigration, therefore, did not cause the Reichsvertretung der Juden in Deutschland (the representative organization of the German Jews) to refer to emigration in terms of a wholesale and mass phenomenon in its memorandum to the Evian conference.[26] This organization and many others that had presented memoranda of their own still regarded the Evian conference and, principally, President Roosevelt's leadership as their main hope in an increasingly darkening world.[27]

Of the thirty-three countries invited to Evian, twenty were Latin American. The potential of these countries to absorb immigration had increased since 1935 because the economic crisis had by then waned in Latin America. Research on Argentina indicates that in 1938 the impact of new industry was leading to a growing need for professionals.[28] That same need, though of different dimensions, was also felt in the other more advanced countries of the region. Each participating government was required to furnish a statement of its immigration laws and of its practices regarding the reception of immigrants as well as a general statement of the number and type of immigrants it would be prepared to receive. Let us consider closely four of these statements by Latin American representatives, two representing the main Euro-American countries and the other two representing countries classified as Indo-American.

Statements of Policy

Tomás A. Le Breton, Argentine ambassador to France, represented his country at the conference. "The Argentine is, above all, an agricultural

25. Strauss, "Jewish Emigration," 318 (Table III b), 338–346.
26. S. Adler-Rudel, "The Evian Conference on the Refugee Question," *Leo Baeck Institute Yearbook* 13 (1968): 261–271.
27. Arthur D. Morse, *While Six Million Died* (New York: Ace Publishing, 1967): Chap. XI; D. S. Wyman, *Paper Walls: America and the Refugee Crisis 1938–41* (New York: Pantheon, 1968); Henry L. Feingold, *The Politics of Rescue* (New York: Holocaust Library, 1970) were the first and best-known works on the subject. Roosevelt's real purpose in convening this conference is revealed in the comprehensive research on the Holocaust as well as in monographs dealing with specific related subjects.
28. Avni, *Argentina,* 429.

country," he declared. "Experienced agriculturists will, naturally, and for a long time to come, find numerous opportunities in a vast and fertile territory such as ours. . . . Our industries, the development of which has, up to the present time, been on a moderate scale only, have at their disposal all the labor required. Immigration into the Argentine must, therefore, be directed toward agricultural work and certain specialized forms of employment." This limited willingness to accept immigrants was subject to another reservation which Le Breton defined in a diplomatic but very unequivocal manner: "Those who intend, whilst living in our territory, to remain permanently bound by the special conditions derived from their country of origin, would do well to abandon their intention." These limitations, although they were implicitly directed at Jewish refugees, did not prevent the Argentine ambassador from concluding his statement with the encouraging promise that "we are fully determined to cooperate within the limits of what is possible. Those limits provide an ample field for the noble work of the present Conference. It is with this determination that we shall collaborate in studying and solving this problem."[29]

The Brazilian representative, Helio Lobo, was more precise than his Argentine colleague. The Brazilian policy, as specified in its constitutions of 1934 and again of 1937, was determined by the "concern for the defence of the labor market at home . . . [which] was associated with concern for assimilation of the immigrants." The yearly quota of 2% enabled 42,000 people to immigrate annually, "and it is certain the state of São Paolo [alone] needs almost as many for rural activities every year." The new immigration law of 1938 enabled the transfer of quotas from one national group to another and, eventually, allowed the minimum of 100 immigrants per country to increase up to 3000. However, "it should be observed that 80% of each quota has to be earmarked for agricultural immigrants or technical experts in agriculture and that no member of these later categories may change his occupation until four years after his arrival in the country." Helio Lobo concluded this detailed declaration with some encouraging remarks: "Brazil recognizes . . . that as regards German and Austrian refugees, the question is urgent. She is prepared to respond to the noble appeal of the American government and to make at this critical moment her contribution toward a favorable solution of the problems within the limits of her immigration policy."[30]

The representative of Ecuador, A. Gastelú, indicated the willingness

29. *Proceedings of the Intergovernmental Committee, Evian, July 7th to 15th, 1938.* Verbatim record of plenary meetings of the Committee, Resolutions and Reports, July 1938, 21–22.
30. *Proceedings,* 17–18.

of his country during the previous few years to accept immigrants as well as its favorable disposition toward the solution of the refugee problem. He mentioned, as proof thereof, the reception of a group of university professors at the time of Inman's visit in 1935. "As, however, Ecuador is an essentially agricultural country, we must take actual facts and national necessities into consideration, and these would not admit of too great an influx of intellectual workers." He nevertheless added, "My government is fully prepared to help in this humanitarian task."[31]

Primo Villa Michel, representative of the other Indo-American country, Mexico, surpassed his Ecuadorian colleague. "My country has always observed a tradition of hospitality and comprehension with regard to political refugees," he declared. In this spirit, the Mexican government hastened to accept President Roosevelt's invitation, and it was "prepared to contribute, within the measure of its legal, social and economic possibilities, toward the solution of the immense problem of justice, humanity and civilization, which we are now considering."[32]

The apparent willingness of the Latin American countries to accept Jewish refugees as indicated in these comments suggests they were ready to overcome many difficulties in order to comply with their humanitarian impulse to help the suffering refugees. Reality, unfortunately, was quite different.

Actual Policies

Argentina had expressed her willingness to absorb immigrants when, at its own initiative, it reached an agreement with the government of Denmark for the organized immigration of Danish peasants to Argentina. This agreement, signed on September 21, 1937, was preceded by similar agreements signed with the governments of Holland and Switzerland. The Argentine foreign minister, Nobel Peace Prize winner Carlos Saavedra Lamas, regarded these agreements, which were to provide Argentina with Nordic agricultural workers, as a very important achievement.[33]

The presidential elections of September 7, 1937, brought to power the radical liberal Roberto M. Ortiz in February 1938; many hopes for a more open immigration policy were then entertained, but these were to be disappointed. As Tomás Le Breton was presenting his statement showing an

---

31. *Proceedings,* 28.
32. *Proceedings,* 28.
33. The embassy in Buenos Aires to Anthony Eden, 21 October 1937, no. 440, British Public Record Office, FO 371, 20599.

encouraging slant at Evian, new and more severe immigration regulations were being prepared in Buenos Aires. Drastic limits were put on the scope of immigration and were applied retroactively, including those candidates for immigration who were already in the process of receiving their permits. Several scores of Jewish candidates who had been singled out by the JCA for agricultural settlement were now also excluded. The pretext given for these draconian regulations was apparently the economic situation, as Le Breton confided to the technical committee of the Evian conference on July 12, 1938. But Le Breton himself could serve as an example of the real motives causing the new limitations. As indicated by us elsewhere, these motives were connected with the impact of racism and anti-Semitism upon people like Le Breton in Argentina. The reference to the "nonassimilable" immigrants who were also undesirable in Argentina, which he had chosen to include in his statement, was an indication of a much more substantive element in the Argentine immigration policy.[34]

The real attitude of Brazil toward the immigration of Jewish refugees at the time of the Evian Conference was clearly expressed in a detailed letter written by the Foreign Minister, Oswaldo Aranha, to the Brazilian ambassador in Berlin, Ciro de Freitas Vale, on January 5, 1940. It came in response to the continuous complaints of the ambassador that, in spite of all the restrictions, Jews managed to infiltrate into Brazil. In his communications, the ambassador had accused the foreign ministry and other authorities of being responsible for that breach of the prohibitions. He directed the same complaints to President Getulio Vargas. The foreign minister was compelled to deny these accusations by comparing the situation regarding Jewish immigration at the end of 1939 to earlier developments. "According to the calculations of the Department of Immigration, 88,000 individuals of Semitic origin entered Brazil in the years of 1934–37," he wrote. "In the face of this situation, the Foreign Ministry dispatched the secret circular No. 1127 of June 7, 1937, forbidding the Consulates to grant visas on passports of individuals of Semitic origin. When dealing with persons of distinction in society and in the world of business, the Consulates must consult with the Secretariat of State before refusing the visa."[35]

The existence of this secret circular was known to Jews, although it was denied time and again until it was officially cancelled in February 1951, after the war was over.[36] According to Oswaldo Aranha, innumerable ap-

---

34. Avni, *Argentina*, 426–438, 521–524.
35. "Carta de Aranha mostra posição do Brasil na entrada de Judeus," *Jornal do Brasil*, 7 April 1973.
36. Elias Lipiner, *Breve historia dos Judeus no Brasil* (Rio de Janeiro: Ediçoes Biblos, 1962), 149.

plications for special permits flooded the Foreign Ministry, coming from a variety of directions. When he first took up his duties on March 15, 1938, he found that complete chaos reigned. "I gave orders, therefore, that the granting of visas should be limited only to those cases which were strictly justified or that were presented in the form of solicitations coming from the Presidency of the Republic, from the other Ministries and from the governments of the States (of Brazil)." This was the position at the time the Evian conference convened but it was not at all echoed in Helio Lobo's statement.

The leaks in the dam of prohibitions were mended by elevating the rank—and thus limiting the number—of officials who could intervene on behalf of the refugees; but the Brazilian government was not content even with these measures. In September 1938, "at the inauguration of the Council for Immigration and Colonization," continued Oswaldo Aranha, "I asked [the Council] to study the ways by which this wave of immigration could best be controlled." That was indeed the first problem the Council discussed; its proposals for the regulations controlling the immigration of Jews were then submitted, later approved by the president of Brazil, and were included in another secret circular, No. 1249, of September 26, 1938. The outcome of these efforts, according to Oswaldo Aranha, was reduction of the number of Jews who succeeded in entering Brazil by 50%, from 9263 in 1937 to 4900 in the critical year 1938.[37]

The sympathetic comments of the Ecuadorian representative regarding the willingness of his country to accept Jewish refugees also veiled a more contradictory reality. He could refer to the agreement the Ecuadorian government had signed in 1935 with a Jewish organization, which envisaged the absorption of up to 50,000 Jews. This agreement aroused controversial reactions in the Jewish world and was never put into practice. Voices were raised against the immigration of Jews in Ecuador as early as in 1936, at the time the agreement was still in existence. The German legation in Quito hastened to report this opposition, indicating that it brought about the expression of opinions "which allow me to conclude [the existence of] an increasing understanding of the Jewish problem in Germany."[38] The arrival of the first refugees in Ecuador during 1937 enhanced local opposition, and it became known in January 1938 that the Ecuadorian government intended to expel all Jews who were not engaged in agricultural work. This

---

37. "Carta de Aranha"; Mark Wischnitzer, in *To Dwell in Safety* (Philadelphia: Jewish Publication Society of America, 1948), 540, estimated the number of Jewish immigrants to Brazil in 1937 and 1938 at 2003 and 503(!) respectively; Arthur Ruppin in *The Jewish Fate and Future* (London: Macmillan, 1940) mentions 2,000 immigrants for each of these years.

38. The German minister, Quito to Berlin, 5 September 1936, JM/2257 (K325) K 34340, Yad Vashem archives, Jerusalem.

intention was not implemented but the very fact of its conception indicates an attitude diametrically opposed to the one encountered by Inman two and one-half years earlier.[39]

The short and pathetic words of the Mexican representative did not reflect the complicated circumstances that determined the level of Mexican willingness to accept Jewish refugees. President Roosevelt's invitation to Mexico to participate in the Evian Conference was followed by a consultation between the Mexican Ministries of the Interior and Foreign Affairs on the policy to be adopted. At its conclusion, Primo Villa Michel, who at that time was stationed in Geneva, was instructed by the Mexican government as follows: "You can discuss basic facilities [which] Mexico will give particularly [for] the entrance of agriculturists, outstanding professionals, technical workers, experts. You have to take into account the tables of quotas in order to establish the number of immigrants who can be received, which could be enlarged in case of necessity. The respective legislation will be modified in case of need, in order to amplify the facility [of immigration]. (Signed) Eduardo Hay."[40] The tables of quotas were published annually and those for 1938 envisaged the immigration of 5000 people from each of several countries; Germany and Austria were among them.[41] Substantial tension reigned at that time in the relations between the United States and Mexico. The leftist regime of President Cardenas had from its inception caused suspicion in the United States, and in March 1938, when Cardenas nationalized the foreign oil companies, relations deteriorated considerably. The invitation to the Evian Conference seemed to offer the Mexican government the opportunity to consider making a gesture of good will in order to alleviate this tension. The instructions given the Mexican representative were probably therefore flexible, reflecting the readiness of the Mexican government to change immigration legislation, if pressured.

The expectation for a clear and definite request on the part of the United States to permit large-scale immigration of refugees was widespread. So testified the Mexican delegate when the conference was over: "All the delegations were afraid," he reported, "that an attempt would be made to bring pressure upon them to receive refugees; so were mainly the delegates of the Ibero-American countries to which President Roosevelt's appeal was ostensibly addressed." To everyone's relief, the United States did not bring such pressure to bear. This could be felt in the wording of the cable that

---

39. Notes of 19, 23, 25 January, 1938, JM/2221, K 215553–215563; Yad Vashem archives; *Mundo Israelita* (Buenos Aires), 5 February 1938, p. 3, indicated that some 500 Jews were involved.

40. Cable no. 51186, 21 June 1938, III 1246-9 (part 1), Mexican Foreign Ministry archives.

41. *Diario Oficial* (Mexico City), 19 November 1937, Vol. 105, No. 17, p. 1.

Villa Michel hastened to dispatch: "The American government . . . limited its expectations of the Evian meeting to obtaining in principle from the participating countries certain reports, which almost none of them gave in detail, and to create a permanent committee in order to systematize, coordinate and render effective the distribution of Jewish emigrants from Germany and Austria. . . . Things did not reach the point of concrete negotiations envisaged in your cable of instructions."[42]

Mexico thus managed to satisfy the United States' requests while at the same time not committing itself to any special and far-reaching steps on behalf of the refugees. Mexico joined the Intergovernmental Committee, in the words of its representative, "in order to defend ourselves, if we so wish, [and] in order to maintain ourselves within an adequate proportion of the role which the other American countries will play."[43]

Four patterns of attitudes emerged from the confrontation between the declarations and the real intentions that have been reviewed. Brazil represented a sheer contrast between words and deeds. The somewhat encouraging statements of its representatives concealed, by omission, the harsh fact of a systematic anti-Jewish policy pursued at that time by the Brazilian government. Argentina exhibited a pattern of slippery diplomatic vagueness, which was intended to smooth over the contradictions in its policy. The apparent openness to immigration, though limited and conditioned, was in reality only a facade for newly erected additional barriers, implicitly aimed at impeding the immigration of Jewish refugees. Ecuador, with its welcoming and benevolent declarations, constituted in fact an arena of conflicting tendencies that had not yet been galvanized into unequivocal policy. This situation clearly opened some perspectives of outside interference that might have induced the Ecuadorian government to live up to its declarations. Mexico offered a positive disposition toward the refugees, which, although presented in humanitarian terms, was based on cold political considerations. This opening, however, was not taken advantage of by the United States.

Only in the case of one Latin American country, the Dominican Republic, did the official statements reflect deeds. Its representative, Virgilio Trujillo Molina, declared at the conference on July 9, 1938, that "the Dominican government would be prepared to make its contribution by granting specially advantageous concessions to Austrian and German exiles, agriculturists with an unimpeachable record." A few weeks later, when the

---

42. Primo Villa Michel to Hay, 18 July 1938, cable no. 155, 15 July 1938, III 1246-9 (part 1), Mexican Foreign Ministry archives.

43. Primo Villa Michel to Hay, 18 July 1938, cable no. 155, 15 July 1938, III 1246-9 (part 1), Mexican Foreign Ministry archives.

Intergovernmental Committee created in Evian began its work, the Dominican government indicated that the number of refugees it was willing to receive might reach 100,000. The encouraging statement was thus, in this case, sincere. It was put into effect with the Dominican authorities' help, in the form of the agricultural colony at Sosua; this was established by the Dominican Republic Settlement Association (DORSA), a subsidiary of the Agro-Joint, the agricultural branch of the JDC. The willingness of the de facto president of the Dominican Republic, Rafael Leonidas Trujillo Molina, to receive Jewish refugees, which had been reported by Inman early in 1935, had not changed by 1938.[44]

Conclusion

Although McDonald had attempted to persuade the Latin American nations to undertake a major share in the solution of the refugee problem, he later tried to water down its Jewish aspect. McDonald emphasized the non-Jewish portion of the German refugees, and the Evian Conference was convened officially to discuss the problem of "political refugees" from Germany.[45] His Latin American interlocutors were not deceived and regarded the issue that was brought before them as concerning, first and foremost, the immigration of Jewish refugees. Latin America's attitude toward the Jewish refugees has thus been revealed at an important point in Holocaust history. This is so even though in early 1935 the future victims had still not grasped the severity of the danger to which they were exposed, nor were the Jewish and non-Jewish international communities aware of it.

At that time, taken as a whole, the willingness of the Latin American countries exceeded the Jewish demand for emergency immigration. Upon examining each country separately, we find that the governments of the two largest nations, Brazil and Argentina, in spite of their considerable potential to absorb large numbers of refugees, were profoundly opposed to Jewish immigration. Mexico, the third largest Latin American country—and the prototype of an Indo-American society—was also practically closed to Jewish immigration; furthermore, alarming news of its imminent expulsion of Jewish immigrants already in the country were appearing in the Jewish press abroad.[46] The situation in all the other countries, however, was dis-

---

44. Mark Wischnitzer, "The Historical Background of the Settlement of Jewish Refugees in Santo Domingo," *Jewish Social Studies* 4(1) (January 1942), 45; Hyman J. Kisch, in "Rafael Trujillo—Caribbean Cyrus," *Judaism* 29(3) (Issue 115) (1980), 368–377, discusses in detail Trujillo's motives.

45. *Proceedings*, 7; Bauer, *My Brother's Keeper*, 232.

46. *Idische Zeitung* (*Diario Israelita*) (Buenos Aires), 2 May 1935.

tinct, as shown by Inman's reports: "In none of the countries that I visited alone, did I find any overpowering barriers. Few of these governments have any legal restrictions, the ones made being conveyed by orders to the consuls concerning visas and passports. In every case, the President or Minister of Foreign Affairs indicated his desire to interpret very liberally or to waive regulations when applied to the German refugees."[47] Underdevelopment and economic difficulties appeared to be the main causes limiting this benevolent attitude. Although it would have been very difficult for external parties to interfere with the local immigration policies of the large states, it would have been quite possible to induce the smaller countries to absorb immigrants by helping them to create new economic facilities.

Quite a different reality was disclosed at the Evian Conference in July 1938. Nationalistic arguments were brought forward by most of the Latin American countries; restrictions on immigration and, more particularly, on urban immigration were emphasized rather than provisions for the reception of immigrants. Unwillingness to attenuate prohibitions was the rule.

The reasons for this evident change in the willingness of many countries to accept refugees should be sought in several areas. Internal political and, eventually, also ideological factors were important in determining the attitude of each nation. The civil war in Spain and the consequent increase in the prestige of the fascist and totalitarian powers in Europe made an impact on Latin America. Xenophobic feelings and resentment at the United States' increasing influence in the region, which were hindered from expressing itself in fields of major interest for the dominant *coloso del Norte*, may have also played a role, particularly given the lack of a determined U.S. policy on the refugee question.

Reasons for the reluctance of many Latin American nations to receive refugees in 1938 should also be sought in the economic sphere. Between McDonald's mission and the Evian Conference, three years had elapsed during which no major development project had been undertaken regarding the migration of refugees. Apparently, no substantial impact on any Latin American economy during those years could be traced to the direct activity of refugees on their behalf. In July 1938, with World War II only fourteen months ahead, time had run out and no major project could be established for the absorption of a great number of immigrants. Preliminary preparations for the agricultural project planned in the Dominican Republic were concluded only in 1940.[48]

47. High Commission for Refugees Document no. A/136, A 107/231, Central Zionist Archives.
48. "Agreement with the Dominican Republic" in *Concerning Refugee Settlement in Dominican Republic* (New York: Dominican Republic Settlement Association Inc.), 30 January 1940, 21–26.

The internal balance of political power, the equilibrium among contradictory external influences, the economic situation as perceived by various segments of the host societies (some of which feared the eventual competition of the immigrants), and the potential development projects that the immigrants or their sponsors might have implemented are all factors to be taken into consideration when analyzing the willingness of each Latin American country to receive Jewish refugees. But another factor that should not be overlooked is the role of individuals in determining the acceptance of refugees. Individuals in the various echelons of local officialdom, among the personnel of each country's diplomatic service, among interested commercial parties, and, last but not least, the leading personalities of the Jewish communities played varied roles.

The combination of all these factors shaped the willingness of each nation to accept Jewish immigrants. The number of refugees actually accepted was determined not only by this willingness, but also by the objective potential of the country to absorb newcomers and by the extent of the Jewish demand for immigration that was generated by a perception of the real need to emigrate on the part of the persecuted Jews and world Jewish organizations.

It has been estimated that, as a whole, 100,000 Jews managed to immigrate to Latin America during the Holocaust era.[49] These data are far from firm, however, and more extensive research on each country is still required before final figures can be obtained. When elements such as those identified in the analysis of the McDonald mission are used as guides for future studies, they will enable us to grasp the significance of the figures not just in terms of what was accomplished but also in terms of what was not done to promote the resettlement of Jews in Latin America at a time when immigration meant rescue.

---

49. Louis Sobel, "Jewish Community Life and Organization in Latin American," *The Jewish Social Service Quarterly*, 20(4) (June 1944), 180. His estimate of 50,000 refugees for Argentina should be corrected to 31,900–39,441. See Avni, *Argentina*, Appendix 2, 542–545.

III
Comparative Dimensions

5
Adaptive Strategies of Jews in Latin America

Robert M. Levine

Introduction

This chapter considers the ways in which Jewish immigrants to Latin America dealt with the exigencies of their new homelands. To some degree, generalizations about the immigrant experience pose problems, because the conditions faced by newcomers to Euro-American countries such as Chile, Argentina, or Uruguay differed significantly from conditions in Indo-American countries such as Mexico or Peru. In the Southern Cone (and to some extent in the southern states of Brazil), Jews were received as elements of immigrant waves, a function of the rapid urbanization and social transformation of that region. Elsewhere, Jews remained for the most part in enclave communities, isolated and with relatively unchanging social patterns.

Sephardic Jewish migrants, pariahs in their Mediterranean homelands, generally impoverished and unskilled, tended to choose Latin American destinations because of the linguistic similarities between their home language (Ladino or Judezmo) and modern Spanish and because family cohesiveness meant more to them than the opportunity for upward economic mobility. Ashkenazic Jews, who made up the bulk of Jewish immigrants after 1920, chose Latin America for more ambiguous reasons. Most were precluded by restrictive legislation from entering English-speaking North America, the preferred destination and already the home of thousands of European and Russian Jews. They believed that their sojourn in places such as Cuba or Mexico would last only a year or two, until they could obtain the necessary visas for the United States. In fact, Jews arriving in Cuba in the early 1920s called the island *Akhsanie Kuba,* (Hotel Cuba).[1] But legal entry into the United States remained closed, and although some did manage to enter, most remained in the countries that had taken them in. These were then joined by refugees from Nazism and by still newer arrivals after World War II and creation of the State of Israel.

On the surface, there are similar patterns to Jewish life throughout the Diaspora. But for the approximately one-fourth of a million Jews who came to Latin America between 1920 and 1947, conditions differed markedly from those encountered by other Jewish immigrants in the United States and Canada. With the exception of those who went to Argentina, Jewish immigrants to Latin America found themselves in premodern and preindustrial societies unfamiliar with urban peoples. Throughout Latin America, society clung to the legacy of more than three centuries of legal barriers against Jews and *conversos*. The Jews found cultures largely devoid of secular national symbols, scornful of menial labor and enterprise. Access to decision-making power depended on ascriptive criteria such as family connections, communion with the Roman Catholic Church, and ownership of land. The public and private educational systems lacked any mandate to integrate foreigners and turn them into good citizens. As Judith L. Elkin has observed, the new cultures tended to be based on philosophies that had been rejected by Jews and that were hostile to them.[2]

Jews arrived in the New World intending to remain, bringing with them their families but little prestigious baggage in the form of skills or language. Under the circumstances, they had to work hard or go under. However, unlike the situation in English-speaking North America—where the Protestant ethic rewarded individual initiative and where acquisition of material goods brought, on the whole, social respectability—Jews in Latin America faced a confusing environment in which access was relatively open, but only to Catholics. As a result, Jews remained outsiders. Immigrants to the United States learned to discard their foreign mannerisms and to seek "Americanization" while at the same time preserving and even strengthening their identity as Jews within a pluralistic society; Latin American Jews who wished to retain their ethnic identity had to accept a mantle of vulnerability created by others' perception of their resistance to assimilation.

History shows that Jewish caution in entering Latin America was well

---

1. The best detailed overview of Jewish immigration to Latin America and the subsequent Jewish experience is Judith Laikin Elkin's *Jews of the Latin American Republics* (Chapel Hill: University of North Carolina Press, 1980).
2. See Judith Laikin Elkin, *Jews of the Latin American Republics,* Chap. 10.

founded. Although Jews did prosper economically and win acceptance during periods of political stability and economic expansion, nevertheless, when the skies darkened (as in 1919, during the terrible days of *la semana tragica*, when hundreds of Jews were killed in xenophobic rioting) Jews again became scapegoats, second-class citizens of societies that were uncomfortable with or even hostile to cultural and religious diversity. As time passed, Jews became the targets of new forms of anti-Semitism, which attacked them by challenging their patriotism, calling them "cosmopolitan garbage" (as in Argentina) or "enemies of the Revolution" (as in Mexico and Nicaragua) or allowing virulent anti-Zionism to mask anti-Jewish attitudes. In Argentina and Uruguay (but not Brazil), nativist campaigns charged Jews with being unassimilable. The historic dilemma first posed in post-Napoleonic Europe—assimilate or be assumed to be potentially disloyal—arose again in twentieth-century Latin America as these countries sought to affirm their national identities.

In the United States, most Jews and other immigrants managed to become absorbed into the primary groups of their host society, receiving the same political rights as native-born Americans and earning acceptance into all social contexts, although it might have taken more than one generation to achieve. This was not the case in Latin America. Most Jews there passed the adjustment stage successfully and achieved *integration,* an intermediate state in which they continued to be regarded as representative of an alien ethnic group.[3] But *assimilation* (a condition in which individuals are no longer regarded as members of a special ethnic group, although they may still share its values) rarely, if ever, occurred. This was especially true if one looks at centers of decision making. Latin American Jews ultimately prospered economically, but they remain excluded from the inner circles of power.

Sources for the study of adaptive strategies discussed in this chapter include questionnaires filled out by Jewish former residents of eight different Latin American countries, in-depth interviews with several dozen Jewish and non-Jewish former residents of Cuba, the standard literature on Latin American Jewish history, and articles in specialized journals in the fields of sociology, migration studies, and psychology. The responses showed eight strategies to have been those most commonly employed by Jews arriving in Latin America after the first World War: ghettoization, resistance to full assimilation, caution and conservatism, borrowing from the host society, isolation within a Jewish infrastructure, outmigration, occupational alienation and creativity, and an emphasis on education.

---

3. See Lars Henrik Ekstrand, "Migrant Adaptation: A Cross-Cultural Problem," *Educational and Psychological Interactions,* 59 (Jan. 1977), 14, citing Eisenstadt and others.

Ghettoization

The Buenos Aires neighborhood where Jews settled was "determined by preference within the boundaries of necessity."[4] Immigration followed a serial pattern: Family members and covillagers followed one another, new arrivals were taken in by extended family units, and mutual aid associations helped out. Residing in the Jewish quarter provided linguistic relief and psychological reassurance. Most of the first Jewish neighborhoods were established in old and deteriorating urban districts, forming a small insular nucleus generally served by a synagogue and soon joined by burial societies, credit unions, and social clubs. Jewish immigrants brought their urban community institutions, such as the *kehilla*, with them and maintained the tiny, closely knit fraternal societies of their former neighborhoods. In Buenos Aires, Plaza Lavalle functioned in the early 1900s as an open-air labor exchange, similar to the *chazar mart* ("pig" market) of New York's Lower East Side of that time or the present-day *feira* in Rio de Janeiro's Quinta de Boa Vista, where impoverished migrants from the rural Northeast sell their labor. The Ashkenazic immigrants also preserved their Old World work methods, importing the sweatshop to the New World and employing fellow Jews at the lowest wages paid to any immigrant group.[5]

Even within Jewish districts, subgroups preserved their Old World identities and remained segregated from one another. Researcher Harriet S. Lesser identified seven distinct and relatively isolated ethnic groups within Mexico City's small Jewish colony: Arabic-speaking Sephardim from Aleppo; Ladino-speaking Sephardim from Turkey, the Balkans, and Italy; German-speaking Ashkenazim; and Yiddish-speaking Ashkenazim, among others.[6] In the tiny Jewish community of Salvador, Bahia, Bessarabian Jews mixed little with Galician Jews. Throughout Latin America, a gulf separated the Sephardim (who tended to be patriarchal, less well educated, and more religiously observant) from the Ashkenazim (who were upwardly mobile and relatively secularized, and who permitted women to work).

From the initial days of their arrival, the ethnic subgroups remained isolated from one another. The Sephardim tended to consider the Ashkenazim to be crass, irreligious, and willing to exploit their wives (whose

---

4. Eugene F. Sofer, *From Pale to Pampa: A Social History of the Jews of Buenos Aires* (New York: Holmes & Meier, 1982), 6.

5. See Sofer, *Pale to Pampa*, 102–103. The Argentine Jewish community is also treated, less thoroughly, in Daniel J. Elazar, *Jewish Communities in Frontier Societies*, Part Two (New York: Holmes & Meier, 1983).

6. Harriet Sara Lesser, "A History of the Jewish Community of Mexico City, 1912–1970." Ph.D. diss., Jewish Theological Seminary and Columbia University, 1972, 40–55. Cited in Elkin, *Jews of the Latin American Republics*, 168.

working scandalized them). The East European Ashkenazim, for their part, regarded the Sephardim as lazy, backward, ostentatious, and uncultured. German Jewish refugees disdained both groups, especially the Ostjude (East European Jews). English-speakers living in small colonies in Havana and Mexico City ignored all the other Jewish immigrants, apparently embarrassed by them. Language differences and the lack of widespread opportunity for education and occupational mobility maintained this distinction, although exceptions occurred over time.

Ghettoization survived beyond the first immigrant generation. Although Jewish residential patterns did become more varied as vertical mobility increased the range of residential choice, Jews in Latin American cities tended to socialize with one another and therefore favored certain neighborhoods on the basis of propinquity. Reliance on religious schools and social associations added to the convenience of living close by these institutions. There was another reason as well: Ghettoization served as a source of positive self-identification, counterbalancing the unwritten rules of a host society that barred outsiders from social intimacy.

Resistance to Full Assimilation

Pluralism never has been accepted in Latin America; consequently, Jews attain the status of a tolerated minority but are not granted access to power within the government, the armed forces, the judiciary, or the law. Consequently, it is understandable that the community as a whole distanced itself from the majority. The result, unfortunately, preserved historic distrust and caused tolerant non-Jews to turn on them in exasperation. Among those who never understood the unwillingness of Jews to abandon their Jewishness was Juan B. Justo, the Argentine socialist leader. Married to a Jew himself, Justo wrote in an article in the Jewish magazine *Vida Nuestra* that Jews "remained enigmatic and suspicious" to him, and that only if Jews "abdicate their secret pride" would they lose their distasteful image.[7]

Because the organized community was tightly knit and did not tolerate intermarriage, it is difficult to estimate how many Jews "disappeared" through making that choice. More men than women emigrated, and many must have married Catholic women and drifted away. Some cases are known of Jews, for the sake of convenience, accepting the designation "German" or "Dutch" (in the case of Ashkenazim) or "Turk" or "Arab" (in the case of Sephardim). But their identity survives in Catholic families with surnames of Cohn and Levy. In the interior of the Brazilian state of Bahia, a

---

7. Quoted in Sofer, *Pale to Pampa*, 35.

researcher found two cases of *coroneis* (rural political and economic bosses) named Jose Abraao Cohim and Joao David Fuchs, both of whom attained prominence in the 1920s.[8] In frontier regions, so few Jewish families could be found that intermarriage was inevitable.

Caution and Conservatism

Historians of immigration have demonstrated that living under paternalistic governments encourages dependency and compliance.[9] Often lacking democratic protections and living in the midst of societies with traditions of differential justice, Latin American Jews tended to accommodate to the status quo by adopting a safe political conservatism, seeking to conform to the norms of the elites whose standard of comfort they wished to reach.

As a result, some Latin American Jews became vulnerable to political upheaval. Of the 12,000 Jews living in Cuba on the eve of the Revolution of 1959, only 800 acknowledged Jews remained in 1984. Smaller-scale but equally traumatic exoduses occurred from Sandinista Nicaragua, Chile under Allende, and Mexico during the 1981–1982 fiscal crisis. Second- and third-generation youth, however, exposed to the Marxist and venomously anti-Zionist atmosphere of the universities, tended in great numbers to opt for radical ideological positions. Mainstream Jews remained conservative and even timid, as typified by the Argentine Jewish community which, during the military dictatorship of the later 1970s, denied the allegations of Jacobo Timerman that the military regime was pointedly anti-Semitic. Unfortunately, revelations about the high proportion of Jewish victims among the *desaparecidos* in the aftermath of the Alfonsin victory have rendered most of these protestations hollow. In fear of retaliation, the communities tend to be extremely cautious, to the extent of blocking international efforts to call attention to violations of human rights.

On the other hand, the low-profile stance of the Jewish communities has permitted quiet, behind-the-scenes negotiations for the security of Jews. David Landau, diplomatic correspondent for the *Jerusalem Post*, revealed early in 1984 that Israeli diplomats and Argentine Jewish leaders, taking advantage of the military relationship between Israel and Argentina, collaborated between 1976 and 1983 in a secret rescue operation named *Milut* (salvage) in which Jewish political prisoners were released from custody

---

8. See Esther Regina Largman and Robert M. Levine, "Jews in the Tropics: Bahian Jews in the Early Twentieth Century." *The Americas.* Vol. XLIII, no. 2 (October 1986), pp. 159–170.

9. Edgar Goldstein, "Psychological Adaptations of Soviet Immigrants," *The American Journal of Psychoanalysis* 39(3) (1979): 258.

and allowed to proceed to Israel.[10] Such clandestine acts could not have succeeded had the Argentine Jewish community not avoided controversy and cooperated with the military junta. In other countries, right-wing regimes have sought out public expressions of support from their Jewish communities, as if they knew that being accepted by Jews amounted to a badge of good conduct in international circles. Thus, General Augusto Pinochet makes a point of visiting a Santiago synagogue each Yom Kippur. Jewish community spokesmen acquiesce in the symbolism.

Borrowing from the Host Society

Besides taking the safe political path, Jews in Latin America to some degree adopt stances that are more consistent with local practice than with progressive trends elsewhere. Religious expression, where it did not disappear altogether, remained traditional, discouraging the rise of reform or progressive Judaism. With the exception of those who came from Germany in the mid–1930s, most Jews remained nominally orthodox, reflecting the unreformed Catholic world around them. In contrast with the North American experience, women rarely sought a role in religious affairs, just as within the Latin Catholic Church women rarely demanded reform. Borrowing did not extend, however, to intragroup behavior: Jews for the most part have resisted the sexual double standard that prevails among the Latin American upper class, thus preserving Jewish family life to a considerable degree.

Isolation within a Jewish Infrastructure

To a greater degree than in the United States, Latin American Jews tended to create a Jewish world and remain within it. The psychological need to maintain the comfort afforded by ethnic enclaves helped first-generation Jews accept the sweatshop. As they became more successful, Jews gravitated toward group behavior of a different sort: Affluent Mexican Jews, conscious of not "feeling" Mexican and of being considered foreigners, now travel to Houston and Los Angeles to buy their clothes and to seek medical treatment. As a result, they contribute to the persistence of the stereotype of themselves as outsiders. Poorer Mexican Jews mixed more with non-Jews, but economic improvement is generally accompanied by a

---

10. Cited in *The Jewish Advocate* (Boston), 16 February 1984, 5.

narrowing of extragroup contacts until, at the top of the economic pyramid, virtually all contacts are with other Jews.

Ironically, some of the communal institutions developed to provide social and cultural reinforcement, such as the Hebraica clubs and the Macabi sports teams, became increasingly secular with time, maintaining a symbolic Jewish identity while ignoring Jewish substance. In Argentina, the Jewish clubs played an important role during the military repression, serving as a place where members could converse without fear. Perhaps in compensation, the clubs adopted a more Jewish stance during this period and in the aftermath of the return to civilian rule.

Outmigration

Perhaps as many as one-third of the Jews who arrived in Cuba and the Dominican Republic before 1930 subsequently entered the United States, by legal or illegal means. Following creation of the State of Israel, more Jews emigrated from Latin America than from any other part of the Diaspora.

Occupational Alienation and Creativity

Most Jewish immigrants to the New World lacked marketable skills and, as a result, like other immigrants they were forced to take the least desirable jobs in their new society. Jews, especially Ashkenazim, combatted this form of alienation either by adopting a hard outer personality shell, demonstrating the very characteristics for which Jews were disliked, or by escaping into hyperactivity, working night and day, often at the cost of physical health.[11] That the Sephardic Jews drove themselves less is not surprising, because they experienced far less cultural disorientation in coming to the New World.

Sephardim (like the Russian Ukranians of Misiones or the Japanese agriculturalists of Brazil) embraced a form of adaptation that emphasized security and reliability over risk-taking and profitability.[12] It has been shown that immigration creates a sense of personal distress that is greatest for

---

11. I. A. Listwan, "Mental Disorders in Immigrants: Further Study," *World Mental Health* 12 (1960): 38–45, cited in M. L. Kovacs and A. J. Cropley, "Alienation and the Assimilation of Immigrants," *Australian Journal of Social Issues* 10(3) (1975): 227.

12. See Leopoldo Jose Bartolome, "The Colonos of Apostoles: Adaptive Strategy and Ethnicity in a Polish-Ukranian Settlement in Northeast Argentina." Ph.D. diss., University of Wisconsin, Madison, 1974.

persons emigrating from cultures that differ most.[13] For Ashkenazic Jews, the cultural distance from Eastern Europe to Bolivia, Guatemala, or Cuba was staggering. Few had experienced the brilliant colors, the heat, or the humidity of subtropical climates. Although most were of lower-class origin, most were literate or even yeshiva-trained, and they found nonliterate lower-class life in Latin America utterly foreign. German Jewish refugees disdained the *swartz arbeit* (in polite translation, dirty work) initially available to them, but most took whatever work they could find, whether on jungle railway construction or selling soft drinks and ice cream on the streets. From carrying the heavy boxes filled with dry ice strapped to their chests in the broiling Havana sun, the Cuban Jews earned the nickname of "Eskimo Pie."[14] Jewish men were humiliated by the life of itinerant peddling so many were forced to lead, whereas Jewish women, imported to Latin American cities for the purpose, were forced to earn their living as prostitutes.[15]

Just as in North America and elsewhere, some Jews sought to escape from poverty through extralegal activities, ranging from acquiescence in corruption to racketeering and criminal activities. Official corruption and the open toleration of favor buying encouraged this option, to which all successful businessmen had to accommodate. Even peddlers who prospered and managed to rent commercial space for retail stores had to deal with the need for police protection in an environment where the practice of *la botella* (bribery) from the one side and the monopolistic practices of merchants from the other squeezed them mercilessly.

In much of Latin America, Jewish merchants (as well as the Syrio-Lebanese who emigrated to the region during the same period) created new domestic markets by selling simple clothing, trinkets, and religious pictures on credit to lower-class housewives formerly unable to buy such merchandise. This risky enterprise propelled the successful among them to great heights. In Cuba, for example, Jewish immigrants within a generation of arrival became manufacturers of shoes, creating an industry that supplied the island where previously no shoes at all had been manufactured for domestic consumption. The relative absence of stimuli for social mobility among native-born elites, already rewarded by the ascriptive basis of traditional society, left the way open for immigrants to fill the rapidly changing

---

13. Bertram J. Cohler and Morton A. Lieberman, "Ethnicity and Personal Adaptation," *International Journal of Group Tensions* 7 (1977): 35.
14. See *Havaner Lebn*, 12 October 1934, cited in Elkin, *Jews of the Latin American Republics*, 106; videotaped interview with Jaimie Schuchinsky, Miami, available on tape from University of Miami Richter Library.
15. See Sofer, *Pale to Pampa*, 68; Elkin, *Jews of the Latin American Republics*, 108.

needs of urban-industrial life and thereby to improve their status dramatically.

But entrepreneurship at all levels necessitated pragmatic business practices. In Cuba, importers had to pay customs inspectors thousands of dollars for each shipment of goods they brought into the country—part of a system in which the inspectors then falsified declarations of value in order to be able to siphon off the difference for themselves. According to import merchants, corruption in Cuba extended to the presidential palace itself, where, during the 1940s, the family of the chief of state took its cut of the illegal fees. *La botella* was another reason Jews were unable to gain status as insiders. Only persons with connections received coveted positions in the private or public sector. Such jobs often required little or no work, but paid very well. Latin American Jews, unlike their counterparts in North America, saw no point in striving to enter mainstream professions or the bureaucracy. As the system did not open itself to outsiders, they channeled their energies into commerce, which was disdained by the upper class. Jews also tended to accept the status quo rather than fight it with organizations such as the Anti-Defamation League of B'nai Brith or the American Jewish Committee. Nor did they enter political life in democratic countries as representatives of voting blocs. Ethnic politics was largely unknown in Latin America, and as a result community leaders lacked political influence. The few Jews who gained elected or appointed government posts did so as unhyphenated nationals and did not carry the weight of Jewish voters behind them.

As Jews prospered, more of their children were able to enter the professions. Jewish youths of the second and third generations became physicians, architects, and engineers. Although some developed general clienteles, most practiced within the Jewish community. Few young men and women entered the law, however, because its practice in Latin America depends largely on social networking. In addition, legal skills are not portable in case of the need to emigrate. As Juan Plaut of the Latin American division of B'nai Brith put it during the 1960s, the percentage of Jewish lawyers in any society presents an "index of comfort."

Not all the immigrants or their children have prospered. In Brazil, a certain percentage of Jews in Rio de Janeiro, São Paulo, and smaller cities remain on the margin of the lower middle class, earning their livelihood as bus drivers, cab drivers, and petty merchants. Eugene Sofer found that in Argentina more than a third of the Jewish community remained in the working class into the third generation, whereas many others who had managed to rise fleetingly out of the working class actually slid back, experiencing downward mobility and economic failure.[16] Not all profited by eco-

---

16. Sofer, *Pale to Pampa*, 96.

nomic advancement over time. Peddlers became obsolete within a generation as mainstream commercial houses hired their own traveling salesmen. New labor laws regulated street vending, limited retail hours, and forced merchants and factory owners to fire immigrants in order to hire given percentages of native-born workers (in Machado's Cuba, for example, at least 50%). But on the whole, Latin American Jews experienced remarkable economic prosperity, especially after World War II.

Although Latin American societies exerted greater pressures for conformity than did North America, Jews were nevertheless prevented from taking their place as assimilated equals in their adoptive societies to the south. The terms in which the choice was presented, as Sofer has demonstrated, were more urgent than the terms offered by societies such as the United States, which were more tolerant of cultural and religious diversity.[17] Elkin quotes an Ecuadorian woman, describing herself as a "Catholic Jew," holding the role of a subordinated minority permitted to occupy a well-defined but circumscribed social niche in which "expressions of creativity emerging from a specifically Jewish tradition are stifled by law, by social pressure, or by self-censorship."[18] This has remained true even while upward economic mobility loosened traditional forms of behavior within the Jewish community itself.

For many of the Jewish immigrants from the Old World, tropical America produced traumatic shock. In the words of a Yiddish poet who came to Cuba from Poland in 1924:

> On my first night in Havana I went to walk on San Isidro Street, where women were selling themselves openly, sitting behind glass windows, calling to passersby for their attention. I was unprepared for this: I was of another morality. I thought: "How can girls sell themselves like animals?" I remember the big stores selling liquor in which girls were sitting, drinking with the American Marines. The girls drank Coca Cola, and the Marines drank and paid for schnapps. I remember the impression when I first saw the pianola on the street and a black-colored man dancing. I never saw a black man before. He was diseased, but he was dancing with real talent. I was wearing a jacket, which my parents had to pay for after I left Poland, and it had a closed collar. It was so hot that sometimes it burned my skin, but I had to wear it because I thought, "how can I throw it out if they still have to pay for it on credit?" You don't understand, you don't know what it will be like to come to such a place. . . . You left a home, parents, sometimes brothers, a bed, your village, you left a life. And here you find yourself speechless, without words, in a strange new type of life. Instead [of] a life, I would call it a tragedy.[19]

17. Elkin, *Jews of the Latin American Republics*, 244.
18. Ibid.
19. Transcript of Schuchinsky interview for film on the life of Jewish immigrants, *Hotel Cuba*, produced by R. M. Levine and Mark kD. Szuchman. Coral Gables: University of Miami, 1984, 46-minute videotape, available from University of Illinois Film Center.

For most, desolation did not last. Other strategies helped the newcomers adapt to their new environment and cope with their new lives. Latin American societies were far more tolerant than those the emigrants had fled. Newcomers saved up money to send for brothers, sisters, and cousins, a chain migration pattern that strengthened family ties and provided an internal support system.[20] The Jewish community was strengthened by this commitment to family integrity and by the insistence on educating its children. Intergenerational and intercommunity ties among Jews remained stronger in Latin America than in pluralistic North America, where the emphasis on diversity and geographic mobility acted to fragment and disperse family units. The fact that Ashkenazic women worked the same long hours as their husbands helped counter the tensions caused by loneliness in a confusing and alienating environment and accelerated the process of absorption by forcing working men and women to learn the language of their new country and to deal with non-Jews, however hard they were to understand.[21]

Emphasis on Education

Jewish insistence on formal education for the community's children provided a major boost for upward mobility. Immigrants sent their children to school despite financial hardships. By the 1970s, 20.4% of São Paulo Jews had earned a post-secondary degree, compared to 1.4% of the general population of the State. In Argentina, where public schools tended to be of high quality, Jews competed for positions in them. The disproportionately high percentage of educated professionals within the Jewish community and its generally unyielding emphasis on schooling characterized Jewish life throughout the region and distinguished it from most other ethnic groups.

Conclusions

One of the first historians to measure the human impact of immigration, Oscar Handlin, described the immigrant experience as traumatic and potentially devastating in terms of alienation, emotional instability and loss

---

20. See Suzanne Ziegle, "Family Unit and Internal Migration," *International Migration Review* 11(3) (Fall 1977): 326; Dorothy E. Mandel, "Aspects of the Adaptive Process in Migration." Ph.D. diss., United States International University, San Antonio, 1982.

21. Corinne Azen Krause, "Urbanization without Breakdown," *Journal of Urban History* 4(3) (May 1978): 302; Margarita Melville, "Mexican Women Adapt to Migration," *International Migration Review* 12(2) (Summer 1978): 232.

of self-esteem.[22] But revisionists, including Handlin himself, have found the original premise to be unduly pessimistic. Not all psyches were shattered by the crossing and some amazingly successful adjustments were made. Immigrants also maintained some parts of their former cultures, preserving values that strengthened them. Most accomplished the transition without significant symptoms of personal maladjustment or breakdown of family life.[23] In Latin America, Jews managed to cope even though fear preserved old feelings of mistrust and their small number limited their ability to overcome the perception of themselves as alien. As in North America, most Jews in Latin America (but not all; see Sofer's writings) achieved middle-class status and relative affluence after one generation.

To be sure, they shared the same psychological terrors induced by the Nazi period as their fellow Jews throughout the world. It would be unfair to fault them for inflexibility or for accommodating to the existing political and social system when their options were so severely limited. Latin American Jews caught too far out either end of the spectrum suffered. Ideological radicals who entered local Communist or subversive groups were persecuted for their ethnic origin as well as for their politics; those who aligned themselves with the Somozas and the Batistas had to flee their adoptive homelands as a consequence of political insurgency.

The Jews who rationalized their decision to accommodate politically did so lacking the safety net of guaranteed liberties and legal safeguards that are offered in more democratic nations. There are serious consequences to making the wrong political choice in so volatile an environment. Ironically, the parents and grandparents of these Latin American Jews had had to make similar choices in earlier generations—in Poland, Russia, or the Turkish Empire. The waning of ethnic pluralism in Latin America, especially in the Southern Cone where Italians, Germans, Poles, Spaniards, and even Japanese more or less intermingled with the larger society, marked Jews as in some ways their country's only surviving ethnic group (at least in the minds of non-Jews). The effort to retain a Jewish identity caused strained relations with the majority society and exacerbated stereotyped views of the "unassimilable" Jews.

For the Jews themselves, Latin America was far more like postwar Europe than the United States or Canada were. The measures taken by these Jews to relate to their host societies were very similar to those adopted by European Jews, especially those living in Catholic nations. Yet when the

22. Oscar Handlin, cited in Krause, "Urbanization," 291–292.
23. See the work of Oscar Lewis on Mexico, for example. Also Krause, "Urbanization," 292–294; Jean-Clause Lasry and John J. Sigal, "Influences sur la santé mentale de la durée de séjour, de l'instruction, du revenu personnel, et de l'âge, chez un groupe d'immigrants," *International Review of Applied Psychology* 25(3) (1976): 215–223.

1982 Israeli invasion of Lebanon raised angry anti-Semitic demonstrations throughout Latin America and Europe, these communities reacted differently. In Italy—where the community of 35,000 Jews was buffeted by anti-Semitic desecrations, near-riots stirred up by labor unions and the press, beatings, and a synagogue bombing—the organized Jewish community met with political leaders, labor officials, university leaders, and other organized groups in an effort to improve Jewish–Christian relations.[24] This effort was led by Chief Rabbi Elio Tuoff, who dealt personally with government officials, meeting the issues of the conflict head on. By contrast, the Latin American communities feared to respond, maintaining their traditional silence. The outpouring of anti-Semitism masked as anti-Zionism met no collective reaction. Friends of the Jewish community were not enlisted in support of Jewish rights. Instead, Latin American Jewish spokespersons sought to minimize the conflict. As a result, they earned an uneasy sense of security in the short term, but failed to prepare themselves for possible difficulties later.

In summary, one may conceive of a three-fold proposition. Jewish immigrants in Latin America, especially Ashkenazim, retained a great measure of their ethnicity. The societies in which they settled rejected pluralism and therefore tended to exclude Jews as outsiders, although this was less true of the urban industrialized areas. On the whole, Jews achieved economic prosperity in Latin America but remain isolated behind social and political barriers from true access to assimilation, even assuming that they desire it.

Second, as they evolved, the Latin American Jewish communities on one hand cultivated a safe political conservatism and on the other hand sponsored strong emigration movements to Israel, the United States, or even back to Europe. At the same time, many Jewish youths, reflecting their polarized social and political environment, became much more radicalized than their North American counterparts.

Finally, most Jews did prosper, albeit within a more defensive, less idealistic posture than North Americans. They survived under conditions lacking any public commitment to diversity or to social democracy or to what Lionel Trilling called, in the United States context, the adversary culture. Latin American societies, defining themselves according to the rigid standards of singularity, exercise a great deal of pressure against their Jewish nonconformists. Thus Jews continue to live under a real threat of disruption.

---

24. See Adam Goldgeier, "After-Shock in Rome," *Present Tense* 11(2) (Winter 1984): 57–58.

6
Demographic Trends of Latin American Jewry

Sergio DellaPergola

Introduction

In the course of the last several years, the question of how many Jews live in Latin American countries, especially in Argentina, has attracted renewed attention on the part of observers of the Jewish community scene. The principal stimulus to this debate—or, occasionally, controversy—was provided by the publication of two things: first, a theoretical critique[1] and, shortly after, a large amount of new empirical evidence[2] that rejected the then-prevailing Jewish population estimates for the entire region and, more particularly, for its larger Jewish communities. The revised population estimates suggested much lower figures and, more importantly, pointed to an entirely different course of demographic development than had previously been assumed.

---

1. U. O. Schmelz, "Evaluacion critica de las estimaciones de población judia en la Argentina," in *Comunidades Judias de Latinoamerica, 1973–1975*, ed. J. Kovadloff (Buenos Aires: Comite Judio Americano, 1977), 198–223. The original Hebrew version appears in *Gesher* 68–69 (1971): 32–51. For a more recent exposition of revised Jewish population estimates in Latin America in the context of demographic changes among world Jewry see U. O. Schmelz, *World Jewish Population: Regional Estimates and Projections* (Jerusalem: The Hebrew University, Jewish Population Studies, Vol. 13, 1981). See also U. O. Schmelz and S. DellaPergola, "The Demography of Latin American Jewry," *American Jewish Year Book* 85 (1985): 51–102.

2. U. O. Schmelz and S. DellaPergola, *The Demography of the Jews in Argentina and in Other Countries of Latin America* (Tel Aviv: Tel Aviv University, David Horowitz Institute, 1974), (in Hebrew).

The major new piece of evidence was a thorough analysis of the detailed computer records of Jews enumerated in the 1960 census of Argentina. By relying on accepted techniques of data processing and demographic analysis and by relating the census returns to other, more fragmentary existing data, it was possible to provide a detailed picture of Jewish population characteristics and trends in Argentina around 1960. A further effort was invested in an attempt to reconcile the 1960 census findings with available data on Jewish population size and movements since the establishment of Jewish settlement in Argentina in the late nineteenth century. These analyses of recent and retrospective population changes rejected as fallacious the periodic augmentation of Jewish population figures that had been routine practice since the post–World War II period. The new findings indicated that, after reaching a peak of slightly over 300,000 persons, Argentinian Jewry was approaching a point of numerical stagnation. Extension of current trends over time would produce numerical decline. Similar diagnoses, though based on far less detailed data, were suggested for other Jewish communities in Latin America.[3] The revised demographic picture implied a thorough reassessment of the general position of the Jewries in the region and bore major implications for the evaluation of the level of activity of the main Jewish communal functions and organizations.

It is not surprising, therefore, that the debate around the more likely size of Jewish population in Argentina and elsewhere on the continent should become a prominent aspect in the broader discussion of the current status of Latin American Jewry. Clearly, however, a correct perception of the demographic picture cannot focus only on population size, which results from the complex interplay over time of several factors of population change. The determinants of each structural and dynamic component of demographic processes should be assessed before addressing their ultimate consequences. Moreover, at least from a demographic point of view, Latin American Jewry should not be seen in isolation, but rather should be evaluated in the wider context of sociodemographic trends that have been shaping contemporary world Jewry.[4] Substantial similarity now exists among

3. Some of the main findings of the Schmelz-DellaPergola monograph were also reported by David Schers and Hadassah Singer, "The Jewish Communities of Latin America: External and Internal Factors in Their Development," *Jewish Social Studies*, 39(3) 1977: 241–258; and by Judith Laikin Elkin, *Jews of the Latin American Republics* (Chapel Hill: The University of North Carolina Press, 1980), which includes extended discussions of sociodemographic trends. See also J. Laikin Elkin, "A Demographic Profile of Latin American Jewry," *American Jewish Archives* 34(2) (1982): 231–248.

4. R. Bachi, *Population Trends of World Jewry* (Jerusalem: The Hebrew University, Jewish Population Studies, Vol. 9, 1976); U. O. Schmelz, "Jewish Survival: The Demographic Factors," *American Jewish Year Book* 81 (1981): 61–117; S. DellaPergola, *La trasformazione demografica della diaspora ebraica* (Torino: Loescher, 1983).

most Western communities with regard to several basic socioeconomic patterns, such as high levels of urbanization, high educational attainment, and concentration in selected sectors of the occupational structure. Secularization and assimilation processes are known to affect, to varying degrees, the social evolution of Western Jewries. Several communities in Western countries share a background of relatively recent and large groups of immigrants from Eastern Europe, whose descendants now constitute the bulk of local Jewish populations. Although the data available for assessing the demographic consequences of these processes have often been insufficient in Latin America, some inferences can be made by looking at the demographic situation of other communities for which such documentation exists and that share with Latin American Jewry important structural features. Awareness of the global picture may provide the student of Latin American communities with a better sense of the more likely range of population trends.

This chapter discusses several of the major demographic features of Latin American Jewry. Although the principal data, estimates, and projections on Jewish population size will be presented, the chapter will also focus on aspects of internal sociodemographic stratification and change that are not directly related to Jewish population size. Most of the materials presented concern Jews in Argentina, whose demographic trends have decisively affected the total Jewish population balance in the region.

Jewish Population Size: Data and Hypotheses

Size and Geographical Distribution of Latin American Jewry

According to revised Jewish population estimates prepared at the Hebrew University's Institute of Contemporary Jewry, 465,000 Jews lived permanently in Latin American countries at the end of 1982. Latin American Jewry accounted for about 5% of the total Diaspora (see Table 6.1). In the early 1980s, world Jewry was estimated to have reached a level of around zero population growth as a result of low birth rates, population aging, and erosion caused by mixed marriages and assimilation. More accurately, between 1980 and 1982 the world Jewish scene presented contrasting developments, with a two-year Jewish population increase of 2.8% in Israel and an estimated loss of −0.9% in the Diaspora. While North American Jewry was minimally increasing (+0.2% between 1980 and 1982), mostly as a consequence of immigration, the number of Jews declined by −1.9% in Central America and by −2.3% in Southern America. This yearly loss of about −1% was determined by negative balances of international migration and of natural and affiliative changes.

The Jewish geographical distribution differed substantially from that

Table 6.1
Estimated Jewish Population Distribution in the World and in the Americas, End of 1982

Region or country	Jewish population			Percentage change 1980–1982
	Absolute numbers	Percentage of world Jewry	Percentage of diaspora Jewry	
World	12,988,600	100.0	—	+0.0
Israel	3,374,300	26.0	—	+2.8
Diaspora	9,614,300	74.0	100.0	−0.9
The Americas, total	6,477,700	49.9	67.3	+0.1
North[a]	6,013,000	46.3	62.5	+0.2
Central	46,800	0.4	0.5	−1.9
South	417,900	3.2	4.3	−2.3

Source: U. O. Schmelz and S. DellaPergola, "World Jewish Population, 1982," American Jewish Year Book 84 (1984): 247–258.
[a]The United States and Canada.

of the general population of the continent: 61% of the Jewish population lived in the countries of the temperate cone versus 11% of the total population of Latin America, 29% versus 55% lived in tropical South America, 9% versus 26% in the isthmian countries, and 1% versus 8% in the Caribbean countries. The detailed Jewish population estimates reported in Table 6.2 rely on a variety of sources of quite unequal quality. Unfortunately, for no Latin American country are indisputably reliable data available (as shown by the absence of A ratings in the last column of Table 6.2). The largest Jewish population, Argentina's, was estimated at 233,000 at the end of 1982; the other larger communities were in Brazil (100,000), Mexico (35,000), Uruguay (30,000), and Chile and Venezuela (20,000 each). Only in Uruguay did the Jews possibly constitute more than 1% of the total population. In Argentina their share of the total was 8 per 1,000 inhabitants, and elsewhere they consisted of tiny minorities of 0–3 per 1,000 of the total population.

Jewish Population Growth in Argentina, 1895–1960

From the establishment of the modern Jewish settlement in Argentina to the present, changes in the size of the Jewish population have been documented through a moderate amount of statistical data, some of doubtful reliability.[5] The first national census of Argentina, in 1895, covered

---

5. For a full list of relevant publications see *Demography and Statistics of Diaspora Jewry, 1920–1970; Bibliography,* ed. U. O. Schmelz et al., Vol. 1 (Jerusalem: The Hebrew

slightly more than 6000 Jews, mostly in rural colonies in the country's interior. The subsequent growth of the Jewish population was estimated by S. Weill, a well-informed leader of the Jewish community who had access to the official statistical data on immigration to Argentina and to detailed figures on the development of Jewish agricultural settlements. Weill, relying on certain assumptions concerning the level of Jewish birth rates and ignoring the Jewish emigration factor, presented a set of yearly estimates of Jewish population size until the mid-1930s[6] (see Table 6.3). Several years later, the demographer I. Rosenswaike, on the basis of a detailed analysis of the 1936 municipal census of Buenos Aires, suggested that Jewish birth rates assumed by Weill were too high and that Jewish emigration could account for as much as one-eighth of Jewish immigration. He accordingly revised the Jewish population estimates for the total country.[7]

Immigration had been a leading factor of Jewish population growth until the late 1930s, among other things because of the stringent quotas that limited migration to other countries. A marked slowdown characterized the World War II period, after which migration to Argentina did not resume at the prewar pace. The 1947 census pointed to a total of 249,000 Jews, which was believed to be an underestimate of the actual Jewish population size. In fact, considering that many Jews had immigrated illegally and feared expulsion, Rosenswaike suggested a corrected figure of between 265,000 and 275,000 in 1947. Substantially higher figures, however, were beginning to circulate among the Jewish community. Implicitly assuming that the rhythm of Jewish population growth would be the same or greater than among non-Jews in Argentina, these conventional estimates swelled from a postwar figure of 350,000 to 400,000 in 1958, 450,000 in 1962, and 500,000 in 1968. These estimates lacked the backing of any empirical research.

Published results of the 1960 census included a figure of about 276,000 Jews aged five and over.[8] The full total, obtained from a special computer processing of the original census records, was close to 292,000.[9] This ad-

---

University, Jewish Population Studies, Vol. 7, 1976); and the three annotated bibliographies by P. Glikson, for 1961–1968, 1969–1971, and 1972–1980, respectively, in *Jewish Population Studies 1961–1968, Studies in Jewish Demography—Survey for 1969–1971*, and *Studies in Jewish Demography—Survey for 1972–1980*, ed. U. O. Schmelz and P. Glikson (Jerusalem: The Hebrew University and London: Institute of Jewish Affairs, 1970, 1975, and 1983).

6. Simon Weill, *Poblacion israelita en la republica Argentina* (Buenos Aires: Bene Brith, 1936).

7. Ira Rosenswaike, "The Jewish Population of Argentina, Census and Estimate, 1887–1947," *Jewish Social Studies* 22(4) (1960): 195–214.

8. Republica Argentina Instituto National de Estadistica y Censos, *Censo nacional de poblacion, 1960*, vols. 1–9 (Buenos Aires: n.d.).

9. Schmelz and DellaPergola, "The Demography."

Table 6.2
Estimated Jewish Population Distribution in Latin America, Corrected Estimates, End of 1982

Region or country[a]	Total population		Jewish population		Jews per 1000 population	Accuracy rating[b]
	Number	Percentage	Number	Percentage		
Latin America	367,343,000	100.0	464,700	100.0	1.3	
Middle America	94,385,000	25.7	41,750	9.0	0.4	
Costa Rica	2,271,000		2,200		1.0	C1980
Guatemala	7,481,000		900		0.1	D
Mexico	71,193,000		35,000		0.5	C1970
Panama	1,940,000		3,500		1.8	C1982
Other[c]	11,500,000		150		0.0	C1982
Caribbean	28,873,000	7.9	5,050	1.1	0.2	
Bahamas	248,000		500		2.0	B1970
Cuba	9,717,000		700		0.1	D
Dominican Republic	5,581,000		100		0.0	D
Haiti	5,104,000		100		0.0	D
Jamaica	2,220,000		300		0.1	B1982
Netherlands Antilles	261,000		700		2.7	D
Puerto Rico and Virgin Islands	3,242,000		2,500		0.8	D
Other[d]	2,500,000		150		0.1	D

Tropical South America[a]	201,779,000	54.9	134,900	29.0	
Bolivia	5,755,000		1,000	0.2	C1982
Brazil	121,547,000		100,000	0.8	B1980
Colombia	28,776,000		7,000	0.2	B1977
Ecuador	8,644,000		1,000	0.1	C1982
Paraguay	3,268,000		700	0.2	C1982
Peru	18,279,000		5,000	0.3	C1982
Surinam	397,000		200	0.5	D
Venezuela	14,313,000		20,000	1.4	D
Temperate South America	42,306,000	11.5	283,000	6.7	
Argentina	28,085,000		233,000	8.3	C1960
Chile	11,294,000		20,000	1.8	C1970
Uruguay	2,927,000		30,000	10.2	D

Source: Adapted from U. O. Schmelz and S. DellaPergola. "World Jewish Population, 1982," *American Jewish Year Book* 84 (1984): 247–258.

[a]Countries with estimated Jewish population of 100 or more are shown separately.

[b]A, Base figure derived from countrywide census or reliable Jewish population survey; updated on the basis of full or partial information on Jewish population movements in the intervening periods. B, Base figure derived from somewhat less accurate countrywide Jewish population investigation; partial information on population movements in the intervening period. C, Base figure derived from less recent sources and/or partial coverage of Jewish population in country; updating according to demographic information illustrative of regional demographic trends. D, Base figure essentially conjectural; no reliable updating procedure. In categories A, B, and C the year for which the principal base figure was obtained is also reported.

[c]Belize, El Salvador, Honduras, and Nicaragua.

[d]Barbados, Dominica, Grenada, Guadeloupe, Martinique, St. Lucia, St. Vincent, Bermuda and the Grenadines, and Trinidad and Tobago.

[e]Including Guyana.

Table 6.3
Estimates of Jewish Population in Argentina, 1895–1980

Year	Official censuses	Weill[a]	Rosenswaike[a]	Conventional estimates[a]	Schmelz, DellaPergola, Bloch[a,b]
1895	6,085	10,100			
1900		15,600		6,700	14,700
1905		25,400		22,500	24,700
1910		68,700		55,000	68,100
1915		116,300		100,000	115,600
1920		126,900	120,000		126,700
1925		171,400	160,400	200,000	162,300
1930		218,500	200,200	215,000	191,400
1935		253,500	226,400	260,000	218,000
1940					254,400
1945				350,000	273,400
1947	249,326		265–275,000	350,000	285,800
1950				360,000	294,000
1955				360,000	305,900
1960	291,877			400,000	310,000[c]
1965				450,000	296,600[d]
1970				500,000	286,300[d]
1975				475,000	265,000[d]
1980				300,000	242,000[d]

Sources: Argentina, Comision Directiva del Censo, *Segundo censo de la Republica Argentina, Mayo 10 de 1895*, vol. 2, *Poblacion* (Buenos Aires: 1898); Direccion General del Servicio Estadistico Nacional, *IV censo de la nacion, 1947; Comparacion de los resultados del censo de la poblacion* (Buenos Aires: 1951); Republica Argentina Instituto Nacional de Estadistica y Censos, *Censo nacional de poblacion, 1960*, special computer processing of the census records of individuals reporting the Jewish religion (Buenos Aires, n.d.); S. Weill, *Poblacion israelita en la republica Argentina* (Buenos Aires: Bene Brith, 1936); I. Rosenswaike, "The Jewish Population of Argentina, Census and Estimate, 1887–1947," *Jewish Social Studies* 22(4) (1960): 195–214; U. O. Schmelz and S. DellaPergola, *The Demography of the Jews in Argentina and in Other Countries of Latin America* (Tel Aviv: Tel Aviv University, David Horowitz Institute, 1974) (in Hebrew); B. Bloch, *The Development of the Jewish Population in Argentina, 1900–1980* (Jerusalem: The Institute of Contemporary Jewry, Division of Jewish Demography and Statistics, 1977) (manuscript in Hebrew); *American Jewish Year Book*, various issues, 1901–1981.

[a]Estimates relate to January 1 of indicated years unless otherwise specified.
[b]Base date 1960. Before 1960, backward projection; after 1960, forward projection.
[c]Census date.
[d]December 31.

mittedly was an underestimate, which omitted some Jews reporting "no religion" or leaving the question on religion unanswered. Examination of detailed tabulations of the Jewish population by age and sex actually revealed an excess of females among young adults, which probably derived from stronger identificational erosion among their male contemporaries.

Several checks with other partial demographic evidence on the Jewish community close to census date were performed before a raising factor could be suggested for the original figure. Among other things, a comparison was performed of the detailed geographic distribution of reported Jews and of persons with no and unreported religion. The two distributions were totally unrelated, both across the twenty-four Argentinian provinces and in Buenos Aires's twenty electoral districts. Eventually, a raising factor of 6.2% was adopted, slightly more than the general countrywide 5.1% of persons with no and unreported religion. A corrected countrywide estimate of 310,000 was therefore suggested for 1960; the more than 18,000 "missing" were allocated differentially to each detailed age–sex subgroup, in accordance with the hypothesized stronger identificational erosion among younger males.

Demographic processes unfold over time as the sum of an uninterrupted flow of individual events—vital, migratory, and, in the case of an ethnoreligious group, identificational. Figures on population size do not stand out in isolation but, at any given point in time, depend on population size at a preceding date and on the type and amount of changes in the interim. Therefore, the 1960 corrected estimate of the size of Argentinian Jewry, to be acceptable, should stand a test of consistency with accepted population data and estimates for earlier years and with the available—though partial—history of population changes. Census data include much retrospective information on past demographic events, such as year of birth, sex, place of birth, and year of immigration of the foreign-born. Such information was utilized as the basis of a backward projection, through which U. O. Schmelz, this author, and B. Bloch tried to determine what Jewish population sizes would be consistent at various earlier dates with a figure of 310,000 in 1960, given the detailed population composition provided by the census.[10] Clearly, although the population characteristics of the survivors at census date are indicative of the volume and timing of past population inflows, the same census data tell us nothing about contemporary population outflows such as deaths and emigration. Mortality patterns were estimated on the basis of known figures for Jewish burials in Argentina, and of available life-tables for other Jewish communities in Eastern and Central Europe. Partial emigration figures existed for some countries of destination—such as Palestine/Israel, and until 1943, for the United States. For the rest, they had to be estimated. Our backward projection was performed for each five-year age group and for each five-year period, starting in 1960 and

10. B. Bloch, *The Development of the Jewish Population in Argentina, 1900–1960* (Jerusalem: The Institute of Contemporary Jewry, Division of Jewish Demography and Statistics, 1977) (manuscript in Hebrew).

Table 6.4
Estimated Jewish Population Evolution in Argentina by Components of Change, 1900–1960[a]—Absolute Numbers and Rates per 1000

Years (January 1)	Initial population	Natural movement[b]			International migration			Total change	Final population
		Births	Deaths	Balance	Immigrants	Emigrants	Balance		
Absolute numbers									
1900–1905	14,700	4,300	2,300	2,000	8,400	400	8,000	10,000	24,700
1905–1910	24,700	9,500	5,000	4,500	40,000	1,100	38,900	43,400	68,100
1910–1915	68,100	17,000	8,300	8,700	41,000	2,200	38,800	47,500	115,600
1915–1920	115,600	19,700	9,400	10,300	1,600	700	900	11,200	126,700
1920–1925	126,700	21,200	9,700	11,500	34,000	9,900	24,100	35,600	162,300
1925–1930	162,300	24,000	9,700	14,300	32,800	18,000	14,800	29,100	191,400
1930–1935	191,400	23,500	9,600	13,900	17,300	4,700	12,600	26,500	218,000
1935–1940	218,000	23,500	9,600	13,900	23,300	800	22,500	36,400	254,400
1940–1945	254,400	25,000	10,000	15,000	4,400	300	4,100	19,100	273,400
1945–1950	273,400	25,200	9,200	16,000	5,800	1,100	4,700	20,700	294,000
1950–1955	294,000	23,700	10,900	12,800	2,900	3,800	−900	11,900	305,900
1955–1960	305,900	18,200	12,000	6,200	2,100	4,900	−2,800	3,400	309,300

Yearly rates per 1000 Jewish population

1900–1905	45.5	24.5	21.0	87.9	4.2	83.7	104.7
1905–1910	46.4	24.6	21.8	195.2	5.1	190.1	211.9
1910–1915	38.3	18.8	19.5	92.5	5.0	87.5	107.0
1915–1920	32.5	15.6	16.9	2.7	1.1	1.6	18.5
1920–1925	29.5	13.5	16.0	47.4	13.7	33.7	49.7
1925–1930	27.2	11.0	16.2	37.3	20.4	16.9	33.1
1930–1935	23.0	9.4	13.6	17.0	4.6	12.4	26.0
1935–1940	20.0	8.1	11.9	19.8	0.7	19.1	31.0
1940–1945	19.0	7.6	11.4	3.4	0.3	3.1	14.5
1945–1950	17.8	6.5	11.3	4.1	0.8	3.3	14.6
1950–1955	15.8	7.3	8.5	1.9	2.5	−0.6	7.9
1955–1960	11.9	7.8	4.1	1.4	3.2	−1.8	2.3

Source: B. Bloch, *The Development of the Jewish Population in Argentina, 1900–1980* (Jerusalem: The Institute of Contemporary Jewry, Division of Jewish Demography and Statistics, 1977) (manuscript in Hebrew).

^aBackward projection; base date 1960.
^bIncludes affiliative changes to and from Judaism.

going back to 1900. Each backward step consisted of eliminating those who had been born or had immigrated in the more recent quinquennium—whose numbers were known from the 1960 census data corrected for underreporting—and age-specifically "reviving" those who had died or emigrated during the same interval.

Tables 6.3 and 6.4 present the main results of the backward projection: estimates of Jewish population size and absolute numbers and rates of population change, by components, in each five-year period. Although the actual computations were performed from the 1960 baseline backward, we may read the tables in forward chronology. Our backward projection and Weill's estimates are nearly identical until 1920 and show very rapid population growth, mostly resulting from immigration. Although with regard to immigration the projection was fed with Weill's data, the other components of change also coincide in the two estimates. Between 1920 and 1935, the two sets of data diverge: Weill's imply a doubling of the Jewish population over these fifteen years whereas the backward projection shows slower growth and, with relatively minor differences, turns out to be very much in line with Rosenswaike's corrected estimates. Although substantial immigration continued during this period, birth rates were falling rapidly. It should be noted that the very high birth rates appearing in the backward projection for the earlier years of the twentieth century do not differ significantly from the rates for Jews in Eastern Europe in the same period. The rapid fertility reduction obtained for Argentinian Jews is also quite similar to parallel changes occurring in Europe and in North America.[11] Moreover, the backward projection suggests a relatively large amount of Jewish emigration from Argentina during the interwar period, especially during the 1920s. Much of it was probably directed to other countries in the continent, with minorities going to the United States or returning to Europe.

The projected total of 285,800 Jews for 1947, after several years of slower growth, suggests that the amount of underreporting in that census was even greater than had been previously assumed. The 1950s witnessed a reversal in the international migration balance, which, with few new immigrants arriving, became negative for the first time. The Jewish birth rate was rapidly dropping, too. Consequently, the rate of Jewish population growth declined from a yearly average 14.5 per 1000 between 1940 and 1950 to 8 per 1000 in 1950–1955 and to a mere 2 per 1000 in 1955–1960. Close to the time of the 1960 census, Argentinian Jewry was attaining zero population growth.

With all the unavoidable limitations of the basic data and methodology of the backward projection, its results seem to fit surprisingly well with

11. DellaPergola, *La trasformazione demografica*.

most other reliable empirical evidence that exists for the sixty years it covers. These findings provide a very strong backing to the 1960 estimate of 310,000: Given the structure of Jewish population revealed by the census, a higher or lower figure would be grossly inconsistent with all other pieces of evidence concerning the modern demographic history of Argentinian Jewry.

The Enlarged Jewish Population in Argentina

The various adjusted estimates presented so far relate to the Jewish population of Argentina, including its identificationally marginal sectors, but excluding the non-Jewish members of the respective households. These non-Jewish relatives are known to exist, in connection with mixed marriages; together with the Jewish population proper, non-Jewish spouses, children, and other relatives form an "enlarged" Jewish population, that is, the total demographic aggregate of Jews and their household members.

The data in Table 6.5 may help establish the size and composition of such an "enlarged" Jewish population in Argentina in 1960. The figures reported in the table's upper line relate to the total membership of households with Jewish heads. The table's second line reports the known Jewish population totals according to the uncorrected census returns. The third line provides a "difference" between the preceding two figures, which we may provisionally consider as the number of non-Jewish members of Jewish households. The proportion of such figures out of the larger totals was about 10% for the total country; it was somewhat higher in the provinces than in Greater Buenos Aires.

This provisional estimate should now be critically evaluated, and two correctives should be introduced into it. First, the larger totals reported in Table 6.5 do not include Jewish members of households whose heads were not Jewish or were Jewish but did not report as such in the census. Account-

Table 6.5
Persons in Households with Jewish Household Heads by Declared Religion and Place of Residence, Argentina, 1960

	Total		Greater Buenos Aires		Provinces	
Declared religion	Number	Percentage	Number	Percentage	Number	Percentage
Total persons in households with Jewish household heads	324,021	100.0	256,452	100.0	67,559	100.0
Jewish population	291,877	90.1	231,987	90.5	59,890	88.6
Difference	32,144	9.9	24,465	9.5	7,669	11.4

Source: 1960 Census of Argentina, author's processing.

ing for these people and their household members increases the proportion of non-Jews in the "enlarged" Jewish population by several percentage points. On the other hand, it has been suggested already that the original census figures should be increased to take into account a reasonable estimate of Jews who did not report as such. Some of these were probably included in the total membership of households with Jewish heads. This tends to reduce the percentage of "non-Jews" in Jewish households.

We have no means of knowing, on the basis of available data, which of the two opposed corrections should be stronger. If we assume that they should be of equal magnitude, we can return to the percentage distributions of "Jewish" and "other" household members in Table 6.5 and utilize them to compute a tentative estimate of the "enlarged" Jewish population in 1960. The basic figure of 310,000 Jews, suggested in our previous discussion, would correspond to an "enlarged" total of 344,000 persons (of whom 34,000 were non-Jewish) based on the reported countrywide rate of Jewish household membership of 90.1%.

Although highly tentative, the latter figure is somewhat closer to the conventional Argentine Jewish population estimates that circulated during the late 1950s and early 1960s. But, evidently, one should avoid inconsistent handling of the concepts of Jewish and "enlarged" Jewish population and confusion between the quantities respectively involved.

Jewish Population Changes in Argentina, 1960–1975

In the absence of more recent comprehensive data, the 1960 census constitutes the main operative data source upon which an assessment of the current size and structure of Argentine Jewry can be based. The Jewish population in 1960, broken down by sex and five-year age groups and corrected for underreporting in each age–sex subgroup, served as a basis for the computation of projections up to 1975.[12] Such estimates utilized all available information on Jewish population change, namely numbers of Jewish burials in Greater Buenos Aires[13] and numbers of Argentine emigrants to Israel. It was necessary to estimate other components of demographic change on the basis of the trends unveiled retrospectively by the 1960 census, of partial data available for small local communities for later years, and of assumptions.

12. Schmelz and DellaPergola, "The Demography."
13. Asociacion Mutual Israelita Argentina, Instituto de Investigaciones Sociales, *Estudio historico de la mortalidad en las comunidades de capital y Gran Buenos Aires, 1963* (Buenos Aires: AMIA, 1964); *Datos estadisticos de la mortalidad en la comunidad de Buenos Aires, 1964; 1965; 1966* (Buenos Aires: AMIA, 1965–1967); and unpublished data.

Table 6.6
Estimated Jewish Population Evolution in Argentina by Components of Change, 1960–1975[a]—Absolute Numbers and Rates per 1000

Years (December 31)	Initial population	Natural movement[b]			Emigration[c]			Total change	Final population
		Births	Deaths	Balance	To Israel[d]	Other	Total		
Absolute numbers									
1960–1965	309,300	15,700	15,500	200	8,200	4,700	−12,900	−12,700	296,600
1965–1970	296,600	15,300	18,800	−3,500	4,200	2,600	−6,800	−10,300	286,300
1970–1975	286,300	14,300	19,300	−5,000	10,600	5,700	−16,300	−21,300	265,000
Rates per 1000 Jewish population									
1960–1965		10.5	10.4	0.1	5.4	3.1	−8.5	−8.4	
1965–1970		10.5	12.9	−2.4	2.9	1.8	−4.7	−7.1	
1970–1975		10.5	14.1	−3.6	7.7	4.1	−11.8	−15.4	

Source: Adapted from U. O. Schmelz and S. DellaPergola, *The Demography of the Jews in Argentina and in Other Countries of Latin America* (Tel Aviv: Tel Aviv University, David Horowitz Institute, 1974) (in Hebrew).

[a]Forward projection, base data 1960. Assumes continuation of known fertility levels, assimilation, and emigration.

[b]Includes affiliative changes to and from Judaism. No special allowance was made for disappeared persons (*desaparecidos*) in the deaths column.

[c]These data and estimates reflect assumptions relating to net migration balance. Figures are presented as if immigration (including return migration) were nil. If some immigration is assumed, the same amount of migrants should also be added to the figures of emigration to destinations other than Israel.

[d]Actual figures supplied by Israel Central Bureau of Statistics.

Table 6.6 reports the results of the main Jewish population estimates for 1960–1975. The numbers of Argentine Jewry, after reaching a peak around the 1960 census, were to start declining, mainly because of increased emigration—especially to Israel—in the early 1960s (see subsequent discussion of patterns of *aliya*, or emigration to Israel). The balance of Jewish births and deaths was still minimally positive between 1960 and 1965, but became negative during the late 1960s. Jewish births do not include children of out-married households not identified as Jewish by their parents. We estimated, on the basis of 1960 census data, that such was the status of about 25% of the children born between 1955 and 1960 to couples involving at least one Jewish spouse. Emigration from Argentina increased in 1970–1975. We assumed the gross number of immigrants to Israel to be slightly less than two-thirds of the total (negative) international migration balance of Argentine Jewry.

According to these estimates, the Jewish population declined from the initial level of 310,000 in 1960 to 297,000 in 1965, 286,000 in 1970, and 265,000 in 1975. Of the total decrease of 45,000 persons, 36,000 pertain to emigration and 9000 to the excess of deaths over births and to assimilation.

Along with this main projection, two further sets of estimates were prepared, one ignoring the effects of emigration and the other ignoring both emigration and assimilation. The aim of these exercises was to evaluate the relative strength of the different possible factors of erosion in Jewish population. The results show that, even ignoring emigration, the natural and identificational balance alone was conducive to Jewish population decline from 310,000 in 1960 to 303,000 in 1975. In the absence of both emigration and assimilation, the Jewish population would have increased to 330,000 by 1975. However, these working hypotheses contradict the well-established reality. Not only was the Jewish population of Argentina declining, but the pace of decline was accelerating.

Jewish Population Estimates in Other Latin American Countries

Our discussion of problems related to the interpretation of data available for Argentinian Jewry also illustrates the deficiencies of the existing data base for other communities on the continent. A few further comments may be made with regard to Jewish population estimates in the three other major communities for which some official census data exist: Brazil, Mexico, and Chile (see Table 6.7).

Wide discrepancies have often appeared among figures on Jews from national censuses and estimates circulated by Jewish community sources. Usually the latter were substantially higher. It can be reasonably assumed that population censuses tend to underreport the Jewish group, but the

Table 6.7
Estimates of Jewish Population in Brazil, Chile, and Mexico, 1900-1980

	Brazil		Chile		Mexico	
Year	Census	Conventional	Census	Conventional	Census	Conventional
1900	819		a		134	1,000
1910	a	3,000	92c		254	8,972
1920	a	6,100	2,138	3,300	a	500
1930	a	30,000	3,697	2,000	9,072	16,000
1940	55,666	40,000	8,333	3,697	14,167	20,000
1950	69,657	115,000	11,496d	40,000	17,574	25,000
1960	96,000b	125,000	15,827	30,000	100,750e	26,000
1970	a	150,000	16,359	35,000	49,277e	35,000
1980	91,795	160,000	a	30,000	61,790e	37,500

Sources: Brazil, Instituto Brasileiro de Geografia e Estatistica, *Recenseamento geral do Brasil*, various years; Chile, Direccion General/Servicio Nacional/Instituto Nacional de Estadisticas, *Censo (general) de la poblacion*, various years; Mexico, Direccion General de Estadistica, *Censo (general) de poblacion*, various years; *American Jewish Year Book*, various issues 1901-1981.
aNo census figure available.
bIncluding more than 10,000 in rural areas.
c1907.
d1952.
eIncluding large figures in provincial localities.

magnitude of such underreporting should be carefully evaluated. In Brazil, where earlier conventional estimates had been lagging behind the actual Jewish population growth, a very large correction was introduced between 1940 and 1950: from 40,000 to 115,000.[14] This is quite inconsistent with the known volume of Jewish immigration to Brazil during the same years, which was relatively low. The high postwar estimate subsequently served as base line for more upward revisions, which, however, lacked the backing of empirical research. A Jewish-sponsored sample survey and census of the Jewish community in São Paulo in 1968 supplied population figures much closer to the official census than to the higher conventional estimates.[15] Around 1980, again, a systematic effort by the São Paulo Jewish community to set up a comprehensive file of local Jews produced a figure very close— actually somewhat below—the 1980 census results, which were much

14. See a review of American Jewish Year Book population estimates for various Latin American countries in Schmelz and DellaPergola, *The Demography*.
15. H. Rattner, "Census and Sociological Research of the Jewish Community in São Paulo 1968," in *Papers in Jewish Demography 1969*, ed. U. O. Schmelz, P. Glikson, and S. DellaPergola (Jerusalem: The Hebrew University, Jewish Population Studies, Vol. 4, 1973), 289-303; H. Rattner, *Tradiçao e mudança; A comunidade judaica em São Paulo* (São Paulo, Federaçao Israelita de São Paulo e Instituto de Relaçoes Humanas do Comite Judaico Americano, 1970).

lower than other conventional estimates.[16] According to the 1980 census, there were 92,000 Jews in Brazil; it can be reasonably suggested that the actual total should be close to 100,000. In Chile, too, conventional Jewish population estimates were usually higher than official census figures and probably exaggerated, even if censuses may have been affected by significant underreporting of the Jewish group.

Occasionally, population censuses in Latin America have generated oddly exaggerated figures of Jewish population size. This occurred in Mexico in 1960, when a census figure of over 100,000 "Jews" was arrived at, compared with local community estimates of 26,000; in 1970, when the figures were 49,000 and 35,000, respectively; and in 1980, when they were 61,790 and 37,500. An analysis of the computer tapes of the 1970 Mexican census revealed that much of the difference was due to erroneous attribution to the Jewish group of relatively large numbers in provincial localities, where the number of known Jews is small. In Mexico City and the surrounding urban area, too, a few thousand ethnic Mexicans, some of them *descalzos*[17] and with large proportions of children, were included with the "Jewish" group.[18] A similar problem plagued the 1960 Brazilian census, whose total figure of 96,000 Jews included about 10,000 persons with extremely high fertility levels in remote rural areas. The same feature, but to a much smaller scale, reappeared in the 1980 census of Brazil.

These examples illustrate the obstacles incurred by demographers in their quest to provide reasonable estimates of the size (and other characteristics) of the Jewish population. The contrasting effects of underreporting and overreporting must be adequately accounted for. The additional empirical evidence that would be necessary to perform these corrections does not usually exist. The estimates adopted throughout this chapter are the result of our attempt to present an informed and critical view of Jewish population characteristics and trends in Latin America.

Main Demographic Patterns

Age Structure

Having outlined the major orders of magnitude and determinants of change in Latin American Jewish populations, we will examine a few demo-

---

16. C. Milnitzky, ed., *Apendice estatistico da comunidade judaica do estado de São Paulo* (São Paulo: Federaçao Israelita do Estado de São Paulo, Departamento de Estatistica e Pesquisa Social, 1980); Instituto Brasileiro de Geografia e Estatistica, *IX recensamento geral do Brasil, 1980*.

17. Barefoot. A question on adult footwear was included in the census questionnaire.

18. See S. DellaPergola and U. O. Schmelz, *The Jews of Greater Mexico City According to the 1970 Population Census: First Data and Critical Evaluation* (Jerusalem: The Institute of Contemporary Jewry, 1978).

graphic variables in greater detail. The structure of population by age groups is a revealing indicator of major demographic processes, as it is shaped by the prolonged effects of natality and mortality levels, age-selective migration movements, and identificational changes. In turn, age composition operates as an important structural factor in determining the overall frequency of events affecting population change. Table 6.8 presents a rather detailed choice of data and estimates of Jewish age structures in different cities and countries over the past fifty years.

In this broad time perspective, comparison reveals that the major trend is the slow and uninterrupted aging of the population. The median age of Argentine Jewry increased from 25–27 in the 1930s to 31 in 1947, to 35 in 1960, and to over 40 in the mid-1970s; in Brazil, it rose from 30.5 in 1950 to 34.5 in 1980. Declining fertility and emigration of young adults underlie these changes. At the same time, there are significant differences among the communities. Jews in Chile, Argentina, and, by inference, Uruguay appear to be aging more than Jews in Brazil and in some of the smaller communities in tropical American countries. Nevertheless, in each instance, median ages are substantially higher among the Jewish than among the general population. It should be noted that the very high proportions of Jewish children reported in some of the data, such as those for Mexico (1970) and for the rural population in Brazil (1980), unmistakably point to deficiencies in the respective sources.

Data on age composition also provide an indirect quality check of the 1960 Argentine census concerning the Jewish population. A comparison between our backward projection estimates for 1935 and the results of the 1936 municipal census of Buenos Aires shows highly consistent age distributions for both foreign and Argentine-born Jews. This is further proof of the reliability of the 1960 census.

Nuptiality

Table 6.9 presents the main marriage patterns among Argentine Jewry. Percentages of never-married persons at different ages illustrate levels and variation in age at marriage and overall propensities to marry among selected sociodemographic subgroups.

Jewish age at marriage has usually been higher than among the general population. This is shown by relatively higher proportions of singlehood among males at age 25–29 and among females at age 20–24. On the other hand, singlehood rates among older adults are substantially lower among Jews than among the general population. Jews, therefore, do not conform to the general pattern in a region in which, apart from frequent *uniones de hecho*, actual singlehood is widespread. Very few Jews in Argentina reported being in consensual unions in 1960.

The data in Table 6.9 suggest that the transition of Argentine Jewry

Table 6.8
Selected Jewish Populations in Latin America by Age, 1935–1980—Percentages

Country and locality	Year	Type of source[a]	Age group						Total	Median age	Jewish population size
			0–14	15–29	30–44	45–64	65+				
Argentina											
Total	1935	C	30.5	29.5	24.2	7.7[b]	8.1[c]		100.0	25.2	218,000
Foreign-born	1935	C	7.9	25.3	39.2	13.4[b]	14.2[c]		100.0	35.6	120,700
Argentine-born	1935	C	59.0	35.0	5.3	0.3[b]	0.4[c]		100.0	12.3	97,300
Buenos Aires (capital)	1936	A	28.3	28.2	26.2	14.7	2.2		100.0	27.0	120,195
Foreign-born	1936	A	7.9	23.9	40.1	24.6	3.5		100.0	35.9	73,588
Argentine-born	1936	A	60.4	35.0	4.4	0.2	0.0		100.0	12.4	46,589
Total	1947	C	24.6	24.8	25.6	19.7	5.3		100.0	31.4	285,800
Total, original	1960	A	20.5	21.3	21.5	28.5	8.2		100.0	35.4	291,877
Total, corrected	1960	A, C	20.5	22.0	22.2	27.5	7.8		100.0	34.7	310,000
Greater Buenos Aires	1960	A	20.2	21.3	21.7	28.7	8.1		100.0	35.5	231,955
Capital	1960	A	19.5	21.2	21.2	29.5	8.6		100.0	35.9[d]	193,799
Suburbs	1960	A	23.6	21.7	24.1	24.4	6.1		100.0	32.7[d]	38,188
Provinces, total	1960	A	21.7	21.1	20.9	28.0	8.3		100.0	34.8[d]	59,890
Rosario	1960	A	18.6	21.8	21.4	29.1	9.1		100.0	36.2[d]	8,384
Córdoba	1960	A	22.2	24.9	20.9	24.7	7.2		100.0	33.3[d]	7,822
Córdoba	1970	B	20.9	24.5	21.4	26.1	9.9		100.0	35.1	(4,513)[e]
La Plata	1960	A	17.3	24.6	19.8	30.2	8.0		100.0	35.9[d]	3,491
Santa Fe	1960	A	21.0	21.1	21.5	28.3	8.0		100.0	35.0[d]	3,196
Tucumán	1960	A	23.5	23.7	20.1	25.6	7.1		100.0	32.8[d]	2,882
Tucumán	1962	B	26.4	—	—	—	—		100.0	—	3,140
Tucumán	1974	B	20.8	23.8	19.2	23.2	13.0		100.0	34.0	3,395
Jewish colonies[e]	1960	A	21.6	17.7	19.2	30.3	11.1		100.0	36.9[d]	9,573
Quilmes	1968	B	24.7	21.9	23.1	24.1	6.2		100.0	31.1	(1,169)[e]

104

Buenos Aires, Sephardim	1968	B	23.1	22.8	22.2	23.1	8.8	100.0	33.9	8,600
Greater Buenos Aires[f]	1973–1974	B	18.2	20.6	16.0	29.2	16.0	100.0	40.0	(1,059)[k]
Bahia Blanca	1975	B	21.9	19.3	18.7	29.8	10.3	100.0	36.9	(2,444)[k]
Total[g]	1965	C	17.3	21.6	22.5	28.0	10.6	100.0	37.6	296,607
Total	1970	C	15.4	21.1	21.6	28.4	13.5	100.0	39.7	286,345
Total	1975	C	15.4	18.1	21.2	28.6	16.7	100.0	41.6	265,047
Brazil										
Total[b]	1950	A	23.8	25.5	22.0	23.3	5.4	100.0	30.5	69,657
Total	1980	A	20.2	23.5	19.1	23.1	14.1	100.0	34.4	91,795
Urban	1980	A	19.8	23.5	19.1	23.3	14.3	100.0	34.6	89,969
Rural[i]	1980	A	40.1	24.9	17.5	11.6	5.8	100.0	19.2	1,826
São Paulo (city)	1968	B	21.6	24.8	19.4	24.9	9.3	100.0	33.2	28,498
São Paulo (state)[j]	1980	A	20.8	23.2	19.1	22.7	14.2	100.0	34.0	44,378
Rio de Janeiro (city)	1960	A	23.1	21.1	21.3	27.5	6.9	100.0	33.3	29,382
Rio de Janeiro (state)[j]	1980	A	17.1	22.6	19.3	24.9	16.1	100.0	37.9	29,139
Rest of country[j]	1980	A	21.9	25.7	19.2	22.2	11.0	100.0	31.7	16,452
Chile										
Total[b]	1952	A	22.8	18.8	22.2	27.7	8.5	100.0	36.3	11,496
Colombia										
Bogota	1977	B	25.3	24.4	17.6	21.3	11.4	100.0	30.5	3,261
Mexico										
Federal District[i]	1970	A	31.7	25.2	17.9	17.1	8.1	100.0	24.9	25,191
Mexico (state)[f]	1970	A	44.2	22.4	21.1	9.6	2.6	100.0	17.9	5,608
Guatemala										
Total[b]	1963	B	30.8	18.5	20.1	21.0	9.6	100.0	30.6	970

(*continued*)

Table 6.8 (Continued)

Country and locality	Year	Type of source[a]	Age group						Median age	Jewish population size
			0–14	15–29	30–44	45–64	65+	Total		
Panama Total[b]	1960–1961	B	29.6	22.6	21.3	20.2	6.3	100.0	28.4	1,807

Sources: Argentina: B. Bloch, *The Development of the Jewish Population in Argentina, 1900–1980* (Jerusalem: The Institute of Contemporary Jewry, Division of Demography and Statistics, 1977) (manuscript in Hebrew); Municipalidad de la Ciudad de Buenos Aires, *Cuarto censo general, 1936*, vol. 3 (Buenos Aires: 1939); Republica Argentina Instituto Nacional de Estadistica y Censos, *Censo nacional de poblacion, 1960* (Buenos Aires: n.d.); U. O. Schmelz and S. DellaPergola, *The Demography of the Jews in Argentina and in Other Countries of Latin America* (Tel Aviv: Tel Aviv University, David Horowitz Institute, 1976) (in Hebrew), and unpublished tabulations of the 1960 census records by the authors; H. Jaimovic, *Main Findings from the Survey of Jews in Cordoba* (Tel Aviv: Tel Aviv University, David Horowitz Institute, 1973) (in Hebrew); *Primer Censo de la poblacion judia de la provinci de Tucuman: datos y comentarios* (Buenos Aires: AMIA, Instituto de Investigaciones Sociales, 1963); I. Blumenfeld, *La poblacion Israelita de la provincia de Tucuman: segundo censo* (Tucuman: Sociedad Union Israelita Tucumana, 1976); R. Kastelboim and L. Rabinovich, *Censo de la comunidad judia de Quilmes, 1963* (Buenos Aires: AMIA, Instituto de Investigaciones Sociales, 1968); E. I. Rogowsky, E. Widuczynski, and F. K. de Winograd, *Demographic Study of the Spanish Speaking Sephardic Community* (Buenos Aires: The American Jewish Committee, Social Research Studies, 1969); J. Fischerman, *Censo de la comunidad judia de Buenos Aires (informe de tareas realizadas al 30-11-1974)* (Buenos Aires: AMIA, 1974) (unpublished typescript); L. M. Sidicaro and R. Bag, *Estudio sociodemografico de la comunidad israelita de Babia Blanca* (Buenos Aires, Oficina Sudamericana del Comite Judio Americano, 1975). Brazil: Instituto Brasileiro de Geografia e Estatistica, *Recenseamento geral do Brasil, 1950*; *Recenseamento geral do Brasil, 1960*; and *Recenseamento geral do Brasil, 1980*; H. Rattner, "Census and Sociological Research of the Jewish Community in São Paulo, 1968," in *Papers in Jewish Demography, 1969*, ed. U. O. Schmelz, P. Glikson, and S. DellaPergola (Jerusalem: The Hebrew University, Jewish Population Studies, 1973), 289–303. Chile: Servicio Nacional de Estadistica y Censos, *12° censo general de la poblacion y 1° de vivienda, 1952* (Santiago). Colombia: M. De Dajes and J. Sapoznikow, *El censo de la comunidad judia de Bogota—1971: estructura, caracteristicas y perspectivas* (Bogota: Bnai Brith, 1978). Mexico: S. DellaPergola and U. O. Schmelz, *The Jews of Greater Mexico City According to the 1970 Population Census: First Data and Critical Evaluation* (Jerusalem: The Institute of Contemporary Jewry, 1978). Guatemala: F. De Tenenbaum, *La comunidad judia de Guatemala: estadisticas compiladas del censo de la comunidad en 1963* (Guatemala: Organisacion Sionista, 1964). Panama: C. Zelenka, *La comunidad de Panama: datos estadisticos compilados de censo de la comunidad en 1960–1961* (Panama: Bene Berith).

[a]A, Official census; B, Jewish-sponsored census or sample survey; C, forward or backward projection based on 1960 census corrected data. Correction allocates to each age group varying proportions of Jews who it is assumed were not reported as such in the 1960 census.
[b]45–54 age group.
[c]55+ age group.
[d]Average age.
[e]Not all relevant population included here.
[f]Sample of AMIA members, plus affiliated and nonaffiliated relatives.
[g]Forward projection corresponding to the figures in Table 6.6.
[h]Age groups 45–64 and 65+ adjusted from somewhat different original groupings.
[i]Very unreliable data.
[j]Urban population only.

Table 6.9
Percentage of Never-Married Jews by Sex, Age, and Selected
Sociodemographic Characteristics, Argentina, 1960

Characteristics	Males		Females	
	25–29	45–49	20–24	45–49
Argentina, general population	46.3	14.1	55.6	13.4
Total Jewish population	55.1	8.9	65.2	6.0
Place of residence				
Greater Buenos Aires	55.3	8.3	65.4	6.4
Provinces	54.2	11.0	64.6	4.7
Birthplace				
Argentina	55.9	10.2	66.4	8.8
Other Western country	45.9	8.7	49.1	3.5
East Europe	45.3	7.3	40.4	2.4
Africa and Asia	69.8[a]	8.3	43.8[a]	7.0
Educational attainment				
Primary	57.7	9.9	62.1	5.3
Secondary	49.1	7.2	60.5	7.7
University	58.7	7.5	80.7	12.0

Source: 1960 Census of Argentina, author's processing.
[a]Based on small absolute numbers.

from an immigrant group to a predominantly local-born group with higher levels of educational attainment has been associated with later marriage ages and lower overall propensities to marry.

Mixed Marriage

The extent of mixed marriage—a rather crucial variable in the demographic balance of any subpopulation—has been very inadequately investigated among Latin American Jews. The 1960 Argentine census does not provide any direct information in this respect. What it does provide are detailed figures of married Jews by year of marriage. After some (minor) correction to take into account migration movements and mortality, these data can be compared with the yearly figures available from Jewish communities on Jewish marriage ceremonies. With regard to Greater Buenos Aires, 1960 census figures on the number of persons married during the late 1950s—including persons married in a Jewish or other type of ceremony—were larger by about one-third than the Jewish community marriage records for the same years.[19] This should not be straightforwardly construed as an estimate of the frequency of mixed marriage because the difference

---

19. AMIA, Instituto de Investigaciones Sociales, *La nupcialidad de la kehila de Buenos Aires* (Buenos Aires: AMIA, 1962); *Datos estadísticos de la nupcialidad en las comunidades de Capital y Gran Buenos Aires, 1963* (Buenos Aires: AMIA, 1965).

between figures from the two sources includes an unknown number of civil marriages between Jewish spouses. More detailed comparisons indicate relatively greater incidence of marriages without a Jewish ceremony among foreign-born, less-educated, blue-collar Jewish adults. This suggests that financial considerations may have affected the preference for less-expensive civil marriage ceremonies on the part of persons at lower levels of income.

In view of the relationship that exists between the frequency of mixed marriages and the proportion of non-Jews in Jewish households, some further inference on trends in mixed marriages can be suggested on the basis of the data in Table 6.5. The estimated proportion of about 10% non-Jewish household members in Argentina in 1960 is greater than the 7.5% found in the United States in 1970–1971, when the current percentage of individual Jews marrying an unconverted non-Jewish spouse had just passed the 20% mark.[20] This suggests an earlier and stronger increase of mixed marriages among Argentine Jews; the incidence around 1960 was perhaps in the range of 20–25% of all Jewish individuals marrying and in all probability has increased in subsequent years. Possibly another 5–10% of Jewish spouses were marrying a Jewish partner in a civil ceremony only.

Besides its significance in the assessment of demographic patterns, the fact that the number of marriages involving Jews in Buenos Aires around 1960 was substantially larger according to the census than according to Jewish community records is further proof of the reliability of the former source. The data presented clearly contradict the claim of large undercoverages of the Jewish population in the Argentine census of 1960.

Fertility

The recent low levels of Jewish natality and their implications for Jewish population size and age composition have already been mentioned. Table 6.10 shows the variation in the average numbers of children born to Jewish women in Argentina up to 1960 by age and other characteristics. Because only ever-married women are considered and the incidence of Jewish unmarried mothers is virtually nil, it appears that cumulative fertility was already falling below the minimum required for demographic replacement and population stability in the long run. Jewish marital fertility levels were not substantially different from the ones prevailing among the general population of Buenos Aires, which are among the lowest in Latin America.

Jewish fertility was somewhat higher in the provinces than in Greater Buenos Aires among foreign-born women with lower educational attainment, not currently in the labor force, and married at relatively younger ages. But the changes that have been occurring in the sociodemographic structure of Argentine Jewry in recent years clearly affect each of the vari-

20. U. O. Schmelz and S. DellaPergola, "The Demographic Consequences of U.S. Jewish Population Trends," *American Jewish Year Book* 83 (1983): 141–187.

Table 6.10
Average Number of Children Born to Ever-Married Jewish Women by Selected Sociodemographic Characteristics, Argentina, 1960

Characteristics	Age in 1960			
	Up to 29	30–44	45–64	65+
Argentina, general population	1.9	2.6	3.2	4.1
Buenos Aires, general population	1.3	1.9	2.3	3.5
Total Jewish population	1.2	2.0	2.2	3.3
Place of residence				
Greater Buenos Aires	1.2	2.0	2.2	3.1
Provinces	1.3	2.2	2.5	3.9
Age at marriage				
Up to 19	1.6	2.5	3.0	4.2
20–24	1.2	2.2	2.4	3.5
25–29	0.7	1.8	2.0	2.7
30–34	—	1.3	1.7	2.4
35+	—	1.0	1.3	2.3
Birthplace				
Argentina	1.2	2.0	2.1	2.9
Other Western country	1.4	1.9	1.6	2.2
East Europe	1.5	2.1	2.2	3.4
Africa and Asia	1.8	2.6	3.8	4.2
Educational attainment				
Primary school	1.4	2.1	2.4	3.4
Secondary school	1.2	2.0	1.8	2.2
University	0.9	1.9	1.7	1.9
Currently in labor force				
Yes	1.0	1.9	2.0	2.6
No	1.5	2.2	2.4	3.6

Source: 1960 Census of Argentina, author's processing.

ables mentioned, associating them with lower fertility levels. Greater female participation in the labor force probably constitutes a particularly significant factor in decisions to postpone or not to have (further) children.

All the data reported refer to children of Jewish women, regardless of the children's own religious affiliation. Mixed marriages and the presumable lack of Jewish identification among a majority of children of outmarried couples[21] were further factors in lowering "effectively Jewish" fertility,

---

21. Because Jews constitute one half of the spouses in Jewish marriages, half of their children should be Jewish. Higher or lower proportions imply, respectively, "gains" or "losses" to the Jewish group. In most Western countries for which appropriate documentation exists, fewer than 50% of children of mixed marriages are Jewish. See S. DellaPergola, "L'effet des mariages mixtes sur la natalité dans une sous-population: quelques problèmes et résultats concernant la diaspora juive," in *Démographie et destin des sous-populations* (Paris: Association Internationale des Démographes de Langue Française, 1983), 223–236; Schmelz and DellaPergola, "The Demographic Consequences."

compared to the averages reported in Table 6.10. Such effects were weaker or stronger according to the different frequency of mixed marriages in each sociodemographic subgroup.

Generational Correlates of Sociodemographic Characteristics

Although 1960 Argentine census data may now seem rather outdated, comparison of the sociodemographic characteristics of different age groups provides an illustration of intergenerational changes that had occurred or were in the making by census date—thus suggesting the direction of changes that were to occur in subsequent years (see Table 6.11). Most prominent was the virtual stoppage of Jewish immigration to Argentina and the consequent growing numerical predominance of the local-born. The latter, in 1960, represented 63% of total Argentine Jewry; their share had increased from a mere 3% of those aged 65 and over to nearly 98% of the children below age 15. Some of the demographic correlates of this generational transition have already been mentioned.

A further, rather obvious indicator of an individual's life-cycle stage is his or her relationship to the head of the household, by age. Family structures were dominated by relatively small nuclear families comprising various combinations of heads, spouses, and children. Other relatives and nonrelative household members were quite infrequent. Only among the elderly were such other relations (especially mothers of household's heads) more frequent. A visible minority of "children" aged 30 and over indicated a trend among adults to postpone marriage and to continue living in the parental dwellings.

The educational attainment of Argentine Jewry was rising rapidly from the rather low standards of the elder generation. The proportion of persons with postsecondary education was more than doubling from each broad age group to the next younger one. The partial evidence that is available shows that this trend continued for the next twenty-five years.[22]

Intergenerational occupational change, too, was substantial. The greatest absolute decline could be observed in the sales category, including the once-prominent *cuentanik* group (Jewish traveling salesmen selling on account). In relative terms, the decline in agriculture was even greater. Also declining were the mostly blue-collar manufacturing and service sectors. Nevertheless, the combined manufacturing, service, and agriculture occupations accounted for 27% of the 30–44 age group—quite a high percent-

22. See the list of sources given in Table 6.8.

Table 6.11
Jewish Population in Argentina by Age and Selected Sociodemographic Characteristics, 1960—Percentages

		Age in 1960				
Characteristics	Total[a]	0–14	15–29	30–44	45–64	65+
Absolute numbers	291,877	59,764	61,849	62,692	83,075	23,824
Sex	100.0	100.0	100.0	100.0	100.0	100.0
Male	49.8	50.4	48.2	48.1	51.4	51.3
Female	50.2	49.6	50.8	51.9	48.6	48.7
Birthplace	100.0	100.0	100.0	100.0	100.0	100.0
Argentina	62.7	97.6	93.9	69.4	26.4	2.9
Other Western country	6.4	1.5	3.4	6.7	9.9	13.0
East Europe	27.6	0.4	2.2	22.0	57.0	74.3
Africa and Asia	3.3	0.5	0.5	1.9	6.7	9.8
Period of immigration[b]	100.0	100.0	100.0	100.0	100.0	100.0
Up to 1919	23.3	—	—	1.1	20.6	53.7
1920–1929	35.8	—	—	34.6	42.6	26.4
1930–1939	28.8	—	41.3	44.7	29.5	14.0
1940–1960	12.1	100.0	58.7	19.6	7.3	5.9
Educational attainment[c]	100.0	—	100.0	100.0	100.0	100.0
None	5.3	—	0.6	1.1	7.1	23.4
Primary school	51.3	—	27.7	55.6	63.6	60.8
Secondary school	32.1	—	50.6	30.9	23.8	13.6
University	11.3	—	21.1	12.4	5.5	2.2
Percentage in labor force[c]						
Male	80.4	—	65.0	98.5	88.7	47.4
Female	19.7	—	32.6	20.3	12.6	4.7
Occupation[d]	100.0	—	100.0	100.0	100.0	100.0
Professional	11.1	—	14.0	14.2	7.5	3.7
Managerial	9.5	—	4.4	11.5	11.4	10.2
Clerical	13.2	—	26.6	11.7	5.9	3.6
Sales	37.2	—	28.7	35.4	43.3	49.7
Manufacturing	22.3	—	19.1	21.9	24.9	22.9
Services[e]	4.5	—	5.9	3.7	4.1	4.7
Agriculture	2.2	—	1.2	1.6	2.9	5.2
Occupational status[d]	100.0	—	100.0	100.0	100.0	100.0
Employer	36.2	—	14.0	39.1	48.7	49.9
Employee	43.4	—	72.2	40.6	27.4	19.6
Self-employed	19.4	—	11.9	19.8	23.4	29.6
Family help	1.0	—	1.9	0.5	0.5	0.9
Household size[f]	3.5	—	3.0	4.1	3.5	2.5
Relationship to household head	100.0	100.0	100.0	100.0	100.0	100.0
Head	29.1	0.2	8.2	39.0	51.9	51.4
Spouse	23.1	0.5	14.9	40.0	35.0	15.9
Child	35.2	90.2	64.1	11.5	1.4	0.3
Other family member	6.9	5.9	5.7	4.8	5.5	22.7
Other household member[g]	5.7	2.9	7.1	4.8	6.2	9.7

Source: 1960 Census of Argentina, author's processing.
[a]Including age unknown.
[b]Foreign-born population.
[c]Population aged 14 and over.
[d]Gainfully employed population.
[e]Including transportation.
[f]Including non-Jewish members. Age of head of household.
[g]Including lodgers, servants.

age compared to other Western Jewish communities in the 1960s.[23] Partial evidence from later years points to a rapid shrinking of these sectors of the Jewish labor force.[24] At the same time, managerial and especially professional and clerical activities were rapidly increasing. The latter reflected the greater participation of younger Jewish women in the labor force. Life-cycle effects of occupational mobility confound the picture for younger adults: The profile of the 15–29 age group, in particular, remains subject to substantial change, particularly because of the later joining of the labor force on the part of those with a prolonged curriculum of studies.

A more disaggregated presentation of Jewish occupational structure would show the persistence of characteristic Jewish concentrations in the liberal professions, management, commerce, and the clothing industry.[25] The structure of the Jewish labor force by occupational status was rapidly shifting from a predominance of employers and self-employed to a greater share of employees.

Ecological Correlates of Sociodemographic Characteristics

Provincial Differences

Regional, provincial, and local differentials in the distribution of sociodemographic characteristics offer a further important perspective on past and recent changes among the Jewish population. We first turn to examining the major differences between Jews in the Greater Buenos Aires metropolitan area and in Argentina's interior in 1960. Data for the five principal provincial communities, as well as for the aggregate of Jewish agricultural colonies, are presented in detail (see Table 6.12). More disaggregated data for Greater Buenos Aires are shown below.

Jews in Greater Buenos Aires (80% of Argentina's total) constituted a more visible share of the total population: 3.4% versus 0.5% in the provinces and slightly more than 1% in other major cities. By contrast, the much-diminished Jewish population in the rural colonies still constituted a

---

23. S. DellaPergola, "Some Occupational Characteristics of Western Jews in Israel," in *Papers in Jewish Demography 1977*, ed. U. O. Schmelz, P. Glikson, and S. DellaPergola (Jerusalem: The Hebrew University, Jewish Population Studies, Vol. 12, 1980), 255–281.

24. See list of sources given in Table 6.8.

25. Schmelz and DellaPergola, "The Demography." Some of these data have been reanalyzed by Moshe Syrquin, *The Economic Structure of the Jews in Argentina and Other Latin American Countries*, Discussion paper 7507 (Ramat Gan: Bar Ilan University, Department of Economics and Research Committee, 1975); see also J. Laikin Elkin, *Jews of the Latin American Republics*.

Table 6.12
Jewish Population in Argentina by Place of Residence and Selected Sociodemographic Characteristics, 1960—Percentages

Characteristics	Greater Buenos Aires	Rest of Argentina, total	Place of residence					
			Rosario	Córdoba	La Plata	Santa Fe	Tucumán	Colonies[a]
Absolute numbers	231,987	59,890	8,384	7,822	3,491	3,196	2,882	9,573
Percentage of Jews in total population	3.4	0.5	1.3	1.3	1.0	1.2	1.0	55.0[g]
Sex	100.0	100.0	100.0	100.0	100.0	100.0	100.0	100.0
Male	49.6	50.6	50.3	49.7	49.8	49.7	50.7	50.5
Female	50.4	49.4	49.7	50.3	50.2	50.3	49.3	49.5
Birthplace	100.0	100.0	100.0	100.0	100.0	100.0	100.0	100.0
Argentina	60.6	70.7	70.9	72.0	64.1	73.4	72.1	72.3
Other Western country	7.3	3.8	3.3	3.1	2.5	3.2	1.7	3.5
East Europe	28.6	22.5	23.2	20.7	31.6	21.7	21.0	23.0
Africa and Asia	3.4	3.0	2.6	4.2	1.8	2.1	5.2	1.2
Period of immigration[c]	100.0	100.0	100.0	100.0	100.0	100.0	100.0	100.0
Up to 1919	20.8	43.2	37.3	17.7	15.4	35.5	27.9	62.7
1920–1929	35.8	30.5	38.8	47.7	43.1	37.2	40.5	21.3
1930–1939	30.2	20.6	19.3	22.4	36.5	22.2	27.6	13.6
1940–1960	13.1	5.7	4.6	12.1	4.9	5.0	4.0	2.4
Educational attainments[b]	100.0	100.0	100.0	100.0	100.0	100.0	100.0	100.0
None	5.4	4.7	4.4	3.5	3.5	5.2	4.9	7.5
Primary	51.0	52.3	45.4	42.2	47.5	51.0	46.2	69.6
Secondary	32.3	31.1	33.5	36.1	29.1	33.1	33.8	19.4
University	11.2	11.8	16.7	18.2	19.9	10.8	15.1	3.5
Percentage in labor force[b]								
Male	80.3	80.7	75.7	77.6	76.7	77.4	79.0	84.9
Female	19.9	19.1	16.9	21.8	22.8	20.3	21.0	12.7

(*continued*)

Table 6.12 (Continued)

Characteristics	Greater Buenos Aires	Rest of Argentina, total	Place of residence					
			Rosario	Córdoba	La Plata	Santa Fe	Tucumán	Colonies[a]
Occupation[a]	100.0	100.0	100.0	100.0	100.0	100.0	100.0	100.0
Professional	10.5	13.4	14.8	16.3	18.7	12.5	14.9	7.7
Managerial	10.0	7.6	9.5	7.9	6.2	9.7	10.1	3.8
Clerical	13.8	10.6	13.9	13.1	14.0	13.8	9.5	8.1
Sales	35.7	43.2	39.3	44.2	40.1	45.7	51.9	28.7
Manufacturing	25.2	11.1	12.7	13.9	15.1	12.2	8.5	8.6
Services[e]	4.5	4.7	4.5	3.9	4.7	5.0	4.5	5.2
Agriculture	0.3	9.3	0.9	0.7	0.4	0.8	0.6	38.0
Occupational status[d]	100.0	100.0						
Employer	34.2	43.9						
Employee	45.8	34.5						
Self-employed	19.4	19.7						
Family help	0.6	1.9						
Household size[f]	3.5	3.7						

Source: 1960 Census of Argentina, author's processing.
[a]Not all relevant population included here.
[b]Population aged 14 and over.
[c]Foreign-born population.
[d]Gainfully employed population.
[e]Including transportation.
[f]Including non-Jewish members.
[g]Rough estimate computed from H. Avni, Argentine Jewry: Its Social Political Status and Organizational Patterns (Jerusalem: The Hebrew University, Institute of Contemporary Jewry, 1972), Table 3.

majority of local residents.[26] Greater Buenos Aires expectedly had a higher proportion of foreign-born and of more recent immigrants. Provincial localities absorbed much of the earlier Jewish immigration to Argentina and had seen the growing up of an earlier generation of Argentine-born Jews. Gradually, however, the effects of Jewish internal migration and of the continuing inflow of immigrants were to be felt mainly in Buenos Aires.[27] The differential countrywide Jewish population distribution, by birthplace and period of immigration, clearly reflects these developments, with the Jewish colonies at one extreme and Buenos Aires at the other. The more heterogeneous composition of more recent, as compared to earlier, immigration to Argentina produced a relatively greater incidence of non–Eastern European Jewish immigrants to Buenos Aires. The more recent development of the communities of Córdoba and La Plata, as compared to the other provincial urban communities, emerges from these data.

The age structures of Argentina's Jewish communities (reported in Table 6.8) were affected, too, by their different seniority and pace of growth. In 1960 Córdoba, then apparently a growing community, displayed a relatively younger Jewish population structure; on the other hand, the declining Jewish colonies featured greater aging. Different composition by age in turn affected the socioeconomic characteristics of the Jewish population in local communities significantly.

No major differences appeared, on the average, between educational attainment distributions in Greater Buenos Aires and in the provincial total. The latter, however, compounded the quite different characteristics of local communities. The proportion of Jews with higher education was relatively high in some of the major provincial communities, especially in La Plata and Córdoba, where it exceeded that found in Buenos Aires; it was lowest in the Jewish colonies.

With regard to occupational characteristics, Jews in Greater Buenos Aires included larger proportions of managers and of persons employed in manufacturing; relatively more professionals, salesmen, and, expectedly, farmers appeared in the interior. Consequently, the proportion of employers, as contrasted to employees, was significantly higher in the provincial communities than in Greater Buenos Aires. The percentage of self-employed was the same in Buenos Aires and elsewhere. These occupational differentials, and to some extent the differences in educational attainment that underlie them, reflect the varying complexity of employment markets

---

26. Estimate based in part on H. Avni, *Argentine Jewry: Its Social Political Status and Organizational Patterns* (Jerusalem: The Hebrew University, Institute of Contemporary Jewry, 1972) (in Hebrew).

27. Schmelz and DellaPergola, "The Demography."

related to the general population size of localities. The greater range of activities in Buenos Aires resulted in a more modern and complex occupational structure of its Jewish population, whereas in smaller localities the Jews were more concentrated occupationally, especially in sales and certain liberal professions. Jewish agriculture was still visible in 1960 in the colonies, where 38% of Jews gainfully employed were farmers.

Jewish Population Distribution in Major Metropolitan Areas

Before we turn to discussing sociodemographic differences between Jews living in different sections of the greater Buenos Aires metropolitan area, a brief description of the general characteristics of Jewish urban population distribution is in order. The chronology of immigration waves and the general sociodemographic characteristics of the Jews in large cities tended to promote dense Jewish residential concentrations. The latter's particular location has been affected by, among other things, the general direction of development of new housing at times of greater Jewish residential mobility, the general residential differentiation among various social classes and ethnic groups, and, more specifically, the spatial distribution of Jewish institutions over the urban territory.

Substantial residential concentrations emerge among the Jews in some of the largest communities in Latin America. According to the available computer records of the 1970 census of Mexico—whose limitations have already been mentioned—61% of the Jewish population of the Federal District lived in only two of its twenty-four statistical areas (Mexico City's eighth and ninth quarters); a further 15% lived in two adjoining quarters (the tenth and eleventh). These four districts, together with the municipality of Naucalpan in the neighboring State of Mexico, formed a territorial continuum stretching westward and northward from the western part of the town's center and contained about 75% of the total Jewish population of the Greater Mexico City metropolitan area.[28]

A detailed processing of the Jewish community records in the São Paulo metropolitan area in 1978 indicates that 20% of Jewish households were situated in Bom Retiro, 15% in Santa Cecilia, 12% in Consolaçao, and 12% in Jardim Paulista. A contiguous territory stretching from northwest of town center to the southwest included five of Greater São Paulo's forty-three subdistricts, with 66% of the Jewish population; another 15% lived in four adjoining subdistricts.[29]

28. DellaPergola and Schmelz, *The Jews of Greater Mexico City*.
29. C. Milnitzky, ed., *Anuario estatistico da comunidade judaica do Estado de São Paulo* (São Paulo: Federaçao Israelita do Estado de São Paulo, Departmento de Estatistica e Pesquisa Social, 1978).

The Jewish population of Greater Buenos Aires seems to be far more dispersed over the urban territory than in the two preceding examples; nevertheless, its distribution is distinctly different from that of the general population. In 1960, Jews formed 3.4% of the total Greater Buenos Aires population, 6.5% of the inhabitants of the city of Buenos Aires (Capital Federal), 14.2% of the residents of the major area of Jewish settlement between Balvanera Norte (the Once district) and Villa Crespo, 24.5% of the total in the Once district itself, and higher percentages in smaller areas, down to single blocks or houses. Over 85,000 Jews (44% of the local Jewish population) lived in the more Jewish north-central sections of the capital, which extended over about one-seventh of the municipal territory.[30]

These robust patterns of concentration constituted an important factor of interaction and continuity in Jewish community life in Latin America. At the same time, population redistribution over the metropolitan area was producing a net transferral to the suburbs and greater dispersal of the Jewish population over the urban territory.

Sociodemographic Differentiation by Neighborhoods

Ecological variation in Jewish population characteristics can be studied for Greater Buenos Aires on the basis of detailed data from the 1960 census. We devised a typological classification of neighborhoods into six groups (five in the capital and one for the eighteen adjoining *partidos* (suburbs) of the Province of Buenos Aires) on the basis of the general socioeconomic characteristics of each area and of territorial distribution of the Jews (see Table 6.13).

Sociodemographic differentiation of Jewish neighborhoods is significant. In 1960, northern areas of Buenos Aires included visible concentrations of immigrants from Western countries, of more educated persons, and of managers and professionals. The main north-central Jewish residential concentration was of predominantly Eastern European origin, was aging, had been in Argentina for many years, and was relatively less educated, with high proportions employed in manufacturing. Jews in manufacturing were even more prominent in western neighborhoods, and a higher proportion employed in sales appeared in south-central and southern neighborhoods. The latter included some of the older, poorer sections of Buenos Aires, which also showed higher proportions of Jewish immigrants born in Africa and Asia. Suburbs had a younger and more frequently Argentine-born Jewish population; their socioeconomic status was somewhat lower than in the better sections of the capital itself.

Even though they relate to 1960, these data provide some indication

---

30. Schmelz and DellaPergola, "The Demography."

Table 6.13
Jewish Population in Greater Buenos Aires by Neighborhood of Residence and Selected Sociodemographic Characteristics, 1960—Percentages

		Neighborhood of residence					
		Federal Capital					
Characteristics	Total	North[a]	North-Central[b]	West[c]	South-Central[d]	South[e]	Suburbs of Greater Buenos Aires
Absolute numbers	193,799	25,222	85,029	34,080	25,822	23,646	38,188
Percentage of Jews in total population	6.5	4.3	14.2	8.1	4.5	3.0	1.3
Sex	100.0	100.0	100.0	100.0	100.0	100.0	100.0
Male	49.4	48.8	49.1	49.8	49.3	50.4	50.6
Female	50.6	51.2	50.9	50.2	50.7	49.6	49.4
Age	100.0	100.0	100.0	100.0	100.0	100.0	100.0
0–14	19.5	19.1	18.7	22.1	18.8	19.3	23.6
15–29	21.2	19.0	20.9	22.2	20.9	23.6	21.7
30–44	21.2	20.6	20.4	23.3	21.3	21.9	24.1
45–64	29.5	31.2	30.9	26.1	29.8	27.6	24.4
65+	8.6	10.1	9.1	6.3	9.1	7.6	6.1
Average	35.9	37.1	36.6	33.5	36.4	34.9	32.7
Birthplace	100.0	100.0	100.0	100.0	100.0	100.0	100.0
Argentina	59.7	53.9	58.1	62.3	62.7	64.6	65.9
Other Western country	7.1	22.4	4.5	5.5	6.5	3.9	8.6
East Europe	29.7	19.5	34.8	30.6	25.7	25.2	22.9
Africa and Asia	3.6	4.2	2.9	1.6	5.1	6.3	2.6

Period of immigration[g]	100.0	100.0	100.0	100.0	100.0	100.0	100.0
Up to 1919	21.2	16.2	21.4	16.9	27.9	25.7	11.7
1920–1929	36.2	19.3	39.6	38.7	36.3	41.3	31.2
1930–1939	29.5	40.4	27.7	31.8	24.0	25.0	34.8
1940–1960	13.1	24.1	11.3	12.6	11.8	8.0	22.3
Educational attainment[b]	100.0	100.0	100.0	100.0	100.0	100.0	100.0
None	5.7	3.4	6.5	5.5	4.8	6.2	4.2
Primary school	50.7	33.7	52.5	55.0	48.7	58.4	52.8
Secondary school	32.3	47.3	30.1	30.0	33.6	26.3	32.3
University	11.3	15.5	10.9	9.6	12.8	9.1	10.7
Percentage in labor force[b]							
Male	79.9	78.7	79.5	80.9	80.2	80.8	82.6
Female	20.1	20.0	20.3	18.3	21.4	20.0	18.9
Occupation[i]	100.0	100.0	100.0	100.0	100.0	100.0	100.0
Professional	10.4	14.3	9.9	8.6	12.3	8.0	11.5
Managerial	10.2	14.9	9.7	9.9	11.2	6.7	8.7
Clerical	14.1	13.3	14.1	13.9	15.3	13.4	12.5
Sales	35.3	35.3	33.4	31.9	38.3	44.0	37.4
Manufacturing	25.4	16.7	28.2	31.7	18.3	23.7	24.2
Services[j]	4.3	5.0	4.5	3.6	4.2	4.1	5.2
Agriculture	0.3	0.5	0.2	0.3	0.3	0.1	0.5

Source: 1960 Census of Argentina, author's processing.

[a]*Secciones electorales* 14, 19, and 20 and northern half of 16, 17, and 18.
[b]*Secciones electorales* 7 and 11, northern half of 9, southern half of 17 and 18, and eastern half of 15.
[c]Western half of *seccion electoral* 15 and southern half of 16.
[d]*Secciones electorales* 5, 6, 8, 10, 12, and 13 and southern half of 9.
[e]*Secciones electorales* 1, 2, 3, and 4.
[f]Eighteen *partidos* of Buenos Aires province.
[g]Foreign-born population.
[h]Population aged 14 and over.

of the changes that must have occurred ever since. Different age distributions by neighborhood provide an indication of the major axes of Jewish population redistribution. The main directions of growth of the capital's more recent Jewish settlement extended from the south and from the east to the west, with ramifications to the north and northwest. Western and suburban quarters presented substantially greater proportions of Jewish children, whereas central and northern areas of the capital displayed greater concentrations of elderly people. Quite similar findings obtain with regard to the territorial distribution of the foreign-born by periods of immigration.

Aspects of Latin American Aliya

The important role of Jewish emigration from Latin American countries over the last quarter of a century has already been mentioned. It is not inconceivable that Jewish emigration may be equally significant in future years. Of the various countries of destination, only Israel supplies adequate information on the size and characteristics of Latin American Jewish immigrants.[31] What proportion of the total Jewish emigration *aliya* represented cannot be specified, but there is common agreement that this proportion has been substantial. Clearly, the characteristics of Jewish migrants to Israel and to alternative destinations—within Latin America or elsewhere in the Western world—should not be expected to be identical. Nevertheless, close inspection of *aliya* from Latin America can provide useful insights into the determinants and characteristics of population movements in the past and may help in trying to assess likely future patterns.[32]

Country Differentials

On the whole, slightly more than 68,000 immigrants came to Israel from Latin America between 1948 and the end of 1983. Of these, 39,900

---

[31]. Israel's Central Bureau of Statistics publishes yearly data on immigrants by country of origin and other characteristics. See *Immigration to Israel, 1948–1972:* Part 1, Special Publication 416 (1973); Part 2, Special Publication 489, (1975); *Immigration to Israel* (yearly publication). Since 1969–1970, a periodical follow-up of new immigrants has been performed through the Central Bureau of Statistics Immigration Absorption Survey. See, among several other publications, *Imigrantes de America Latina un año y tres años despues de le immigracion; arribados entre 1969/70–1973/74,* Special Publication 652 (1981). See also *Statistical Abstract of Israel* (yearly publication).

[32]. *Aliya* from Latin America was analyzed by M. Sicron, "Immigration to Israel from Latin America," in *Papers in Jewish Demography 1973,* ed. U. O. Schmelz, P. Glikson, and S. DellaPergola (Jerusalem, The Hebrew University, Jewish Population Studies, Vol. 10, 1977), 347–354. See also F. Peñalosa, "Pre-migration Background and Assimilation of Latin American Immigrants in Israel," *Jewish Social Studies* 34(2) (1972): 122–139; D. L. Herman, "Israel's Latin American Immigrants," American Jewish Archives 36(1) (1984): 16–49.

came from Argentina, 8400 from Brazil, 7800 from Uruguay, 5000 from Chile, 2600 from Mexico, 1300 from Colombia, 1000 from Venezuela, over 700 each from Cuba and Peru, 330 from Bolivia, and over 100 each from Panama, Ecuador, and the aggregate of remaining smaller communities in the region. These absolute figures of migrants to Israel reflect quite different emigration propensities by country. After controlling for average Jewish population sizes over the period considered, the following rough typology of *aliya* propensities emerges (by declining intensities):

High: Cuba, Bolivia, Uruguay, Chile
Medium: Colombia, Argentina, Peru, Ecuador
Low: Brazil, Mexico, Venezuela, Panama

Country *aliya* differentials are the product of varying longer-term average migration propensities, of the different timing and intensity of periodical crises in each country, and possibly also of the different proportions moving from each country to Israel versus other destinations. In general, it can be stated that countries offering more favorable economic opportunities and greater political stability also featured a stronger holding power over their Jewish communities. Lower *aliya* countries, such as Brazil, Mexico, Venezuela, and Panama, continued to attract some Jewish immigration—often from neighboring countries—in contrast to the consistently negative migration balances of communities displaying more frequent *aliya*.

The more interesting aspect of Latin American *aliya*, however, is related to its irregular and asynchronic unfolding over time. The yearly immigration figures for the five largest communities are shown in Figure 6.1. The original data were transformed into standardized scores to allow for easier comparisons. For each country, the 1953–1983 yearly average number of immigrants was given a value of 0 and the standard deviation over the years was given a value of 1. Therefore, the graphs point to the rhythm and intensity of *aliya* fluctuations, regardless of the quite different absolute numbers of migrants involved.

Aliya peaks and troughs seem to reflect quite accurately some of the main political and economic events in Latin American societies. The historical maximum of *aliya* from Argentina in 1963 clearly reflects a national economic recession accompanied by anti-Semitic outbursts. The later peaks in 1973 and 1977 correlate with important changes in the country's political power structure: Peron's return to power and the establishment of the military junta. Uruguay's *aliya* chronology displays a first peak in 1963 (similar in nature to the one seen for Argentina), a second one in 1973 when the military regime was established, and a third one in 1983, a year of

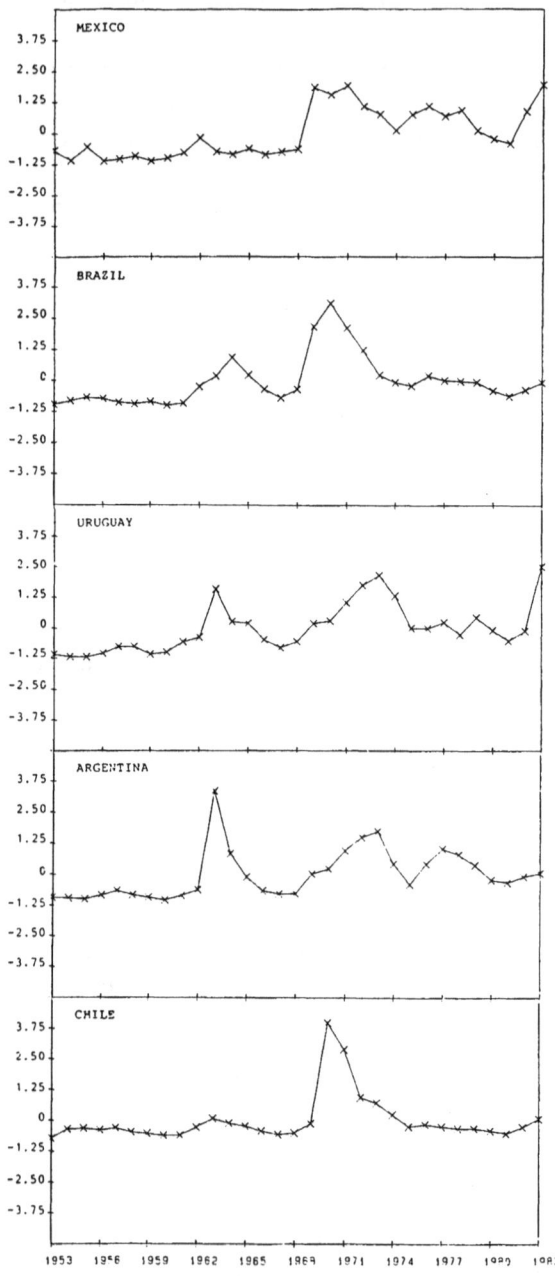

Figure 6.1. Yearly numbers of immigrants to Israel from selected countries in Latin America, standardized scores, 1953–1983. For each country, the average number of immigrants over the years was set equal to 0, and the standard deviation over the years was set equal to 1. Z scores in the diagrams measure yearly *aliya* levels in standard deviations from the country's overall average.

continuing economic adversity and of mounting public political protest.[33] Brazilian *aliya* seems to have responded to the taking of power by the military in 1964 and especially to the strengthening of the military government in 1969–1970. Mexico's generally more stable *aliya* levels reached an all-time peak in connection with the financial crisis of 1982–1983. Finally, Chile's *aliya* profile is dominated by one event, the 1970 election to power of the Allende administration. A similar, even sharper pattern would obtain for Cuba after the 1961 political changes there.

It should be realized that some of these reactions to a peculiar political or economic conjuncture were not typical of the Jews only, but were generally shared by the public at large. However, given the very peculiar socioeconomic structure of Jewish populations and the Jews' concentration in certain occupational classes and sectors of the political public opinion, their vulnerability when confronted by actual or (correctly or incorrectly) expected changes may have been at times greater than that of other population groups. It should be stressed, moreover, that all of the data presented here refer to gross migration to Israel, irrespective of return migration. The latter is hard to figure out on a yearly basis because of limitations of available data. It can be roughly estimated that—according to year of immigration—between 18% and 25% of Latin American migrants to Israel reemigrated within three years of their arrival, either to the respective countries of origin or to other countries. This means less reemigration and a higher Israeli retention rate of *aliya* from Latin America than from other Western countries, particularly those in North America.[34]

Summing up the patterns in Figure 6.1, it clearly appears that the major driving force in the quantitative fluctuations of Latin American *aliya* has been the alternation of hold and push factors that operate in the countries of origin rather than the balance of pull and repel factors that may be perceived as operating in Israel. The latter should not be ignored: Increases in *aliya* can be generally observed following the 1967 Six Day War, reflecting the augmented centrality of Israel in the perceptions of Diaspora Jews. However, such increases are by far smaller than those generated by local events in each country. By the same token, expectations of declining *aliya* in 1982–1983, resulting from high Israeli inflation rates and the heavier defense burden connected with the Lebanon war, are systematically disproven by actually increasing migration figures. These trends appear to be

---

33. R. Roett, "Democracy and Debt in South America: A Continent's Dilemma," *Foreign Affairs* 62(3) (1984): 695–720.

34. Israel Central Bureau of Statistics, Immigrants Absorption Survey, various publications.

generally applicable to a country-by-country analysis of Western *aliya*.[35] Yet push factors more emphatically affected migration from Latin America, which was, between 1953 and 1983, on the average four to eight times greater (per 1000 Jewish population in the countries of origin) than the total of *aliya* from free emigration countries.

Characteristics of Migrants

A further important aspect of Latin American (and other) *aliya* is the great selectivity in the personal characteristics of the migrants, compared to the characteristics of nonmigrant Jews in the countries of origin and, conceivably, of Jews who migrate to other destinations. Some of the characteristics of more recent *olim* (immigrants to Israel) will be briefly assessed here.

Age

The following percentages compare the age distributions of Latin American immigrants to Israel in 1982 and of the Jewish urban population of Brazil in 1980.[36]

Population group		0–14	15–24	25–34	35–44	45–64	65+
Latin American *olim*, 1982	(a)	20.8	32.2	15.8	10.0	13.1	8.1
Brazilian Jews, 1980	(b)	19.8	16.2	14.4	12.0	23.3	14.3
Relative percentage difference	(a−b)/(b)	+5	+99	+10	−17	−44	−43

Assuming the age structure of Brazil Jewry is fairly representative of that of total Latin American Jewry, the 15–24 age group is nearly twice as numerous among *olim* than would be a random cross-section of the Jewish population in the countries of origin. The 25–34 age group and children below 15 are overrepresented, too. Although it is a general finding that young adults may display lesser residential stability and higher return migration, it is also clear that *aliya* substantially affects the demographic balance by driving out some of the forces that might contribute to future Jewish population growth in Latin America.

---

35. S. DellaPergola, "On the Differential Frequency of Western Migration to Israel," *Studies in Contemporary Jewry* 1 (1984): 292–315; S. DellaPergola, "Aliya and Other Jewish Migrations: Toward an Integrated Perspective," in *Scripta Hierosolymitana—Studies in the Population of Israel in Honor of Roberto Bachi*, ed. U. O. Schmelz and G. Natan (Jerusalem: Magnes Press, 1986), 172–209.

36. Israel Central Bureau of Statistics, *Immigration to Israel 1982*, Special Publication 723 (1983); Instituto Brasileiro de Geografia e Estatistica, *IX recensamento geral*.

Family Structure

In 1982, 39.5% of Latin American migrants to Israel arrived alone as compared to 50.5% of North American *olim*.[37] The corresponding percentages for some individual countries were: Argentina, 33.3%; France, 57.4%; USSR, 23.7%. Lower percentages of immigrants arriving alone point to more frequent transferral of entire households and to greater stability of settlement in Israel.

Occupation Abroad

Occupations of Latin American *olim* indicate a substantially lower share of salespersons than that probably existing among Jews in the countries of origin; the proportion of professionals and managers is probably higher than in the original Jewish population. The following data, pointing to changes in the occupational structure of Latin American *olim* over time, indirectly confirm the changes occurring in the countries of origin, namely greater professionalization and a declining share of blue-collar workers. The data also illustrate the different developmental stages reached by Jewish occupational structures in Latin and North America.

Population group	Professional, managerial	Clerical	Sales	Blue-collar
Latin American *olim*, 1966–1971	40.7	15.0	16.2	28.1
Latin American *olim*, 1982	54.1	14.8	14.3	16.8
North American *olim*, 1982	73.5	10.1	6.3	10.0

Ideological Characteristics

Aliya disproportionately draws from the more strongly identified sections of Diaspora Jewry. Data on the level of activity of Latin American *olim* in Jewish organizations abroad confirm this general pattern. On the other hand, the predominantly secular character of Latin American Jewish communities is reflected in the religious characteristics of new immigrants.[38]

Latin American olim, 1969–1974	High	Medium	Low
Activity in Jewish organizations abroad	53.3	18.3	28.4
Religious observance abroad	8.4	38.4	53.2

37. Israel Central Bureau of Statistics, *Immigration to Israel 1982*.
38. Israel Central Bureau of Statistics, *Immigrantes de America Latina*.

Compared to their North American peers, Latin American *olim* display greater past Jewish community involvement (53.3% of highly active members versus 46.3%) but far less religious observance (8.4% of religious versus 46.3%).

Locality of First Referral

Patterns of settlement in Israel provide further insights on the ideological characteristics of Latin American immigrants.

Population group	Jerusalem	Tel Aviv, Haifa	Other urban	Kibbutz	Other rural
Latin American *olim*, 1982	11.9	11.9	52.8	21.6	1.8
North American *olim*, 1982	37.9	11.3	38.0	10.4	2.4

The far greater incidence of kibbutz-oriented *aliya* from Latin America seems to reflect the importance of pioneer Jewish youth movements there. The more religious orientation of North American *aliya* is consistent with its greater concentration in Jerusalem.

Absorption Patterns

Latin American *olim* display a relatively poorer initial knowledge of Hebrew than do North American immigrants. Among new arrivals between 1969 and 1974, 15.1% of Latin Americans, versus 21.4% of North Americans, were fluent or almost fluent in Hebrew.[39] However, after three years of stay in the country, 63.8% of Latin American *olim*, versus 58.5% of North Americans, could speak Hebrew quite satisfactorily. Satisfaction with housing and employment was high, between 80% and 90%, without significant differences between Latin and North American immigrants. Though less satisfied with social life in Israel (57.4% versus 85.5%) and having less interaction with veteran immigrants and with the Israel-born (24.2% versus 37.4%), Latin American *olim* after three years in Israel thought more definitely of staying permanently in the country (81.9% versus 78.2% of North Americans). And, as already mentioned, Latin American *aliya* retention rates were actually higher.

Concluding Remarks

This brief profile of Latin American migration to Israel points to a number of distinctive patterns of the major determinants of movement and characteristics of movers. Changes in the sociopolitical fabric of the conti-

---

39. Israel Central Bureau of Statistics, *Immigrantes de America Latina*.

nent, such as those that occurred in Argentina in 1984, might moderate Jewish migration levels and alter its composition. Doubtless, however, over the past decades emigration such as that portrayed here has significantly affected, both quantitatively and qualitatively, the sociodemographic structure and the patterns of Jewish life of those choosing to stay in Latin America. Through the shedding of the younger, more educated, and more Jewishly motivated, emigration has had—and may continue to have—markedly erosive consequences for the regional Jewish demographic equation.

Jewish Population Projections, 1975–2000

The task of projecting future population trends of Latin American Jewry is especially problematic, in view of the unsatisfactory nature of the information available on current trends. An even greater obstacle is the general fluidity in the position of Jewish communities. More so than in other geopolitical regions, there exists a rather broad range of conceivable developments, especially with regard to the future intensity and direction of international migrations. Despite these basic limitations, population projections may fulfill a useful role in the framework of assessing recent population trends. Indeed, projections show the longer term implications of *current* trends by magnifying dynamic features that risk passing unnoticed if observation is limited to a momentary snapshot of population characteristics. Further, population projections can provide useful guidelines to observers of the Jewish scene interested in looking in advance at the more likely general directions of change in the size and composition of the community.

Several sets of Jewish population projections were prepared by U. O. Schmelz at the Institute of Contemporary Jewry for various countries and regions in the Diaspora and for world Jewry.[40] Different alternative hypotheses were considered for each of the main relevant variables: fertility, international migration, and assimilation. The base year of the projections is 1975; quinquennial changes were computed according to five-year age groups and for each set of assumptions until the year 2000. Two of these alternative projections will be presented here in some detail: for Jews in Argentina (see Table 6.14) and in the other countries of Latin America (see Table 6.15).

One set of assumptions projects a continuing over time of the observed comparatively low levels of fertility and mortality, of the estimated current levels of assimilation, and of levels of international migration similar to those observed in the recent past. Migration levels have been estimated

---

40. Schmelz, *World Jewish Population,* and unpublished data.

Table 6.14
Projected Jewish Population Evolution in Argentina, by Components of Change, 1975–2000—Absolute Numbers and Rates per 1000

Years (December 31)	Initial population	Natural movement			International migration balance	Total change	Final population
		Births[c]	Deaths[d]	Balance			
Absolute numbers							
Medium projection[a]							
1975–1980	265,000	10,900	19,500	−8,600	−20,300	−28,900	236,100[e]
1980–1985	236,100	8,000	19,400	−11,400	−17,300	−28,700	207,400
1985–1990	207,400	6,300	18,900	−12,600	−9,200	−21,800	185,600
1990–1995	185,600	5,600	18,200	−12,600	−8,100	−20,700	164,900
1995–2000	164,900	4,900	17,000	−12,100	−7,200	−19,300	145,600
Medium projection, no migration[b]							
1975–1980	265,000	11,500	19,900	−8,400	—	−8,400	256,600
1980–1985	256,600	9,500	20,900	−11,400	—	−11,400	245,200
1985–1990	245,100	8,200	21,400	−13,200	—	−13,200	232,000
1990–1995	232,000	7,900	21,500	−13,600	—	−13,600	218,400
1995–2000	218,400	7,500	20,900	−13,400	—	−13,400	205,000

Period	Births	Deaths	Natural increase	Net migration	Total change
Yearly rates per 1000 Jewish population					
Medium projection[a]					
1975–1980	8.7	15.6	−6.9	−16.2	−23.1
1980–1985	7.2	17.5	−10.3	−15.6	−25.9
1985–1990	6.4	19.2	−12.8	−9.4	−22.3
1990–1995	6.4	20.8	−14.4	−9.3	−23.7
1995–2000	6.4	22.0	−15.6	−9.2	−24.8
Medium projection, no migration[b]					
1975–1980	8.8	15.3	−6.5	—	−6.5
1980–1985	7.6	16.7	−9.1	—	−9.1
1985–1990	6.9	18.0	−11.1	—	−11.1
1990–1995	7.0	19.0	−12.0	—	−12.0
1995–2000	7.1	19.8	−12.7	—	−12.7

Source: U. O. Schmelz, unpublished data.

[a] Low fertility, low mortality, moderate assimilation, and medium net migration.
[b] Same assumptions as in *a*, but nil net migration.
[c] Effectively Jewish births, net of non-Jewish children of mixed marriages.
[d] Includes losses that are due to adult assimilation.
[e] The Jewish population estimate reported in Table 6.3 for 1980 is higher because of revised estimates of international migration balance.

Table 6.15
Projected Jewish Population Evolution in Latin America (other than Argentina), by Components of Change, 1975–2000—Absolute Numbers and Rates per 1000

Years (December 31)	Initial population	Natural movement			International migration balance	Total change	Final population
		Births[c]	Deaths[d]	Balance			
Absolute numbers							
Medium projection[a]							
1975–1980	257,000	13,900	16,900	−3,000	0	−3,000	254,000
1980–1985	254,000	12,700	18,500	−5,800	0	−5,800	248,200
1985–1990	248,200	10,800	19,100	−8,300	−6,000	−14,300	233,900
1990–1995	233,900	8,900	19,100	−10,200	−5,500	−15,700	218,200
1995–2000	218,200	7,800	18,700	−10,900	−5,000	−15,900	202,300
Medium projection, no migration[b]							
1975–1980	257,000	13,900	16,900	−3,000	—	−3,000	254,000
1980–1985	254,000	12,700	18,500	−5,800	—	−5,800	248,200
1985–1990	248,200	11,000	19,300	−8,300	—	−8,300	239,900
1990–1995	239,900	9,400	19,500	−10,100	—	−10,100	229,800
1995–2000	229,800	8,500	19,500	−11,000	—	−11,000	218,800

Yearly rates per 1000 Jewish population

Medium projection[a]				
1975–1980	10.9	13.3	−2.4	−2.4
1980–1985	10.1	14.7	−4.6	−4.6
1985–1990	8.9	15.9	−6.9	−11.9
1990–1995	7.9	16.9	−9.0	−13.9
1995–2000	7.4	17.8	−10.4	−15.2
Medium projection, no migration[b]				
1975–1980	10.9	13.3	−2.4	−2.4
1980–1985	10.1	14.7	−4.6	−4.6
1985–1990	9.0	15.8	−6.8	−6.8
1990–1995	8.0	16.7	−8.6	−8.6
1995–2000	7.6	17.4	−9.8	−9.8

Source: U. O. Schmelz, unpublished data.

[a] Low fertility, low mortality, moderate assimilation, and medium net migration.
[b] Same assumptions as in *a*, but nil migration.
[c] Effectively Jewish births, net of non-Jewish children of mixed marriages.
[d] Includes losses that are due to adult assimilation.

on the basis of the known incidence of *aliya* and of assumptions on the relative distribution of migrations from Latin American countries to Israel and elsewhere. The second set of projections assumes no international migrations and therefore focuses on the consequences of a continuation of recent internal demographic changes within local Jewish populations. It should be noted that projected figures of births in Tables 6.14 and 6.15 refer to *effectively Jewish* natality, after discounting losses of children born to mixed couples and not imputed to the Jewish group; projected figures of deaths incorporate the assumed net effects of adult assimilation. Therefore, data in the birth and death columns actually reflect, respectively, the overall positive and negative components in the natural and identificational balance of the Jewish population.

It can be seen from Tables 6.14 and 6.15 that both major sections of Latin American Jewry can be expected to lose population in the foreseeable future if demographic trends that predominated around 1975 continue, regardless of emigration. Such projected losses are relatively more significant in Argentina than in the remaining communities. A fall of 23% in Argentine Jewish population would occur between 1975 and 2000, reflecting a decline in absolute numbers from 265,000 to 205,000 Jews. Jewish population in the rest of Latin America would be expected to decline from 257,000 in 1975 to 219,000 in the year 2000, a reduction of 15%. Within this general trend, substantially greater stability should be assumed in countries such as Brazil, Venezuela, and Mexico, whereas relatively greater population losses may be incurred by Jews in Uruguay, Chile, and some of the other smaller communities in the continent.

Taking into account emigration, Argentine Jewry might decline by 42% between 1975 and 2000 (to an absolute figure of 146,000), as against a projected decline by 21% in the rest of Latin American Jewry (to a total of 202,000 at the end of the century). Judging on the basis of migration trends between 1975 and 1984, reality may fit somewhere in between these various hypotheses, pointing to sustained—though not extreme—Jewish population decline in Latin America. It should be realized, in any case, that the low effectively Jewish birth rate is inducing a process of uninterrupted aging in the Jewish population structure. This is conducive to more frequent cases of Jewish deaths than of Jewish births and to reduced Jewish population size, irrespective of the additional effects of international migrations.

Conclusions

In spite of serious limitations in the data available for the sociodemographic study of Latin American Jewry, and in spite of the conjectural character of some of the materials presented, the evidence on Jewish population trends seems to be quite consistent. The overall demographic development of Argentine Jewry until 1960 and the trend of decline characterizing Latin American Jewry since the early 1960s were outlined with the help of various data resources. Even if a corrective must be introduced in some of the data reported or hypothesized on Jewish population size and characteristics, that corrective should not be too large. Recent Jewish population reduction, however, has not been indicated here as the only feature worth attention. A number of further distinctive sociodemographic patterns were pointed out. Some effects of generation, life-cycle status, and residential redistribution on basic characteristics of the Jewish population were discussed. Some of these mobility processes indicate the persistence of Jewish distinctiveness and cohesion, in spite of population decline.

These factors should be kept in mind when evaluating other aspects of the current and expected development of Latin American Jewry, particularly the interplay of various factors internal to the community (Jewish education, Jewish organizations, Jewish wealth, and so on) and the relationship between Jewish populations and surrounding majority societies. Demographic changes underlie each of these internal and external factors and are likely to be increasingly felt at various levels of communal decision making. The latter, therefore, should rely on solid, detailed, updated evidence on the major relevant population characteristics and trends. And yet, notwithstanding the variety of data presented here, it should be realized that there can be no serious alternative to a fresh new round of empirical data collecting if the existing demographic picture is not to lose much of its relevance in the near future. In the absence of satisfactory Jewish data bases derived from official population censuses, development of such new data resources will have to be the primary responsibility of Jewish institutions in Latin America, possibly in collaboration with the Division of Jewish Demography and Statistics at the Hebrew University's Institute of Contemporary Jewry. Such an empirical updating has unfortunately met various obstacles associated with institutional developments within the Jewish community and more generally with the unfavorable economic conditions prevailing in the region. One can hope that these difficulties will be overcome in the near future so that a realistic approach to Jewish population trends and their consequences may become possible. Such an approach is necessary if the exacting, manifold problems that epitomize the contemporary Jewish experience in Latin America are to be met adequately.

7
The Origins of Zionism in Latin America

Haim Avni

Introduction

Zionism, the modern ideology of the national resurrection of the Jewish people, took organizational form only late in the nineteenth century. It was first established as a loosely confederated body of local societies of Lovers of Zion (*Hovevei Zion*) founded in 1884 and later as the World Zionist Organization created in 1897 under the leadership of Theodor Herzl. By that time the national movements of Western Europe and Latin America already had achieved territorial autonomy and political independence. In contrast, Zionism's ideology and program—the return to the land, to a majority Jewish society, to Jewish language and culture—preceded political independence. The achievement of Zionism's goals depended on the Jews in the Diaspora who sought to recover first their national identity and ultimately their national home.

The study of Zionism in Latin America is important for Jewish history, as well as for Latin American history, because the contradictions posed for Jews of the Latin American diaspora were acute. As newly arrived immigrants, struggling for economic survival and to strike roots in their new host societies, the Jews of Latin America might well have seemed able to devote little energy and material support to the realization of a national program so very distant from them. Moreover, the intensity of the challenge posed by the Jewish national movement must have been perceived by the host societies of Latin America, given the visibility of Jewish immigrants in religious, national, and cultural terms. The reactions to Zionism in the host societies of Latin America undoubtedly influenced the development of Zionism in Latin America and thus the dynamics of the relationships between those societies and their Jewish communities.

In spite of its importance, the history of Zionism in Latin America has been only partially studied by a small number of scholars. In *Latin American Jewry: A Research Guide,* Martin H. Sable lists only twenty-six bibliographical items, three of which could be classified as research works and only an additional five as systematic and analytical reports.[1] In *Jews of the Latin American Republics,* Judith Laikin Elkin discusses Jewish political movements briefly.[2] Victor A. Mirelman,[3] Margalit Bejarano,[4] Nachman Falbel,[5] the author of this chapter,[6] and particularly Silvia Szenkolewski,[7] are among those who contributed some of the scholarly works available and their investigations have supplemented the mainly descriptive or biographical summaries by Nathan Bistritzky,[8] Moisés Joselevich,[9] Yeshayahy Austri-Dan,[10] Samuel Malamud,[11] and others. Yet it can be concluded that the

    1. Martin H. Sable, *Latin American Jewry: A Research Guide* (Cincinnati: Hebrew Union College Press, 1978), 302–312.
    2. Judith Laikin Elkin, *Jews of the Latin American Republics* (Chapel Hill: University of North Carolina Press, 1980).
    3. Victor A. Mirelman, "Zionist Activities in Argentina from the Balfour Declaration to 1930," in Y. Bauer, M. Davis, I. Kolat (ed.), *Studies in the History of Zionism, Presented to Israel Goldstein* (Jerusalem: Hassijouya Ha ziyonit, 1976), 188–223 (in Hebrew with summary in English).
    4. Margalit Bejarano, "Ha-Tziyonut ha-Sefaradit" (Sefardic Zionism), in "Ha-Kehila ha-Sefaradit shel Buenos-Aires" (The Sephardic community of Buenos Aires). Master's thesis, Hebrew University of Jerusalem, 1974 (in Hebrew), 132–142.
    5. Nachman Falbel, "O Sionismo e os Judeos no Brasil," *Shalom* (São Paulo) (April 1980), 12–23.
    6. Haim Avni, *Ha-Tzyonut ve-Hanchalata be-America ha-Latininit* (Zionism in Latin America), in *Publications of the Study Circle on World Jewry,* M. Davis (ed.), 8th Series, No. 3 (Jerusalem: The Institute of Contemporary Jewry, The Hebrew University of Jerusalem, 1976) (in Hebrew).
    7. Silvia Szenkolewski, "Di Tzionistische Bawegung in Argentine, 1897–1917" (The Zionist movement in Argentina, 1897–1917), in *Pinkes fun der Kehile/Anales de la Comunidad Isralita de Buenos-Aires, 1969* (Buenos Aires: Asociacion Mutual Israelita Argentina, 1969), 101–130, (in Yiddish); S. Szenkolewski, "Ha-Tenua ha-Tzionit ve-ha-Miflagot be-Argentina, 1936–1943 (The Zionist movement and parties in Argentina, 1936–1943) (in Hebrew). Ph.D. diss., Hebrew University of Jerusalem, 1985.
    8. Natan Bistritzky, *Al-ha-Yahadut vé-ha-Tzyonut be-America ha-Latinit* (Zionism and Judaism in Latin America) (Jerusalem: Jewish National Fund, 1947) (in Hebrew).
    9. Moisés Joselevich, *Jornadas Pioneras, Apuntes para una historia del movimiento jalutziano de America latina* (Jerusalem: Departmento de la Juventual y del Julutz de la Organización Sionista Mundial, 1957).
    10. Yeshayahu Austri-Dan, *Di Tzionistische Bawegung in Mexico* (The Zionist movement in Mexico) (Mexico: The Zionist Federation, 1957) (in Yiddish).
    11. Samuel Malamud, *Do arquivo e da memória* (Rio de Janeiro: Bloch Editores, 1983).

study of Zionism in Latin America, taken as a whole, requires considerable development.

This chapter attempts to highlight three sets of issues involved in Latin American Zionism: first, the role played by Latin America in the history of the Zionist movement; second, the impact of Zionism on Latin American Jewish life and institutions; and third, the position of Latin American Zionists within the World Zionist Organization. Because of the uneven coverage of the existing research, more conclusive remarks will be offered regarding the earlier parts of this history, whereas more unanswered questions will be raised with respect to later developments.

The Early Years of Zionism

The encounter between the Zionist movement and Latin America preceded by six years the establishment of the World Zionist Organization. In the summer of 1891, it became known that Baron Maurice de Hirsch had decided to invest in an extensive agricultural colonization project in the Argentine Republic the enormous sum of fifty million francs (U.S. $10 million), which had been set aside by him to solve the plight of Russian Jewry. Some young Lovers of Zion, such as Shemaryahu Levine, tried to raise a popular protest against this decision, arguing that the exclusive target of such a project should be the Jews' ancestral land, Palestine, whereas the official leadership of the movement attempted to persuade Baron de Hirsch to invest some of his funds *also* in Palestine. Indeed, they obtained a pledge from him to match any funds they would raise to finance an exploratory mission to "Asiatic Turkey." Following an economically favorable report on such a mission, the Baron promised to participate in the establishment of an agrarian bank through which the financing of the settlement in Palestine could be carried out. This pledge was, however, accompanied by a detailed note in which the Baron contrasted the merits of Argentina to those of Palestine in the establishment of a large Jewish settlement. He concluded this document by a statement definitely in favor of the Latin American country.[12]

In 1891 and in the following years, Argentina and Palestine were frequently weighed against one another by all the Zionist leaders. Colonel Albert A. Goldsmid, one of the most colorful personalities of the Lovers of

---

12. "Baron de Hirsch's Memorandum on Palestinian Colonization, 1891," Appendix II in Kurt Grunwald, *Türkenhirsch, a Study of Baron Maurice de Hirsch, Entrepreneur and Philanthropist* (Jerusalem: Israel Program for Scientific Translations, 1966), 122–125; originally published in *The Maccabaeans* (London: March 1904), 125–127.

Zion in Great Britain, was offered by Baron de Hirsch the position of director general of his project in Argentina—to turn into reality the Baron's dream of settling tens of thousands of Russian Jews every year in Argentina; he apparently went through some deep soul searching before accepting that offer. He sought the advice of Rabbi Shemuel Mohliver, the religious leader of the Lovers of Zion movement since its inception, and received his blessing wrapped in a casuistic homily: "As the letter 'A' in the alphabet leads to the letter 'Z', so will the enterprise in 'A'rgentina end up in 'Z'ion."[13]

The other founder of the movement, the nonreligious physician Leo Pinsker, was in 1891 more inclined toward Argentina. Disappointed by the poor results obtained in the movement's colonization work in Palestine, he dictated from his sick bed, barely three weeks before his death, a new introduction to an English edition of his booklet *Auto-Emancipation,* in which he agreed to the idea that the great Jewish national project could eventually be established in Argentina. Among the secular Lovers of Zion there were, thus, those who were ready to have Palestine replaced by Argentina. But traditional Lovers of Zion, such as Achad Ha'am and some of his followers, as well as religious leaders, were prepared to accept Argentina only alongside Palestine. For both factions, the remote Latin American country became an ideological challenge.[14]

Four years after Baron de Hirsch initiated his project, another encounter occurred between Zionism and Argentina. On June 2, 1895, Baron de Hirsch received Theodor Herzl, the future founder of political Zionism, in his Paris mansion. The meeting was a failure and this very fact rendered it a meaningful event in the history of the Zionist movement. On the face of it, Herzl had every chance of gaining the Baron's support for his vision of Jewish statehood, because the Baron himself had had very similar ideas in 1891. It seems, however, that this similarity was precisely the reason that prevented the latter from feeling much enthusiasm for Herzl's proposals.

The Baron de Hirsch, then 64 years old and one of the richest men in the world, had, for several years, been engaged day in and day out in the realization of his great project. Herzl, aged 35, was younger than the Baron's son Lucien would have been had he lived, and at the time he was only known as a journalist and playwright, though a successful one. Herzl regarded the Baron as a "moneyed Jew" who lacked a real and far-reaching vision. He presented to him ideas evolving out of his own original thinking, which were similar to those the Baron had long before then conceived and was trying to implement. The Baron was apparently unable to regard Herzl

---

13. Haim Avni, *Argentina, "Ha-Aretz ha-Yeuda"* (Argentina, "the Promised Land") (Jerusalem: The Magnes Press, 1973), 122–123 (in Hebrew).

14. Avni, *Argentina,* 302–303.

as anything other than "a man of plans" of a type he had often encountered in his lifetime. Herzl must have reminded him of one in particular, Dr. Wilhelm Löwenthal, whom he resembled physically. Dr. Löwenthal had been the Baron's first representative in Argentina and the very person who had induced him to choose that country as the target for his project. Having severely disappointed his employer by his overoptimistic judgments and unrealistic actions, he had been ruthlessly discharged.[15]

Herzl's abortive meeting with Baron de Hirsch marked a turning point in the former's Zionist activities. His failure to gain the support of the Jewish aristocracy, personified by Hirsch, induced him to direct his efforts toward the Jewish masses. The notes he had prepared for his meeting with Hirsch formed the basis for his epoch-making pamphlet *Der Judenstaat* (*The Jewish State*), which became the cornerstone of the World Zionist Organization. But even in that booklet the encounter with Argentina continued. "Argentina oder Palestina?" reads one of the headings in Herzl's booklet and its author, as Baron de Hirsch had done barely four years earlier, proceeded to analyze the advantages of each country. Unlike the Baron, however, Herzl inclined toward "our historical fatherland" rather than toward the one that was "by nature, one of the richest countries in the world." But he left the final decision to the "Jewish Company," which, according to his plan, ought to be established, and asserted that "it will take whatever it will be given and whatever the public opinion of the Jewish nation will favor."[16]

By the time the First Zionist Congress was convened two years later, all doubts had been dissipated as to the preference of the Jewish people. But even then, Argentina, unique among all the diasporas old and new, held a special position in the Zionist mind. In his memorable opening address to the First Zionist Congress, Herzl referred to "the practical forerunners of today's Zionism" who had established Jewish agricultural settlements, saying: "Of these colonization projects in Palestine and in the Argentine, we all shall not speak but with a sincere gratitude. But they were only the *first*, not the last word of the Zionist Movement."[17]

Argentina was on the agenda of the Second Zionist Congress, which met in Basel in August 1898. Henrique Son, the delegate of the Argentine Zionists, a colorful but dubious personality, brought before it the plight of the Jewish settlers in the Jewish Colonization Association (JCA) colonies. A move to request an Argentine government inquiry was then supported by

15. Avni, *Argentina*, 99–107.
16. Herzl, *Der Judenstaat* (The Jewish state) (1895; reprint, Berlin: Jüdischer Verlag, 1918), 34.
17. *Stenographisches Protokoll der Verhandlungen des Ersten Zionisten Kongresses August 25–31* (Stenographic minutes of the deliberations of the First Zionist Congress, Aug. 29–31) (Vienna: Verlag des Vereines "Erez Israel," 1898), 6.

some delegates but was killed by Herzl's firm leadership.[18] A more serious discussion of the JCA, its work in general and in Argentina in particular, was engendered at the Fifth Zionist Congress in 1901 by Israel Zangwill, the famous writer and, later, territorialist. He proposed to prosecute the JCA in the courts of law for its alleged failure to execute its founder's will. It took all of Herzl's statesmanship to avoid such a legal confrontation, but the discussion disclosed the still-prevailing sensitivity of many Zionists to the role of Argentina in the history of their movement.[19]

The fact that Zionism was deeply ingrained among the Jewish colonists in Argentina gave the Zionist leaders cause for much pride. Warm applause greeted the announcement at the Third Zionist Congress in 1899 that local societies had been established in almost every colony, grouping together full "shekel"-paying members of the World Zionist Organization. "This is a striking proof that our aspirations for colonization directed toward Palestine find understanding and adherence also among the colonists on the other side of the ocean," declared the rapporteur, Oscar Marmorek, before the applauding Congress.[20]

In the question of "Palestina oder Argentina" Palestine obviously prevailed, but Argentina left its definite mark on the early history of Zionism.

The Early Years of Latin American Jewry

Zionism was also present in the early history of the Latin American communities. The first appearance of any Jewish organizations in Argentina dates back to 1862. The French Alliance Israelite Universelle was the most influential institution until Zionism was established in 1897. By then the increasing number of Eastern European immigrants had changed the character of the growing Jewish community and Zionism had become a widespread tendency, even when the number of members affiliated with Zionist societies did not constitute a significant proportion of the total Jewish population.[21]

In Brazil, the first signs of organized Jewish life had preceded those in

18. *Stenographisches,* Second Congress, 130–135.
19. *Stenographisches,* Fifth Congress, 324–327. Zangwill, like many other critics of the JCA, was unaware of the radical changes the Baron introduced in his plans during the year preceding his death. See Avni, *Argentina,* 256–264.
20. *Stenographisches,* Third Congress, 29. The same declaration was repeated in the Fourth Congress (*Stenographisches,* Fourth Congress, 72). *Shekel,* a biblical monetary unit (and also the present Israeli currency), was the symbolic name of the fees and membership card of the Zionist Organization.
21. Szenkolewski, "Di Tzionistiche Bawegung," 108–116.

Argentina by several decades; but because of the smaller number of Jews involved, their dispersion throughout the enormous territory, and, for many, the temporary nature of their stay in the country, Jewish communal life had to be renewed time and again. The first manifestation of a Zionist organization was evidenced in 1901 and came from remote Manicoré, in the heart of the tropical state of Amazonas. In a letter addressed to Dr. Max Nordau by "the Hebrew Colony" of that town, the modest sum of 150 francs, collected among the local Jews, was enclosed with a request to be kept regularly informed on all matters concerned with Zionism.[22] This response to the Zionist call was read at the Fifth Zionist Congress, along with another, emanating from Chile. There, too, a group of Zionists reported their initiative to form an association and explore the ways in which a firm relationship with other Zionist associations could be established. This apparently preceded any known organized Jewish life in Chile, the first organization registered there only came into being in 1906.[23]

Zionism in Brazil gained an impressive public position in 1915 when two intellectuals, David José Perez and Alvaro de Castillo, a Jew and a non-Jew, established an "organ for the interests of the Jewish people in Brazil" in Rio de Janeiro named *A Columna—Ha'Amud* (*The Column*; the title was printed both in Portuguese and in Hebrew). Its first issue carried a long article on Theodor Herzl written by David Perez, and later numbers included contributions by Max Nordau and other Zionist leaders. Although not the official organ of Tif'ereth Zion, the Zionist Association in Rio de Janeiro, or of any other of its type, the periodical constituted a rostrum for Zionism and its work in Palestine. *A Columna* received a warm welcome from Zionists in many and remote parts of Brazil.[24] When the Balfour Declaration was made public, David Perez and other activists started to prepare a nationwide Jewish Brazilian Congress, similar to the one that took place in Argentina in 1916. One of its main purposes was to foster Brazilian support for the Zionist claim to establish Palestine as a Jewish national home. The need for this political demonstration on the part of the Jewish community diminished when two members of the Brazilian parliament declared their

---

22. The first synagogue in Brazil was established in 1824 in Belém, State of Pará. See Egon Wolff and Frida Wolff, *Judeos nos primórdios do Brasil republicana* (Rio de Janeiro: Biblioteca Israelita H. N. Bialik, 1979), for details of the wide dispersion of Jews in Brazil; see also *Stenographisches*, Fifth Congress, 12–13.

23. *Stenographisches*, Fifth Congress, 12–13; Moises Senderey, *Historia de la colectividad israelita de Chile Editorial Dos Ydische Wort* (Santiago: 1956), 55–58.

24. *A Columna*, No. 1, 14 January 1916, 5–8; No. 2, February 1916, 24–25; Hebrew letter by S. T. Nigrin, 29 June 1916, requesting that the periodical be published in Hebrew, Central Archives for the History of the Jewish People, David Perez Files Doc. 121A; see other letters written in a Zionist vein in these archives.

own willingness to bring that very demand before Brazil's Congress. The Jewish Conference was postponed and later cancelled; attention was redirected at celebrating the Balfour Declaration of 1917 and stirring up diplomatic activity in its support.[25]

"Under the influence of the overwhelming emotion caused by the official intimation which the leaders of the Sionism have had the kindness to communicate to us . . . " wrote David Perez and Jacob Schneider (the latter a well-known Brazilian Zionist leader) to Sir Arthur Peel, the British minister in Brazil, in an obviously Portuguese-influenced English, "the Israelites of this Capital, interpreting collectively the sentiments of their Brethren throughout Brazil, beg hereby to approach your Excellency for the purpose of expressing their most grateful recognition and offering, at the same time, their entire solidarity to the Government of His Britannic Majesty. . . . The Jewish colony in Brazil is not large and strong like its co-sister of the United States, but it feels, nevertheless, the same enthusiasm as that co-sister does." The two leaders were granted an interview with Sir Arthur Peel in order to congratulate the British Government on the capture of Jerusalem by the British forces. The minister later informed them that their communication, submitted to him on that occasion, "has been duly laid before His Majesty, King George V, and . . . His Majesty desires me to convey an expression of his thanks for their message."[26]

Not all Jews living in Brazil shared this enthusiasm for Zionism. "I am Jewish but, in the first place, German" wrote M. Rothschild of São Paulo to the editor of *A Columna* upon returning to him the September–December 1917 issue of the paper. "As a German, I am in total disagreement with the tendency of your *revista*, in which I see my fatherland, Germany, treated with maximal injustice."[27] That number of *A Columna* was also the last to be printed, and its temporary suspension became final. Nevertheless, Zionism in Brazil continued on its course and was reinforced manifold when a larger wave of immigration reached that country in the years following World War I.

In Argentina also, the Balfour Declaration and the events preceding it had a significant impact upon Jewish public life. In a meticulous study of this period, Victor Mirelman indicated the surprising involvement of the Congregación Israelita de la Republica Argentina (CIRA) in Zionist matters in the years 1917–1918. This communal organization, the oldest of Argen-

---

25. Letter to Moyses J. Abensur in Umarizal-Fox do Javary, Amazonas, 12 February 1918, Central Archives, Perez Files Doc. 148; the members of Congress referred were Mauricio de Lacerda and Gonçalves Maya.

26. Address to the minister, 11 December 1917, Central Archives, Perez Files Doc. 146; letter from Sir Arthur Peel to Perez, 1 April 1918, Central Archives, Perez Files Doc. 150.

27. *A Columna*, No. 24, September–December 1917, 1; M. Rothschild to Perez, 2 February 1918, Central Archives, Perez Files Doc. 147.

tine Jewry, had always been under the influence of the non-Zionist JCA, but it sponsored a group of volunteers for the Jewish Legion of the British Army, which had been organized by the radical Zionist leader Zeev Jabotinsky. In this and other matters, the CIRA stood in open rivalry with the Zionist Federation, the official Zionist body, which did not entirely welcome this sudden independent Zionist zeal. The veteran Zionists and their newly gained sympathizers also entered into close contact with the British official representatives, thus responding to new challenges and acquiring more prestige.[28]

The same situation also existed in the small community of Cuba. The Balfour Declaration inspired David Blis, an ardent Zionist and an ex-student of the Theological Seminary of Breslau and later of the Hebrew Union College in Cincinnati who was working at that time as agent of a jewelry dealer, to try to induce the Cuban Senate to pass a resolution supporting the Jewish National Home. Through the daring use of his contacts, he indeed succeeded.[29]

The enthusiasm that the Balfour Declaration generated among the veteran and new Zionists had its maximum impact on Chilean Jewry. This very young community—whose first symptom of organized life, a public prayer, dated back to only eleven years before the Balfour Declaration—had been one of the most intimidated and timorous communities in Latin America. Although the first, and weak, organization founded on August 8, 1909, in Santiago, carried the name Union *Israelita* en Chile, the much stronger second one preferred to hide under the name Sociedad Centro-Comercial de Beneficencia (Society of Commercial Center of Charity). According to its statutes, this society's membership was open to people who were "merchants or industrialists of the same faith as the founders and members of the first Board of Directors," thus carefully avoiding the use of the word Jews or Jewish. On September 15, 1914, the Union agreed to merge with the Center, on the explicit condition that Article 2 of the merger agreement be implemented: "The Sociedad Centro-Comercial de Beneficencia promises that within 90 days from this date, it will enter the word 'Israelita' in the name of the Institution." This compromise, however, was only fulfilled after the publication of the Balfour Declaration more than three years later. The same phenomenon of neo-Marranism was also evidenced in Temuco, where the community's organization, mainly composed of immigrants from Monastir in Macedonia, had chosen to hide under the name Centro Macedonico.[30]

Almost immediately after the Balfour Declaration became public, this

---

28. Mirelman, "Zionist Activities," 202–206.
29. Boris Sapir, *The Jewish Community of Cuba, Settlement and Growth*, Jewish Teachers' Seminary and People University Press (New York: 1948), 17–22.
30. Documents presented to President Zalman Shazar on his state visit to Chile in June 1966, agreement of fusion, Central Archives; see Senderey, *Historia*, 69–72.

situation began to change. The small nuclei of Zionists, which until then, had been on the fringes of the community now formed a Comité Nacional Judío. During the second half of 1918, under the extraordinary influence of Dr. Ber Epstein, an emissary of the World Zionist Organization, Zionism emerged from its marginal state. The first anniversary of the Balfour Declaration was celebrated by the whole community of Santiago in a central theater, with the participation of representatives of the government, congressmen, and members of the diplomatic corps. Shortly thereafter, the now-renamed Centro Israelita decided to convene a nationwide Jewish Chilean Congress; when it met on September 18–20, 1919, with the participation of thirteen organizations from Santiago and from five other cities, it founded the Federación Sionista (the Zionist Federation) as the all-inclusive representative of Chilean Jewry, and from 1920 onwards the annual nationwide meeting of Chilean Jews was named the (Chilean) Zionist congress. Chile was the only country in Latin America where the Zionist Organization became officially identified with the whole Jewish community.[31]

A Formative Decade

The decade following the end of World War I in Latin America constituted a period of consolidation of the Jewish communities, as in the case of Argentina, or of their preliminary formation, as was the case in several other countries. In spite of the small size of all these communities, the fact that they were composed of recently established immigrants, mainly from Eastern Europe, meant the persistence in the new Diaspora of almost all the political and organizational differences that had prevailed in the Old Country. The history of Zionism and of its various parties in each country thus must be studied alongside the history of anti-Zionism there.

A starting point for carrying out an overall review of Zionism in the subcontinent during the 1920s may be found in the Keren Hayesod's report on the contributions received during the first eight years of its existence (1922–1930). The fifty-three countries listed included seven Latin American ones. Four of these (Cuba, Mexico, Panama, and Peru) appeared at the bottom of the list because, in the case of the three latter countries, their contributions had amounted to less than £500 and, in the case of Cuba, to less than £800. At that time, each of these four communities comprised only a few thousands or even hundreds of Jews, but their contributions equaled or even exceeded that of Hungary, which was then the home of some 445,000 Jews Chile, which had an estimated Jewish population (in 1935) of

---

31. Senderey, *Historia*, 72–77.

9000 and whose contribution amounted to £9,394, ranked above such prosperous and old communities as those of Switzerland and Italy, which had 17,973 (in 1930) and 47,825 (in 1935) Jews, respectively. The Brazilian community, which possibly comprised only 50,000 Jews, contributed the sum of £13,222; next on the list came France, whose contribution was only £15,749, although the number of Jews was estimated at around 260,000, many of whom were the most wealthy Jews in Europe. Argentina, ranked eighth on the list, came immediately after Rumania, which had a Jewish population three times larger, as well as after Poland, which at that time had the largest Jewish diaspora in Europe. Argentine Jews, some 200,000 individuals, gave the Keren Hayesod £73,439, only one-third less than Polish Jews, whose numbers were more than fifteen times greater.[32]

Keren Hayesod was only one of the two main financial instruments of the Zionist Organization and was possibly less popular than the Jewish National Fund, Keren Kayemeth. Other funds related to specific institutions in Palestine—for instance, the Hebrew University—also appealed to the pocket and energies of the Latin American Zionists. The Keren Hayesod data are sufficient, however, to suggest that Zionism in Latin America was considerably more vigorous than it was in several other larger and wealthier communities. On the other hand, the testimony of some of the Zionist emissaries who visited these communities and were instrumental in launching these campaigns seems to contradict this hypothesis. Leib Jaffe, one of the most outstanding among these delegates, spoke warmly of his Latin American hosts with whom he spent many months in 1923, but also criticized the lack of a thorough Zionist education and questioned the possibility of survival of Zionism there. Jaffe and other emissaries concluded that the local communities did not possess an appropriate leadership and that they should, therefore, be helped by the Zionist Organization on a more permanent basis than by sending them temporary campaigning visitors. The few studies that have been carried out until now support the claim that during the 1920s and even in the following decade Latin American Zionism leaned heavily, even for organizational initiatives, on "physicians from abroad."[33]

32. *Report of the Executive of the Zionist Organization Submitted to the XVI Zionist Congress at Zurich, July–August 1929* (London: 1929), 140; for population estimates see Arthur Ruppin, *The Jewish Fate and Future*, Macmillan (London: 1940), Table II, 31–32. Argentine Jews, however, fared much worse than those of South Africa (72,000 Jews in 1926 contributed £269,721) or of Canada (156,000 Jews in 1931 contributed £147,327).

33. Mirelman, "Zionist Activities," 206–211. These characteristics apply even more to the Sephardic communities in Argentina; see Bejarano, "Ha-Tziyonut," 132–136; see also I. L. Gorelick, *Be-Eretz Nod* (In the land of wanderings) (Buenos Aires: 1943), 132–134, for articles written in the 1920s lamenting the lack of a real Zionist zeal and the dependence on "physicians from abroad."

The Holocaust Era

The waves of Jewish immigrants and refugees that reached Latin America during the 1930s and also partly after World War II had broken out reshaped the Zionist map of the subcontinent. Small groups of Jews, sometimes made up of only a few individuals, settled in small and remote places where no Jews had lived before. Their existence was revealed by the systematic screening for eventual contributors to the Zionist funds. These were conducted by some indefatigible emissaries, among whom was Dr. A. S. Yuris, who campaigned on behalf of Keren Hayesod. In 1941 he visited sixteen towns and villages in Colombia, out of which in only four—Bogota, Baranquilla, Cali, and Medellín—some Jews had lived before the Holocaust era. Isolated Jews in small towns in Venezuela, Bolivia, Ecuador, and Guatemala were visited by him, as well as by Leib Jaffe, Manuel Graiver, and others, who brought back the humble donations for Palestine and Zionism from these Jews. The list of towns which were visited by Yuris and Graiver in Uruguay and Mexico included, in the first country, Montevideo and seventeen other localities, and in the second, Mexico City and nine provincial centers.[34] Aside from the tremendous dispersion of the Jews throughout Latin America, the emissaries' reports also attested to a widespread awareness of Zionism. "Being here isolated and unable to take part in the Zionist campaigns," wrote Samuel Szomstein in September 1945 from the small town of Coro in Venezuela to the editor of the *Haynt* in Warsaw, "we seized the opportunity of being assembled for the festivals of New Year and the Day of Atonement, and collected among us the small sum of 22 dollars." The initiators, Samuel and his wife Cirile Szomstein, requested the *Haynt* to send the money to the headquarters of the Jewish National Fund (JNF) in Jerusalem, which was indeed done.[35]

Almost a year later, in Caracas, a group of Sephardic and Ashkenazic Jews, prompted by Manuel Graiver, announced the founding of the Zionist Organization in Venezuela. The sum collected on that occasion and transferred to the Keren Hayesod was £592, which exceeded eight years' contributions in the 1920s of the communities of certain countries. Nevertheless, political upheavals in 1938 and the fear of government repression disrupted the normal development of Zionism in Venezuela. The regular campaign was suspended and the frightened activists hastened to send back to Jeru-

---

34. Yuris to Lauterbach, 11 October 1941, S53/468, Central Zionist Archives, Jerusalem; letters by Graiver, A349/95, Central Zionist Archives; L. Jaffe "to friends," 24 November 1942, S25/1872, Central Zionist Archives.

35. Letter from JNF in Poland to Jerusalem, 17 November 1935, KKL5/982, Central Zionist Archives; S53/468 Yuris to Lauterbach, various letters, KKL5/982, Central Zionist Archives; Graiver to Jerusalem, 17 July 1940, A349/95, Central Zionist Archives.

salem the shekels they had previously received, together with a request to refrain in future from sending them Zionist publications by mail.[36]

Turbulent political circumstances temporarily disturbed the normal Zionist activities in other Latin American countries also, but nowhere did they have as lasting and deep an effect as in Brazil. "After the 'golpe de estado' of 1937, the Federal Government proclaimed as illegal any political activity related to . . . foreign corporations. The head of the police and of the DOPS [department of security] claimed that Zionism was included in that prohibition. . . . Zionist activities were thus suspended until the end of World War II," according to Samuel Malamud, a leading Brazilian Zionist. According to him, the police tolerated private meetings of the Zionist leadership, and fund raising for Zionist purposes was incorporated into the operations of the Comite Hebreu-Brazileiro Pro-Vitimas da Guerra (Hebrew–Brazilian Committee for the Victims of the War), which functioned under the auspices of the Brazilian Red Cross and of which Malamud was one of the vice presidents. Open and ordinary propagation of Zionism was, however, impossible during eight crucial years.[37] The impact of that situation upon the character of Brazilian Zionism—as well as the impact of the total prohibition of the publication of newspapers and periodicals in foreign languages, which closed down the Yiddish press—has not yet been studied. It may be assumed, nevertheless, that its results were far-reaching not only because of the singularly important period of Jewish history in which it occurred, but also because of the intensive developments to which Zionism was exposed during those years.

As the only diasporas that were spared the pain of direct involvement in the war, the Latin American Jewish communities attracted attention of world Jewish organizations during that time. As shown elsewhere, the Zionist Organization, together with the World Jewish Congress (the Zionist-led world political representation of the Jewish communities), surpassed the non-Zionist American Joint Distribution Committee (JDC) and the American Jewish Committee (AJC) in gaining the support of Latin American

---

36. José Battan to JNF, Jerusalem, 28 July 1936, KKKL5, Central Zionist Archives; Fortunato Benacerraf and José Battan to JNF, 19 October 1938, S5/2049, Central Zionist Archives.

37. Malamud, *Do arquivo*, 36, 40, 42. Whether or not Brazilian Zionists could have avoided the ban on their activities, as has been argued by Rachel Sefardi Yarden (the New York–based promoter and coordinator of the committee's "Pro-Palestina Hebrea") has as yet to be studied. See Memorandum, "Zionism Comes of Age in Latin America," Summer 1945, S5/698, Central Zionist Archives; R. S. Yarden's testimony, Oral History Division of the Institute of Contemporary Jewry, The Hebrew University of Jerusalem, 15(171). Robert Levine, "Brazil's Jews during the Vargas Era and After," *Luso Brazilian Review*, 5(1) (June 1968): 45–58, provides a detailed background without dealing with this issue.

Jews.[38] Through their special emissaries and their European members who immigrated to the subcontinent, the Zionist parties deepened their influence and while competing with each other put up a common front against the anti-Zionist Communists and Bundists. Although almost all the factions were campaigning for funds and the main issue at stake for all emissaries was contributions they could collect in each community, this same activity helped to enhance and deepen the Zionist (or anti-Zionist) attitudes.

In spite of this process, several observers complained bitterly of the poor state of Zionist education, both for adults and youth, and of the ideological shallowness of the Latin American Zionists. They criticized the carelessness with which the Zionist Organization had until then dealt with these problems. Among these critics the most outspoken was the author Nathan Bistritzky, who for five years had served as the JNF emissary to Latin America and had spent long periods in almost every country there. In lengthy reports, memoranda, and later a booklet, he expressed his criticism and far-reaching proposals. He also dedicated much of his time to fostering Zionist education and to the preparation of basic texts in Spanish.[39]

In November 1945, Maximo Yagupsky, a well-known Argentine Jewish intellectual and educator, who was the head of the American Jewish Committee's Office in Buenos Aires from 1948 to 1961, submitted to this North American non-Zionist organization a "Survey of Jewish Life in Argentina and Other Latin American Communities, Existing Conditions and Future Possibilities." The purpose of this memorandum was to outline the possibility of the eventual operation of the committee in Latin America. In the detailed information he gave on Argentine Jewry and its institutions, leading personalities, and conflicting interests, Yagupsky underlined that almost all factions "support Zionist activities." When he formulated his "suggestions for a program in Buenos Aires," therefore, Yagupsky advised that the AJC should "in particular . . . be very careful not to give the impression that it is hostile to the spirit or goals of Zionism, but rather it should indicate its sincere interest in the realization of the Jewish National Homeland." The importance of not adopting a stance hostile to Zionism had previously been stressed by Morris D. Waldman, vice chairman of the AJC's executive committee, in his report on a trip to Latin America a year earlier. At the end of World War II

---

38. Haim Avni, "Patterns of Jewish Leadership in Latin America during the Holocaust" in *Jewish Leadership during the Nazi Era: Patterns of Behaviour in the Free World*, ed. R. L. Braham (New York: Institute for Holocaust Studies of the City University of New York), 87–130.

39. Bistritzky's final report, 1945, S25/2037, Central Zionist Archives; his report from Buenos Aires, 29 December 1942, S53/468, Central Zionist Archives; Bistritzky to Granowsky, 14 November 1943, S53/474, Central Zionist Archives.

Zionism thus was described, within the framework of even a non-Zionist organization, as a dominant factor in Latin American Jewish life.[40]

The first Latin American Zionist Conference, which convened in Montevideo in March 1945, also shows the commitment of many Latin American Jews to the Zionist ideology. The conference attested not only to the importance of Zionism in Latin America, but also to the new position held by Latin American Zionists within the World Zionist Organization.

"[In] view [of the] great importance of this Conference please urge Jewish Agency send prominent delegate from Palestine representing the Jewish Agency [and] Zionist Organization," cabled Kurt Blumenfeld and Leib Jaffe from New York to the Keren Hayesod headquarters in Jerusalem. Its director, Arthur Hantke, beseeched Eliezer Kaplan, then the treasurer of the Jewish Agency, to attend that conference (and thereafter to inaugurate the Keren Hayesod campaign in Argentina). "After the destruction of European Jewry," he wrote Kaplan, "the importance of the South American community has increased manyfold. . . . This Diaspora is almost second in size to the Jewish community of the United States and we ought to invest [in it] much educational work."[41]

The conference was convened by the Central Zionist Council of Argentina with the approval of the Jewish Agency in New York. Some 300 delegates and 50 alternates from twelve Latin American republics assembled. The festive sessions and ceremonial events were attended by Uruguayan officials headed by the Uruguayan vice president, Dr. A. Guani. Multitudes of Jews and non-Jews were present at the public sessions. The resolutions adopted also reflected the spirit of a widening movement that was called upon to undertake new tasks and was confident in its ability to respond to that call. One resolution demanded the establishment of a Central Zionist Office in Buenos Aires, which should be "headed by an authorized representative of the Zionist Executive" and directed by an executive council of local leaders and would centralize all the "political, organizational propaganda and cultural activities" in Latin America. Its creation would have implied decentralization of the Zionist Organization's functions and a demand for a larger share in international Zionist activities for Latin American Zionists.[42]

---

40. Maximo Yagupsky, "Survey of Jewish Life in Argentina and Other Latin American Communities, Existing Conditions and Future Possibilities," Archives of the American Jewish Committee, New York, Foreign Affairs Department, 12 November 1945, 8, 23–24; Morris D. Waldman Papers, Report, November 1944, American Jewish Archives, Cincinnati.

41. Cable by Blumenfeld-Jaffe, 27 December 1944, S53/468, Central Zionist Archives; A. Hantke to Kaplan, 12 January 1945, Central Zionist Archives.

42. S5/719, Central Zionist Archives; resolutions of the conference in Montevideo, S5/698, Central Zionist Archives; Rachel Yarden, "Zionism Comes of Age," Summer 1945.

Although they raised the fundamental issues of the respective responsibilities of and the relations between the local and the delegated leaderships, the Conference's decisions indicated unmistakably that Latin American Zionists were confidently facing the new era then opening that led to the establishment of the State of Israel. Their help would soon be needed, mainly in the political sphere.

The Establishment of Israel

The potential importance of Latin America in an international organization that would replace the League of Nations had already been recognized by the New York Office of the Jewish Agency in 1943. A small Latin American department headed by Rachel Sephardi Yarden was set up there in November 22 of that year, and within a few weeks lists of hundreds of leading Latin American intellectuals and statesmen had been compiled, mainly with the help of local Zionists. This new department initiated a concerted effort to gain the support of prominent individuals by providing them with adequate information about Zionism in Spanish. Before long, local "pro-Palestina Hebrea" committees, headed by distinguished political and literary personalities, were established in Mexico, Cuba, and Uruguay. Somewhat later, Argentina, Chile, Colombia, and Costa Rica followed suit, and efforts were made to extend the network of these committees to all other Latin American nations.[43] The San Francisco Conference of 1945 and the 1946 Paris Peace Conference demonstrated the unique importance of the Latin American states, which formed the largest bloc in the United Nations. The promotion of Zionism in the subcontinent among the governing classes and public opinion at large became a vital necessity. Arab propaganda, based in many countries upon the local communities of Arab immigrants, presented the Zionists in each country with a new and special challenge.

Some of the local Zionist leaders became the promoters and virtual organizers of the pro-Palestina committees, although they remained behind the scenes. The attempts to gain the support of gentile personalities also attracted some dormant Zionists within the Jewish communities. Enrique Dickman, the Argentine Jewish socialist and member of Congress, had written in favor of Zionism in 1918 and now came forward to participate in the new Zionist political effort. Alberto Gerchunoff, the famous Argentine Jewish writer, whose *Los Gauchos Judios* (1910) had endorsed complete Jew-

---

43. Report of the Latin American Department of Jewish Agency, December 1943–31 March 1944, S5/698, Central Zionist Archives.

ish "argentinization," toured the Latin American subcontinent trying to enlist the support of leading intellectuals and politicians for the Zionist cause.[44]

The main Zionist activity, however, assumed a more direct form. Petitions were signed and addressed to heads of state, public meetings were held in support of the Jewish state, written protests against the British White Paper in Palestine were circulated among the public and published at press conferences, and so on. All these activities, moreover, accompanied the Zionist diplomatic campaign in the international political arena and the armed struggle in Palestine during the years 1946–1948. The importance of the Zionists' activities in Latin America cannot be determined, however, without analyzing each of them thoroughly and comparing them with other, non-Zionist communal activities. The influence of the Latin American Zionists upon the vote of their respective governments on the United Nations Resolution on Palestine of November 29, 1947, still has to be studied and assessed. At this point, however, it can be stated that the only important diplomatic achievement of the World Zionist Movement since the ratification of the British Mandate by the League of Nations in 1922 was rendered possible by the Latin American nations. They provided thirteen out of the thirty-three votes cast in favor of the Plan of Partition (of Palestine) with Economic Union; only one Latin American nation (Cuba) joined twelve other states to vote against it, whereas the other Latin American countries were among the ten abstaining. Without Latin American support, the resolution would not have received the required two-thirds of the votes.[45]

The United Nations Resolution of November 29, 1947, had an enormous impact on Jews all over the world, exceeding that of the Balfour Declaration thirty years earlier. Enthusiastic Jewish multitudes in Argentina, Brazil, and elsewhere in Latin America celebrated the event by mass gatherings with singing and dancing. Sincere sympathy was expressed by supportive gentiles. In contrast to 1917, the Jewish people followed up the Zionist diplomatic success by raising large sums of money. The onslaught of the Palestinian Arabs on the 600,000 Jews in Palestine, which started on the day following the United Nations' vote and was supported by seven independent Arab states, caused a major manifestation of Jewish solidarity. The Soviet Union's endorsement of the United Nations' plan of partition, essen-

---

44. Enrique Dickman, "Sionismo y socialismo," 1 October 1918, and "El estado de Israel," 1 October 1948, in *Recuerdos de un militante socialista* Editorial La Vanguardia (Buenos Aires: 1949), 442–447; report by Alberto Gerchunoff, 10 June 1947, S25/7502, Central Zionist Archives.

45. United Nations, "Future Government of Palestine," *Official Records of the Second Session of the General Assembly Resolutions, 16 September–29 November 1947* (Lake Success, New York), 181(II).

tially motivated by its anti-British policy, enabled leftist Jews to participate in the United Jewish Emergency Appeal as well. The sums collected in 1948 in Argentina exceeded, according to one source, by almost eight times the contributions raised in all the Zionist campaigns in that country only a year earlier.[46]

The unusual alliance between the Zionists and the leftists, their bitter opponents in the Jewish community, was extremely short-lived in Latin America, as elsewhere. The uniformity of behavior of this sector of Jewish opinion throughout the world suggests that the reasons for the rift and the later renewed animosity had their origin in the changes of policy of the Soviet Union toward the Jewish state. The adherence of the other sectors of the Jewish community in Latin America to the cause of Zionism and to the State of Israel, however, remained unchanged. "Venezuela always presented an organizational problem to the World Zionist Organization, not because people are not Zionists, but because practically everybody claims to be one," reported Benno Weiser, a Viennese journalist and writer who spent the war years in Ecuador and later became one of the architects of Israel's relations with Latin America. Following his visit to Venezuela in 1952, he reported, "the Jewish communities dealt with the requests of the Jewish Agency, when they received them, and from its ranks the Magbit [The United Jewish Appeal] Committees were appointed."[47] In Buenos Aires, the Zionist parties, campaigning in the communal elections as a bloc or in competition with each other, conquered the main institutions and became the dominant political power.[48] In Mexico, too, the previously strong anti-Zionist disposition ebbed after 1948 and Bundists and other non-Zionists joined gradually in almost unanimous support of Zionism and of the Jewish state.

At the same time, another undeniable phenomenon took place: the

---

46. "[Organized] Zionism, however, did not sufficiently participate in this campaign," later complained one of the Zionist Argentinian leaders. "For various reasons, the campaign was led by a group of non-Zionist Jews, on the one hand, and by elements of the Leftist circles on the other and the impression was created that they were the actual masters," he and other Zionist leaders lamented, adding: "It should, however, be emphasized that the Leftist circles had done their work wholeheartedly." Minutes of a meeting of the Central Zionist Council of Argentina, 7 December 1948, S41/165, Central Zionist Archives, at which Eliahu Dobkin, member of the Zionist Executive participated. Quotation from Moshe Kostrinsky's opening statement; Itzhak Harkavi and other participants spoke in the same vein. See also *Orientacion* 10 July 1946 (Buenos Aires), a declaration by the Jewish Committee of the Communist Party in Argentina supporting the Jewish struggle in Palestine while criticizing the official Zionist leadership for its endeavors to gain the support of the Truman Administration.

47. Report on Venezuela, August 1–5 1952, Z6/341, Central Zionist Archives.

48. Haim Avni, "Argentine Jewry: Its Socio-Political Status and Organizational Patterns," *Dispersion and Unity* (Jerusalem) 13–14 (1972): 192–200.

increasing tendency on the part of the governments and general societies in Latin America to regard their Jewish communties no longer as *rusos, polacos,* or *turcos* ("Russians, Poles, or turks" according to their countries of origin) but as the local branches of an Israeli Diaspora. Memoirs of some of the Israeli ambassadors amply attest to this phenomenon.[49] Explicit evidence is provided by a letter written in 1958 by the Bishop of Misiones in northeastern Argentina, Msgr. Jorge Kemerer, to Dr. Leon Kubovi, then the Israeli ambassador to Argentina, requesting Kubovi's immediate intervention with the leaders of two local Jewish societies who, according to the bishop, were the ambassador's *compatriotas* (compatriots). A new provincial constitution was being discussed at that time and the Union Israelita de Misiones (The Union of Misiones' Jews) together with the Asociación Israelita de Socorros Mutuos (the Jewish Association for Mutual Assistance) appealed to the Constituent Assembly requesting that racial discrimination and the teaching of religion at governmental schools be made unconstitutional. The bishop regarded the latter request as an unfair intervention and, quoting the Israeli law regarding the teaching of religion in Christian schools in Israel, he concluded that the "israelita societies of Misiones are, in Argentina, less tolerant toward [Christian] Argentinians than their own compatriots are toward foreign [!] Christians in Israel."[50]

The substitution of the stigma-burdened name *Judios* by the less disturbing *Israelita,* which was frequently done by the founders of the Jewish communities, facilitated, after 1948, this confusion between Israelitas and Israelis. The deeper reasons for this occurrence, however, still must be investigated. It may be that only a change of nomenclature took place within an existing system in which the adherence of immigrants and their descendants to their *madre patria* is commonly accepted. In that case, the establishment of Israel might have "normalized" the position of the Jews in Latin America by providing them with a visible and logical *madre patria,* similar in kind to the one of the Italians, Germans, or other immigrant ethnic groups. It might, however, indicate a new stratum in the special attitude toward the Jews, whose fundamental difference from the host society in religious terms was always obvious and whose alienation in national terms, hitherto only suspected, was now definitely corroborated. In that case, a local diaspora of "Israelis" could be respected and tolerated but not regarded as an intrinsic part of the general society.

49. Natanel Lorch, *Ha-Nahar ha-Lochesh* (The whispering river) (Tel Aviv: 1969), 132–136, Maanachot Editorial, The Ministry Defense; Jacob Tzur, *Ketav Haamana Mispar Arba* (Accreditation number four) Sifriyat Maanir (Tel Aviv: 1981), 144–150.

50. Haim Avni, *Emantzinatzia ve-Chinuch Yehudi, 1884–1984* (Emancipation and Jewish education: a century of Argentinian Jewry's experience 1884–1984) (in Hebrew) (Jerusalem: The Zalman Shazar Center, 1985), 132–133.

The predominance of the Zionists in Latin American Jewish life might have also enhanced their position in world Zionism. A first point of inquiry would be an analysis of the scope of the representation Latin American Zionists gained in the central organs of the World Zionist movement. Although in 1939 there were no Latin American members of the Zionist Executive and, in 1946, only one full member and two alternates, the first Zionist congress to convene after the establishment of the State of Israel elected four full members and six alternates from Latin America, who constituted 6.25% of the total number of members and alternates.[51] At subsequent congresses, this representation grew considerably both in size and importance. Since 1956, Latin American Zionists have been among the members of the Zionist Directory; in 1978, one of them, Arye (Leib) Dulzin, was elected chairman of the Executive of the World Zionist Organization.

The significance of these data, however, should not be overestimated. The major changes in the importance of the World Zionist Organization following the establishment of the State of Israel and the scarcity of formal affiliation with the organization compared to the widespread support of the Zionist cause suggest a need for less institutionalized indicators of the role of Latin American Zionists in world Zionism. The scope of fund raising, immigration and settlement in Israel, investments, and other material contributions to the Jewish state might serve as indicators. When examined in context and compared with data on other diasporas, such indices will help in assessing the impact that Latin American Zionists have had on the course of Zionism since 1948.

Conclusion

Latin America played a role at two points in the history of Zionism: in its early days, when Argentina presented a serious challenge to Palestine, and in 1947, when the Latin American nations were the decisive factor in the adoption of the United Nations resolution granting international support and recognition to the establishment of Israel. Zionism was an important factor in Latin American Jewish life almost from its inception, not in spite of the fact that the communities were composed of immigrants, but rather because of this fact. Zionism intensified in the second and third generations of Jewish life in Latin America, a development whose causes must be sought

---

51. *Hachlatot ha-Kongress ha-Tzyoni* (Resolutions of the Zionist Congress): the 21st Congress (Geneve, 16–25 August 1939), 29–32; the 22nd Congress (Basel, 9–24 December 1946), 52–55; the 23rd Congress (Jerusalem, 14–30 August 1951), 53–56 (Jerusalem: World Zionist Organization, 1940, 1947, 1952) (in Hebrew).

in the impact on Latin American Jewry of events both in world Jewish history and in the Latin American societies.

It is clear from this review that much research in the role of Latin American Zionism remains to be done. Early Zionist stirrings in the first years of the century have yet to be fully documented. The relative strength of Zionism and anti-Zionism in Latin America compared to other diasporas in the decade following World War I has yet to be determined. The growth of Jewish identification with Zionist ideology in Latin America during the Nazi period has not yet been studied in depth, which is also true of the activities of Zionists in the immediate post–World War II period and of their impact on the Latin American position in the 1947 United Nations vote. The complex process through which Latin American Jews have not only continued but increased their identification with Jewish nationalism and statehood while living in nationalistic Third World societies poses a theoretical challenge with major implications for understanding the dynamics of both Jewish history and Latin American societies.

8
Jewish Education in Latin America

Daniel C. Levy

The Context

Jewish education in Latin America carries a historic burden. This is to guard—in what is now the major Third World center of Jewish population—a people's unique success at preserving group identity in the face of dispersion and persecution. Of course, religious conviction, so intertwined with education, has often carried the burden in other times and places and plays a role in Latin America today. But Latin American Jewry has been notably secular. Therefore "the non-centrality of the synagogue" is juxtaposed to "the centrality of the school."[1] Moreover, the diminished importance of Zionist federations after the establishment of the State of Israel in 1948 has weakened an alternative binding institutional structure for Latin America's Jewish communities. The social club may be the only institution that matches the school in the breadth of commitment attracted, but it cannot claim an equal tie to a specifically and traditionally Jewish content. Moreover, the Jewishness of even the Jewish family itself is open to serious question.[2]

---

1. Jaime Barylko, "In Latin America, We Are What We Are Plus What Latin America Is," *Jewish Frontier* (March 1981), 16. Also see Eduardo Rauch, "Latin American Jewry: An Introduction," *Jewish Frontier* (March 1981), 8–9.
2. The David Horowitz Institute for the Research of Developing Countries, *Brazilian Jewry: The Jewish School System of Rio de Janeiro* (Tel Aviv: 1980), 93. David Schers, the project director of this report, was also the author of a shorter piece, "Jewish Education in Rio de Janeiro," to be published in a forthcoming volume (*World Jewish Education: Cross-Cultur-*

The importance of Latin America's Jewish schools is further suggested by the substantial share of the Diaspora's school-aged children (6–17 years old) that they educate. The Diaspora total, according to the most complete estimates available, is 1,325,500, not including the USSR (where no formal Jewish education exists). Although Latin America's 65,050 children are only 5% of the total, several relevant factors must be considered. First, the United States alone holds roughly 63% of the total and Eastern Europe, where probably only 1% of Jewish children attend any Jewish school, holds another 12%. Latin America has fully one-fifth of the remaining population; Argentina itself has the fifth largest school-age Diaspora population, Brazil the seventh.[3] Still, even these data tell only part of the story, because the percentage of Jewish students who attend Jewish schools is much higher in Latin America than in the Diaspora generally, and this contrast is greatly intensified if we focus not on any Jewish schooling, including part-time or "supplemental" schooling, but only on Jewish *day schools*, those where students go for all their school hours. Latin America could approach half of the cohort group in day schools, whereas the Diaspora generally reaches only 13%, with 24% more in supplemental schools.[4] Thus, Latin America accounts for roughly 18% of total day school enrollments in the Diaspora, *including* the United States. This apparently places Latin America slightly

---

al Perspectives) edited by Harold Himmelfarb and Sergio DellaPergola in connection with the Project for Jewish Educational Statistics of the Hebrew University of Jerusalem. On São Paulo, see sections on education in Henrique Rattner's excellent study *Tradição e mundança: A comunidade judaica em São Paulo* (São Paulo: Atica, 1970).

3. Computations made from Harold S. Himmelfarb and Sergio DellaPergola, *Enrollment in Jewish Schools in the Diaspora, Late 1970s* (Jerusalem: Hebrew University, Institute of Contemporary Jewry, Project for Jewish Education Statistics, 1982), 14, 16. United States figures estimated from share of North American total enrollments, ages 3–17, applied to North American total ages 6–17, the cohort group shown for Latin America. The Himmelfarb and DellaPergola work (*Enrollment*) is now easily the best source on enrollment data and it draws from earlier reports. For an earlier set of estimates, see Organización Sionista Mundial, *Educación judía en la diaspora* (Jerusalem: 1971), which gives estimates for 1967.

4. Although Himmelfarb and DellaPergola (*Enrollment*, 14) tentatively placed the 49% figure in the day-school column, they were reluctant to divide it into day and supplemental. At the Albuquerque conference, however, DellaPergola affirmed the basic day-school orientation. The major exception found in their report concerns the pre-primary level (mostly in Argentina and Brazil) ages 3–6, whereas the data on page 14 deal with ages 6–17. Historically, supplemental schools were common in the Southern Cone, but day schools dominate there today. On Brazil, see Horowitz Institute, *Brazilian Jewry*, 47, 172; on Argentina, see Yaacov Rubel, "Jewish Education in Argentina," 5–9; and on Uruguay and generally, see Efraim Zadoff, "Other Countries in Latin America," 7–8, both mimeos to be published in Himmelfarb and DellaPergola, *World*.

ahead of Western Europe, ranking behind only the United States in Diaspora day school enrollments.

A few more words on enrollments are required here. First, the figure of 65,050 does not include the pre-primary level (under 6 years old) and would otherwise be much higher. For example, Argentina might add 5684 to its 12,891 contribution to the total. In any case, totals for Latin America's enrollments come overwhelmingly from a few nations. Next to Argentina, Brazil is the only other giant, providing roughly 10,000 students, or more than 7000 without the pre-primary level. Very roughly rounded and estimated, Mexico follows with 6000, followed by Venezuela, Uruguay, Chile, Colombia, and Peru, all somewhere between 1000 and 3000, whereas nations such as Guatemala, Ecuador, and Paraguay are closer to just 100 each.[5] Expectedly, the list grossly parallels the rank ordering of nations by Jewish populations.

On the other hand, the proportion of Jewish students who attend Jewish schools varies across nations. From less than one-third in nations such as Uruguay and Chile, the share rises to roughly one-half for nations such as Brazil and Colombia, to the great majority, roughly 90% or more, in nations such as Peru and Venezuela.[6] Much of the variation may be explained by examining national situations in juxtaposition to the reasons that individual Jewish families choose Jewish schools versus other options. Finally, note that there are roughly 150 schools in question, not including the pre-primary level.[7]

The question of how well Latin America's Jewish schools are managing is too broad, and the answers too complex, to address adequately in this chapter. Nevertheless, an overview can now touch on several basic themes and point the interested reader to more detailed explorations of individual nations. Among the subjects that receive perfunctory or no treatment here are nonformal education, the historical development of Latin America's Jewish schools, pedagogy, higher education, and, as already mentioned, the reasons that parents choose or reject Latin America's Jewish schools.[8] It should also be noted that many existing studies are dated, deal with only

---

5. Based on Himmelfarb and DellaPergola, *Enrollment,* 33–38.

6. Among many sources, see Himmelfarb and DellaPergola, *Enrollment,* 33–38; Organización Sionista Mundial, *Educación,* 6.

7. Estimate of Sergio DellaPergola, Albuquerque, March 1984; also see Organización Sionista Mundial, *Educación,* 46.

8. For a rare view of the informal side, see Israel Even-Shoshan, Chapter 14 in this volume. For more on the past, see Judith Laikin Elkin, "History of the Jews in Latin America in the Nineteenth and Twentieth Centuries." Ph.D. diss., University of Michigan, 1976 (especially pages 255–298). Another dimension I do not deal with is the impressive ORT network.

one nation, are institutional reports, are properly concerned with public relations as well as analysis, or are in Hebrew.[9]

This chapter focuses on two theses, or central tensions, of interest to both Latin Americanists and Judaic specialists. These themes are important not only in order to relate Latin America's Jewish education to broader issues, but also to provide contexts within which to evaluate that education. Without such contrasts, evaluation tends to be ephemeral. A major concern here is to assess the constraints exogeneously imposed upon the Jewish community and then to assess how well the community itself functions within those constraints.

One thematic question is the degree of Jewish autonomy within the political constraints imposed by dominant groups and the state. For Latin Americanists, this theme relates to basic issues in state–society relations. Among these are the degree of freedom that various societal actors enjoy in organizing their own affairs and in establishing institutions that can fashion their own goals and policies. During the 1970s, the most influential literature on Latin American politics and society held that the state tended to be strong, to the point that civil society had little breathing room. Substantiation for this view derived mostly from those nations where "bureaucratic" or "modern" authoritarian regimes held sway. These are highly repressive regimes that coercively impose demobilization and a sharp reduction of latitude for organized autonomous action.[10] Combined with the more traditional dictatorships of Central America, Paraguay, and other places, the advent of these military regimes left few democracies or even fairly open politics in place. Further, the four most prominent bureaucratic authoritarian regimes reigned in Argentina, Brazil, Chile and Uruguay, nations holding the majority of Latin America's population—and more than four-fifths of the Latin American Jewish population. Redemocratization in the 1980s, most notably in Argentina, Brazil, and Uruguay, has changed such figures dramatically, and it is decreasingly common to define authoritarianism as Latin America's modal type.

Limits on societal space, however, have been associated not only with particular regimes but also with broader linkages between the state and

---

9. I cite here works in English, Spanish, and Portuguese; there are also sources in Hebrew, whereas Yiddish sources are mostly historical. One important Hebrew work, a manuscript in progress by Haim Avni, concerns Argentina. Also on Argentina, see the bibliography by the Centro de Documentacion e Información Sobre Judaismo Argentino, *Educación judía en la Argentina* (Buenos Aires: 1984).

10. See, for example, Guillermo O'Donnell, "Reflections on the Patterns of Change in the Bureaucratic-Authoritarian State," *Latin American Research Review* 13(3) (1977): 3–38; David Collier, ed., *The New Authoritarianism in Latin America* (Princeton: Princeton University Press, 1979).

society. Most influential among these has been corporatism, which, as contrasted to pluralism, suggests a system of carefully restricted and monitored organizations. Some authors have even postulated corporatism to be deeply rooted in Latin American history and culture, based largely on Catholic traditions antithetical to variegated identities, groups, and institutions; other authors have emphasized the structural and economic bases of corporatism.[11] Compared to several years ago, however, fewer observers now regard corporatism as the Latin American modal type. At the same time most observers would find politics and society much more corporatist, and much more authoritarian, in Latin America than in the diaspora settings of the United States or Western Europe. Within such a context, what are the constraints on the autonomy of institutions such as Jewish schools? In responding to that question, it will be useful to view Jewish schools within the broader elite private school phenomenon found in most of Latin America. A similar comparison can be rooted in Jewish history. Against the contextual backdrop of centuries witnessing such a wide range of persecution and tolerance of Jewish educational institutions, where does contemporary Latin America fit?

The second thematic tension is more sociologically concerned with group identity and assimilation. This tension is certainly related to the first tension, but I will focus here on how well the community meets identity challenges within the bounds of the political freedom accorded it. Although pressures toward assimilation have been powerful before, contemporary pressures are unusually strong, strong enough to justify the preoccupation of Jewish leadership throughout most of the Diaspora. This preoccupation is properly focused largely on education. From a Latin Americanist perspective, important issues include the socialization of a distinctive minority—how well Jewish schooling preserves Jewish identities within societies where various expectations compete as to how groups should orient themselves to a national identity. Latin American societies are highly stratified, with Jews mostly belonging to the relatively select category of the middle class to the upper middle class. Ethnically and culturally, however, one may be struck by either the stratification (as between *mestizos* and those of European heritage) or by the relative homogeneity (as in the preponderance of Spanish-speaking Catholics). Both stratification and homogeneity present challenges and opportunities for Latin America's Jewish efforts to preserve a group identity through schooling.

11. See, for example, Howard J. Wiarda, ed., *Politics and Social Change in Latin America: The Distinct Tradition* (Amherst: University of Massachusetts Press, 1974); also, Collier, *New Authoritarianism*. Alfred Stepan refers to "organic statism," suggesting a powerful state and a holistic society, in *The State and Society: Peru in Comparative Perspective* (Princeton: Princeton University Press, 1978).

Governance: Contours of Autonomy

State–School Relations

The basic fact about state–school relations is a positive one. Evidence gathered from many Latin American nations strongly suggests a substantial degree of school autonomy from the state as well as other political actors outside the Jewish community. Obviously, this evidence could run counter to expectations simply derived from theories of authoritarianism or corporatism and will merit our attention.

The evidence also runs counter to what one might postulate on the basis of a strong political–educational tradition of bureaucratic centralism, sometimes tied to the *estado docente* (teaching state) concept wherein education is to be run by the national ministry. Indeed, educational statutes reflect this centralist bias even as they give license to private schools. These licenses, to judge by laws and statutes identifying where the formal authority lies, leave the schools little autonomy. Because the Jewish school, legally speaking, is merely one type of private school, it must incorporate itself into the national system whose recognition it needs. As Smith's in-depth study of Colombia shows, the ministry holds wide authority over school foundation, curriculum, degrees and titles, records, and so forth. Private schools must submit annual records to the ministry and receive state approval for all changes in organization and curriculum. Failure to comply can result in forced school closings. For all this, the ministry's Inspection Department possesses authority delegated by the state itself.[12] In fact, bureaucratic centralism means that even private schools must adopt the basic curriculum spelled out by the ministry. Compared to the U.S. educational system, then, Latin American systems go much further in standardizing curriculum not only for public schools but even for private ones. Additionally, certain Latin American states limit autonomy over the admissions process in their pursuit of nondiscriminatory access; for example, some Jewish schools have to take in a quota of non-Jewish students.[13]

Statutory authority and actual governance are two different things,

---

12. John Kenneth Smith, "Jewish Education in Colombia: Group Survival Versus Assimilation." Ph.D. diss., University of Wisconsin, 1972, 120–121, 134; "Mexico," in *Comunidades judías de latinoamérica* (Buenos Aires: American Jewish Committee, 1972), 166; "Panama," in Abraham Monk and Jose Isaacson, eds., *Comunidades judías de latinoamérica* (Buenos Aires: Editorial Candelabro, 1968), 103; Zadoff, "Other Countries," 2.

13. Colombian law, on the grounds of prohibiting discrimination, forces Jewish schools to accept Catholic students (and then, because of their presence, the school must offer three hours per week of Catholic religious instruction from a teacher approved by the local bishop). However, almost all Jewish children who want entry are accepted (Smith, "Jewish Education in Colombia," 125–126).

however, as has been shown in studies of both European and Latin American educational bureaucracies.[14] In practice, most states have exercised only limited interference in Jewish school governance. Curriculum is probably the major exception, and in Peru, for example, schools are restricted in manifesting their "affinity to Jewish history, Zionism or Israel, except through strictly religious channels."[15] But nearly all Jewish schools are free to develop whatever Jewish content they desire once they have provided the basic public school content; this results in a Jewish school day considerably longer than the public school day. Even the insistence on standardized curriculum does not greatly limit autonomy, because most Jewish schools *want* to provide basic secular studies. Indeed, they often choose to provide more than required and they often innovate within the standardized programs, and Jewish school personnel sometimes achieve national influence (e.g., as advisors to national ministries).[16] Add to this the fact the Jewish schools generally reach high academic prestige and do not draw on state subsidies, and we can partly explain the state's laissez-faire approach. This finding parallels findings about the autonomy of Latin America's elite private universities from state control and would surely apply to other elite private schools as well. There are even cases where national political leaders send their children to Jewish schools, though certainly not to the extent they use other elite private schools and universities.[17]

Evidence from nations like Colombia and Mexico helps concretize such findings on autonomy. There is a "give-and-take" relationship between the Colombian government and the Jewish schools.[18] The government does not enforce all regulations. It allows the exhibition of Jewish symbols, such as the Israeli flag and pictures of Israeli alongside Colombian leaders, which violates the letter of the law. Although inspections can occur unannounced,

14. See Burton R. Clark, *The Higher Education System: Academic Organization in Cross-National Experience* (Berkeley, Los Angeles, London: University of California Press, 1983), 107–134; Daniel C. Levy, *The State and Higher Education in Latin America: Private Challenges to Public Dominance* (Chicago: The University of Chicago Press, 1986).

15. Leonardo Senkman, "Latin American Jewry between Revolution and Reaction," *Jewish Frontier* (March 1981), 12. Ironically, an increased government role sometimes promotes Jewish education. In the 1960s, the increased number of hours in Uruguay's standardized curriculum squeezed supplemental schools, leading to their replacement by the day-school network; see Zadoff, "Other Countries," 8. Similarly, pressure from the Argentine government in 1970 hurt supplemental schools at the primary level, thereby promoting day schools; see "Argentina," in *Comunidades judías* (1972), 35.

16. Zadoff, "Other Countries," 5–6.

17. Marc Turkow found examples at Panama's Albert Einstein and Venezuela's Herzl-Bialik schools. Institute of Jewish Affairs, *Proceedings of the Experts Conference on Latin America and the Future of its Jewish Communities* (London: 1973), 147.

18. Smith, "Jewish Education in Colombia," 128–133.

they actually occur when the school's directors request them, typically only once every few years. The chief consequence of the inspections is not state interference but rather high marks and prestige for the Jewish schools. Again, this parallels the pattern found when Latin American national ministries license or inspect other elite private educational institutions; the institutions emerge with their autonomy intact, their public legitimacy and therefore their security and ultimately autonomy itself enhanced.

Whereas autonomy in Colombia obtains in a system of notably close church–state ties, in Mexico it obtains in a political system formed with antireligious zeal. Even in the revolutionary 1920s and 1930s, the state remained comparatively indifferent to Jewish schooling (in contrast to its powerful assault on Catholic schooling) probably because the former was not tied to a strong political threat; nonetheless, there were difficulties. Subsequently, the "institutionalized" regime has become generally tolerant of religious institutions, looking the other way amid myriad violations of constitutional restrictions on religious activity. Ministerial approval and inspections are required but easily handled because the schools more than meet standardized requirements.[19] As in other nations, the ministry requires that 5% of admissions be reserved for needy scholarship cases, but this hardly infringes on school autonomy, especially as the *becarios* (scholarship recipients) can be Jewish.

Naturally, variation exists according to era and nation. One area worth investigation is how the different political orientations of Jewish communities affect their relationships with the state.[20] Another, about which some general points can be made here, is the effect of different regimes. I will not focus on moderate democratic regimes here, mostly because they present the least problematic circumstances for autonomous Jewish institutions.

A major concern at the 1972 conference on "Latin America and the Future of Its Jewish Communities" was that Jewish institutions (elite, private, or religious) would be in for hard times under spreading leftist or populist regimes. Chile was a key example. The Marxist coalition under Salvador Allende launched a national unified school program that threat-

---

19. On the revolutionary threat, see Zevi Scharfstein, "Jewish Education in Latin America," in *The Jewish People: Past and Present*, vol. 2 (New York: Central Yiddish Culture Organization, 1948), 177; Zadoff, "Other Countries," 5. Mexico's first Jewish school was created in 1924 but in 1927 changed its name and dropped religious studies; the state's ban on religious studies was not rolled back until 1940. On the contemporary state role, Ierajmiel Barylka, director of the Colegio Yavne, Saul Lokier, ex-administrator at several Jewish schools, Heni Rosen, director of the Colegio Israelita, and Jaya Tórenberg, ex-director of the Colegio Israelita, separate interviews with author, each in September–October 1983 in Mexico City.

20. For example, the Brazilian community is generally reported as more outspoken than the Mexican and, as Schers has argued, Jewish schooling should be seen in such wider contexts. David Schers, interview with author, Tel Aviv, January 1984.

ened all private schooling. The Instituto Hebreo might have been forced to accept local non-Jewish applicants before Jewish applicants from outside the neighborhood.[21] In practice, the coalition was characteristically split on the initiative and, also characteristically, faced a center-right opposition that dominated in most nongovernmental power centers and ultimately in the legislature. The overall plan was withdrawn, and, specifically in the Jewish case, negotiations avoided serious consequences. Concerns therefore surround (1) what might have been had the leftist regime been stronger and (2) the damaging effects on Jewish education of the general political–economic crisis, which drove many Jews to flee the country. School enrollments fell and remaining university graduates faced reduced professional employment opportunities.

Similarly, Peru's leftist military regime threatened all private education, and Jewish education faced serious problems. But, here again, opposition (including Jews joined with Catholic school teachers) thwarted the state's initiatives just as a wider opposition thwarted most of its educational initiatives.[22] Potential problems were also feared in Argentina, where peronismo was making its comeback, though it was unclear how much power its left wing would wield.

Of course, leftist regimes were not without precedent. As just mentioned, the Mexican revolution produced some problems but not crippling ones for Jewish schools. But the major precedent, because it has persisted, is the Cuban experience. Although the revolution has been largely above the rank anti-Semitism that characterizes many communist regimes, its policies have pushed the great majority of Jews into exile. Revolution meant the end of most private institutions, not just economic but also social ones. Thus private schooling virtually disappeared at all levels. Yet the Jewish Albert Einstein School was allowed a little special status. Though turned into a public school, it could accept Jewish students from outside its neighborhood and some Jewish studies were optionally available in the late afternoon. Apparently, however, the breathing room was reduced in 1975, when all Jewish children were forced to attend their local public school.[23]

---

21. On the 1972 conference, see footnote 17; on Chile, Zadoff, "Other Countries," 4; Kathleen Fischer, *Political Ideology and Educational Reform in Chile, 1964–1976* (Los Angeles: Latin American Center Publications, 1979), 93–117; Joseph P. Farrell, *The National Unified School in Allende's Chile: The Role of Education in the Destruction of a Revolution* (Vancouver: University of British Columbia Press, 1986).

22. Senkman, "Latin American Jewry," 12; Zadoff, "Other Countries," 3. Beyond Jewish education, see Erwin Epstein's fine analysis, "Peasant Consciousness under Peruvian Military Rule," *Harvard Educational Review,* 52(3) (1982): 280–300.

23. Everett Gendler, "Holy Days in Havana," *Conservative Judaism* 23(2) (1969); Zadoff, "Other Countries," 2, reported that the name changed from Herzl to Einstein after the revolution. The 1979 Sandinista takeover in Nicaragua led to the nearly complete exodus of that nation's tiny Jewish community.

How misplaced the fear of a leftist tide appeared by the mid–1970s! The right proved dominant. And anti-Semitism under Argentina's military regime posed chilling threats to Jewish institutions. Still, despite these threats and despite some tragic consequences, Jewish schools have generally fared well under modern (bureaucratic) authoritarian regimes on the right. Without analyzing the reasons in depth, the following hypotheses are suggested. These regimes are especially sensitive to some of the factors identified as crucial to school autonomy in the face of bureaucratic centralism. They (1) limit expenditures on public schools and are therefore happy for self-financed private education to thrive; (2) let the public system deteriorate, thus possibly bolstering private enrollments; (3) look favorably on elite, prestigious education and less favorably on some mainstream concerns about equity; (4) concentrate their repression disproportionately on lower classes while seeking the support of middle and upper-middle classes for their political legitimacy; and (5) treat tolerantly many social organizations that are not politically oriented.[24]

It is important to realize that although individual Jews, including intellectuals involved in leftist causes, have been politically active, they have rarely framed their political participation in Jewish terms, and Jewish communities per se have not usually taken political positions, except in protecting their people and specific "Jewish freedoms." These freedoms include the right to a Jewish education and the right to attend synagogue, observe holidays, promote cultural organizations, and support Israel. No such Jewish freedom threatens rightist regimes. Moreover, as noted frequently at the 1972 conference, Latin America's Jewish educational and economic successes are not nearly matched by political power;[25] Jewish organizations pose virtually no political threat.

Whatever the mix of such reasons, a paradoxically favorable climate for Jewish school autonomy often arises. It is paradoxical insofar as it arises under regimes that notoriously use coercive state power to undermine the autonomy of many societal institutions. The Chilean junta, since 1973,

24. In the repressive destruction of public life, as in Chile, there could be a social–religious parallel to the Catholic situation, in which some youth turn to the Church to avoid the horrors of public life (although others turn to the Church because it becomes a lonely bastion of political–social consciousness). The most significant case for Jews would be in Argentina, where many Jewish youths turned toward political leftism in the early 1970s; with the ensuing regime's brutal repression came a turn not only toward the democratic political center but also, in some measure, toward Jewish identity and institutions, as Even-Shoshan's chapter (Chapter 14 in this volume) points out in regard to nonformal education and the Conservative religious movement.

25. See also Irving Louis Horowitz, "Jewish Ethnicism and Latin American Nationalism," *Midstream* 18 (November 1972), 24–27. Probably the most important exception, albeit partial, is Brazil; see Schers, "Jewish Education," 3–4.

might be the most zealously pro–private education (and enterprise) regime in Latin American history. Though policies have lagged well behind original intentions, Zadoff has pointed out there is diminished state supervision, just as he has pointed to a relaxation in Peru by 1976.[26] The latter date is immediately subsequent to the military regime's lurch to the right. Similarly, we have noted Mexico's more secure climate for Jewish schools since the revolution institutionalized itself (about 1940) along conservative lines. Concerning Brazil, Schers has described the favorable climate set for the last two decades by the junta, notwithstanding its nationalist doctrines, and has contrasted this to Vargas's populist regime decades earlier—with, for example, its ban on teaching foreign languages in schools.[27]

There are of course limits on Latin America's Jewish school autonomy under rightist military regimes. When many Argentine Jewish schools were organized largely on political lines, mostly to the left, they were vulnerable to such regimes; thus the regime change of 1930 led to the closing of some schools. In more recent times, most limits on Latin America's Jewish schools have stemmed from general restrictions that necessarily affect academic freedoms. Jews are citizens, after all, and often among those most dedicated to democratic debate, human rights, and liberal tolerance. Jewish professors and teachers are obviously not exempt from restrictions on free speech or other broad freedoms. Jewish educators sensitive to the contradictions between a religious–cultural tradition of open debate and a repressive political system cannot freely discuss such contradictions in class.[28]

Further, great variation has existed even among modern authoritarian regimes. In general, the Argentine, Brazilian (until the mid–1970s), Chilean, and Uruguayan regimes have been more repressive than the Brazilian (since the mid–1970s), the Peruvian, or certainly the Mexican.[29] Also, Jewish schools are imperiled where these regimes preside over widespread economic failure. Leftist regimes have no monopoly on the economic problems that affect Jews, even those that drive them to emigrate. In Argentina, severe

---

26. Zadoff, "Other Countries," 4–5; by 1981, the government considered a new law to promote private education.

27. Schers, "Jewish Education," 2, 4.

28. On the Argentine history, see Scharfstein, "Jewish Education in Latin America," 173. Focusing on contemporary regimes, the compromises Jewish schools must make parallel those made by other Jewish institutions. Just as Chile's President Pinochet is received at synagogue on Yom Kippur, so his photograph, like that of any president in power, hangs on the wall of Santiago's Instituto Hebreo; Rabbi Peter Tarlow and sociologist Elio de la Vega, interviews with author, Santiago, May 1982.

29. See Daniel C. Levy, "Comparing Authoritarian Regimes in Latin America: Insights from Higher Education Policy," *Comparative Politics* 14(1) (1981): 31–52. The Uruguayan military regime may defy the laissez-faire pattern; Zadoff ("Other Countries," 5) reported tough controls on private schools, including close monitoring of teachers' political "qualifications."

problems predated but also continued after the military takeover of 1976. By the 1980s, Chilean economic woes spread from the lower into the middle classes. And even in Mexico, where the middle and upper-middle classes had enjoyed relatively sustained benefits for decades, the economic crises of the 1980s have created a new atmosphere—stimulating emigration and other problems for Jewish schools.

Allowing for the qualifications, however, Latin America's rightist authoritarian regimes have generally not directly attacked the autonomy of Jewish schools. The case of these schools may suggest that many Jewish institutions often can function well, within the limits touched on here, under what have sometimes been defined as authoritarian rather than revolutionary or certainly totalitarian regimes.[30] And so Latin America has had but few regimes that have defied the basic patterns of relations between the state and Latin America's Jewish schools, which have encompassed substantial autonomy.

Finally, if the relative autonomy of Latin America's Jewish schools from the state can be understood largely within the context of elite private education more generally, this is not to minimize the achievement. Latin America's Jewish schools differ from Latin America's other elite schools in that they are Jewish institutions and function as such within a religiously alien setting, one not always separated from the state apparatus. Additionally, whatever status Latin America's Jewish schools enjoy, they have earned. Immigrant schools have become elite schools. They have coped intelligently with the considerable turmoil often characterizing the wider environment and have secured their autonomy through financial self-reliance.

Financial Autonomy

If the state usually allows considerable autonomy to Jewish schools, despite bureaucratic centralism, then the orientations that Jewish schools assume depend mostly on policies forged within the community. The locus of decision-making power lies there.

To analyze which groups wield what power, it is useful first to determine how the community finances its schools. Although finance does not necessarily dictate how private nonprofit institutions are governed, correlations tend to be strong. In fact, to work backwards for a moment, we already know that the state governance role is limited, so it is not surprising that its

---

30. For Juan Linz's seminal work on this distinction, see "Totalitarian and Authoritarian Regimes," in F. Greenstein and N. Polsby, eds., *Handbook of Political Science*, vol. 3 (Reading, Mass.: Addison-Wesley, 1975), 175–411.

financial role is limited. Here then is a further blow to corporatist notions depicting a societal context in which private institutions—if they exist—are run and financed by the state. Instead, Latin America's Jewish schools, following the rule for most Latin American private schools and higher education institutions, are quite financially independent of the state. Each Jewish school has its own *patronato* (financial board), responsible for ensuring the school's financial well-being, and the exceptions regarding the state role are only partial, as in Chile and Colombia.[31] This again appears to parallel broader state–private education patterns; Chile became, by midcentury, the Latin American nation most identified with public money for private education. Within nations, religious schools are more likely than lay private schools to get state money, but that relates partly to the fact that Catholic schools tend to attract a lower socioeconomic clientele; this is manifestly untrue of Jewish schools.

In the absence of direct subsidies, the major financial question concerning the state role in nonprofit institutions often concerns provisions for tax deductions and exemptions. Although more information is needed on Latin America's Jewish schools, we do know that donations are generally tax-deductible, providing a special incentive for voluntary giving. Such giving is crucial to Latin America's Jewish schools, as tuition alone is inadequate to cover costs. Typically for Latin America's private educational institutions, donations are especially important beyond recurrent annual expenses. Buildings and facilities basically depend on donations.

As is common for religious schools, donated services have played a large role in financial solvency. Sneh described their particular historical importance in Argentina where *activistas sociales voluntarios* provided their free labor.[32] Also, many teachers and administrators have worked for low salaries. In terms of direct financial contributions, individuals play a role, as reflected in fund-raising drives (often run by parents) and in the plaques that adorn the walls of many schools.

The other major domestic sources are the community institutions. By the 1920s, with the major influx of Jewish immigrants, these institutions helped pool the community's resources to build schools. These feats are remarkable when one remembers how most of the immigrants from Eastern Europe were workers and artisans, neither highly educated nor wealthy. The school board of Buenos Aires and the Unión Israelita of Belo Horizonte

31. See, for example, Zadoff, "Other Countries," 313, and Schers, "Jewish Education," 2–3.

32. Simja Sneh, "La red escolar judía en la República Argentina," in Monk and Isaacson, *Comunidades judías,* 130. Yet not all is rosy on the giving side; for example, some believe that Mexican Jews give more readily to causes other than education. Annette Jusidman, director of the Colegio Hebreo Tarbut, interview with author, Mexico City, October 1983.

(Brazil) provided early examples, Venezuela's Unión Israelita de Caracas a later one. Such organizations assume special importance in troubled times, as did those in Buenos Aires in the early 1970s when enrollments were threatened. The role of such community organizations also varies by nation. For example, the role appears much greater in Argentina than Brazil. Scharfstein found that the board accounted for one-third of the income of the Buenos Aires Jewish schools in 1947, and Barylko gave an updated figure of greater than one-half, even for the operating budget. Yet Schers, focusing on Rio, found that perhaps 90% of school income comes from tuition, with the rest raised by parents and school personnel more than community organizations. Then, too, community support does not necessarily refer to organizations based on the entire community. In Mexico, for example, the Ashkenazi schools are helped by the Kehilá Nidje Israel as well as by the Centro Deportivo Israelita, the Sephardic community supports its own, and the Aleppo (Syrian) community recently began to construct its own lavish school.[33]

Nor do donations come only from domestic organizations. The World Zionist Organization (WZO) plays a role by sending both money and teachers as well as by training teachers and assisting in developing the content of Jewish studies in Latin America's Jewish schools. Although data are not available to establish the proportional importance of the WZO, knowledgeable observers like Jacobo Kovadloff feel that it is substantial.[34] Other international actors include ORT (Organización, Reconstrucción y Trabajo, the Organization for Rehabilitation through Training) and Israel's own education ministry. Schers outlined major areas of Israeli aid, including direct financial contributions; technical assistance, the most important aid, through programs, training courses, and the services of teachers; and integration networks, such as those linking various communal institutions. Understandably, some Israelis resent the fact that hard-pressed Israel must subsidize institutions catering to well-to-do communities.[35]

What donations do not cover, tuition must. Just as no authoritative

---

33. On Argentina, see Scharfstein, "Jewish Education in Latin America," 174; J. Barylko, "Kehillah and Education: Fundamental Ideas in Jewish History" (Buenos Aires: AMIA, 1983), 21; Sneh, "La red escolar," 130. On Brazil, see Schers, "Jewish Education," 7 (Rio) and "Belo Horizonte," in Monk and Isaacson, *Comunidades judías,* 160. On Venezuela, see Mario Nassí F., *La comunidad ashkenazí de Caracas* (Caracas: Unión Israelita de Caracas, 1981), 12–13, 24–25. On Mexico, see Samuel Schmidt, correspondence with author, 11 July 1983; also Ana Portnoy, "Cultura e intelectuales judíos en México." Licenciado thesis, Universidad Iberoamericana, Mexico City, 1977, 65–66. Panama's school is supported by three religious congregations; see "Panamá," in Monk and Isaacson, *Comunidades judías,* 103.

34. J. Kovadloff, Director of the South American Section of the American Jewish Committee, telephone conversation with author, New York City, December 1983.

35. Horowitz Institute, *Brazilian Jewry,* 121.

figure shows what percentage of total donations comes from what sources, so no such figure shows the donation–tuition balance. But informed estimates are possible. These generally run between 60 and 90% of recurrent expenses (much less of total expenses).[36] The amount of tuition is obviously held in check by the donations, not just of money but also of services. Other factors include the relatively low salary paid to teachers compared to other professionals. Schers has reported that in Rio teachers receive only "the very low minimum salary fixed by law." More than 80% are female, many teach while finishing university studies, and many teach in two or more schools.[37]

Other factors, however, make tuition substantial. In fact, tuition at Latin America's Jewish schools tends to be roughly comparable to tuition at other prestigious private schools.[38] This means that it can exceed tuition at Latin America's elite private universities. For one thing, however inadequate teacher salaries are, they usually match those found at other prestigious private schools, thus exceeding Latin American public standards. For another, Latin America's Jewish schools assume the double burden of providing Jewish studies on top of the required public curriculum. This means hiring specialized teachers, developing more programs, and simply running a long school day. Third, high quality implies high costs in terms of laboratories, computers, and libraries. Fourth, following the movement of Jews to well-to-do neighborhoods, beautiful campuses are built in very attractive settings (e.g., within Caracas, Mexico City, and Rio) where land tends to be expensive. Such facilities often visibly outstrip what is found at most Latin American higher education institutions.[39]

Another factor that increases tuition in some cases is the state requirement that a percentage of students be *becarios*. This raises issues of equity and responsiveness. But, of course, Jewish schools have traditionally been

36. On Mexico, interview with I. Barylko; on Rio, Schers, "Jewish Education," 7; generally, Zadoff, "Other Countries," 13, 20.
37. Schers, "Jewish Education," 28–29.
38. Horowitz Institute, *Brazilian Jewry*, 56.
39. On shifting campuses see, for example, Nassi, *La comunidad ashkenazi*, 14, 24, and Horowitz Institute, *Brazilian Jewry*, 44, 46. So far, high costs have been related to positive features. However, judging by the Mexican case, negative features may also come into play. Chelminsky wrote that the Jewish schools persist with antiquated financial policies; others have pointed to "traditional" rather than professional administration. Another complaint heard in Mexico concerns the duplication of institutions. One case involves the Colegio Israelita (1255 students in 1983) and the Nuevo Colegio Israelita (473), where the latter may no longer be so different from the original. Tzila R. de Chelminsky, "La educación judía en México," in Jose Isaacson and Santiago E. Kovadloff, eds., *Comunidades judías de latinoamérica* (Buenos Aires: Editorial Candelabro, 1970), 227; interviews with I. Barylko and Tórenberg; enrollment figures from correspondence with Schmidt.

preoccupied with their felt responsibility to provide education for all Jewish students regardless of their means; this is, after all, a tradition that insured universal education when the concept was still alien to most surrounding societies. To what extent are Latin America's Jewish schools attending and accountable to the lower economic strata? The situation varies. Tuition was historically and necessarily low in immigrant-based Argentina; according to Chelminsky it should be higher than it is for most Mexican Jews.[40] Because (at least most) Latin America's Jewish schools have a policy of not rejecting any Jewish student on financial grounds, there might not appear to be a problem. First, however, there is the stigma of having to ask. The head of Santiago's Instituto Hebreo stated that middle-class "borderline cases" may be most reticent to ask and to reveal their problems.[41] Beyond admission, there is the problem of meeting the status costs within the schools. These include buying "in" clothing, going on trips, and various expensive forms of socializing. Thus, those who govern schools face problems regarding both admission and subsequent status costs that are faced by other Latin American Jewish nonprofit organizations, such as country clubs. But issues of group identity and perpetuating Jewish traditions are especially potent in the schools.

In sum, school *patronatos* draw off various actors to sustain a school system that, for many reasons, represents a substantial financial burden. That burden has been dangerously intensified with the widespread economic crises of the 1980s. But at least until now, Jewish financing of Jewish schools has reflected the vibrancy of group identity.

Power Holders

Although it is difficult to pinpoint the distribution of power among Jewish actors—especially as it varies according to finance, personalities, time, and place—certain generalities are possible. In any case, like finance, governance is all in the family.

The major role of parents suggests a special vibrancy, a *widespread* commitment to something Jewish. It is, after all, the parents who assume responsibility, through tuition alone, for the bulk of ongoing costs; in turn, this commitment is naturally accompanied by a strong role in governance. Again, a political–economic pattern emerges similar to that generally found in elite private schools. Parental power is maximized by a financial role as

---

40. Sneh, "La red escolar," 130; Chelminsky, "La educación judía," 228.
41. Abraham Megendzo, director of the Santiago school, interview with author, Santiago, May 1982; on Rio, see Schers, "Jewish Education," 24.

consumers in a free-market context where ample choice is often available. The first choice is, of course, whether to go to a Jewish school at all; as pointed out, going to a Jewish school is far from a given in most nations, and either public or, more commonly, other private options are also used. The second choice, in the larger Jewish communities, is which Jewish school. As schools desire to attract more students and tuitions, parents are in solid positions to demand what they want, especially where transfers among Jewish schools are common. This is the case in Mexico and parents appear quick to vote with their children's feet. As an ex-director of Mexico's oldest Jewish school engagingly put it: "The traffic jams you see in Mexico City, they are the Jewish mamas driving their kids to and from school." She pointed to an overlapping bus system where each of several schools sends its buses to various neighborhoods.[42]

In other words, parents have power because they can choose those institutions willing to be accountable to them, can maintain their voice within those institutions, and retain an exit option. It therefore comes as little surprise that Smith found Jewish parents often viewing themselves as the "owners" of Colombia's Jewish schools. They even directly intervene, entering the school to voice their complaints. By contrast, the director of Mexico's Colegio Hebreo Tarbut has reported that power comes less through active participation than indirectly, as their parental opinions are known. In any case, Zadoff concluded that parents form the single greatest power in Latin America's Jewish schools generally.[43]

Further, some other forces have a strong parental component. In Colombia, for example, fathers elect the administrative boards (*juntas*) and, of course, parents can make up the boards themselves.[44] Depending on the set-up, something similar may hold for *patronatos*, although it is common for nonprofit *patronatos* to represent especially the donors. Whatever the combination of these two basic types of boards, they typically set general orientations and assume financial responsibilities, including raising the necessary donations and hiring and firing personnel. Such boards frequently seek to hire effectively enough that daily administration and academic affairs can be turned over to trusted administrators and teachers. It appears that the boards' direct governance role has diminished over time, as often happens when nonprofit organizations become institutionalized. Yet this is partly because delegation has been successfully achieved and the boards

42. Interview with Tórenberg.
43. See Albert O. Hirschman, *Exit, Voice and Loyalty* (Cambridge, Mass.: Harvard University Press, 1970) on the concepts; Smith, "Jewish Education," 109–110; interview with Jusidman; Zadoff, "Other Countries," 20.
44. Smith, "Jewish Education in Colombia," 106.

need intervene only when schools fall off track or are not accountable to the concerned community.

A more overarching authority is the community board of education, or *vaad*. The *vaad* is often influential, especially when it is needed to ensure financial solvency. A major governance question, then, is the power distribution between the local community and school boards. The Argentine–Brazilian comparison suggests great variation and reflects the differences found in financial roles.

The Argentine case, most notably in Buenos Aires, shows strong pushes toward centralization. The community's supreme governance authority, or *kehillah*, the Asociación Mutual Israelita Argentina (AMIA), created a department named Vaad Hajinuj Hamerkazí (Central Education Council) to subsidize, coordinate, and supervise Jewish education. The *vaad* assures access, minimum standards, and some standardization across schools. It also works to increase financial security, enrollments, and commitments, and even runs some institutions, such as a model school. *Vaad* influence has sometimes led to resentment in individual schools. A related Vaad Hakehilot for Argentina's interior has worked to establish Jewish schooling in smaller communities. But the Brazilian case demonstrates that the *vaad* does not always achieve much centralization. In fact, Rio de Janeiro's Jewish schools retain considerable autonomy despite the existence of the Vaad Hachinuch (Central Education Council). Most Jewish schools in Rio have two main governing bodies. One is a sponsoring body composed mostly of founders, former presidents, and other dignitaries; the other is a parents' committee. Although the former holds most formal, legal, and general authority, the latter actually wields considerable power. Since 1977 the *vaad* has tried to increase its role in order to decrease duplication and competition among Jewish schools, but, even faced with possible hard times, the schools have opted to preserve their autonomy. This situation demonstrates a pointed correlation between the financial and administrative limits on a community board. School autonomy is further heightened in Brazil, and Latin America generally, because schools are not tied to synagogues.[45] It is also heightened as central board power is restricted because of cleavages among Jewish schools that reflect cleavages within the Jewish

---

45. On Argentina, see Rubel, "Jewish Education in Argentina," 3, 12–13; J. Barylko, "Kehillah," 19–25; Vaad Hajinuj Hamerkazí, "Informe de actualidades: Año lectivo 1982" (Buenos Aires, 1982), mimeo; Scharfstein, "Jewish Education in Latin America," 174; Sneh, "La red escolar," 129–133, 140; the Sephardic network has come in much more slowly. On Brazil, see Horowitz Institute, *Brazilian Jewry*, 47–48; Schers, "Jewish Education," 6–10. Zadoff, "Other Countries," 16–17, found that the role of Latin America's Jewish umbrella organizations is limited.

community. Bases for these cleavages (some of which will be discussed) include the importance of religion, nation of origin, Ashkenazic or Sephardic identity, language, and social and political orientations.

Finally, let us consider the role of school directors. Were these professionals merely delegates of the boards that appoint them they would not much affect power distributions. In practice, however, the power of directors varies, even within nations. Such is the case in Mexico, depending, obviously, on how powerful the school boards are. Discord between directors and boards may have increased as schools have modernized and the parental supervision of boards composed of the immigrant generation has passed. According to Schers, the director is the central figure in Rio's schools— a new figure not so culturally and ideologically tied to the school's founders, a university graduate educated in Brazil rather than Europe or the Middle East.[46] In some settings, board–director tension is especially sensitive because the directors are not Jewish. This is so in Colombia. The appointment of Catholics might be seen as a vehicle for state interference, especially as the rationale for these appointments relates to the preponderance of mandated material over Jewish curriculum; indeed the directors, who are powerful, are also the supervisors of the standard curriculum.[47] Yet Colombia's Jewish parents are committed to biculturalism and therefore favor many such links to the broader society.

More common than non-Jewish directors are non-Jewish teachers handling the standardized curriculum. Depending on the union structure, this can create problems for boards or directors in terms of hiring, curriculum, responsibilities to parents, and discipline. There is also the matter of non-Jewish students, often *becarios*, but it appears that most are happy to be in quality schools. According to both the director and ex-director of Mexico's Colegio Israelita, many even take the Hebrew and Yiddish subjects.[48]

Probably the most common governance tension, however, relates very directly to the issues of identity that will be discussed shortly. Directors, possibly with board support, often promote Jewish identity as much as possible, whereas parents and especially students are more willing to trade off identity for a more secure standing in society at large. This is a classic identity–assimilation tension. The director of the Santiago school has concluded that he cannot make his school more Jewish for fear of alienating the clientele; some parents are afraid that children who feel their Judaism "too"

---

46. Schers, "Jewish Education," 27; Horowitz Institute, *Brazilian Jewry*, 48.
47. However, Jews are found in other administrative positions; Smith, "Jewish Education in Colombia," 58–59, 61, 115.
48. Interviews with Rosenberg and Tórenberg.

intensely may want to move to Israel. The director of Mexico's Yavne School has reported that the great majority of his students are less religious than the school's curriculum and basic orientation would suggest.[49]

To summarize, the autonomy of Latin America's Jewish schools, restricted very little by the state, is more restricted by other extra-school authorities. This is typical for Latin American private educational institutions. It hardly limits the autonomy of the Jewish community, however, because most of these extra-school authorities represent the community itself. To explore an exception, or rather an extension, of what community means, more attention should be devoted to the role of international Jewish actors, such as the World Zionist Organization.[50] But for the most part we find a rather classic pattern of private school governance, characterized by direct accountability to rather narrow constituencies. Within that context, governance patterns vary in large part because these constituencies vary. One of the variations concerns the orientation toward identity and assimilation. Operating autonomously, how do Jewish communities handle this basic question within their schools?[51]

Group Identity

We have already considered some indicators of the performance of Latin America's Jewish schooling. The Jewish community has managed to operate substantially autonomous and self-financed schools, attracting roughly half the potential Jewish students.[52] But to what extent do these institutions contribute to the identity of their tiny and (for the most part) atypical group within Latin American societies? If the (nebulous) answer is that the record is mixed, the following sections try to make that answer more meaningful. The first analyzes the ambivalent missions Latin America's Jewish schools have had concerning Jewish identity. The second tries to specify the principal successes and failures.

Mixed Missions

To judge Latin America's Jewish schools by how well they have preserved Jewish identity is to judge by only one of their missions. However

---

49. Interview with I. Barylko.
50. See Organización Sionista Mundial, *Educación*; Zadoff, "Other Countries," 21–22.
51. Zadoff, "Other Countries," 31–32, posed this as a major question for future research and for his own policy recommendations; if the legal and material bases of Latin America's Jewish education are sound, the challenge is ideological commitment.
52. I have not dealt with failed attempts to create Jewish schools, such as early attempts in Cali, Colombia (Smith, "Jewish Education in Colombia," 38).

important that mission is, it has usually been forced to compromise itself with other missions.[53] There are, of course, continual debates among Jews about what is or should be intrinsic to a Jewish identity and how much it ought to be intertwined with concerns of the broader society. Latin America's Jewish schools have set missions tied not only to academic excellence or good job-market prospects, but also to given political or social persuasions, even pointedly secular ones.

It is against such a background that one should judge the success of Jewish schools in preserving Jewish identity. Elkin found that many Argentine Jews who emigrated from early Eastern Europe and wanted a traditional religious education were pushed by international Jewish agencies that favored education for rapid assimilation.[54] Sneh wrote of two waves of immigration to Argentina, the first traditionally observant, the second clustering as urban workers and artisans and characterized by its "militant and laical orientation." The second clustering helped produce schools organized around political parties—Israeli political parties. Moreover, these orientations shaped not only schools but other community organizations also, so the schools fit into a wide network. The socialist–Zionist fervor of Eastern Europe, so instrumental in shaping the state of Israel itself, had a powerful impact in Argentina, and also in nations such as Uruguay and Brazil.[55] Over time, as it did in Belo Horizonte and other parts of Brazil, leftist secularism declined, although variably. Major factors included the growing prosperity of most Jews and the momentous turns of Mideast politics. In any case, religion was not generally established as the centerpiece of Latin America's Jewish schools.

Most frequently, Latin America's Jewish schools assumed mixed missions: simultaneously to preserve a distinctive Jewish identity and to stimulate integration into surrounding societies. Importantly, given the stratification of these societies, integration has generally meant *integration into privileged strata*—economically and, without doubt, educationally. This reflects the substantial achievements of Jewish immigrants. Matters would be much different if assimilation were to imply integration into Latin America's mainstream.

Smith's work on Colombia lists a variety of founding missions, including helping students to be Jews and love God without neglecting secular concerns, social mobility, and Colombian patriotism. In short, the effort to build biculturalism and a Colombian–Jewish identity is seen as the major

---

53. Naturally, many of those who attend non-Jewish schools also have Jewish identities, and a Jewish identity need not imply a religious commitment, as many Israeli kibbutzim attest.
54. Elkin, "History of the Jews in Latin America," 263–264; Sneh, "La red escolar," 129.
55. On the general East European background, see Amos Elon, *The Israelis: Founders and Sons* (New York: Bantam Books, 1972).

issue for Colombian Jewish schools. On balance, according to Smith, the schools seem to have done fairly well, although with notable differences among the three major communities studied. For Latin America's Jewish schools in general, the perceived balance of identity and assimilation naturally will vary significantly. For example, the Theodor Herzl School in Belo Horizonte, Brazil, seems to emphasize integration, although with Jewish values. In Rio, two of six Jewish schools identify themselves as religious, but even there most of the constituent families are not observant. More evidence is needed to compare goals, much less achievements, across nations.[56]

Promoting Identity?

Leaving aside the issue of mixed missions, the ways in which Latin America's Jewish schools have or have not in practice promoted Jewish identity are of interest. To start on the negative side, *religious* identity has not been effectively promoted. A broad, if imprecise, proof of this lies in the very secular nature of Latin America's Jewish adult life, of the lives of Latin America's Jewish school graduates. For those who see the historical preservation of the Jewish identity intertwined with preservation of religious identity, this is a profound preoccupation. It is largely by this standard that the director of the University of Chile's Center for Judaic Studies has judged his nation's Jewish schooling to be a major failure. Most Chilean students and graduates do not go to synagogue, read Jewish books, or care about Jewish as opposed to "pragmatic" matters; Jewish educational life is "underdeveloped." Similarly, especially since the 1960s, doubts have arisen about the acclaimed Mexican system: Graduates do not enter Jewish community life.[57] And there is evidence from several nations that religious orientation declines as the immigrant generation passes. Yet even much of the immigrant generation had limited religious orientation. For example, the early struggles in Colombia's Jewish schools did not concern the religious–secular balance; a consensus toward secularism dominated. In Argentina, religious institutions were not crucial to schooling; on the contrary, secularism was often antireligious.[58]

---

56. On Colombia, see Smith, "Jewish Education in Colombia," 17, 54–57, 153, 190–192; on Brazil, see Schers, "Jewish Education," 15; "La comunidad judía en Belo Horizonte," in Monk and Isaacson, *Comunidades judías,* 161–162. Identity does not necessarily weaken over time. It may be, for example, that Santiago's Instituto Hebreo has stronger Jewish studies today than it did twenty years ago.

57. On Chile, see Gunter Böhm, Director of the Center of Judaic Studies, University of Chile, interview with author, Santiago, January 1982; on Mexico, see Chelminsky, "La educación judía," 228; Portnoy, "Cultura e intelectuales," 67; Mexico probably fares better than most of Latin America, however.

58. On Colombia, see Smith, "Jewish Education in Colombia," 46; on Argentina, J. Barylko, "Thoughts on Jewish Education in Argentina," mimeo, 11.

One partial consequence of weak identity, which then is a cause of further weakened identity, is the inability to produce sufficient teachers of Jewish studies. On the one hand, there is the general curriculum, accounting for the bulk of classroom hours and taught mostly by non-Jewish teachers. In Colombia in 1970, only five of twenty-six teachers at Cali's Jewish school and forty-one at Barranquilla's were Jewish. From a political or organizational studies perspective, this makes Latin America's Jewish schools vulnerable to those in the environment who often do not share institutional goals of identity. This is especially dangerous in times of political turmoil, when the general society may be at pointed odds with the Latin American Jewish school. Zadoff cited Mexico in the 1930s and Peru in the early 1970s.[59]

On the other hand, Latin America's Jewish schools have had great trouble providing Jewish teachers even for their Jewish studies. Argentina is the significant exception. Graduates of teaching training programs there often follow up with study in Israel before returning to Argentina and various other Latin American nations. Mexico has also boasted a teacher training institute. It has helped, but has not saved Mexico from typical problems. Strikingly, the teaching profession, even when involved in Jewish studies, lacks prestige. Indicatively, most teachers have been women, and many quit after a few years. Beyond that, women's liberation has opened more attractive opportunities elsewhere. Therefore it is increasingly the Sephardic women (e.g., in Mexico, those from Aleppo) who previously did not work outside the home who fill the teaching ranks. Problems are less acute at the upper secondary level than at the primary level.[60]

For the most part, teachers of Jewish studies must be imported. Before World War II, they came from countries such as Poland. Since then Israel has been the main supplier. The *shlichim* (Israeli teachers) surely make great contributions, but major problems exist. Among these are (1) the expense incurred in transportation, settling, Spanish language training, and rapid turnover; (2) language problems, especially if "by the time they learn Spanish, they've gone"; (3) parental fears that the *shlichim* in effect recruit their children to immigrate to Israel.[61] Yet the most devastating problem of

59. Zadoff, "Other Countries," 17; on Colombia, see Smith, "Jewish Education in Colombia," 40, 44.
60. On Mexico, see Ira T. Lerner, *Mexican Jewry in the Land of the Aztecs* (Mexico City: B. Costa-Amic, 1973), 50–51; interviews with Lokier, I. Barylko, and Jusidman; Miguel Abruch, UNAM sociologist, telephone interview with author, Mexico City, October 1983. Also see Rubel, "Jewish Education in Argentina," 24; Zadoff, "Other Countries," 18.
61. Respectively on these three points: Smith, "Jewish Education in Colombia," 83; interview with Böhm; Elkin, "History of the Jews in Latin America," 273. For more on the teacher problem, see Alexander Pushkin, "Resultados y conclusiones du un estudio comparativo de las escuelas de capacitación de maestros judíos en la diaspora," in Organización Sionista Mundial, *Educación,* 11–12.

all may lie in the open demonstration that these mostly autonomous and well-to-do communities cannot produce professionals willing to assume one of the most important roles in preserving group identity.

The performance of Latin America's Jewish schools is more encouraging, although not always overwhelmingly so, on most other counts. Curriculum is a critical one. Of course, as we have seen, most time is budgeted for general studies, basically following the standardized content and texts used in non-Jewish schools. Latin America's Jewish schools have more autonomy over their Jewish studies, although Israeli and international Jewish organizations have promoted some uniformity.[62] The schools manage to allocate considerable time for Jewish studies by extending the school day well beyond the number of hours required by the state. In São Paulo, for example, the 35–40-hour week is one-third beyond the minimum. The percentage of time devoted to Jewish studies varies by school but especially by grade, decreasing at higher levels. Rio's Jewish primary schools spend roughly one-third of their time on Jewish studies versus roughly one-tenth for secondary schools. According to Zadoff, interschool variation appears greater at the primary level, some schools devoting less than one-third of their time (4–10 hours weekly) to Jewish studies, others up to half their time (13–18 hours weekly), and most secondary schools allocating between one-tenth and one-fifth of their time (3–9 hours weekly.)[63] Given secularism, pressures to attend (non-Jewish) universities and to otherwise assimilate, and parent and student reservations about the importance of Jewish studies, these figures are impressive. As a rule, to attend a Latin American Jewish school is to receive a comparatively substantial Jewish education.

Of course, the time added to the state curriculum contributes to a Jewish identity only if it truly deals with Jewish subject matter. It does. Subjects include Hebrew, Yiddish, and Jewish religion, culture, and history. Also important is attention to Israel. The Israeli connection shows how efforts to build Jewish identity extend beyond the formal curriculum. Many of Latin America's Jewish students participate in organized trips and interchanges with Israel. This is the case at Peru's Colegio León Pinelo, for example, and eleventh graders at Chile's Instituto Hebreo are encouraged to spend two months in the Holy Land. Sneh reported that Argentina's Jewish schools helped mobilize the community to active support for Israel in the

---

62. Smith, "Jewish Education in Colombia," 180–181; Zadoff, "Other Countries," 12.
63. On São Paulo, see Federacão Israelita do Estado de São Paulo, Departamento de Estatística e Pesquisa Social, *Apêndice Estatístico de São Paulo 1980* (São Paulo), 24; on Rio, see Horowitz Institute, *Brazilian Jewry*, 172. Chelminsky, "La educación judía," 222, found that Mexican schools devote 9–12 of their 35 weekly hours to Jewish studies. Zadoff, "Other Countries," 24–25.

1967 war. Further, Latin America's Jewish schools organize after-school and summer events, from lectures to day camps, with strong Jewish content. As Smith has shown for Colombia, Latin America's Jewish schools promote the celebration of Jewish holidays, and not only by their students but also by the Jewish community at large.[64] Finally, even cursory observation reveals the wide extent of Jewish symbols, notices, events, and so on prominently displayed on the walls of Latin America's Jewish schools.

At least as impressive, certainly in comparison with the U.S. diaspora experience, is the Latin America's Jewish school role in maintaining the chief languages of identity. Most Jewish immigrants arrived in Latin America speaking neither Spanish nor Portuguese but Yiddish. Communities have been deeply divided over its preservation. For many, Yiddish is a crucial link to their cultural heritage in Europe. For others, Yiddish is not necessary to the Jewish identity; Hebrew is. Naturally, some assimilationists care little to preserve either language. Such divisions, profoundly affecting the role of Jewish schools, are of course nothing new for Jewish communities; to illustrate, consider the intense debates that raged within Europe's Jewish community between the world wars.[65] In Latin America, the political left tended to support Yiddish over Hebrew, the religious language. Since World War II, however, Yiddish has lost considerable ground while Hebrew has gained. Yet even amid widespread notices of its impending death, Yiddish is being sustained by several of Latin America's Jewish schools. This is notably true in Mexico, for example. Spurred by the birth of Israel and its inspiring revival of Hebrew as a vibrant language of daily use, Latin America's Jewish schools made Hebrew the basic language of instruction for their Jewish studies.[66] Although data are lacking, it appears that many graduates of Latin America's Jewish schools speak Hebrew.

An important point thus far deleted from the language discussion raises some related issues about group and subgroup identity. Most Sephardic immigrants spoke not Yiddish but Judezmo—a variant of Spanish that has survived since the Expulsion from Spain in 1492. With little stake in

---

64. Yaacov Hasson, "Elementos para un estudio histórico y pedagógico de la educación judía en el Perú," in Isaacson and Kovadloff, *Comunidades judías de latinoamérica*, 243; Abraham Megendzo, director of the Santiago school, interview with author, Santiago, January 1982; Sneh, "La red escolar," 132–133; Smith, "Jewish Education in Colombia," 75–79, 97. The Horowitz Institute report, *Brazilian Jewry*, 108–143, gives a detailed account of the Israeli impact on Rio's schools.

65. See, for example, Yehezkel Kaufman, "The Hebrew Language and Our National Future," in Arthur A. Cohen, ed., *The Jew: Essays from Martin Buber's Journal der Jude, 1916–1928* (University: University of Alabama Press, 1980), 97–111.

66. For some indication of variability by nation, see Monk and Isaacson, *Comunidades judías*.

preserving Yiddish, these immigrants helped promote schools where Hebrew has been the uncontested language of Jewish identity.

Language is only one factor separating schools for Ashkenazim and Sephardim. The Jews of the Middle East and North Africa brought with them somewhat different traditions from those of their more numerous counterparts from Europe. To generalize, the Sephardic schools probably have tended to be more religiously oriented, more inward looking or attached to their Jewish identities, and more conservative. But such cleavages are not clear cut. In Mexico the Colegio Israelita de México, Colegio Hebreo Tarbut, and Colegio Yavne are associated with the Ashkenazi community and the Colegio Hebreo Sefaradí and Colegio Hebreo Monte Sinai are associated with the (Turkish and Syrian) Sephardic community, but one could also divide Mexican Jewish schools along Ashkenazi, Sephardic, and religious lines (e.g., Colegio Emek, Colegio Beth Yaacov and the Keter Tora Albert Einstein), for example.[67] Moreover, many schools have both Ashkenazim and Sephardim. This occurs where communities have been too small to manage more than one school,[68] and it increasingly occurs as subgroup identities diminish across generations, just as national ones do (e.g., Hungarian and Polish Jews in Chile). Thus, Latin America's Jewish schools have sometimes protected subgroup identities within Judaism, but, by and large, protection of the group identity of Judaism proves challenging enough. The tendency, in education as in other aspects of Latin America's Jewish life, is toward the decline of subgroup identities.

Conclusion

Stepping back and seeking a general conclusion about Jewish education in Latin America, I am struck by parallels to a crucial paradox in Jewish political history. This concerns the challenges posed for Jewish group identities where the dominant society builds a relatively tolerant environment, one receptive to the Jew who wants to be part of it. Analysts of Jewish civilization continually discuss this paradox, often related historically to the liberalizing reforms instituted in Napoleonic France or, in the contemporary diaspora, to democratic life in Western Europe and the United States.

But Latin America? Notwithstanding powerful traditions of authoritarianism and corporatism, the near monopoly of Catholicism, and a tragic

---

67. Schmidt correspondence and Lokier interview; "Mexico," in Monk and Isaacson, *Comunidades judías,* 95; Lerner, *Mexican Jewry,* 106–113, including divisions according to the emphasis on Israel.

68. "Venezuela," in Monk and Isaacson, *Comunidades judías,* 124.

degree of socioeconomic stratification in which Jews are widely identified among the privileged—notwithstanding all this, Jews who want to subordinate their Jewishness have often been welcomed as Brazilians, Uruguayans, and so forth.[69] As Eduardo Rauch put it: "If Latin America has not been a great place for Judaism, it has been a magnificent haven for Jews."[70] The lure is especially strong because it is focused not on the socioeconomic mainstream but on a privileged niche. This makes for a very important contrast to the U.S. experience. Thus, for example, whereas the U.S. public school has been a major vehicle for assimilation, the lack of good Latin American public schooling has often hindered assimilation.[71] Not only has the use of Jewish schools been much greater in Latin America, but the chief alternative now is the elite private secular school.

Of course, on the one hand, we must not underestimate anti-Semitism and intolerance, nor the fact that these have varied by epoch and nation. On the other hand, whatever problems dominant society poses for Latin America's Jewish education by allowing Jews not to be Jews, it also grants Latin America's Jewish education space to operate successfully by allowing Jews—to some uncertain degree—to be Jews. More specifically, it allows considerable autonomy to Jewish schools, despite the limits already discussed and the strong dose of bureaucratic centralism in the educational system; further limits (including some that help make Jewish universities seem impractical) relate to the fact that being "too" distinctively Jewish severely limits acceptance and mobility.

Taken on balance, then, the environmental context is simultaneously tolerant and challenging in a way that leaves the fate of Jewish identity largely in Jewish hands. Within that context, Latin America's Jewish education would not get high marks were Latin America's Jewish communities fully committed to promoting their distinctive identities. But the communities are not so committed. Both secularism and a desire for acceptance into the dominant society mix with concerns for identity. If the consequent weakness of other Jewish institutions in promoting Jewish identity places a special responsibility on Latin America's Jewish schools, it also imposes trying handicaps. The school cannot do much more than the community wants of it. The school can be much more Jewish than the family only at

---

69. Space prevents elaboration of the possible explanations, some touched on already, so I just mention a few. Liberal and plural traditions share the scene with authoritarian and corporatist ones; Catholicism is not always the basis for social and political action, let alone exclusionary action, especially when lay traditions are strong. Few leftist regimes reign long enough to restructure class relations. The politics of most other regimes favor the bourgeoisie. Bureaucratic centralism is more formidable on the books than in practice.

70. Rauch, "Latin American Jewry," 70.

71. Elkin, "History of the Jews in Latin America," 255.

considerable risk to its very existence.[72] Schools are not independent entities. However autonomous they are from the state, Latin America's Jewish schools are much less autonomous from their Jewish communities.

Therefore, within the full context within which Latin America's Jewish education functions, it does an impressive job. That full context includes not only the perhaps surprising degree of autonomy permitted by the dominant society, an autonomy earned and creditably maintained, but also the attractiveness of that society, which is to say some of its privileged strata, to the Jewish communities. Naturally, the high academic quality of Latin America's Jewish schools is one very laudable achievement. Yet most other schools attended by Latin America's Jewish students also offer high quality and, regardless of school, quality provides the social capital with which to function in the dominant society. What Latin America's Jewish schools—basically self-financed—provide distinctively, for all the restrictions, is something markedly more Jewish than anything found in other schools. Overall, those who want a Jewish education get it, those who do not do not, and those who want some probably get somewhat more than they want. Much more could not reasonably be expected.

---

72. Although the Horowitz Institute report (*Brazilian Jewry*, 29–31, 72–84, 144–166) reached a carefully mixed verdict on how well Rio's schools promote a Jewish identity, it reached a clear conclusion that the parents are very satisfied.

IV
Adaptation and Evolution

9
Economic and Social Mobility of Jews in Brazil

Henrique Rattner

Introduction

The study of the occupational structure and social mobility of immigrants and their descendants supplies a series of indicators for the evaluation of the extent and degree of integration into the adoptive society. A successful economic career is frequently a necessary (although not a sufficient) condition for admission into the elite segments of society that share, control, and distribute wealth, prestige, and power. On the other hand, poverty nearly always indicates the failure of attempts to move upward in the social stratification system, because the normal path of social mobility—higher education, business success, and political protection—is not accessible to the poor.

From this point of view, the economic and social trajectory of Jews who migrated to Brazil beginning in the first decades of the twentieth century can be considered an outstanding success. Although most of them left their countries of origin without financial resources and under generally precarious conditions, within two generations they not only managed to acquire positions of wealth and prestige, but also succeeded in integrating with the cultural and political elites of the country. Contrary to the picture painted by historians of the Jews of Europe—only a small minority of whom succeeded in penetrating the economic, political, and cultural life of the elite while the majority of Jews remained oppressed in the lower strata of the social pyramid—in Brazil Jews have situated themselves in the upper ranks of society in terms of income per capita, educational achievement, life-style, and political identification.

Empirical evidence seems to suggest that people who attain new positions tend to use their greater power and prestige to establish defense barriers against the aspiring segments that have remained behind. The concrete result of this attitude is the persistence of the status quo and a significant trend toward increasing inequality in the social structure.[1]

If mobility depends on occupation and job rank, which in turn depend upon employment level and creation of new jobs, then we must look at the dynamics of the overall social development in its demographic, economic, political, and cultural aspects if we wish to understand and interpret the achievements of an immigrant group. The study of the rapid upward social mobility of Jews in Brazil presents an optimal combination of structural and individual factors in a given historical period through which we may augment our understanding of the role of immigrants in social and economic development.

The Brazilian Context

The transformation of Brazil from a rural to an urban society during the course of the twentieth century introduced great changes into the social structure, creating a large middle class. Urbanization and industrialization created new jobs and occupations in the secondary and tertiary sectors, and these very changes created opportunities for seemingly unlimited upward mobility. And yet, even before the advent of the present economic crisis, which stopped industrial expansion and thus exacerbated urban tensions to incredibly high levels, there remained large areas of rural and urban poverty, malnutrition, lower income, marginality, and poor quality of life for the majority of the more than 120 million people of Brazil. Despite enormous growth since the 1950s, the majority of the people of Brazil remain extremely poor.

Following a period of economic growth centering on World War II, structural bottlenecks, inflation, and the international economic situation initiated a period of economic instability and political unrest in Brazil, culminating in the military coup d'etat of 1964. The following twenty years brought profound political and institutional changes to Brazilian society. Economic stagnation came to an end in the second half of the decade with the massive entry of foreign investments and the creation of new direct and

---

1. D. Wrong, "The Functional Theory of Stratification: Some Neglected Considerations," in E. O. Laum et al. (eds.), *The Logic of Social Hierarchies* (Chicago: Macmillan, 1970).

indirect employment opportunities. The measures taken to restore economic growth included increased intervention by the state in the economy, improvements in the fiscal and financial systems, incentives to savings, compulsory loans, and large foreign investments attracted by the comparatively low wages. All this stimulated a powerful economic boom, best expressed by the average annual growth rates of more than 10% of the gross domestic product over several years. The booming economy speeded up internal migration, housing construction, and public works projects, which had a significant multiplier effect on the labor market and the overall economy.

In the middle of the 1970s, inflation, foreign and internal debts, and the spreading worldwide recession put a stop to the Brazilian miracle. Increasing unemployment and continuous drops in real wages and purchasing power of the workers and urban middle class, combined with overwhelming evidence of corruption in the ruling technocracy, brought about public manifestations of dissatisfaction and political pressures that weakened the authoritarian regime, which finally embarked on the political *abertura* (relative democratization).

Occupation and Social Stratification of Brazilian Jews

Study of the occupational structure and mobility of Brazilian Jews provides a profile of the economic activities of a minority group whose immigration and acculturation into the mainstream of the adoptive society are relatively recent. The bulk of Jewish immigrants to Brazil established themselves in the principal cities of Rio de Janeiro and São Paulo during the period between the two world wars and again shortly after World War II. These two periods, but especially the 1950s, coincided with a very intensive and rapid expansion of the urban–industrial system, based initially on the accumulated wealth of São Paulo's coffee planters.

Undoubtedly, Jews participated in the process of economic growth and industrialization out of proportion to their number within the population. Urban dwellers for centuries, some of them craftsmen and others with experience in small business and trade, they entered the new world with a set of qualifications that enabled them to achieve economic mobility and social integration into the emergent urban-industrial society, which badly required qualified labor and managerial talent, entrepreneurs and tradesmen for the expanding economy.

Sociological studies of industrial entrepreneurs in Brazil reveal the decisive participation of immigrant members of minority groups in the establishment of industries and commercial enterprises, arguing that this kind of activity and economic behavior may have been the only path open to them for achieving upward social mobility in a predominantly agrarian and traditional society which only a few decades earlier had abolished slavery.[2]

In the case of São Paulo's industry, there is evidence that more than 80% of pioneer entrepreneurs were immigrants or their descendants of not more than two generations.[3] The research data do not reveal the specific identity of those immigrants in terms of ethnic origin or religious affiliation. We know only that approximately 25% of them came from Central (Germany, Austria, Czechoslovakia, Hungary) and Eastern (Poland, Russia, Rumania) Europe, which suggests a very high proportion of Jews among them. Prior to their immigration, many Jews had been craftsmen, industrial workers, or small merchants, and others had been bankers, lawyers, or members of the liberal professions. For some, immigration held the promise of "America," whereas for others it implied the loss of privileged position. But once arrived and settled, both classes prospered as merchants, industrial entrepreneurs, and professionals.

The favorable conditions encountered by immigrants on the Brazilian shores from 1920 onward, with the steady expansion of industry, made their progress easier, facilitating their integration into the country's economy. The growth process was accompanied by parallel development of the urban middle class, which became one of the most important segments of the emerging social structure.

Not by accident, Jews with a long historical tradition of life in urban environments and with aspirations to middle-class status fitted neatly into the new functions and positions of the urban–industrial society. This was particularly true for the Brazilian-born second generation, whose occupational choices tended toward the liberal professions, management of private and public firms, trade, and industry. The immigrants who started their careers as peddlers and salesmen applied themselves with diligence and hard work to the task of "making America."

Through savings and long hours of work, their small shops grew and expanded, and here and there the first attempts at establishing manufactur-

---

2. Luis Carlos Bresser Pereira, *Desenvolvimento e crise* (Rio de Janeiro: Zahar Editores, 1968); F. H. Cardoso, *Empresário industrial e desenvolvimento econômico* (São Paulo: Difusao Européia do Livro, 1964); H. Rattner, *Tradiçao e Mudança—A comunidade Judaica em São Paulo* (São Paulo: Editora Atica, 1977); H. Rattner, "Sur judeu e brasileiro: Problemas de identidade sócio cultural no Brasil," *Revista Shalom*, 16 (no. 198) special supplement, June, 1982.

3. Luis Carlos Bresser Pereira, "Origens étnicas e Sociais do Empresário Paulista," *Revista de Administrao de Empresas da Fundação Gehilio Vargas*, 3(3), 1964.

ing enterprises were successful, leading later to the expansion and flourishing of large industrial and commercial enterprises. However, economic and especially social mobility do not depend only upon market opportunities. The individual's economic career and social trajectory are deeply affected by his or her situation at the point of departure or, more specifically, by age at entry into the labor market, initial occupational status, the social origin and cultural capital accumulated by the individual's family, and his or her own educational background. High educational levels correlate with corresponding occupational levels and life-style patterns in a dynamic urban society where the acquisition of technical and professional knowledge almost always assures access to roles and positions of higher prestige and rewards.

Empirical evidence seems to suggest that the age of entry into the labor market depends on the individual's social origin and family background. The lower the social origin, the earlier occurs the entry; the earlier the entry into the labor market, the lower the occupational status of the individual. Adults, especially those in the middle segment of the social stratification system, begin work in jobs of higher status. The later the entry, the better the start and the chance for a prestigious career. A strong educational background is one of the main individual resources for taking advantage of good employment opportunities, which in turn may lead to upward mobility.

People from the lower socioeconomic classes who are illiterate or who have gone through precarious schooling only, or who have had to undergo a process of coexistence of night school and work, find that their low social origin is confirmed through being forced to accept employment in nonqualified work, which in turn keeps them in a lower social position. Youngsters from the upper middle strata who are college bound normally enter the labor market only at age 22. But most Brazilian families are unable to postpone the entry of their children into the labor market that long—long enough to provide them with an adequate education. Thus, the average age of entry can be considered a valuable indicator of social justice: The earlier the entry, the greater the inequality. Social origin thus becomes a serious obstacle to education and occupational mobility. This process is compounded by the introduction of computer education, which is accessible mainly to youngsters from upper middle class families. Children from the lower strata lack the educational background and the cultural environment that would enable them to assimilate abstract computer language, a fact that influences their educational achievement negatively and thus increases social inequality.

With reference to the aforementioned criteria, our 1968–1969 census[4] indicates a 100% frequency of Jewish children in elementary and junior high schools. The proportion of college students was 78.6% for boys and 52% for girls of the respective age groups. Ten years later (1978), the survey conducted by the statistical department of the Federation of Jewish Associations of São Paulo evidenced a proportion of 20.4% of the entire Jewish population with a college degree (16% in 1968–1969) versus 1.4% of the population of the State of São Paulo. Over 80% of the 18–25-year age group were attending an institution of higher education.

During Brazil's years of economic growth, higher education and prosperous businesses combined to form the most important path to upward social mobility. This is due to the fact that in order to delay entry into the labor market for several years, Jewish youngsters dedicating themselves almost exclusively to study must rely on the moral and material support of their families. There is no doubt that family solidarity and traditional Jewish values that stress learning as an important human objective make a significant contribution to the ability of Jewish adolescents to choose their occupations.

The 1968–1969 census and the follow-up survey a decade later determined the distribution of the Jewish economically active population (EAP), (Tables 9.1 and 9.2), showing clearly the increase in the percentage of employers and members of the liberal professions.

Breaking out the three categories of employers, persons in the liberal professions, and executives (Table 9.3) reveals an absolute increase of 10.2% (or a relative increase of 17.7%) among the EAP in the decade 1968–1978. These data reveal not only a clear upward trend in Jewish social mobility, but also significant social stratification, especially when

---

4. Statistical information about Jews in Brazil is scarce, inaccurate, and incomplete. The 1950 Population Census offers only global figures for Jews in the different states of the Brazilian federation, without a breakdown of the data by age, sex, marital status, geographic origin, or occupation. The situation is even worse for the following census years, 1960, 1970, and 1980. The official questionnaire utilized by the Brazilian Institute of Geography and Statistics (IBGE) asked for religious affiliation only for Catholic, Protestant, and "Other," which eliminates the possibility of analyzing the demographic, economic, and social evolution of the Jewish community. Therefore, the data base is precarious and derives almost exclusively from the survey carried out among the Jewish population of the State of São Paulo in 1968–1969 (H. Rattner, *Tradição e mudança—A comunidade judaica em São Paulo* (São Paulo: Editora Ática, 1977), which was partially updated by the department of statistics and social research of the Federation of Jewish Associations of São Paulo in 1978 and 1980. Although Jews live in many localities in Brazil, this bias does not seem to invalidate inferences for the collectivity as a whole because social, cultural, educational, and religious organizations and activities are patterned along the lines of the *paulista* community. In terms of occupation, education, life-style, and cultural behavior, no significant differences can be observed that are due to geographic location.

Table 9.1
Percentages of Occupations of the Jewish Economically Active Population

Occupation	1968–1969	1978
Employers	27.3	35.6
Liberal professions	14.9	26.7
Executives, managers[a]	15.3	5.4
Craftsmen and independent businessmen	8.8	
Employees	12.8	15.6
Workers	0.3	
Retired	7.9	
Other	12.7	

[a]The decrease in the number of executives and managers may be attributed to differences in criteria as between the two surveys; and some overlap with the category of employee.

compared with data supplied by ECLA (Economic Commission for Latin America) on the occupational structure of the country as a whole.[5]

The important contribution of immigrants to industrialization and economic growth in the postwar period has already been mentioned. Even with no specific information available concerning the role played by Jewish entrepreneurs in Brazil's economic development, the evidence that nearly a quarter of all entrepreneurs had their origin in Central and Eastern Europe suggests significant participation by Jews in the process of economic innovation. Jewish businesspeople are found in nearly all sectors of industry, trade, and services. Some have attained leading positions in their respective branches. For instance, paper and cellulose, automotive components, carpets and furniture, building and general construction, plastics, mechanics and electronics, and engineering and consulting firms are some of the areas in which Jews occupy a prominent if not a leading position.

There can be little doubt that occupational structure is closely related to social stratification and income distribution. Based on the available data, we may conclude that about two-thirds of the Jewish community of Brazil belong (in terms of income, occupation, educational level, and consumption patterns) to the upper strata of Brazil's stratification system. Studies of income distribution in Brazil show a clear trend toward the concentration of income in the hands of the upper 5% of the population, whose share in the income distribution—excluding profit from capital investments and

---

5. Carlos Filgueira and Carlos Geneletti, *Estratificación y movilidad ocupacional en America Latina* (Santiago: Cuadernos de la Comisão Económica para a América Latina, 1981).

Table 9.2
Occupational Level of Jews in São Paulo, 1978

Occupational level	Men		Women		Total	
	Number	Percentage	Number	Percentage	Number	Percentage
Employees	1415	13.03	752	25.26	2167	15.66
Crafts and autonomous business	65	0.60	56	1.88	121	0.87
Executives and managers	627	5.77	113	3.80	740	5.35
Liberal professionals	2754	25.36	948	31.84	3702	26.76
Employers	4096	37.72	832	27.95	4928	35.62
Retired	704	6.49	100	3.36	804	5.81
Others	1197	11.03	176	5.91	1375	9.93
Total	10,858	100.00	2997	100.00	13,835	100.00

Source: *Statistical Annuary of the Jewish Community in São Paulo* (São Paulo: Federação Israelita do Estado de São Paulo, 1978).

Table 9.3
Percentages of Occupational Structure in Brazil, 1950, 1960, 1970

	1950	1960	1970
Medium and superior strata, total	15.2	15.3	18.6
Medium and superior strata in secondary- and tertiary-sector occupation	13.2	14.5	17.9
Employers	1.8	1.8	0.8
Managers	—	2.6	1.4
Liberal professionals	0.4	0.7	0.5
Dependent professionals	—	2.5	4.0
Autonomous trade	2.5	0.3	2.9
Sales, crafts, etc.	8.5	6.6	8.4

Source: *Estratificación y movilidad ocupacional en America Latina* (Santiago: Comissão Econômica da América Latina, 1981), 32.

government's share in income—had increased from 28.5% in 1960 to 38.2% in 1970 and to 49% (estimated) in 1980. On the evidence of data about the peculiar occupational structure of the Jewish community, confirmed by additional information on educational level, housing, and conspicuous consumption patterns, it can be assumed that two-thirds of Brazilian Jews belong to the elite who control nearly half of the total personal income and of the country's wealth. This may not be a distinguishing mark of Brazil. Kuznets, in a study of the economic structure of U.S. Jewry, pointed out the higher indices of income, educational level, professional achievement, and so on among American Jews as compared with other ethnic groups or with the total urban population.[6] There is, however, a significant difference in the general background against which the previously mentioned trends occur. In the United States only about 20% of the total population are considered poor and without access to the affluent society, whereas in Brazil the opposite proportion prevails: Almost 80% of the population are "underdeveloped" and nearly half live at subsistence level.

It may be worth observing that the participation of Jews in Brazil's economic growth process has not been restricted or subjected to discriminatory practices. There is also no evidence of movements directed explicitly against Jews or any other minority group in contemporary Brazilian society. The presence of Jews in all spheres of economic, cultural, and political life allows us to make some inferences concerning their complete integration into their adoptive society. We may hypothesize that at a certain

---

6. Simon Kuznets, *Economic Structure of U.S. Jewry: Recent Trends* (Jerusalem: The Institute of Contemporary Jewry of The Hebrew University, 1972).

stage of development into a mature capitalist economy, certain cultural, ethnic, and religious traits are no longer obstacles to penetration into highly diversified economic activities. The proper logic of capital accumulation tends to invalidate, under certain circumstances, attributes such as race, religion, and nationality because the necessity for valorization of capital does not allow such elements to become permanent constraints.

This does not mean that minority groups must sacrifice any or all the specific traits by which they distinguish themselves from the majority of the population. However, in the process of acculturation and social mobility, certain distinctive cultural traits and customs of a group may be abandoned without its members losing their identity. Group identity and solidarity continue to exist, but on a new and different base created by other environmental conditions than those that had sustained the traditional characteristics of the group.

In the last part of this chapter, we will speculate about the social and political consequences of this historically peculiar situation for Brazilian Jews in the light of the trends and perspectives of their adoptive society. What are the implications of this situation in which Jews have attained positions characterized by a strong identification with and participation in the roles and privileges of the ruling elite?

Ideological Aspects and Political Attitudes of Brazilian Jews

For the majority of Jewish immigrants who entered Brazil in the decades since the 1920s, immigration signified, besides the discovery of a novel geographic space, penetration into a new social, economic, and cultural universe. Accustomed to living in small closed communities, they experienced for the first time the opportunities and possibilities of economic and social mobility offered by a society organized in accordance with universalistic and achievement patterns. Life in a dynamic industrial–urban environment (and not, of course, in the traditional agrarian sector of Brazilian society) offered numerous opportunities for the conquest of wealth, status, and prestige. On the other hand, the ongoing changes in the immigrants' economic and social circumstances brought about profound transformations in individual life-style as well as in the community's organizational structure and functions.

One of the consequences of this process of social ascent was the transfer of community leadership from rich but poorly educated merchants to an intelligentsia of liberal professionals, lawyers, engineers, and physicians. This occurred not through conflict but through cooptation and interpenetration of the two groups by marriage. The capital of the elderly merchant might typically be used to open an office or medical clinic for the recently graduated son-in-law. Increasing prosperity and with it social respectability tended to change life-styles and the value orientation not only of individuals but of whole communities. To rise in the social scale and to enter the elite meant for Jews the adoption of behavior patterns of a new reference group whose cultural life of conspicuous consumption imitated patterns imported from affluent societies abroad and that contradicted traditional Jewish restraint and austerity.

The adoption of a hedonistic life-style typical of the upper class in affluent societies, within a social context where the majority of the population are struggling to survive physically, can lead to questioning the legitimacy of such behavior in the light of the Jewish ethical tradition. This tension is felt in the intergenerational relationship, with youth openly challenging their elders and looking for cultural and political alternatives in leftist or countercultural groups.

Finally, the economic and educational achievements of Jews and their subsequent admission to the Brazilian ruling elite conditioned a very strong identification with the political ideas and values of the dominant oligarchies, to the point that the traditionally progressive, liberal democratic, and egalitarian aspirations the immigrants brought with them from Europe have been abandoned.

This reorientation is not a feature peculiar to Jews. Several studies of social stratification and mobility present a clear correlation between occupational and social mobility and the corresponding political orientation.[7] The point made by some authors is that people who move upward tend to become more conservative in their political behavior and values than those who were born in the upper strata. The upwardly mobile seem to obey a strong urge to conform with the norms and rules of the new reference group through choices of political ideologies and options that turn them into respectable defenders of the status quo. The process by which political ideologies and values are transmitted or chosen by different social groups have not been sufficiently studied by social scientists.

West pointed out that the older generation, when economically successful, tends to forget the needs and aspirations of those who remained behind in lower social ranks. Others refer to a feeling of gratitude to the social order that benefited them and that results in their adopting strongly conservative attitudes. Certain types of professional training may also have a strong conservative influence on the political behavior of those who under-

---

7. P. West, "Social Mobility among College Graduates," in R. Bendix and S. M. Lipset (eds.), *Class, Status, and Power* (Glencoe, Ill.: The Free Press, 1953).

go it, and the common preoccupation of the middle class with the accumulation and preservation of property may also result in a conservative political position.

An important factor to be considered in this context seems to be the position of the group concerned within the hierarchy of the sociopolitical structure. Questions such as how they earn their living, with whom they share power, whom they dominate, and what or who may be considered a menace to their privileged position may shed some light on the intricate problems of political choices and values assumed by rising social strata.

With reference to Brazil's economic growth process, it is possible to affirm that Jews have never been made to feel themselves as an obstacle. On the contrary, their constructive and dynamic role is documented in rich detail, reflecting the coexistence of their traditional values with the needs of capital accumulation in an increasingly diffuse community life.

The absence of any signs of marginalization of Jews from dominant economic activities and the open and dynamic stratification system have led to a very strong identification along the line of social class rather than on the basis of common religious or other traditional patterns. Social mobility and economic achievements press toward identification with certain social classes, rather than toward conformity or obedience to cultural patterns dictated by Jewish religious tradition. "Even if not all of them have become great businessmen, or leaders of the civil or military bureaucracies, the ties of common economic and hence political interests are sufficiently strong to define and to identify themselves with the dominant political groups, the regime and its repressive practices, however authoritarian and reactionary those may be."[8]

In light of what has been discussed, it is not an easy task to evaluate and predict the future of the Jewish community in Brazil. The triumphal attitudes and behavior of the ruling technocracy, typical of the period of the Brazilian "miracle," have given way to a profound pessimism and uncertainty about the country's future, with gross domestic product decreasing annually, foreign and internal debts reaching unprecedented levels, and the annual inflation rate surpassing the 200% mark.

There is a general feeling in almost all spheres of Brazilian society that political and economic changes are overdue; this is combined with a profound distrust and even contempt for its (military) rulers.[9] What kind of changes and how and when they will occur are questions that exceed the

8. H. Rattner, "Jewish Entrepreneurs in Brazil's Economic Development" (mimeo, University of São Paulo).

9. When these lines were written, the military was still in control of Brazil. Since that time, elections have been held and governance has passed to civilian hands. Nevertheless, the author's observations remain valid.—Editor

scope of this chapter. However, on the strength of the arguments presented here, it may be assumed that in the case of political upheaval Jews will act in accordance with their economic interest and corresponding social position within the social structure into which they seem thoroughly integrated.

Conclusions

Measured by occupation and income, the majority of Jews belong to the elite 5% who rule the economic and political destiny of Brazil. Their privileged position is more than confirmed by analysis of the level of education within the community. Jews are active in all spheres of cultural life, but not as Jews creating for Jews. Their public is not Jewish and their entire literary and artistic production is not based on or inspired by Jewish motives, traditions, or history. Jews are instead involved in the mainstream of Brazilian culture, where they are well represented among both consumers and producers.

With regard to the political dimension, Jews have been visibly integrated into the ruling system. Both before and after the coup d'etat of 1964, Jews have held prominent positions in government, as elected representatives to Congress, Senate, and state legislative bodies, as municipal counselors and secretaries to local governments, and even in the higher ranks of the armed forces. On the evidence of such facts, it is reasonable to assume that Jews are identified with and integrated into the dominant power structure, to which they give full support and from which they have benefited.

Thus, as allies and supporters of the ruling oligarchies (the old ones and the new ones), Jews tend to remain aloof from (or participate only marginally in) the incipient movements aimed at renovating Brazil's social and political system.

The paradox of making a good life under an authoritarian regime disturbed many members of the Jewish community and led to increasing intergenerational dissent and tension. Discussions reveal a series of complex problems that must be dealt with simultaneously on the basis of an ethical dilemma that cannot be ignored.

In the light of past experience, it seems that the main objectives of Jewish politics in Brazil today concern the defense of specifically Jewish interests—the fight against anti-Semitism and preservation of the State of Israel and of the Brazilian Jewish community's identification with it.

In spite of oscillation in Brazil's foreign policy, especially after the oil crisis intensified dependence on the Arab countries, the military government—for all its "responsible pragmatism"—never allowed discrimination against the Jewish communities at home. However, the *abertura* of the opening years of the 1980s created a new situation. Increasing freedom of the press, labor unions, and public manifestations necessarily included the emergence of pro-Palestinian and anti-Jewish groups. During the years of the totalitarian repression (1969–1975) the military crushed any manifestation considered dangerous to the maintenance of tranquility and public order. But in a more open regime, the possibilities for anti-Semitic attacks increased, especially because of the economic recession, which intensified feelings of envy and competition and the struggle for survival.

Additionally, the Brazilian Jewish community, like others in Latin America, must bear the onus of the unpopularity of Israel's policies—particularly those of the Likud government—among populist and leftist movements. It is certainly no coincidence that the foreign policies of Brazil, Argentina, and Mexico have tended to defend Third World pro-Palestinian, anti-Israeli positions in almost every international forum in the 1980s.

The changes in economic policy that occur during a transfer of power from the military to the civilian sector are anticipated with fear and distrust by the upper strata of society of which the Jewish population is a part. A feeling of uneasiness and insecurity leads to possible ambivalence in the attitudes and behavior of Jews and of their community leaders toward the progressive democratization of Brazilian society. Faced by the corruption and incompetence of the ruling group and threatened by increasing violence of the mass as a consequence of economic depression, unemployment, and galloping inflation, the middle and upper strata—a minority in defense of their privileges—have developed a whole series of stereotyped prejudices and discriminatory attitudes against potential rivals. Although their motivation may be comprehensible, the effects of such rationalizations are disturbing and give cause for the most serious apprehension as to the future of Jews in Brazilian society.

As with other immigrant groups in a dynamic society, there are clearly contradictory trends and tendencies within the Brazilian Jewish community that may either strengthen or weaken the identity of its members. These trends are intensified by the contradictions inherent in the adoptive society's development process, which oscillates between periods of rather timid attempts to establish a more open, egalitarian, and pluralistic system and long periods of authoritarian and repressive military regimes. As long as this situation of uncertainty and potential threat to property rights persists, the need for security and self-defense may reinforce the search for group identity and therefore the cohesion and solidarity of Jews with their community and its organizations. But this hypothesis does not respond to the crucial question of the future of Brazilian Jews should political turmoil sweep Brazilian society in the future.

10
Jews and the Argentine Center: A Middleman Minority

Bernard E. Segal

Introduction

The best evidence available in the 1960s showed that most Argentines were not anti-Semitic and that among those who were, prejudice did not go beyond the acceptance of certain common stereotypes.[1] But Argentina is a country with an odd juxtaposition of social openness and political closure, so although anti-Semitic campaigns have always failed to arouse much popular enthusiasm, the suspicion lingers that such a campaign might succeed if it were coupled with more appealing programs than those of Argentine right-wing nationalism, the source of the country's clearest expressions of xenophobia in general and anti-Semitism in particular.

Could the reason for Argentina's specialized but nonetheless stubborn and occasionally dangerous antipathy toward Jews be something about the Jews themselves? Before answering, we rush to point out that merely considering the question does not mean accepting either calumnies leveled at Jews for centuries or racial slurs current in the modern era. After all, Herzl himself viewed anti-Semitism as the inevitable result of clashes between different but equally legitimate nationalisms, and nearer our own time, a writer as thoughtful as Hannah Arendt pointed out—as the great Argentine socialist leader Juan Justo once had done—that Jews could hardly expect to be anything but vulnerable if "precisely because they were neither part of

---

1. Gino Germani, "Antisemitismo ideológico y antisemitismo tradicional," *Cuadernos de Comentario* 1 (1963).

class society nor of the state's politically active governing clique, the Jews were oblivious to the increasing tension between state and society... driven toward the center of the conflict because they stood between the two as part of neither."[2]

Providing a complete understanding of the reasons Argentine Jews are in the Argentine center and why the center itself is so often so weak is more than can be accomplished in the space allotted here. Nevertheless, that understanding can be enhanced by calling attention to some ways that Argentine immigration and ethnicity relate to the changing dynamics of Argentine class. It is well known that when Argentina's immigrant-based littoral area early became, then long remained, differentiated from the slower-moving interior, the change included economic and political shifts as well as shifts in status, all of which occurred earlier and were farther reaching than in Latin America generally. Where national majorities were unlike Argentina's, being composed largely of regionally encysted and racially distinct indigenous peoples, the differences between their countries and Argentina were particularly marked.

Immigration's role in changing Argentina's social structure prior to the 1930s has been discussed often; the part played by ethnic or racial elements in the Peronist mobilization of native but neglected underclasses has been discussed less. Nevertheless, both are important to the context, and both have been important to Argentine Jewry. They will first be treated briefly and generally, then more specifically, reviewing and evaluating a crypto-Marxian theory of intergroup relations marked by its assertion that in order to explain prejudice against certain center-bound minorities, it is necessary to concentrate on their socioeconomic performance. At first glance, the theory appears to fit Argentine Jewish circumstances. Closer examination, however, shows that it suffers from a generalized flaw in that it illogically explains antiminority behavior by examining the target rather than the source of that behavior. It also suffers from particular flaws in that, as applied to Argentina, the theory leads first to ignoring some important similarities between Jews and other immigrant groups and then to overemphasizing some of their differences while ignoring others that are more important.

Immigration, Migration, and the Decline of Ethnicity

In 1860, when Argentine civil war put an end to governments of misgovernment under *caudillos,* population became critical to the victors' plans for building and strengthening their nation—new people, not just to

---

2. H. Arendt, *The Jew as Pariah,* ed. R. H. Feldman (New York: Grove Press, 1978), 18.

match and provide labor for expected economic growth, but to transform the nation—to turn it, in the well-known phrase, from barbarism to civilization. Barbarism's home was a huge and rich but untapped and underpopulated land, inhabited by a small number of Indians (whom frontier battles would all but exterminate before long), a mass of passive peons, and equally ignorant but undisciplined frontiersmen. All were separated by an unbridgeable gap from the rather small number of educated people in Buenos Aires who regarded themselves as heirs of the Enlightenment. Immigration would bring hard-working newcomers to work farms and ranches, raising grain and cattle to feed the world, civil newcomers to be part of a harmoniously integrated nation, grateful newcomers to identify completely with their new land, adapting quickly and remaining loyal. Immigrants would resolve the demographic and cultural problems simultaneously. Such was the dream of those who became famous as the liberal oligarchy.

The immigrants themselves—and the Jews among them who began arriving shortly before the turn of the century—shared this vision. They came, they said, to make America—not, as in the case of the United States, to make it *in* America, in a place that had already taken on form and shape. Yet the Argentina that yearned for farmers created hired hands. Skyrocketing land values made a few great families richer but also made it impossible for newcomers to buy their own property or make a go of it as commercial renters. One part of the liberal dream vanished in the immigrant cycle: Disembarking in Buenos Aires, they left the city to farm, but, failing, returned to the great port to meet what soon became a larger number of others who had never left it at all. Together they became an urban working class whose problems and imported ideologies clashed with the old liberal dream, although they had one of their own. Most did not move out of the working class until about 1940.

Even the successful among them could not change the top level of society, although a few were co-opted into it. With the middle classes a virtual vacuum, mobility became the immigrants' province, the center of society their space. But this space remained small, for small business and tiny industry in agro-export Argentina were both vulnerable to foreign competition and susceptible to the vagaries of international economic cycles. Nevertheless, with no competing group to block ascent and a growing urban market to be supplied, some ambulant peddlers and independent craftsmen became shopkeepers and some tavern owners became brewers, cooks, or restaurateurs. Ultimately, their children took advantage of an open educational system that was one of the true gems of the old liberal heritage. Unlike the land-holding elite, which was beginning to think of itself as an aristocracy, a good many immigrants were unabashed risk-takers, unashamed of dirty hands. Unlike the lower classes of rural Argentina, who were still locked in backwater provincialism watched over by landlords desiring power more than wealth and prestige more than both, most immigrants learned quickly to understand and use unions if they stayed working class, as most did, or money and markets if they did not.

By 1920, a far higher proportion of Argentine than of U.S. residents was foreign-born, mostly Spanish and Italian. Their Catholic religion and Mediterranean folk culture eased adaptation to this new country, which had risen in part from similar origins. Indeed, the generally Latin character and Catholic faith of most Argentine immigrants were major elements behind their rapid assimilation, and hence of a rather rapid decline in ethnic pluralism.

The same Depression that ended massive immigration in 1930 provided a few people with a new chance to step ahead. In an enclosed national market, immigrant and immigrant-descended entrepreneurs found interstices to fill, this time with new industries to supply domestic consumers with products that could no longer be imported. Thanks in part to these efforts, by 1940 the Argentine economy was becoming more industrial than agricultural for the first time. The obvious economic development and progressivism of the areas where most immigrants settled still offered a sharp contrast to the backwardness and traditionalism of the rest of the country, where most of the native population lived. But the pattern was changing. Attrition of the original immigrants through death, combined with the continuing upward mobility of others and of the descendants of all, meant that the composition of the urban working class was changing as it grew larger.

Argentines from the interior, some of them driven from the land by the agricultural downturn of the 1930s, filled some old ranks and most of the new, and were soon to appear in greater numbers than Argentina's infant industry could absorb. Still a minority of the total population, the native-born were nonetheless a larger proportion of it than in 1930, an increase due largely to their continued high birth rates after those of immigrant urban Argentina had fallen to European levels.

Meanwhile, the far right struck, spearheaded by the military coup of 1943. The brief fascist experiment, including the strongest state-sponsored strictures against Jews that Argentina has ever known before or since, failed. The Argentine lower and working classes were at that time no serious threat to the social order. In the face of just such a threat, classic European fascism enrolled the middle classes. But Argentine fascism assaulted the middle class instead, curtailing the liberties of faith, education, press, and assembly that even fraudulent leaders of the 1930s had not tried to snuff out.[3] A major

---

3. George L. Blanksten, *Perón's Argentina* (Chicago: University of Chicago Press, 1953). See also Robert J. Alexander, *The Perón Era* (New York: Columbia University Press, 1951), especially Chap. 11, "Church and State in Peron's Argentina"; Felix Weil, *The Argentine Riddle* (New York: The John Day Company, 1944).

concession for 1945, the promise of free elections, was thus an apparent victory for that part of Argentine society the immigrants had done so much to make: an urban, middle-class, secular, liberal democratic, urgent, hustling, shoulder-jostling, arriviste portion of a nation just about to capitalize on the resumption of world trade after World War II. A portion of the nation, however, was surely not the whole, and not even big enough to conquer the polls and certify the ascendancy of its values. Instead, Juan Peron intervened.

Peron, who was part of the junta that took over in 1943, began with no program other than the chauvinism then shared by the church, the armed forces, and a few dissident intellectuals. What sort of ideology was it? Consolidated in the 1930s, it was the product of political alienation, with roots in the Depression. Argentine exports had been cut out of European markets; the response of the great agricultural producers was to use Argentine politics to accommodate Britain's demands in order to keep what shrunken market remained. It was a response that angered right-wing nationalist circles. They were not among Argentina's richest people, but they were reasonably well off, drawn from the lower-middle class on up. They were closely linked to the assertively conservative confessionalism then dominant in the Argentine Church. The right-wing nationalist movement was never very large; lacking in mass appeal, it never formed a party because it was too divided into separate and often quarrelsome coteries. Its members' dedication and social status, along with the stamp of religious legitimation, nevertheless gave it influence beyond its numbers.

Right-wing nationalists believed that only a society that was at once national (i.e., native) and moral (i.e., preconciliar Catholic) could overcome the vices of modernity: weakness and selfishness among individuals, shifting standards that allow arrivistes more influence than the older and once better known, and cleverness and stealth, which were everywhere rewarded more than boldness, courage, and strength. This reactionary package combined a yearning for a predemocratic but postcapitalist corporatist order with a search for a universal disciplined morality. Such was—and still is—Argentine fascism. Although it resorted to racist anti-Semitism, it owed more to the Counter-Reformation than to any modern form of bigotry and depended for its ideology on Primo de Rivera and Franco more than on Hitler. Argentine *nacionalismo* was not accompanied by Wagner or Strauss, but played out to the strains of tangos mourning the loss of youth's chaste love and yesterday's dreams. Few chose to dance; many had to listen.

Argentine right-wing nationalism had three targets. One was the landowning oligarchy, now castigated both for its role at the beginning of the nineteenth-century takeoff—when it had been liberal in more than Manchesterian, laissez-faire economics—and for its actions in the present, when, thanks to its dependence on Britain, free trade was the only article of liberalism it still stood for. The oligarchy could protect itself; from 1932 until 1943 the army was its instrument and every national government its creature. The other two targets were more vulnerable. One was political democracy or any organized expression of it—especially the Radical Party, which could still win elections if given the chance, and, further to the left, the Progressive Democrats and Socialists. Both Democrats and Socialists were seen as no different from Communists, since in the right-wing nationalist world view, the choice was simply Christ or Lenin.

The third target was the Jews, a people who obviously chose not to choose Christ. Anti-Semitism was so central to the doctrine of every right nationalist faction that it lent thematic unity to the movement as a whole.[4] For right-wing nationalists, the equation still held: Jews equaled Russians equaled Bolsheviks, a formula tying together the old and the new in Catholic formulations, the two coils of church propaganda of the time. (Elsewhere in this hemisphere, similar views appeared contemporaneously in French Canada, while in the United States they were being disseminated by Fr. Charles Coughlin.) One of these coils was the ancient concern over Jews as subversive nonbelievers; the other, an effort to assign responsibility for a world moving so fast that it appeared to be slipping from the control of those who thought they had the right and the obligation to impose morality upon it. The Argentine right saw the new times as a swirling morass of atomization without guidance or compass. Events seemed to be freeing classes, not just individuals, to act for themselves. Indeed, along with the misery, the Depression had spread cynicism about the old verities of home and honor, dignity and security. As old certainties fell away, right-wing nationalists glimpsed the shadow of the most unspeakable of phantoms, a class war that would forever destroy the ordered harmony among different social ranks.

Juan Peron changed class relations but never threatened class war, in part because he led his movement from the top down. Peron amended right-wing nationalism, adding substance to rhetoric in a class and cultural appeal to low-ranking native Argentinians, in particular to the new migrants to the cities. For eighty years they had been ignored or despised. Now he told them that Argentine authenticity lay with them—the *pueblo,* the folk. He became their benefactor, spokesman, patron, tutor. His Argentina, he promised, would resolve their oppression and turn their shame to pride. He asked only their devotion in return. Devotion is free. The poorest of poor people can give it away, and they gave it to him gladly.

---

4. Marysa Navarro, *Argentine Nationalism of the Right,* Sage Publications, Studies in Comparative International Development, vol. 1, no. 12, 1965.

The flush of Peronist electoral victory was Peron's reward for having learned to play themes of the troubled 1930s as folk music. The far right had conjured up the myth of a past resting on country people of the interior subjugated but intrinsically bold and independent, simple and unsullied, untouched and unstained by modernity's corrupt commerce and compromising politics. This was pure nativism, worshipful of tradition and order, thoroughly anti-Semitic, and treating people as symbols, not as participants. This was the nativism Peron alloyed and strengthened with populism and nationalism, but not, be it noted, with race or ethnicity. Kalman Silvert noted with special emphasis that the absence of racism was an important reason Peronism could not be considered fascist.[5] Others may disagree, unwilling to grant that racism is one of fascism's essentials. But apart from a brief flirtation with anti-Semitism when he was closer to the right-wing nationalists (and which he later disavowed), Peron was not racist, nor did he ever intimate that immigrant Argentina was not entitled to a place in the nation. The entrepreneurs of the 1930s prospered under his regime, expanding their businesses in the industrial boom of his first Presidential term. Peron vilified and offended the rich and powerful; he used force and the threat of force to bend many others to his will, including some of his own lieutenants. He was a bully, a bully who suffered bigots, but he was not one of them.

But what of his opposition and its hatred of his following? Was this not bigotry? Was Argentina really, as Gino Germani once wrote, a country "remarkably free of racial prejudice?"[6] Better-off people in Argentina had looked down on rural native Argentines since at least 1860, to say nothing of the colonial era. Much later, wasn't similar disdain apparent when city dwellers called Peron's migrants *cabecitas negras* (little black heads)? Didn't Jews share it as part of the urban and indubitably white Argentine majority? Wasn't this arguably racial hatred?

At an earlier date, when immigration was supposed to improve inferior native stock, it was conveniently assumed that cultures were products of heredity. Yet there never was a time in late colonial or postindependence Argentina when there was much physical ground for distinguishing native Argentines from others. Argentina did not have a large Indian population like that of Bolivia or Peru, and Argentine mesticization was far advanced as early as the turn of the nineteenth century. Further, even in more Indian

---

5. Kalman Silvert, "Argentina: The Politics of Anti-Nationalism," in K. Silvert (ed.), *Expectant Peoples* (New York: Random House, 1963).

6. Gino Germani, "Argentine Peronism," in *Authoritarianism, Fascism, and National Populism* (New Brunswick, N.J.: Transaction Books, 1978).

parts of Latin America racial assignment is flexible, as much a matter of culture as of physical appearance and resting on variables such as language, dress, work, and money. Consider too that the word *criollo,* so often taken in Argentine usage as synonymous with rural native culture rather than with the culture of urban immigrants, is far more national than racial. Also, there was a great excess of males over females among the immigrants, and many married *criollas,* making populations that were already physically indistinct at their margins even more so. There is no gainsaying that the term *cabecitas negras* does have racial overtones.

Despite all this, and taking into account that the far more common term for the native newcomers in the Peron years was the political one *descamisados* (shirtless ones), it seems safe to conclude that opposition to Peronism, like Peronism itself, rested more on differences of income, status, and political allegiance than on race, ethnicity, or any combination of the two.

A Middle Muddle

The relationship between prejudice and Peronism demonstrates in an especially critical case how class and status, not race and ethnicity, have been the stuff of Argentine political acrimony. Attitudes toward Jews have frequently been exceptions to this rule, however, just as Argentine Jews have themselves been somewhat exceptional. The rapid decline of Argentine ethnic pluralism previously alluded to has had a good deal to do with both exceptions. It left Jews in a position where they seemed in some ways to be Argentina's only ethnic group. They were clearly acculturated, but they also remained internally organized and retained their Jewishness as a core aspect of their group and individual identity. Most other immigrants and their descendants were becoming more completely and more simply Argentinians. Class was becoming the major fracture line of Argentine society.

Back when he was more a Hegelian philosopher than an economist, and while he was probably working through some of his own ethnic self-hatred, the first great spokesman for class conflict had written "On the Jewish Question," noting in one of its less vitriolic passages that "The Jew has emancipated himself in a Jewish manner, not only by acquiring the power of money, but also because money has become, through him and also apart from him, a world power, while the practical Jewish spirit has become the practical spirit of the Christian nations. The Jews have emancipated themselves insofar as the Christians have become Jews."[7] Marx on the Jews would ultimately come to be read, at least by admirers wishing to avoid embarrassment to themselves and their mentor, as having viewed the Jews as no more than secondary actors. In the more abstract formulation, history, having set Jews aside and having kept them apart from the heart of medieval society, had given them the chance to move the present along by eating away at the decay of a rotting feudalism like so many helpful capitalist microbes. They might be condemned for their part in helping introduce the modern era (which conservatives hated as much as Marx did), but could nonetheless join everyone else in that future where all would be caught up in the transformation from capitalism to socialism, a change that would have as one of its side effects the end of all religious obscurantism, Christian as well as Jewish.

Whether for curing the Jewish problem or the problems of society in general, the Argentine right has of course been bitterly opposed to Marx's or anyone else's leftist radical therapy. Nevertheless, though almost surely unwittingly, it adopted and has kept parts of Marx's views on Jews—but only the ones that contained more diagnosis than prescription, that centered more on the Jews than on the class order as a whole, and that therefore may owe more to conservative than to radical thought.

The tenor of accusations against Argentine Jews has been familiar enough: Jews were money managers in a society where money should not matter, covering constant profit searching with the pretense of unique religious practice. If Jewish religion alone was not sufficient evidence of failure to understand the notion of lives devoted to spirit, Jewish arch materialism was, whether it was that of shopkeepers or that of Marxists. Moreover, Jews did not have a nation, and so could not understand national loyalty; or, if they did have a nation, it was foreign, so their loyalty to Argentina was suspect. Because they chose to be outsiders, they had themselves to blame for not feeling secure. Angered and embittered Red Shylocks, in constant hidden battle against Portia and Providence, cultivated shrewdness in order to outwit others in the marketplace, dupe the innocent, and manipulate the powerful.

Of all the distinctions between powerful but decadent Buenos Aires and the genuine but dominated interior, none have ever been sharper or more vicious than the twisted caricatures that contrast naive provincials with conniving urban speculators such as Jews. Although these distortions have clearly been drawn to fit the Argentine context, they have a wider

---

7. Karl Marx, "On the Jewish Question," in Robert C. Tucker (ed.), *The Marx–Engels Reader* (New York: W. W. Norton, 1978), 49.

familiarity, and demonstrate Arnold Rose's thesis that anti-Semitism generally has its roots in city-hatred.[8] As in Russia, France, Poland, and Germany, the nourishing of these stereotypes in Argentina has represented both elitist distaste for the flavor of haggling and the market and an attempt to win the support of the masses for a crusade against their purported exploiters. In the 1920s, members of other groups had been damned on similar grounds, blamed for their rising class standing and their alleged opportunism during the long period of Argentina's growth and expansion. Later, Jews alone were blamed; *judíos* became virtually synonymous with *Rusos* and with "foreign Argentina." Jewish prosperity was seen not as a consequence of generalized economic and social change, but of Jewish clannishness and sharp practice.

Through the 1930s, Jewish race was another alleged source of unwholesome characteristics. Racist views have now gone out of fashion, but not certain other perspectives that explain prejudice by finding its proximate causes in social structure and its immediate ones in the behavior of its victims. Edna Bonacich's essay "A Theory of Middleman Minorities"[9] is a short but influential work of this type. In order to explain a widespread form of prejudice and discrimination, she assayed minorities such as Chinese and Japanese immigrants as well as Jews, but used the latter most extensively in making her argument. To take one example, Bonacich cited Max Weber's reference to Jews as a group typifying more rigorous intragroup than intergroup moral standards. Bonacich did not allude to Argentina or Argentine sources, but offered her work as a general theory, thereby implying that it ought also apply to places she did not mention. Moreover, because Argentine Jews meet her defining middleman criteria—they are neither so poor and controlled as native masses nor so secure and well off as native elites—her work could conceivably be applied to them quite easily. Indeed, if Argentine sources had come to her attention, she could have found a great many comments to support her views, especially items bearing on the suggestion that Argentine anti-Semitism would cease if only Jews forsook ingroup solidarity and aligned themselves with one or another of their country's mainstream political tendencies.[10] Her thesis, in brief, is that majority

---

8. Arnold Rose, "Anti-Semitism's Root in City-Hatred," *Commentary* 6 (October 1948): 374–378.

9. Edna Bonacich, "A Theory of Middleman Minorities," in Norman R. Yetman and C. Hoy Steele (eds.), *Majority and Minority: The Dynamics of Racial and Ethnic Relations* (Boston: Allyn and Bacon, 1975).

10. Juan Jose Sebreli, *La cuestión judía en la Argentina* (Buenos Aires: Tiempo Contemporáneo, 1968); Samuel Tarnopolsky, *Los prejuiciados de honrado conciencia* (Buenos Aires: Editorial Candelabro, 1971). Moreover, "it was . . . a small step for Justo to write another essay entitled, 'Why I Do not Wish to Write for a Jewish Publication,' in which he charged the Jews with opposing the formation of a national consciousness by their stubborn refusal to abandon their Jewish heritage."

hostility toward minority groups who prosper more than native masses but are nonetheless denied entrance to native elites is best explained by the minorities' own qualities. Their socioeconomic orientations and performances, their actions and their successes, are what cause dislike, not their cultural (including religious) and/or racial distinctiveness or their interstitial position as people who maintain commercial but otherwise distant relations with the masses while serving as buffers and scapegoats for elites, which simply heightens their minority vulnerability.

Arguments to support these points commence with what Bonacich calls "sojourning," the idea that middleman minorities do not expect to remain permanently in the countries they enter as immigrants but plan instead to return to homelands either in the countries from which they emigrated or, as in the Jewish case, to a place where they resided long ago before their group scattered. Because of this sojourning, especially if something about the middlemen's old-country culture encourages and enables them to do so, group members in their new societies prefer to enter economic activities of a kind where they can keep their resources liquid. Thus, rather than investing in land or fixed industry, they tend to engage in activities where their own skills are at a premium, using "capital of the mind" rather than material capital to generate assets that are convertible to cash or are more portable and valuable than cash itself. Beginning poor, however, they band together for mutual assistance, relying on kinship and common background to root intragroup trust; simultaneously, to minimize their involvements with others, they avoid local politics and start schools of their own to watch over the socialization of their children.[11] Their social organization promotes their economic activities because emphasis on loyalty to the group, support, cooperation, and informal social control all play an important part in their lives. They specialize in a limited set of business activities such as the garment industry, laundries, rug dealing, grocery distribution, or food preparation and service; group wholesalers sell to group retailers, and both rely on the same sources of group-generated credit. Rapid upward mobility for many group members and an economic standing

---

11. At the outset of their emigration to the West before their acculturation began, full-blown religious orthodoxy, or its remnants in daily life, went a considerable way toward explaining Jews' social solidarity and occupational forms. Jews of the time ate kosher food. Where was it to be found if not in Jewish homes or in a Jewish neighborhood? The Jewish Sabbath, more likely to be honored then than now, was Saturday. Who could honor it without being self-employed or working for another Jew? Bonacich's bare mention of middlemen's old-country cultures in combination with her lack of references to specific cultural details may be pardonable, due simply to lack of space. Nevertheless, the omissions make her case for the purely situational determinants of middleman performances and subsequent native hostility appear stronger than they would be if other relevant matters were considered.

so high for the group as a whole result, despite the presence of some group members who do not succeed as well as others, that most members not only become reluctant to return to their place of origin (as they had originally intended), but remain closely knit to retain economic advantage already won. The group's strong internal cohesiveness therefore becomes one of the reasons for host hostility toward it, manifested in accusations of disloyalty, especially if group members retain ties of sentiment, commerce, or charity to kin abroad. Because the group has prospered, such hostility is intertwined with host antipathy stemming from any or all of three host society segments: clients in the indigenous mass, who feel they have been duped by operators shrewder than themselves; the native laboring class, who object to the group's use of kinfolk, compatriots, or coreligionists working in family firms under conditions that natives may regard as scarcely tolerable and as therefore unfair to "regular" workers (some of whom may additionally resent the ethnic division of labor's solidarity); and actual or prospective host business competitors, who believe they face hurdles that members of a closed group can overcome more easily thanks to the help they reserve for and provide to one another.

Of the many reasons it is unreasonable to account for Argentine anti-Semitism in terms of this theory, several concern unique particulars of Jews as Argentine immigrants; others concern points Jews have in common with others. To begin with the most obvious and least open to dispute: The reputation of Jews in Argentina as clannish dissenters and urban sharp-dealers preceded their immigration to that country, binding them to an image no more based on experience with them then than when Argentina's right-wing nationalists capitalized on it a full forty years later, when most Jews had become significantly acculturated. Note also that an important proportion of the earliest Jewish settlers in Argentina settled on the land, an act of more than symbolic significance—proof of their intention to stay rather than sojourn. In fact, most of the rest of the Jewish Argentine immigrants were not sojourners either. Unlike many of the Spanish and Italian men who came and went with harvest seasons, Jews more frequently emigrated and settled in family units (which explains why relatively few intermarried with natives). Despite the dreams some harbored for Zion, most regarded Argentina as their home from the start; Zionism as geographic nationalism was the ideology of a minority. Argentine Jews were also less likely than other immigrants either to consider or actually to return to their countries of origin, which had scarcely been—especially Czarist Russia—pleasant places for them. Today too, although Zionist sympathies have been far more widespread since World War II than they ever were before, the traditional Passover wish "next year in Jerusalem" remains more a hope for tourist visits than an expression of longing for a new home.

In economic matters, it is probably true, extrapolating from data of the United States of the time, that the bulk of Argentine Jewish immigrants had a somewhat higher level of skill than other Argentine immigrants did. What is more certain and more important, however, is that *all* of the Argentine immigrants, and not just the Jews, had advantages over the native Argentine underclass. The Jews' economic concentration in areas such as the needle trades rested on artisan skills brought with them from Europe, not on a desire for easily liquidated assets. Further, many of the ubiquitous ambulant peddlers had not been tradesmen before, but peddled because there was no market for skills they brought with them. Their gradually increasing prosperity, dependent on investment and reinvestment, was hardly evidence of preparation for their moving on or moving back to where they had originated.

In matters combining class with status group, according to Bonacich, a hallmark of the middleman minority is that economic activity takes a preindustrial capitalist form, oriented to rational profit seeking but bound by kinship, nepotism, and group particularity. In Argentina, however, many observers have noted that the second set of cultural patterns is characteristic of the economy as a whole.[12] But these patterns were never unique among Jews. Further, although Bonacich made much of the economic advantages of continued group membership, her theory cannot explain why most Argentine Jews, who could assimilate if they so choose, remain solidary even now, when most material advantages of group cohesiveness have disappeared and when being identified as Jewish can be economically disadvantageous, closing off certain careers, especially with the state.

Further, in economic activities, social organization, educational preferences, and political participation, Jews were not and are not unique among other immigrants to Argentina and their descendants. Jews were early entrepreneurs, but so were others such as the Basques; others were more responsible than both, because their numbers were larger, for the spread of commerce in Buenos Aires. Similarly, solidary social organization based on ties of kinship and common regional origin were the characteristic forms of all the immigrants' earliest formal social associations. Again, most Jewish youngsters attended public schools, as did the youngsters of other groups; although it may have been true that Jews had more schools of their own than did some other Argentine ethnic groups, there were others who had them and who, if their wealth and standing had risen enough, relied

---

12. Tomás R. Fillol, *Social Factors in Economic Development: The Argentine Case* (Cambridge, Mass.: The M.I.T. Press, 1961). For a more general treatment purporting to cover Latin America in general, see S. M. Lipset, "Values, Education, and Entrepreneurship," in S. M. Lipset and A. Solari (eds.), *Elites in Latin America.*

more than Jews of equivalent rank upon private schools, especially those associated with the Church. And in politics, where no Argentine immigrant groups voted in large numbers, the Jews were also no exception—although later, again parallel to the others, second-generation Jews did become both voters and office holders.

The greatest of the Jews' distinctions from other Argentine immigrants was therefore not that the Jews were middlemen—indeed, until the 1940s, most were workers—but that they were not Latin, not Mediterranean, and, most important, not Catholic. When Jews worshiped, it was not in parish churches; when Jews had private schools, they were not Church schools; when Jews were endogamous, it was to prevent conversion and absorption; and when Jews established charities it was because the state had none, because they had no Church that had any either, and because they were under a religious obligation of their own to do so. In the same vein, it is surely significant that what ultimately became the AMIA, the umbrella organization of the Buenos Aires Jewish community, began not as a business or political association, but as a burial society.

We should also take note of some other atypical immigrant groups in Argentina, groups that ranked too high to be thought of as middlemen at all. Anglo-Argentines had a critical place as managers of railroads, public utilities, packing plants, and major commercial outlets of the domestic market. Culturally distant and socially separate, the Anglo-Argentines were largely endogamous, English-speaking, and Protestant. They continued to call England home even after generations of residence in Argentina. There was always a good deal of Argentine antipathy toward England and the English, but not toward the Anglo-Argentines, despite the transparency of Anglo-Argentine encystedness, disdain for Argentine mass culture, and split loyalties. Indeed, just about the only senses in which Anglo-Argentines were not middlemen were their wealth and influence, the interests they shared with the Argentine elite, and the foreign-owned assets they managed. These were not the only reasons they escaped the sting of discrimination and hatred that Jews experienced, however. Along with Germans and French, who were in many ways similar to them, Anglo-Argentines had a home country that commanded respect. Jews did not. All were of Western European background and so came from a preferred aesthetic and cultural type. Jews did not. All spoke a major foreign language thought useful for well-educated Argentines to know. Jews did not. And of course all of them, including the Protestants, worshiped Christ, whereas Jews did not.

In the end, what is particularly striking about the fact that these groups did not experience prejudice as much as the Jews did is that all three came closer than Jews to fulfilling the specific criterion—economic influence—upon which Bonacich most relied for supplying a rationale for host society prejudice. Her emphasis on economic power is too important to pass over lightly:

> The resistance to assimilation of sojourning middleman communities would be no problem for the host society if these groups were economically isolated. Groups like the Amish, who preserve cultural distinctiveness but combine it with economic self-sufficiency, do not provoke the same concern. However, middleman minorities develop great economic power in a country toward which they feel essentially alien. Such power appears devastating to host members, who believe their country is being "taken over" by an alien group.
>
> I hope the reader is convinced that host members have reason for feeling hostile toward middleman groups. Perhaps you are saying, "Yes, there is a rational component, but the extremity of the host reaction reveals a strong irrational force at work. Middlemen may be felt to compete unfairly, they may even appear dangerously disloyal, but surely the reactions to them are out of proportion to the offense? Usually these groups are tiny minorities with little or no political power. Is it necessary to incarcerate them, as were the Japanese in World War II; to expel them, as were the Asians of Uganda; or to dislocate them, as occurred in the Group Areas Act of South Africa? Surely these acts mark hysteria and deep-seated hatred."
>
> While some irrational elements are probably at work, even the extremity of the host reaction can be understood as "conflict" behavior. The reason is that the economic and organizational power of middleman groups makes them extremely difficult to dislodge. For example, their wealth enables them to use bribery when necessary, another charge often leveled against these groups. The Chinese in Southeast Asia illustrate the point. . . . The difficulty of breaking entrenched middleman monopolies, the difficulty of controlling the growth and extension of their economic power, pushes host countries to ever more extreme reactions. One finds increasingly harsh measures, piled on one another, until, when all else fails, "final solutions" are enacted.[13]

This quotation should be analyzed serially. First, a group "like the Amish" has never been thought other than white or other than Christian. Next, the author's attribution of alien feelings to middleman groups gets converted just a sentence later to alienness as objective, true condition. What might "alien feelings" mean? Many nations have such diverse traditions that it is quite possible for minorities to feel closely identified with one stream of value and belief, such as voluntary assimilationism, and alien with respect to another, such as nationalistic nativism. On this, Argentina is an especially clear case in point.

It is loading the dice to make the irrationality in host hostility only "probable" while middleman power is left unmodified as if it were fact. It is artifice to state that hosts can find reasons for antipathy toward minorities (only fools could not) without considering how accurate are the percep-

13. Bonacich, "Theory of Middleman Minorities."

tions on which the reasons are based. It is slippery conceptual shorthand to call discrimination "conflict" behavior as if the description were an explanation, particularly if the reference reminds readers of Marx, a father of conflict theory and one who never regarded middlemen as any better than unproductive parasites. It is inconsistent first to cite cases of middleman minorities who were easily pushed around and then to follow with a statement that middleman groups are too powerful and too well entrenched to be treated that way; a mistake to suggest, especially when writing of societies in which suborning officialdom is a way of life, that only middleman minorities are rich enough to offer bribes (and an egregious omission to say nothing of the bribe takers); and finally, the sheerest sort of carelessness to write of "final solutions" as if the quotation marks made jailing the same as expulsion, or either one the same as genocide.

Conclusions

Directed against a group that stayed somewhat distinct but made some money, anti-Semitism has been a favorite form of Argentine ethnic antipathy, an exception to the rule of no prejudice, and a use of an ethnic scapegoat in a country almost without others (it is practically without Indians and virtually without blacks). To explain anti-Semitism, Argentine society itself must be examined. Because space limitations prevent a full examination here, a few notes must suffice.

The queen said to have pawned her jewels to pay for Columbus's first voyage to America is known in the Spanish-speaking world as Isabela la Catolica. Her firm attachment to her faith is just one reason for the name. Another is that her husband, in order to unite Spain, expelled the Moors and the Jews, its two quintessential middleman minorities. Argentina's unification campaigns are more contemporary. They have utilized a wide range of justifications for enforcing true belief: religious conviction, racial homogeneity, nativist patriotism, national security, populist consensus, and economic necessity. Each could be and has been defined as a legitimate and even "reasonable" reason for anti-Semitism. But the core of Argentine anti-Semitism, contrary to Bonacich's hypotheses, does not lie with migrant masses, or labor, or prospective business competitors. Instead, it is to be found among people on the nonlaboring, noncommercial right, among people who grind antimodernist and antiliberal axes as weapons for the defense of a well-worked and well-established Weltanschauung with roots in the Counter-Reformation aspect of Hispanic tradition. As for the left, with the exception of a few fanatics who drift from right to left and back again in search of the cleansing fire of national renovation, the threat is less to Jews as Jews than as property owners like others, and to civil liberties, on which Jews depend more than others.

Nearly five centuries ago there were Spaniards in what is now Argentina who were fixated on *limpieza de sangre,* fearing *conversos'* penetration as much as Jewish heresy. In Buenos Aires today, preconciliar spiritual heirs of Torquemada are still capable of believing that moral rot lies hidden in illustrious Argentine families with distant Sephardic forbears who had escaped from Inquisition Spain and Portugal. Such an idea might be dismissed for the absurdity it is if Argentina were a country with a genuinely open political system to match its splendid history of social receptivity to newcomers. As long as it is not such a country, however, the drumbeat of anti-Semitism will go on. Few there have ever marched to it. But those few, covered by a veil of respectability, are occasionally able to whisper in the ears of the powerful, some of whom also dream of a "true" Argentina resting upon a single unquestionable, uniform, and unchanging Argentine identity. Impossible to realize in so various a society, the dream still lingers, offering false hope of closing class fissures and healing political fractures and leaving open to suspicion any whose private loyalties both signal and depend upon attachment to pluralistic diversity.

11
Costa Rican Jewry: An Economic and Political Outline

Lowell Gudmundson

Introduction

The history of the Jewish community in Costa Rica has been basically that of the Polish immigrants of the 1930s and 1940s and their descendants, so much so that today the terms *polaco* (Pole) and *judío* (Jew) are still often used interchangeably in popular speech. Although Costa Rica did receive a small number of late nineteenth and early twentieth century Jewish immigrants of Sephardic origin, as well as some South American Jews after 1970, of the 743 Jews in Costa Rica in 1941 fully 700 were of Polish origin. In the period 1929–1939 nearly 600 Polish Jews migrated to Costa Rica; an additional 200 or so arrived shortly after World War II. In 1978 the population of the Costa Rican Jewish community was estimated at 411 families or 1586 individuals, perhaps 10% of whom were of post-1970 South American origin and the rest of Polish descent.[1]

This comparatively minuscule immigration of Polish Jews in the 1930s led to the formation of a very tightly knit community of several hundred individuals who, by the 1950s, were highly conscious of their shared culture and position in the host society. The solidarity of the community was

---

1. Jacobo Schifter Sikora, Lowell Gudmundson, and Mario Solera, *El judío en Costa Rica* (San José: Editorial Universidad Estatal a Distancia, 1979), 94–95, 146. Initially, children born locally but of immigrant parents were considered to be foreigners as well. For further details and testimony on the myriad community issues not dealt with in this brief overview, consult this work.

further reinforced by sporadic outbursts of creole anti-Semitism, by a shared immigrant experience from residence to initial occupation, and perhaps most importantly by common village origin in Poland. These features of Costa Rican Jewry and its historical development are the focus of this chapter. An attempt will be made to tie these features of past experience to the contemporary situation and prospects of the local Jewish community.

Immigrants and Their Occupational Experience

The first Jews to settle in Costa Rica arrived late in the nineteenth century.[2] They were often associated with Caribbean or North Atlantic trading houses and of Sephardic origin. These few immigrant merchants, perhaps only one or two dozen at most, were uniformly well placed in the local socioeconomic structure, at times even occupying political or civic office in Costa Rica.[3] Moreover, one particular immigrant merchant, from Austria by way of Argentina, played a central role in the early history of the Polish community. Enrique Yankelewitz founded a department store that was perhaps the single major source of cloth and garments on consignment to the ambulatory Jewish merchants within the later Polish emigrant group. Yankelewitz, with his Mil Colores store, was the first employer for a substantial number of the immigrants of the 1930s.

The first few Polish Jews to arrive in Costa Rica came in the late 1920s. They were young men with some resources and industrial or commercial expertise. Whether owners of small shops or artisans in Poland, these individuals brought with them small sums, the tools of their trade, and, most importantly, the commercial and industrial know-how to establish themselves in the host society. These early settlers were soon followed by family and friends, forming a tiny community first to the north of the central

---

[2]. Several Costa Rican authors have claimed that many early colonial settlers were *conversos* (Jews forced to convert to Catholicism in Spain) or Sephardic Jews. Similar references appear in the case of Antioquia, Colombia, an assertion that is used to explain a notable degree of entrepreneurial dynamism. However, no solid evidence is offered for either Colombia or Costa Rica. See Samuel Stone, *La dinastía de los conquistadores* (San José: Editorial Universitaria Centroamericana, 1975); Gonzalo Chacón, *Costa Rica es distinta en Hispanoamérica* (San José: Editorial Trejos Hermanos, 1969); and Ann Twinam, *Miners, Merchants, and Farmers in Colonial Colombia* (Austin: University of Texas Press, 1982).

[3]. Representative figures were Moisés Maduro, a merchant from St. Thomas, Virgin Islands, appointed to public office before 1880; Alfredo Sasso Robles, of Panamanian origin, who became head of the Costa Rican Chamber of Commerce and candidate for national Deputy in 1930; and Max Fischel of the United States. Fischel combined dentistry, retail pharmaceutical sales, and land speculation during the 1920s.

market district of San José and then increasingly south and west of the city center.

Of a group of 210 Polish Jews who emigrated to Costa Rica between 1933 and 1936, the high point of arrivals, fully 38% came from just two Polish settlements: Zellochow (45), a shoemaker's village of 5000 souls (40% Jewish) southeast of Warsaw, and Ostrowietz (35), a city of 50,000 further south of Zellochow. An additional 9% (19) came from Warsaw itself, and no other point of origin could account for over 5% of the sample.[4] The Zellochow group came from an overwhelmingly artisan-based community, which had developed one-piece shoe manufacturing for the Russian peasant market. After Polish independence in 1919, this market was soon lost and the village Jewish community entered a period of crisis and decline, which eventually led to significant emigration to Costa Rica and elsewhere.[5]

The Polish Jews who arrived in Costa Rica during the 1930s were drawn from a traditional *shtetl* (village) background, nonorthodox in religion and politically largely inactive. Their occupational experience ranged from that of laborer in artisanry, to craftsman, to shop or store owner, but the commercial or artisan professions were nearly universal within the group. Their educational attainment had been very limited in Poland, but they brought with them commercial and technical skills that, together with their literacy and immigrant solidarity, provided them with major advantages within contemporary Costa Rican society. Between 1930 and 1950 a similar community occupational structure, ranging from clerk or laborer to shop owner, was recreated in Costa Rica, but it evolved rather quickly toward higher status and greater wealth across the board than had been the case in Poland. Eventually, clerks and laborers became petty shop owners, while at the higher level the ownership of major commercial and industrial enterprises replaced mere shopkeeping as the mark of distinction within the local community.

Upon their arrival in the Costa Rica of the 1930s most adult males worked for a time in the employ of one of the earlier, more wealthy immigrants, or took up ambulatory sales of cloth and garments on consignment from these same individuals. The early Polish arrivals had not all reached this level of activity, to be sure, but the Yankelewitz family and its Mil Colores department store served as initial employer of many of these arriving in the early to mid-1930s. These ambulatory consignee merchants (*buhonero* in Spanish, *klapper* in Yiddish) developed a circuit and clientele they serviced periodically, both to offer new items and, more importantly,

4. Schifter et al., *El judío,* 106.
5. Schifter et al., *El judío,* 102–103, citing Mr. José Rochwerger as the source of this information.

to collect installment payments on past sales. This development of installment credit to the lower orders was by all accounts a Jewish innovation in Costa Rican commerce, and is referred to today generically as *pagos a lo polaco* (Polish payments). It was precisely this practice that helps to explain, in part, such early success and rapid establishment as independent shopkeepers on the basis of ambulatory consignment sales and profits.

The importance of this consignment system for the early immigrants and the speed with which many became independent merchants can be seen in the account books of the period kept by the Mil Colores department store. In 1934 all 99 of the consignees listed were Polish Jews, with an average outstanding balance of over 500 *colones* (about $250). In 1935 about 100 of the 120 consignees were Jewish, 59 of 63 in 1936, 30 of 47 in 1937, and only 27 of 85 in 1939.[6] It appears that the period of greatest profitability for Mil Colores was that of the war years of 1939–1945,[7] and by this period former consignees had also achieved shopkeeper status and withdrawn from the ranks of the door-to-door peddlers. Even so, the colloquial term *polaquear* is still used to describe ambulatory or circuit sales on credit of cloth and garments carried out by both local and immigrant merchants.

The extent of this occupational and proprietary advancement can be further seen in the legislatively mandated census of the Jewish community in 1941.[8] Although 76 of the 218 males registered were still *buhoneros*, fully 99 were independent shopkeepers. In addition, there were 13 artisans, 5 in leatherworking, 3 merchant manufacturers of food products and furniture, and, most importantly, 6 manufacturers of clothing (3 of whom were also major merchants).

Despite the obvious improvement in the economic standing of nearly all members of the community over the 1930s, the differences between shopkeeper and traveling salesman, between manufacturer and shopkeeper, remained and were perhaps magnified in the process of community formation. In an internally generated 1952 census of Jewish employers we capture a glimpse of the great disparity between the few industrialists and the shopkeeper majority.[9] In 1952 Jewish employers were heavily concentrated in two basic activities: clothing manufacture (52% of the 1283 workers employed in the average month by the 146 employers reporting) and

6. Schifter et al., *El judío*, 154.
7. Schifter et al., *El judío*, 155.
8. Schifter et al., *El judío*, 168, citing the San José newspaper *La Tribuna*, 7 March 1941, and its report on the legislative inquiry report.
9. Schifter et al., *El judío*, 170–172, citing data contained in the private archive of the Centro Israelita Sionista de Costa Rica in San José.

clothing and garment retail sales (27%). Without distinguishing between manufacture and retail sales (a distinction that would prove false in practice because major industrialists were themselves merchants first), we can judge the size disparity of community enterprise by the following figures. Those firms that employed fewer than 5 salaried workers accounted for fully 68% (100 of 146 cases) of all firms, but only 16.8% of all workers (214 of 1283). Thus, the typical Jewish shopkeeper employed only 1 in 6 workers, by this time nearly all native Costa Ricans. Those firms that employed 5–20 workers made up 18.5% of all firms, with 23.1% of employees; those few firms employing over 20 workers accounted for 13% (19 cases) of firms but fully 60.2% (773) of workers. The largest of these industrial firms, a clothing manufacturing plant, employed an average of 80 workers per month during 1952, whereas the community-wide employer average was but 2.7 workers.

This story of economic advance, albeit highly uneven and unequal during the 1930s and 1940s, has continued along parallel lines into the present. The few major firms within the community further accelerated their expansion during the 1960s with the stimulus of the Central American Common Market. Today, any further expansion is increasingly based on exports either to the United States or to other nontraditional markets in the Caribbean. Perhaps the single major divergence from the pattern revealed by the 1952 employer census is that of the emergence of a second generation of Jewish professionals and academics since the early 1970s, which will be discussed further.

Anti-Semitism in Costa Rican Politics

Soon after their arrival, Polish Jews became a topic of general social and political commentary, not all of it disinterested or favorable. Those opposed to or simply critical of this immigration did not immediately resort to open anti-Semitism of the kind that later surfaced in the rhetoric of the "Polish plague" or "odious Jew" variety. However, as early as 1936 the political opposition was pillorying three-time President Ricardo Jiménez for his "favoritism" toward questionable immigration and "undesirable" elements. In addition to their attacks on the legality of earlier immigration, the critics alleged that the peddlers carried Communist propaganda in their bundles, that upon entry they had promised to become farmers rather than merchants, and that they were undesirables in general. Ultimately, the commercial competition offered by the newcomers was the source of most irritation. The other charges, immigration irregularities included, were so vague or fanciful as to be easily dispatched with a pamphlet that was equally intended to rebut the charges and ridicule those making them.[10]

This initial polemic over the *polacos* coincided with the 1936 presidential election. The winning candidate, the conservative León Cortés, was closely identified in the public mind with the anti-Jewish position, as well as being viscerally anti-Jiménez. Cortés and his administration (1936–1940) have also been considered by historians as perhaps the high point of Costa Rican anti-Semitism.[11] Cortés did not make the Polish question a major issue early in his term, limiting himself to the naming of a German citizen, Max Effinger, to head the immigration service. Effinger did, on occasion, deny entry to those "not of Aryan race" or the like, but even this policy was circumvented quite frequently by relatives of those already resident in Costa Rica.[12] Nevertheless, Cortés did allow 159 Polish Jews to enter the country over his four-year term, a significant reduction from the 50–80 per year of the earlier administration, but hardly a radical closing of the borders. Moreover, during the 1940 election campaign and thereafter, the Cortés administration was actually criticized by the triumphant candidate, Rafael Angel Calderón Guardia, for having been too lax in this regard.[13]

During the waning months of his administration Cortés had begun to stiffen his policies on immigration and Jewish registration and control in general. In 1939 only 14 Jewish immigrants were admitted and only 2 followed in 1940, a restrictive policy that caused the protest and intervention of Parisian and North American Jewish organizations, to no avail.[14] Cortés argued, as would the incoming President Calderón, that restrictive immigration policies were not anti-Jewish per se, and in any case were needed to maintain the nation's "equilibrium in its social and economic life."[15] At the same time (late 1938 and early 1939), Cortés ordered the registration of all Jewish residents and their domiciles and occupations; this was never achieved, thanks to generalized noncompliance on the part of the affected individuals.

10. Ricardo Jiménez, "¿Por qué y cómo entraron los polacos?" pamphlet from 1936 reproduced textually in Schifter et al., *El judío*, 193–200.
11. See, in particular, Theodore Creedman, "The Political Development of Costa Rica, 1936–1944: Politics of an Emerging Welfare State in a Patriarchal Society." Ph.D. diss., University of Maryland, 1971.
12. The actions taken by Effinger are discussed in T. Creedman, "León Cortés y su tiempo," *Anales de la Academia de Geografía e Historia de Costa Rica* (1967–1969): 149–167.
13. *La Tribuna*, 20 June 1940, 1; *La Tribuna*, 7 March 1941, 1.
14. *Diario de Costa Rica*, 25 Feb. 1939, 1, 6; *Diario de Costa Rica*, 26 Feb. 1939, 1, 4.
15. *Diario de Costa Rica*, 4 March 1939, 1, 8.

The attempt to register and control the activities of Jews in general, and Jewish merchants in particular, was carried forward by President Calderón soon after his inauguration in 1940. In fact, in his inaugural address Calderón accused his predecessor of having allowed "the largest Polish invasion of the country,"[16] and he insisted that "commerce should be the enterprise of persons established in the country, to avoid the possibility of disloyal competition which, in the practice, has been shown to be the greatest threat to Costa Ricans' prosperity."[17] Calderón, as Cortés before him, responded to the clamor on the part of retail merchants in general (Spaniards, Lebanese, and Germans in particular) to limit the peddler trade. Some 120 of these "national" merchants[18] demanded that Calderón open a congressional investigation of the problem; he acceded by naming Deputy Ricardo Toledo to head the investigative commission, which reported its findings in March 1941. This was, in fact, the high point of overt anti-Semitism in Costa Rica up until that time, rather than the Cortés–Effinger era of vaguely pro-Nazi symbolism.

The principal recommendation of the investigative commission was as sweeping as it was unworkable: Jews should only be given residency upon promising not to work in commerce but only in agriculture or industries not yet developed locally. Contradictorily, all Jews, agriculturalists and captains of industry as well as merchants, were to be expelled one year after the conclusion of the war in Europe.[19]

No further steps were taken as a consequence of this legislative–investigative exercise, but the issue did surface again, to a limited extent, in the 1944 presidential campaign. Cortés ran again and attempted to build upon his anti-*polaco* image, whereas the official and winning candidate, Teodoro Picado Michelski, was openly pro-Jewish. Picado, of Polish Catholic background on his mother's side, had long been friendly with individual Jewish families and bitterly denounced Cortés's earlier appointment of Effinger to supervise immigration policy.[20] However, this sudden shift in political alliances, with Jews now increasingly identified with the official party and candidate (*calderonismo*, headed briefly by Picado), was as mis-

16. *La Tribuna,* 20 June 1940, 1.
17. *La Tribuna,* 17 May 1940, 7.
18. *La Tribuna,* 17 May 1940, 1.
19. *La Tribuna,* 7 March 1941. The documentation from this legislative commission is nowhere to be found in the national archive's congressional section. Whether through oversight or deliberate suppression, this important historical record has been lost.
20. *La Tribuna,* 17 Oct. 1943, 5. Picado eventually gained much support from those who would benefit from the substantial sugar and coffee properties taken from the local German colony after 1943. See Schifter et al., *El judío,* 163, note 57.

leading as it was potentially dangerous. With the outbreak of civil war in 1948, Costa Rican Jews were increasingly a captive ally of the official party and a target for attack by certain extreme factions of the opposition.

The 1948 revolutionary movement led by José Figueres opposed the reelection pretensions of Calderón Guardia. The much-disputed election, under the supervision of President Picado's *calderonista* administration, had pitted Calderón against the rightist candidate Otilio Ulate. Figueres and his small band of followers claimed an Ulate victory and election fraud by the pro-Calderón administration. Upon their triumph, they claimed, they would install Ulate as President, but this they in fact carried out only after an eighteen-month interim junta had ruled by decree and rewritten the constitution.

Ulate, a provincial politician and newspaperman, had been associated with some of the most outspoken anti-*polaco* positions during the 1940s. Certain of his followers, as with those of Figueres, were openly anti-Semitic. The outbreak of bombings, the sacking of the Jewish temple in San José, and street graffiti warning the "Jewish dogs" convinced community leaders of the need for direct action in the midst of a civil war that was rapidly developing in favor of the rebels. Two of the community's leaders, Salomón Schifter and David Sikora, made their way to the advancing rebel forces, encamped outside of the capital, to meet with Figueres and discuss the critical situation facing Costa Rican Jewry.[21] Figueres categorically declared his new government's intention to put a stop to the outrages and to respect individual liberties. This was taken as a personal guarantee and greatly facilitated the eighteen-month process of transition. Indeed, many have mistakenly come to believe that Costa Rican Jews are and always have been partisans of Figueres and his movement (Partido Liberación Nacional), just as the roles of Jiménez, Cortés, and Calderón have so often been confused. To be sure, the relatively great popularity of Figueres among Jews dates from this intervention in their favor, but must be seen against the policies of the more intransigent factions within his own rebel following.

Once the Interim Junta led by Figueres returned power to President Ulate in late 1949, the "Polish question" resurfaced and led to the final major wave of anti-Semitism in modern Costa Rican politics. Ulate had clearly expressed his own view of Jews in a 1946 editorial. Therein he praised the earliest Jewish immigrants (Sephardic Jews?),

> who made the coffee groves flourish copiously, contributed to the creation of industry, and if some of them entered into commercial activities they did so in loyal competition, without a desire to absorb everything. . . . Those who have

---

21. Schifter et al., *El judío,* 164–165.

introduced racial distinctions in manners and customs are the Polish Jews. . . . They have a separate social life, they marry without the contamination of creole blood, and even in death they prefer that they be covered in their cemeteries by a dirt different from that which covers other mortals. Those are racial distinctions, and Costa Ricans are not the ones who are making them. . . . They have not come to create wealth but to drain it away and to try to take over national and long-standing foreign trade. . . . Neither have they come to raise up buildings, but rather to make more grave the housing problem for Costa Ricans. . . . They have undertaken mass naturalizations, not out of conviction nor love for the land which shelters them, but out of calculation and with the intervention of the local Communists [the Picado administration?], which ties them to the nation's politics and makes them little loved by public opinion. . . . They do not contribute to solving any problem, . . . [but] constitute one of the greatest plagues which we suffer. . . . You [the Jews] should not be irritated by the complaints of Costa Ricans; you have left them without homes to live in, you are taking from them one of the few prosperous activities of the present day; you do not invest, nor produce; you try to create monopolies in some areas of commerce. . . . Go to the countryside, as you promised when you entered the country; work the land, give evidence that you want to be productive elements.[22]

The vanguard of the anti-Polish campaign was a so-called Junta Patriotica (patriotic junta) of merchants, led by Alejandro García A. This gray eminence of Costa Rican anti-Semitism had relieved himself of all responsibility by arguing that "Jews are repudiated because they themselves are odious in their way of life." Later, he would even claim that José Figueres had sold out to the Jewish colony.[23]

This particular campaign came to a head in late 1951 and early 1952 with public demonstrations against Jewish commerce in May 1952 and bomb attacks against two merchants' stores in June. President Ulate and his foreign minister (and later president) Mario Echandi eventually stopped this campaign, but not until extensive international reporting and a visit by Rabbi Maurice Perlzweig of the World Jewish Congress had made it a political liability. Perhaps the most revealing, and damaging, report was the story appearing in *The New York Times* under the grave title "Costa Rican Jews Under Attack." Sidney Gruson reported that

> the campaign against Costa Rican Jews has developed since the Jewish New Year holidays last September [1951]. Pushed by a group calling itself the Junta Patriotica, the campaign has been marked by virulent newspaper propaganda paid for by the Junta, by anti-Jewish slogans painted on walls, and by a few acts of violence. . . . There is widespread supposition that much of the Junta's

22. *Diario de Costa Rica,* 9 Oct. 1946, 1, 8.
23. *Diario de Costa Rica,* 25 April 1952, 9; *Diario de Costa Rica,* 23 June 1952, 1, 6.

financial support comes from merchants who feel themselves in competition with Jews.... Similar anti-Jewish campaigns in 1934 and 1949 were nipped at the start from the presidential office [by Jiménez and Figueres].

Concluding that both President Ulate and Foreign Minister Mario Echandi were implicated in the campaign, Gruson continued:

> In an interview, Señor Echandi said that the campaign was not against those Jews of non-Polish origin who had "identified themselves with the country by intermarriage" and other ways. "It is against those who have refused to assimilate, those who have no contact with Costa Rica except through their commerce."[24]

After the 1952 affair, anti-Semitism was never so openly expressed or tolerated in Costa Rican politics again. One or two very minor exchanges of opinion between Palestinian and Jewish figures have been reported in the local press,[25] but local commercial competitors have no longer found political forces willing to serve as spokesmen for anti-Semitic views. Moreover, the local Catholic hierarchy adopted a remarkably pro-Jewish position early on and never took any active role in these campaigns.[26] An accurate, if whimsical, reflection of the decline to near irrelevance of the "Jewish question" in Costa Rican politics can be seen in the popular jocularity regarding the local "Arab–Israeli" conflict of 1978. In the presidential election campaign of that year, a major opposition candidate was of Lebanese origin and the wife of the official party candidate was of Jewish descent (of the Yankelewitz family, coincidentally). Such a sense of ethnic humor would have no doubt been hard for many participants of the political battles of the 1930–1952 period to appreciate.

Contemporary Costa Rican Jewry

Since the 1950s Costa Rican Jewry has not only escaped direct political attack, it has also witnessed major internal change. From a colony of

---

24. S. Gruson, "Costa Rican Jews Under Attack," *The New York Times,* 1 June 1952, p. 2.

25. *La Tribuna,* 16 Oct. 1947, 1, for exchanges between the Comité Pan-Arabe de Cuba and the local Zionists over the Palestinian question of the day; *La República,* 26 Oct. 1955, 7, for exchanges between a local Palestinian resident and the Centro Israelita regarding the same question.

26. In this 1955 Palestinian–Zionist exchange, the Archbishop of San José, Rubén Odio Herrera, called for an end to the polemic, basically to avoid touching off further anti-*polaco* campaigns locally; *La República,* 26 Oct. 1955, 7. Moreover, in 1960 the Catholic priest Francisco Herrera titled his editorial homily "The Holy Church Takes the Side of the Jews" (*Diario de Costa Rica,* 2 March 1960, 12).

petty merchants and their families, congregated close to the central market district of San José, the community has evolved toward greater residential and occupational complexity. Perhaps most important has been the rapid development of second- and third-generation professionals far out of proportion to the community's size, leaving behind shopkeeping as the typical Jewish occupation. Moreover, community institutions beyond the synagogue (first founded in 1932 and moved to the present site in 1955) and the Centro Israelita Sionista de Costa Rica (founded in 1931–1932 and reformed definitively in 1934 after some internal discord) have been consolidated, particularly the community school (Escuela Dr. Jaim Weizman, founded in 1960 and now including kindergarten, primary, and secondary schools). This has tended to offset, to some extent, a notable secularization and acculturation of that same second generation of professionals and academics away from traditional religiosity and community insularism.

Both the 1941 and 1952 censuses of Jewish occupations showed an overwhelming merchant–industrial majority among adult males. By the late 1970s, however, Jewish surnames were increasingly prominent in Costa Rican professional circles. In an informal survey of membership among leading professional associations in 1978, Costa Rican Jews, only 0.08% of the national population, accounted for 1.6% (23) of its medical doctors, 2% (3) of its architects, 1.2% (10) of the civil engineers, 10% (10) of the industrial engineers, 2% (3) of the mechanical engineers, but only 0.2% (5) of the more creole-dominated and tradition-bound legal profession.[27] This movement into the free professions has been paralleled, and perhaps even exceeded, in the ranks of university academics, where Jewish men and women of letters have occupied leading positions since the early 1970s. However much this divergent generational experience has tried familial and community harmony, its effect society-wide has been quite positive. In addition to the obvious contribution to the national society and economy, the emergence of a second generation of professionals has radically altered the host society's perception of the Jewish community. No longer limited to the highly visible and coveted activities of retail trade in textiles, Costa Rican Jews have outgrown the scapegoat role in local politics which dogged their footsteps in the 1930s and 1940s.

Today, as in the past, Costa Rican Jewry has tended to adopt a united political stance only vis-à-vis the question of the State of Israel. As early as 1943 there was a local Pro-Palestine Committee, which gained the support of Costa Rican intellectuals.[28] A very few youth actually enlisted in the far-off struggle; most collaborated more indirectly by sending funds to the New

---

27. Schifter et al., *El judío*, 382, note 3.
28. Schifter et al., *El judío*, 366.

York and Palestine headquarters of the movement.[29] In October 1947, Moshé Gurany, representative of the Jewish Agency in Palestine, visited the Costa Rican community and was also greeted publicly by President Picado, who expressed his support for the cause of the Jewish state, which triumphed the following year.[30] This occasion was marked with great festivity and thanksgiving by Costa Rican Jews, as the major local newspapers of the time bear witness.[31] However, none of the more ambitious attempts at a Zionist policy of emigration from Costa Rica to Israel proved notably successful among the youth of the community.

Costa Rica's relations with the state of Israel have been very close and friendly since 1948. Instrumental in this development, as well as in defusing local anti-Semitism after 1948, were Luis Alberto Monge and Benjamín Núñez, Figueres's associates in the founding of Liberación Nacional. Monge (whose wife, Doris Yankelewitz, was the object of the "Arab–Israeli" discussion mentioned earlier) was the nation's first Ambassador to Israel, and he and his wife have remained active in bilateral relations since then. Elected president in 1982, Monge became the first head of state to move his country's embassy in Israel from Tel Aviv back to Jerusalem. Núñez, a Catholic priest and labor organizer, likewise formed part of the 1948–1949 interim junta government of Figueres and later served as Ambassador to Israel. Perhaps the high point of affective ties between Costa Rican Jews and Israel was reached with the State visit of Yitzhak Shamir, then foreign minister and now prime minister, to Costa Rica in mid-1982. Continued amicable relations are, however, based more upon beneficial cooperative arrangements in agricultural and industrial development with the Costa Rican government than upon local Jewish sympathy and support for Israel.

Despite the often-rumored increase in Israeli relations with and arms supply to right-wing regimes in Central America and the anti-Zionist and pro-Palestinian positions of Nicaragua's Sandinista government, Costa Rica's relations with the Jewish state and the local community's ties have not become a national political issue of any significance. Moreover, the allegedly anti-Semitic acts of the early Sandinista period in Nicaragua offer somewhat more of a parallel with Costa Rican revolutionary upheaval in 1948 than with events of today. Not only is the political climate of contemporary Costa Rica radically different from that of its neighbor, but the Jewish community is far larger, more heterogeneous, and more settled in than its ill-fated and minuscule Nicaraguan counterpart.

To be sure, wealth in general—and Jewish wealth in particular—

29. Schifter et al., *El judío*, 164, note 59, and 366–368.
30. *La Tribuna*, 16 Oct. 1947, 1; *La Nación*, 26 Oct. 1947, 4; *La Nación*, 2 Nov. 1947, 4.
31. *La Tribuna, Diario de Costa Rica*, and *La Nación*, 30 Nov.–2 Dec. 1947.

invites political criticism in Costa Rica, as in any other nation with a significant history of anti-Semitic politics. There is undoubtedly considerable potential for a future revival of such anti-Semitism in public life, particularly as part of a rightist radicalism coming out of the pre-1948 oligarchical tradition. Moreover, remnants of that same oligarchy, as well as segments of the urban middle class, maintain a certain degree of resentment toward and estrangement from Jews because of the latter's much-commented-on tendency toward marital endogamy and disproportionate educational and professional achievements in competitive fields. Should these potentially conflictive issues be joined to any lower-class anti-Semitic tendencies, there could be a revival of the debates of the 1930–1952 period. However, there do not appear to exist sufficient elements of cohesion or national political simplicity to make this a likely scenario for the short- to medium-range future.

Costa Rican Jewry and its prospects appear radically different from the fate genuinely and justifiably feared in the mob-ruled spring of 1948. Community stability and permanence will be based first on the legacy of the *shtetl* immigration from Poland as well as on the post-1960 emergence of marked occupational heterogeneity. The consolidation of such a prosperous and pacific community was no doubt the dream that motivated the early immigrants to leave their homeland, the sacrifices of the *klapper* peddler days, and the herculean efforts to bring family members before the Nazi storm broke over Europe. The fulfillment of such a shared vision of a new life in a new land is, in essence, the story of twentieth-century Costa Rican Jewry.

12
Capitalism, Socialism, and the Jews: The View from Cabildo*

Carlos H. Waisman

Argentine Right-Wing Nationalism

The Argentine movement that calls itself Catholic Nationalism originated in the 1920s, and it became a significant political force in the 1930s and 1940s.[1] It was always an elite movement whose leaders belonged to the intelligentsia and whose constituencies were the armed forces, the Catholic church, and the antiliberal faction of the middle classes. In the 1940s, a substantial number of right-wing nationalists joined Peronism, whose doctrine they contributed toward shaping. Through this vehicle, some themes of Catholic nationalist ideology penetrated, in a diluted form, the mentality of large segments of the working and middle classes. Most nationalists, however, remained aloof from or were quickly disenchanted with Peronism, because of its populist organization, eclectic ideology, and pragmatic policies.

Right-wing nationalism persisted over time thanks to the generation of

---

*This is the authentic version of this paper, and the only one whose publication I have authorized. An inaccurate Spanish translation, for which I did not assign copyright, was published in Leonardo Senkman, *El antisemitismo en la Argentina*, vol. 2 (Buenos Aires: Centro Editor de America Latina, 1986). Although that piece appears under my name, I disclaim responsibility for its content.

1. On Argentine Catholic nationalism, see Federico Ibarguren, *Orígones dei nacionalismo argentino 1927–1937* (Buenos Aires: Ceicius, 1969); Marysa Navarro Gerassi, *Los nacionalistas* (Buenos Aires: Jorge Alvarez, 1968); and Enrique Zuiueta Alvarez, *El nacionalismo argentino* (Buenos Aires: La Bastilla, 1975), 2 vols.

a closed subculture. The movement always had its small group of intellectuals, usually drawn from the liberal professions, its small but committed collectivity of activists, its publications, and its network of study groups and ideological institutes. Catholic Nationalism never attained control of the state, but this was not, in any case, its realistic objective. Nationalism is not a political party, but an ideological movement whose goals are to influence the armed forces and the church and to enlarge its constituency among intellectuals, professionals, and students. Since the 1930s, however, right-wing nationalists had a disproportionate access to political power. Nationalist militants held important government positions, both under Peronist constitutional administrations and military regimes (i.e., the whole period since 1930, except for two Radical interludes: 1958–1966 and 1983 to the present). There have been nationalist cabinet members, university rectors and deans, judges, and even presidents under military regimes. Within the military, in particular, nationalist influence has been strong. Since the 1930s, a large faction of the officer corps, especially in the army (and, later, in the air force) has been so labeled. This peculiarity, rather than the size of its membership or the circulation of its publications, is what makes Argentine right-wing nationalism important: There are groups with similar or related ideologies in most countries in Western Europe and Latin America, but nowhere else do they have such an institutionalized insertion in the state.

This chapter studies the ideology of the monthly magazine *Cabildo,* the foremost nationalist publication since the end of the military regime known as the "Argentine Revolution." It first appeared in 1973, when it filled the vacuum left by its predecessor, *Presencia. Cabildo* was banned in 1975 by Isabel Peron's government, as were several other left-wing and right-wing periodicals. It appeared later with a different name, and was banned again. It resumed publication after the military coup of 1976. The following year, *Cabildo* was briefly suspended after a violently anti-Semitic issue in which it blamed Jews for the guerrillas that were operating at that time in Argentina. The accusation itself was a standard element in the ideology of the magazine, but the violence of the language triggered an international protest, which included articles in *Le Monde, The New York Times,* and *Time.*[2] The issue became sensitive because of the campaign in the United States and Western Europe against the massive and arbitrary repression that the military regime was carrying out and the perception in some influential Jewish circles abroad that the Argentine community, one of the largest outside Israel, the United States, and the Soviet Union, could be in danger. The ban was a public relations gesture by the military regime, and *Cabildo* resumed regular publication shortly thereafter. The ideology did

---

2. "Todos contra *Cabildo: Cabildo* por la nación," *Cabildo,* 1977, no. 9:5.

not change, but the language became less strident, especially in relation to the "Jewish question."

During the military regime of 1976–1983, *Cabildo* was one of the few political magazines allowed to appear. In 1980, it claimed to be the one with the largest circulation and readership in the country.[3] Statements made at that time by government officials or military officers—and, as we know now, even by police or security personnel in charge of the illegal prisons of the regime—frequently were diluted, distorted, or toned down versions of material from *Cabildo*. The publisher, Ricardo Curutchet, was then a judge. Retired officers and former government officials write for the magazine, and a former military president, General Roberto M. Levingston, was recently interviewed by it.[4] *Cabildo* has lost its preeminence since the reestablishment of democracy at the end of 1983, but it is still the official organ of Catholic Nationalism, and it circulates widely in the armed forces. It is the center of an organizational network whose components currently include the Restoration Nationalist Movement (a political group), the Our Lady of Mercy Study Center (an institute offering courses and lectures), student organizations, and institutes devoted to international relations.

I will now describe the main themes in the ideology of *Cabildo*.

Conception of the Nation

The identity principle or subject in the ideology of Argentine right-wing nationalism is, of course, the nation, rather than the citizen or the class. One of the central factors distinguishing the ideologies of right-wing and left-wing nationalism is the meaning of the term *nation*. For the Left, nation usually denotes *people*, or the population that inhabits a given territory. When the term has a cultural referent, it usually is the empirically existing culture shared by such population. In right-wing nationalism, on the other hand, territory, population, and culture have a normative rather than an empirical meaning: The boundaries of the national territory are considered an invariant product of history and tradition, the population is a community determined by lineage rather than by birth (by *jus sanguinis* rather than by *jus soli*), and national culture is defined by traditional or ideal values.

The territorial component is very salient in the ideology of *Cabildo*. The magazine devotes an inordinate amount of space to the discussion of

---

3. "La comisión trilateral y el poder internacional del dinero," *Cabildo* extra (Cuaderno No. 1, 1980: 2.
4. "Seguridad y defensa nacionales," *Cabildo*, 1984, no. 73:22–26.

the minor territorial issues faced by Argentina: the disputes with England over the Malvinas/Falkland Islands, with Chile over the Beagle Channel, and with Brazil over the water level in the Itaipu Dam. In addition, there are constant references to the territorial amputations that Argentina would have suffered since independence. Nationalists openly long for the boundaries of the predecessor state, the Viceroyalty of the Rio de la Plata, and talk about an "imperial destiny" (sometimes camouflaged as "leadership") for the country. They are obsessed by Brazil, whom they see as an expansionist power and Argentina's historic rival for hegemony in South America.

However, the central component of the nationalists' conception of the nation is not the territory but the collectivity, which they define on the basis of ethnicity and religion. The application of lineage as a criterion is, of course, problematic in a country of immigrants: Most contemporary Argentines are the descendants of the European immigrants who arrived between 1870 and 1930, and most of these immigrants were of non-Hispanic origin (half came from Italy). But membership in the nation, for *Cabildo,* seems to be limited to inhabitants of Hispanic Catholic ancestry (whites in particular) and to other Catholics, especially those of Latin origin, who assumed a Hispanic identity. This would leave out people of partially or pure Indian or African ancestry (about 15–20% of the population), non-Catholics (about 10%), people who maintain non-Hispanic ethnic identities, and so on.

"We the Hispano-Argentines," says Ignacio B. Anzoátegui, "we who feel the need to call ourselves Hispano-Argentines so that we are not confused with the foreign-Argentines, we the white Hispano-Argentines, who feel the need to call ourselves Hispano-Argentines so that we are not confused with any other products of white miscegenation, we who are authentically Argentine . . . are fed up with the traitors and the mulattoes."[5] The "traitors" are the nineteenth-century Argentine "liberals," whose goals were the integration of the country in international markets, mass immigration, the establishment of democratic institutions, and the repudiation of the Hispanic cultural heritage, in lieu of which they advocated the assimilation of English and French culture. *Cabildo* identifies with the other nineteenth-century tradition, the "nationalist" one, which represented continuity with the anti-liberal Spanish past. The main figure of this tradition is Juan Manuel de Rosas, governor of Buenos Aires province (1835–1852), who is worshipped by *Cabildo* as a major national hero.

In this interpretation, mass immigration is seen as an "uncontrolled and tragic transformation."[6] *Cabildo* writers are ambivalent about immigrants, even about Latin Catholic ones. In a discussion of a Radical politician, Ernesto Sammartino, he is accused of ignoring the alleged antiliberal roots

---

5. Ignacio B. Anzoátegui, "Conquista y reconquista," *Cabildo,* 1973, no. 6:34.
6. Carlos Maria Dardán, "La tradición y el gringuito," *Cabildo,* 1974, no. 19:17.

of his party. The interpretation is that this is due to Sammartino's immigrant ancestry: "His affiliation to the *pampa* [Argentine plains] is still fresh. I would almost say that he still 'smells of the port,' "[7] says a writer (a statement that provoked a response by a nationalist of Italian descent, who explained that what was wrong with Sammartino was his liberal ideology, rather than his ethnicity).[8]

Cabildo is consistent in this regard. "We are heirs to a millenary civilization grounded on Christian revelation, Greek philosophy, and Roman order,"[9] it says, but the Argentine identity is "Hispanic, not Latin."[10] This hispanophilia is surprising, given not only the composition of the Argentine population but also that of the nationalist movement: Its three main contemporary ideologues were Giordano Bruno [*sic*] Gentai, Carlos A. Sacheri, and Julio Meinvielle. None of these surnames is of Spanish origin. Neither is the publisher's, Ricardo Curutchet, nor those of many of the people who write in it. Genta explained this apparent incongruity as follows: "I come from Italians ... at least, we are similar in origin, in history. But ... [Spain] brought us the Religion of Christ.... The privilege of speaking this language ... is really a gift, a priceless gift, as is the Religion of Christ, and besides the fundamental institutions of the natural order (also a gift from Spain)."[11]

However, Hispanic tradition is also dualistic.[12] Argentine right-wing nationalists identify with the tradition of the Counter-Reformation: "America was discovered ... by Columbus and Vespucci, Italians; but it was Spain, Catholic, anti-Semitic, inquisitorial, the one which gave us religion, language, and temperament."[13] This is, also, of course, the Spain of the Falange and Franco, who were ardently supported by Argentine nationalists.

Catholicism is the other component of national identity, but it is the traditional, integrist, antiliberal variety of Catholicism. "The Fatherland—this Passion founded by Spain, was born Catholic and Marian. In the shadow of the Cross, enamored of Christ and of His Mother, strong in Faith, loyal in service," says *Cabildo* with characteristic fervor.[14] Nationalism aims at a restoration, the meaning of which is the subordination of state and culture to religious doctrine: "*Our Restoration* is a return to the Traditional Order, in which political power gets its inspiration from the Imperishable Truths

---

7. Dardán, "La tradición," 17.
8. Carlos Dall'Oca Bianca, "La tradición y el gringuito," *Cabildo*, 1975, no. 21:30–32.
9. Bernardino Montejano, "Acerca de lo 'nacional y popular,'" *Cabildo*, 1973, no. 7:8.
10. R. H. M., "Hispanidad," *Cabildo*, 1977, no. 11:27.
11. Jordán B. Gentai, "Su última conferencia," *Cabildo*, 1974, no. 19:27.
12. G. J. Y., "Cocineros antes que frailes," *Cabildo*, 1977, no. 9:31.
13. Carlos Maria Dardán, letter to the editor, *Cabildo*, 1975, no. 21:32. Dardán was a frequent contributor to the magazine.
14. Alonso Quijano, "Cosas veredes Sancho ... ," *Cabildo*, 1979–1980, no. 30:7.

whose depositary through the centuries has been the Holy Church. [In it] no individual or collective will may attempt against the Rights of God, Family or Nation."[15] As could be expected, *Cabildo* rejects not only leftist or progressive Catholicism, but also the mainstream liberal one, in the strongest possible terms, and it supports Bishop Lefebvre and "traditionalist" movements within the church. These are representative statements: "Modernism and its fruits constitute a properly Satanic situation;"[16] "progressivism is accomplishing a destructive action,"[17] "the liturgical reform [adopted by the Vatican Council] has been directed by Satan."[18]

The Enemy

"The politician's first task, his first duty, is to detect the enemy." Thus starts the 1977 editorial that led to the suspension of *Cabildo*.[19] The list of enemies of Argentine right-wing nationalism is more or less standard, but the explanation or justification of the opposition to them is not. The principle of opposition has a complex structure, for it consists, as in medieval philosophy, of different levels of reality.

At the first level, that of the surface, communism is the central enemy. Following Pope Pius XI, *Cabildo* considers that communism is characterized by two traits: its *"diabolic inspiration*, . . . its Satanic essence" and its "character of *false messianism.*"[20] What nationalists oppose in communism is its antireligious nature, rather than specific characteristics of its economic or political institutions. Nationalists are anticapitalist, and their ideal political system is a dictatorship in which no opposition or dissent is tolerated. But they see communism as the extreme outcome of the process of secularization initiated with the development of capitalism and they reject "totalitarianism," by which they mean exclusively the control or elimination of integrist religion by an atheistic state. For this reason, "any other higher value one may risk, life included, in the war against Marxism, will be well sacrificed."[21] In the typical extremist pattern, the contours of "communism" are, for the nationalists, very diffuse, and the label is freely applied to leftists

---

15. Tomás Cruz, "Nuestra restauración," *Cabildo*, 1984, no. 75:31.
16. Antonio Caponnetto, "El humo de Satán ha entrado en el templo de Dios," *Cabildo*, 1978, no. 19:27.
17. Julio Meinvielle, "Ubicación exacta de la década del 70 en la revolución anticristiana," *Cabildo*, 1973, no. 7:28.
18. Enrique, "Carta de un socerdote a otro," *Cabildo*, 1974, no. 20:20.
19. Editorial, *Cabildo*, 1977, no. 7:3.
20. "A cuarenta años de tres grandes encíclicas de Pio XI," *Cabildo*, 1977, no. 8:29.
21. "Ha muerto un enemigo," *Cabildo*, 1973, no. 6:23.

of all kinds, liberals, nonintegrist Catholics, Jews, intellectuals, journalists, and the like.

Liberalism is another enemy, albeit not a central one. Nationalists oppose liberalism on two grounds: It is also a form of secularization (although milder than communism) and, they claim, it is an inevitable prelude to communism. In their view, the liberal state lacks a "transcendent mission" and also power to impose the "common interests" and prevent the success of particular ones (the former are deduced from the state's "transcendent mission," but nationalists never explain who makes the deduction). Thus, under liberalism, the state ceases to be the "cohesion factor," "intermediate societies disappear," and political parties, "i.e., the free and disharmonic interplay of interests and opinions," become the center of political life. This is the great weakness of democracy.[22] The people can be wrong: "*vox populi* can be either *vox dei* or *vox diaboli.*"[23] This is why "liberal apostasy—itself the daughter of Protestant heresy, is in the origin of the smashing success of communism,"[24] for "democracy is the vulgar procuress [*celestina*] of International Communism. It is the natural, inevitable, obliged road to Bolshevik terror."[25]

Beyond liberal democracy, capitalism itself is defined as an enemy. The first reason is that the development of capitalism is a crucial determinant of, as Weber would say, the disenchantment of the world. Capitalism is "a system which erects profit as the main and ultimate end of life,"[26] on account of which it was rejected by the Catholic church.[27] A second reason is that capitalist concentration leads to the transformation of private wealth into a basis for power. Wealth eventually becomes stronger than the national state itself. Following Maurras (and also as in the Marxist critique, even though the theoretical context of the latter is totally different), *Cabildo* points out that there is "an irreversible process which leads modern democracy to become . . . an oligarchy, and money to become the owner of Power. . . . Money . . . aspires to concentrate all Power . . . to seize the State."[28] Finally, the power of money becomes a supranational force, which threatens the national state also from without: "The 'international imperialism of money' weaves, under countries' apparent autonomies and possible

---

22. M. C., "En el camino de las utopiás politicas," *Cabildo,* 1977, no. 10:18.
23. Bernardino Montejano, "Critica nacionalista," *Cabildo,* 1973, no. 1:5.
24. "A cuarenta años," 29.
25. Antonio Caponnetto, "Patria o democracia," *Cabildo,* 1977, no. 10:21.
26. Adel E. Vilas, "Reflexiones sobre la subversión cultural," *Cabildo,* 1977, no. 9:36.
27. Juan Carlos Monedero, "El anticapitalismo nacionalista y el capitalismo de 'La razón,'" *Cabildo,* 1977, no. 12:19.
28. Editorial, *Cabildo,* 1978, no. 19:3.

antinomies, the fabric of universal rule."[29] From here to the classical fascist theme of plutocracy as the hidden government of the world there is only one step.

Thus, communism, liberalism, and capitalism (and Freemasonry, as one would expect[30]) are the enemies at the surface. At a deeper level, there is a unifying force, which orchestrates the assault on the "natural order": the Jews. "The Jewish problem!" says the editorial of the 1977 issue that provoked international uproar, "the life of nationalism, here, in France, and in Central Europe, consisted in its denunciation."[31]

A first reason for the categorization of the Jews as enemies is that, on the basis of the nationalist definition of the nation, they are alien. And yet, thanks to liberalism and capitalism, they are considered citizens, and as such they can accumulate wealth and power. "Since Carolingian times . . . 'judaeus' and 'mercator' are synonyms. For this reason, in a country converted into a market the traffickers, i.e., the Jews, can act with impunity."[32] When referring to individual Jews, *Cabildo* emphasizes their alien character. For instance, newspaper publisher Jacobo Timerman, one of its *bêtes noires*, is called a "despicable Ukrainian,"[33] a Jew who adopted Argentine citizenship in "a tactical and farisaic gesture,"[34] and who "vomited his hate, his ambition, and his irreverence over the very roots of the nation that so casually had sheltered him."[35] Similar language is used with reference to other prominent Jews: former economy minister José B. Gelbard, banker and alleged supporter of the Montonero guerrillas David Graiver, Rabbi Marshall Mayer, Henry Kissinger.

The magazine diligently keeps track of Jews in government and in prominent positions in all spheres of life, and it exposes them. Because the nationalists' knowledge of Jewish names is extremely imperfect, many times the attribution is erroneous. In one case, their error gave rise to a curious exchange. In 1982, *Cabildo* denounced that a newly appointed secretary of Public Information, Oscar Magdalena, was in fact a Sephardic Jew.[36] Two issues later, it published a letter by Magdalena, who denied the charge and provided documentation: a book with the genealogy of his mother's family (an old Argentine family) and his father's Spanish birth certificate.[37] A com-

---

29. Luis M. Bandieri, "Nacionalismo vs. antiimperialismo," *Cabildo*, 1973, no. 4:22.
30. "La ofensiva masónica," *Cabildo*, 1977, no. 9:41–43.
31. Editorial, *Cabildo*, 1977, no. 7:3.
32. Alonso Quijano, "Cosas veredes Sancho . . . ," *Cabildo*, 1980, no. 30:7.
33. "La revolucizaon socialdemzaocrata," *Cabildo*, 1984, no. 72:8.
34. Editorial, *Cabildo*, 1979, no. 28:3.
35. Editorial, *Cabildo*, 1978, no. 15:3.
36. Raul A. Murcia, "Jacobo Timerman regresa al país," *Cabildo*, 1982, no. 57:12–13.
37. Oscar Magdalena, "Como se pide," *Cabildo*, 1982, no. 58:11.

mon error is the attribution of Jewishness to individuals with "Jewish-sounding names," which in Argentina are all the German and Slavic ones. Frequently, *Cabildo* publishes lists of real or alleged Jews in order to expose their influence in different organizations, even in foreign governments. Thus, there were lists of Jews in the Allende government in Chile,[38] the Carter administration in the United States, (Carter, by the way, was sometimes called Carter Braunstein, and the latter name, apparently one of his last names, sounds Jewish in Argentina),[39] and so on.

A second, and more powerful, reason for the antagonism against Jews is that they are said to control or direct the enemies at the surface, namely communism and capitalism. These alleged linkages are presented with the conventional arguments of the extreme right and on the basis of two types of facts: the overrepresentation of Jews among communists and bankers and the Jewish role in the alleged collaboration between these two groups. Thus, in a typical statement, *Cabildo* lists prominent Jewish Marxists.[40] Also in typical fashion, the roster includes not only Jews such as Marx, Bernstein, or Trotsky, but also gentiles such as Engels and Lenin. The same article asserts that all but four members of the first Soviet Revolutionary government were Jewish. As for the role of Jewish capitalists in the Russian Revolution, *Cabildo* frequently repeats the old story (probably taken from Henry Ford's *The International Jew*, always in print in Argentina) according to which the Russian Revolution was financed by the New York bankers Jacob Schiff and Jacob Warburg.[41]

On the other hand, Jews are said to control the U.S. economy and the world capitalist system as a whole. "The American financial apparatus," says *Cabildo*, "[is] dominated by the servants of the golden calf, the same ones who at the foot of Sinai danced their rites of corruption and moral, intellectual, and physical perversity."[42] International finance is sometimes called "the International Money Power," a code name for international Jewry.

The Graiver affair, which came to light in 1977, was the most important local instance of the purported Jewish–communist–capitalist link. The military regime claimed that Graiver, an international banker and businessman (and Timerman's partner in the newspaper *La Opinión*), was the banker of the Montonero guerrillas. *Cabildo* considered this issue to be comparable to the Dreyfus case: "Both serve to detect the profundity of evil, the perversion of political leaders, the identity of the enemy, and the defen-

38. Boanerges Husita, "Diccionario de un rumiante," *Cabildo*, 1973, no. 7:20.
39. Thomas McIan, "T.I.R.E. Internacional No. V," *Cabildo*, 1978, no. 20:26.
40. "Omitir la historia," *Cabildo*, 1977, no. 8:9.
41. "La Argentina entre el mundialismo y la beligerancia," *Cabildo*, 1978, no. 17:8.
42. R. A. M., "Esta es la super potencia?" *Cabildo*, 1980, no. 33:27.

selessness of two naive nations which were disordered by democracy."[43] It was in this connection that *Cabildo* launched its strongest anti-Semitic attack. With characteristic language, in which morbidity metaphors predominated ("pus stain," "infection," "cancer"), the magazine blamed "Jewish intelligence" and "Jewish finance" for the appearance of the guerrillas. Their objective would be "the destruction of the State" and even "the destruction of the Fatherland." *Cabildo* called for a "national revolution" aimed at "removing" the Jewish danger.[44]

Jewish history is treated in *Cabildo* with the same degree of accuracy accorded to the analysis of the Jewish role in communism and capitalism. Thus, the obituary of former minister Gelbard, who was born in Poland in 1917, reports that apparently all Polish Jews at that time belonged to the bourgeoisie "devoted to traffick, usurary lending and the administration of big landholdings," that they never tried "to disguise their origin with the nationality of the territory where they were born, as was the case in Western Europe and America," that most Jews had a "socialist and Marxist mentality," and so on.[45] The Holocaust, predictably, is called "the Great Fraud of the Century,"[46] even though *Cabildo* recognizes the "excesses" of Nazism;[47] and the information that Anne Frank's diary was published with modifications is interpreted as meaning that the whole diary is a mystification, a part of a "jungle of falsehoods, inventions, vulgar lies and subtle plots."[48]

In this context, some of the references to the State of Israel may appear surprising. There are a few standard conspiratorial statements (e.g., *Cabildo* reprints and automatically endorses an item from the anti-Semitic publication *Spotlight*, according to which the Paris synagogue bombing of 1980 was the work of the Mossad),[49] but most material about the Middle East and Israel is devoid of the conspiratorial logic and the emotional and even violent language that are the magazine's standard fare. The tone of discussions of the Middle East conflict ranges from neutral to mildly pro-Arab (e.g., the assertion that the crossing of the Suez Canal by the Egyptian Army in the Yom Kippur War was "a military feat worthy of study

---

43. Editorial, *Cabildo*, 1977, no. 7:3.
44. Editorial, *Cabildo*, 1977, no. 7:3.
45. "Gelbard: la muerte no da derechos," *Cabildo*, 1977, no. 11:11.
46. Thomas McIan, "Nova et vetera (V)," *Cabildo*, 1983, no. 62:13.
47. Tucidides, "La sombra de Nuremberg," *Cabildo*, 1983, no. 62:13.
48. "Anna Frank: fin de la mistificación," *Cabildo*, 1981, no. 39:29.
49. Alonso Quijano, "Cosas veredes Sancho . . . ," *Cabildo*, 1981, no. 41:17.

in depth"⁵⁰), and there are even isolated pro-Israeli statements: "No one denies [the Israelis'] bravery in the defense of their national cause."⁵¹

References to domestic Israeli politics, even when strongly critical betray an underlying respect. Thus, *Cabildo* accuses Israel of being as racist and as expansionist as the Third Reich,⁵² but it would not mind, to be sure, Argentina being either (even though nationalists deny being racist). It reports about legislation in Israel restricting Christian missionary activity, and this provokes an outburst against the perfidy of the "deicide people."⁵³ But would not *Cabildo* want an outright ban of non-Catholic or even of nonintegrist Catholic religion in Argentina? Occasionally, the language reflects even sympathy. For instance, it describes Menachem Begin as an "ultra-rightist," a "religious man," who "aspired to constitute a national state, independent of . . . Zionist centers in North America" and who thought that local Jews should govern the State "within the parameters of Jewish religion and its expansionist mandate."⁵⁴ A curious projection: Propaganda aimed at liberals and leftists in the West describes Israel as a theocratic, militarist, and expansionist nation. Because these are the very traits *Cabildo* wishes Argentina to have, the effect is this uncomfortable blend of condemnation and respect. (There are other reasons, to be sure: Soviet support for the Arab cause and PLO support for Argentine guerrillas.)

A Metaphysical Battle

There is still a third, more profound, stratum in the structure of the enemy; it is a metahistorical and indeed metaphysical level. Underlying communism, liberalism, and capitalism, and the Jews who are their motor, there is "a reality that is as tremendous as it is complex, a reality which unfolds as much in the temporal historical plane as in the plane of metahistory and theology."⁵⁵ In the nationalist conception of history, the Jews are, in turn, somebody else's instrument.

Why the Jews? As I showed, *Cabildo* identifies them systematically and calls for their elimination from positions of power. Catholic National-

50. Miguel Angel Moyano, "Sadat-Beguin: La paz de los 'halcones,'" *Cabildo*, 1977, no. 12:27.
51. "Hoy-gran pogrom en la Argentina-hoy," *Cabildo*, 1980, no. 38:14.
52. Ulises, "El Estado de Israel: Esa nueva versión del III Reich," *Cabildo*, 1980, no. 36:27.
53. "El 'liberalismo sensato' y 'democracia fuerte,'" *Cabildo*, 1978, no. 19:8.
54. Moyano, "Sadat-Beguin," 26.
55. "Cabildo y el mito antisemita," *Cabildo*, 1977, no. 8:9.

ists, however, reject passionately the "racist" label. "How could we, who worship a God who is Jewish in the flesh, be racist? How can we, who have been grafted in the old stem of Israel . . . be accused of being racist?"[56] These statements may appear tactical, for they followed the international protest caused by the anti-Semitic elements in the denunciation of Graiver, but the argument is repeated over and over in the magazine. Thus, *Cabildo* praises Action Française, Italian fascism, the Spanish Falange, and the Rumanian Iron Guard, but it has reservations about Nazism. It recognizes that Nazism was one of the "great nationalist reactions" to the spread of communism in Europe, but it stresses its "grave errors and deviations." Following Pope Pius XI, Catholic nationalists criticize Nazism on two counts: "paganism" and racism, "the arrogance fed by the belief in racial superiority."[57] The rejection of German racism, of course, is not tantamount to a rejection of racism in general, but Catholic nationalists would equally disavow "Latin" racism. In fact, they claim to accept Jews who convert. For instance, the item reporting the appointment of Monsignor Lustiger, who was born Jewish, as the archbishop of Paris is devoid of anti-Semitic innuendo (even though it bitterly attacks Jews displeased with the designation).[58]

I have quoted statements linking communism and liberal Catholicism with the devil. Satan is behind them, nationalists think, and also behind capitalism and modern culture as a whole. General Vilas, one of the leading figures in the repression of left-wing and liberal intellectuals in the late 1970s, wrote that eighteenth-century "idealism, rationalism, and empiricism" are a "diabolic trilogy."[59] This is where Jews come into the picture: They seem to be the intermediary between Satan and the enemies on the surface. It is through the Jews that the devil carries out his work.

The argument goes back to the charge of deicide: "In the only valid holocaust . . . in history," asserts *Cabildo*, "the perpetrators were Jewish."[60] The editorial of the famous 1977 issue quoted approvingly Father Meinvielle, the leading ideologist of Argentine anti-Semitism, who wrote that "the Jews must work for the extermination of the Christian States."[61] Why is it that they "must" do so? Meinvielle himself, the author of *El judío en el misterio de la historia* (*The Jew in the Mystery of History*) clarifies the statement in an article published by *Cabildo* after his death. The question is one of political theodicy: If communism is evil, why does it spread throughout the world? It is a part of God's design, Meinvielle argues. We are witness-

56. "Cabildo y el mito," 9.
57. "A cuarenta años," 29–31.
58. "Mirador europeo," *Cabildo*, 1981, no. 41:48.
59. Vilas, "Reflexiones," 36.
60. "Hoy-gran pogrom," 14.
61. "Editorial," *Cabildo*, 1977, no. 7:3.

ing the evangelization of the "pagan" peoples. The prophecy is that "only when the pagan peoples enter the church will the Jewish people return [sic] to the Christian faith." For this reason "this is the only concern of the Jews": to prevent the entry of all the peoples into the church. Hence not only communism but also "the heresy of progressiveness" has corrupted Christianity.

The argument is clear so far, but later it appears contradictory. Meinvielle goes on to state that we are living in a very special epoch, that of the second coming of Christ. Now, "as we get close to the parusia, or the coming of the Lord, we are also approaching the manifestation of the Anti-Christ. The Anti-Christ is operating since the beginning of the church. It [the Anti-Christ] would then be a people, the people who, by antonomasia, is the enemy of Christ." There is "a hidden power, a Judeo Masonic plan against Christ and his church." For the time being, this hidden power operates in secrecy, through lodges. What prevents it from appearing publicly is the fact that people still believe in Christ: "As long as Christianity reigns in the world, the Anti-Christ will not come. . . . [he will manifest himself] when the peoples are seized by total secularization."[62]

The contradictory nature of the argument has to do with the Jews. In a dialectical feat Marx would envy, Meinvielle says that, on the one hand, Jews struggle against the evangelization of the "pagans," for this would be the prelude to their own conversion. On the other, he argues that, as long as Christianity reigns, the Anti-Christ will not come. So the Jews are in fact accelerating his coming (and thus their own disappearance) while fighting against their enemy, Christianity. (The best parallel I can think of is Marx's discussion of capitalist behavior: Capitalists, in order to fight a decline in their profits, invest in new machinery, and they thus raise the organic composition of capital and provoke a decline in the rate of profit.) In this transcendent historicism, humans of different ethnicities, religions, and ideologies are just blind instruments of God's cunning, unconscious actors playing roles on the great stage of the universe while believing they take part in trivial secular conflicts.

A Sociological Interpretation

Argentine Catholic Nationalism is not fascist. Rather, it belongs to the "old right," the kind of traditionalist, authoritarian movement exemplified by Action Française. This old extreme right and fascism share several basic traits: strong nationalism, passionate anticommunism, opposition to capital-

62. Julio Meinvielle, "Ubicación exacta," 26–28.

ism and to liberal democracy, and willingness to use large-scale violence against their enemies. They diverge, however, in a series of fundamental respects. Fascism is a "modern" movement, and fascist regimes institutionalized high levels of mobilization. Fascism is based on mass parties, and its objective is the establishment of legitimate rule. The old right, on the contrary, is elitist: Its aim is to influence the military, the church, and the intellectuals, and it does not seek the support of the masses. Its ideal regime is a hierarchical, authoritarian, low-participation dictatorship. Fascists present themselves as revolutionaries, even as socialists of a different kind; "old" rightists openly describe themselves as reactionaries whose objective is to restore a traditional, premodern social order.

Argentine Catholic Nationalism is a small movement, but yet it is influential, as I have noted, among some strategic groups in the society. It should not be considered as a part of the lunatic fringe that exists in all societies. The question is: Why is it that this doctrine, a combination of unwarranted generalizations, petitions of principle, and conspiratorial explanations, has had significant appeal? A first answer is that the doctrine is not disembodied, that it is spread by a small but committed intelligentsia, some of whose members have had access to the military, priests, students and others, that it is supported by an infrastructure of institutes and publications, and so on. This is not a satisfactory explanation, for individuals are not passive recipients of ideas. Ideologies are accepted only when they make sense, when they seem to their carriers to be plausible frameworks for the understanding of their experience. The issue is, then, why did these specific contents seem to provide, to some people, a framework for the interpretation of political reality?

The origin of the movement and the source of its ideas are relatively clear. Catholic Nationalism developed and attained its influence in the 1930s and 1940s. This is when its main intellectual leaders (Genta and Meinvielle, already mentioned, plus Federico Ibarguren and the Irazusta brothers) established their reputations. They combined three sets of ideas. The first, and in many ways central, set is the overall ideological framework, which was provided by the Latin European right. International demonstration effects do not travel at random: They follow specific channels of diffusion. Since the early nineteenth century, Argentine intellectuals were in the periphery of French culture. Even in the twentieth century, after mass immigration from Spain, Spanish cultural influence came second. It is not surprising, then, that Maurras and Action Française would have had such a direct resonance on the Argentine right. The Spanish Falange and Italian fascism provided additional models.

A second set of influences is that of integrist Catholicism, which flourished in Argentina in the 1930s and 1940s. The courses of Catholic culture, in particular, were a mechanism for the fusion of neo-Thomist philosophy, nineteenth-century corporatist thought, and European rightist doctrines. The third ideological influence, finally, was local: the nativist, Hispanicist, anti-immigrant literature of the beginning of the century. This literature represented the reaction of "old Argentines," many from provincial elites, to the massive inflow of European immigrants. These old Argentines felt engulfed by the immigrants, most of whom were non-Hispanic and who concentrated in the most dynamic area of the country, the littoral, where they and their children became the majority of the population.

Nationalist ideologists combined these different strands into a rather coherent doctrine. The logic that underlies their reasoning may seem peculiar to external observers, but it is consistent with the political culture that prevailed in Argentina in the period following the Depression. This political culture is rationalistic rather than empirical, and it frequently resorts to conspiracy theories. These are commonly found in mainstream discourse. The right, Peronism, most of the left, and some segments of the now ruling Radical party have routinely blamed the decline of the country after World War II on hidden outside forces, which are said to have domestic representatives. Thus, what the right calls "communism" is usually a nonempirical, all-powerful, diffuse entity. Perón developed the remarkable concept of "synarchy," a hidden world government that unifies capitalism, communism, Zionism, the Catholic Church, and of course, Freemasonry. "Imperialism" is, in most left-wing political discourse, an equally diffuse force. The latest contribution to the genre is the obscure term *patria financiera* (financial fatherland), which alludes to finance capital and is used freely by most political groups, a segment of the Radicals included.

Catholic nationalist ideas "made sense" to many officers and to some right-wing intellectuals, professionals, and priests as a framework for the understanding of the processes that were transforming Argentina and the regions of the world most closely related to Argentina (Latin Europe and secondarily Latin America) from the 1930s to the 1960s. These processes are three.

The first is international. Argentine right-wing political and intellectual elites conceptualize the dynamics of world politics, from World War I on, as an uninterrupted process of the spread of communism. The critical points in this expansion were the Spanish Civil War—which, because of the composition of the Argentine population, was lived almost as a domestic catastrophe—and the Cuban Revolution. For important segments of the ruling class and the political elite, European fascist regimes, the Franco dictatorship, and military rule in much of postwar Latin America were reasonable responses, "excesses" notwithstanding, to communist expansion.[63]

63. Carlos H. Waisman, *Reversal of Development in Argentina: Counter-Revolutionary Policies and their Structural Consequences* (Princeton: Princeton University Press, 1987).

A second process is the relative decline of Argentina in the international system since the 1950s. The country, which in the first half of the twentieth century had been defined by both citizens and foreign observers as a rich nation, a Latin and southern replica of the United States, stagnated in the second postwar period. Argentina fell behind Europe, and it gradually joined the ranks of the underdeveloped world. At the same time, shifting patterns of world trade and finance led the Argentines to the painful realization that they may have enjoyed European standards of living for two generations, but theirs was nevertheless a peripheral and dependent nation, whose development could be either induced or blocked by European and American import needs and capital flows. This awareness had traumatic consequences for the children of both the proud elite that had built the country in the late nineteenth century and the immigrants who had left Europe in search of economic opportunity.

The third process has to do with changes in the social structure of the country and their political and cultural consequences. The industrialization wave of the 1930s and 1940s not only expanded the size of the bourgeoisie and the working class, but it also changed their ethnic composition and role in society. The new segments of the bourgeoisie were "nationalized": As a large fraction of the immigrant working class moved upward in the class structure, it was replaced by creoles from the interior. Also, industrial classes, due to the significance of manufacturing in the social structure, became central political forces. This change was very important at the level of the upper classes, in which the traditional agrarian elite was gradually displaced by the new bourgeoisie. The tension between them was aggravated by the fact that Argentine manufacturing has a limited ability to compete on international markets, and yet it requires imported inputs that can only be bought with the foreign exchange generated by the agrarians. The latter, as a consequence, feel exploited by the industrialists. Finally, the secular process of dualization of Argentina into a developed littoral and a depressed north intensified during this period.

Let us sum up the combined effects of these simultaneous processes, as they were perceived by officers, old Argentines, impoverished elites and middle classes, individuals and groups with traditional ideologies, that is, the losers in this process of change. On the one hand, communism advanced in the world; on the other, Argentina declined (as a consequence, many Argentines believed, of the characteristics of the world capitalist economy). Domestically, as the working class, the alleged carrier of the communist danger, grew and gained influence, the old Argentine elite was displaced from power, and nouveau riche immigrants, many of them first generation, turned into a central component of the economic elite. Finally, as the country became more industrialized and urbanized, it also became more educated and secularized. Since the 1950s the Argentine university system has expanded to the point that enrollment rates are now at the level of European countries with mass higher education. The structure of the intelligentsia changed, and new types, such as social scientists and psychologists, appeared. In the new ideological discourse, science and technology appeared more central than religion or traditional philosophy. In the culture of the large middle classes, priests were displaced by psychoanalysts. New secular religions, such as socialism, spread among the intelligentsia. Even in the Catholic Church, liberal and leftist trends gained in strength.

Right-wing intellectuals saw these economic, political, and cultural outcomes as a combination of threats and defeats. They began to interpret correlations as causal links, that is, to assume that if all these processes were taking place at the same time, they had to be causally related. From the vantage point of their siege mentality, and with the rationalistic and conspiratorial framework they borrowed from the European Right, it made sense to them to think that, for example, if Argentina declined internationally at the same time as new immigrant wealth was becoming dominant, the latter could be the cause of the former.

Resistance to change, frustration as a consequence of collective and individual downward mobility, resentment because of others' upward mobility: These well-known processes are the stuff out of which receptivity for nationalism developed among sectors of the "old Argentine" middle class and groups linked to the state apparatus. Anti-Semitism, the most irrational element in the ideology, was not just the product of international demonstration effects. The Argentine Jewish community is large, and it is concentrated in the areas of the country where economic, political, and cultural change was taking place. Jews were overrepresented, as usual, in the new industrial bourgeoisie and the left-wing intelligentsia, in the new professions such as psychoanalysis and related fields, and in teaching and research in the expanding university system.

Thus, Jews were very salient in the areas of society where change was taking place at the same time as "old Argentines" were losing power and prestige. Is it surprising that, in their minds, Jews came to symbolize change, that is, everything that was wrong with the world? Was not this resentment explicit when *Cabildo* blamed the Graiver affair on liberal democracy because it had allowed for "the access [to power] of the newcomers and the displacement of old Argentines?" Was not status panic obvious when, in reference to Gelbard, the magazine asserted that the government should prevent forever that "the son of a nomadic old-clothes man may have access to the control of the levers of the economy"? "An old Argentine," it said, "is not, cannot be the same as an upstart Israelite."[64] The backward utopia presented as the "restoration of the natural order" is no more than the

64. Editorial, *Cabildo*, 1977, no. 7:3.

dream of turning back the clock of history and reestablishing the old pre-capitalist stratification system in which, right-wing intellectuals believe, soldiers, priests and themselves had the most prestigious positions. "The restoration of the natural hierarchical order . . . would return wealth to its instrumental and subordinate function. . . . The discipline of arms and the discipline of the priesthood would recover their lost preeminence and exemplar value."[65]

What are the prospects? On the one hand, changes in the structure of society since the 1960s have been conducive to the generalization of the psychological states that feed right-wing nationalism; on the other, several factors may be conducive to changes in its ideology.

Since the 1960s, the Argentine economy has not only stagnated, but it also retrogressed. The high-growth segment of the occupational structure has been, for most of this period, the informal sector. Both the working and the middle classes have been subject to processes of marginalization. The psychological consequences of downward mobility for large segments of the middle class are aggravated by "modernization" itself. According to different estimates and definitions, a fourth to a third of college-age people attend postsecondary institutions now. In a context of economic stagnation, this is bound to produce a highly frustrated professional and intellectual proletariat. To be sure, people in such a situation face several adaptive strategies in addition to political activism (emigration, lowering of expectations, etc.), and most of those selecting political activism are more likely to go to the left than to the right, for most young people prefer to be revolutionary rather than reactionary and to support egalitarian rather than hierarchical ideologies. However, all that an elite movement such as right-wing nationalism needs in order to survive is a critical mass, a small but regular flow of professionals and intellectuals. Social conditions in Argentina are such that a supply of new blood is assured for it in the foreseeable future.

Other factors suggest the possibility of changes in the doctrine of nationalism, in order to render it more "plausible," more consistent with the facts as its carriers experience them. One of these factors is the changes within the Catholic Church. Since the Second Vatican Council, the nationalists' variety of integrism has been delegitimized. A second factor is the disastrous record of military regimes, particularly the one in power from 1976 to 1983. Catholic nationalists place their hopes on an Argentine Franco who would, unlike the Spanish original, carry out their program of national restoration. Hence their focus on the cultivation of a political following among the military. But the recent regime, with its failure in all fronts (economic, human rights, war with England), led to the delegitimation of

---

65. Bandieri, "Nacionalismo," 22.

the armed forces as a political actor among all groups in the society (the ruling class included) and to the demoralization of the military themselves. It will not be easy, in the foreseeable future, to form a social coalition in support of military intervention.

Third, the nationalist conception of the nation is anachronistic today. In the 1930s and 1940s, this conception made sense to radical conservatives, integrist Catholics, and old Argentines: It was the time of the Spanish Civil War and Franco's "national crusade"; it was also a period in which large segments of the immigrant population had a low level of integration into Argentine society. Nowadays, the exaltation of the Spanish reactionary tradition lacks empirical referents, for Spain is a conventional liberal democracy. Also, Argentine society is much more integrated; a generation later, cultural differences between old Argentines and immigrants are fading.

Finally, the Catholic nationalist variety of anti-Semitism is now much less consistent with the "facts," as people perceive them, than when the doctrine was formulated. In the Europe of the interwar period, especially in Germany, Austria, and France, Jews were prominent in finance and in the revolutionary left. In Argentina at the time, these stereotypes could still make sense; the country had to deal with Jewish bankers in the United States and Europe, some of the export companies handling Argentine trade were Jewish, and many Jews were prominent in the left-wing intelligentsia. Later, in the postwar period, as I noted, many of the new industrialists were Jewish. But these stereotypes are inadequate today. Argentina has a staggering foreign debt, the highest in its history, but Jewish bankers do not appear among its main creditors. In fact, the symbol of financial exploitation is now the International Monetary Fund, an intergovernmental agency whose directors in the past period had perfectly "Latin" names. Furthermore, Argentina eventually had its revolutionary attempt, but none of its top leaders were Jewish. In fact, a large contingent of the main guerrilla group, the Montoneros, originated in the nationalist right itself. This major discrepancy between essence and evidence was sadly noted by *Cabildo,* which characteristically attributed the unexpected finding to Jewish perfidy: "If one reads the list of the fallen for 'liberation,' one will note that few last names—almost none—give the track of a Zionist. The reason is that these Zionists, who are so frequently found in the student slates at the University of Buenos Aires, have always behaved à la Timerman: sowing the seed, but never showing the face or holding a machine gun. Regrettably, the blood shed by the sicarians of subversion is preponderantly Creole."[66] At a larger scale, the image of the Jew as a "trafficker" and Marxist makes little sense in the contemporary world: Israel is neither a major financial center nor a revolu-

66. "Preso sin nombre, celda sin número," *Cabildo,* 1981, no. 43:12.

tionary state, and its citizens are stereotyped as soldiers and farmers rather than as moneylenders or radical intellectuals, Israel is allied with the West while the Soviet Union supports the Arabs, there are instances of anti-Semitism in Eastern Europe, and so on.

The leadership of nationalism is changing. The three main ideologues, Genta, Meinvielle, and Sacheri, died in the late 1970s (Genta and Sacheri killed by the guerrillas), and the generation whose ideology crystallized in the 1930s and 1940s is leaving the scene. The new leadership will be as frustrated and resentful as the old one was, and it will be similarly inclined to develop conspiracy theories to account for the decline of the country and their own discontent, but generational changes may facilitate the refurbishment of the doctrine.

V
Defining a New Identity

13
Argentine Culture and Jewish Identity

Leonardo Senkman

Introduction

During the flood of immigration to Argentina in the period from 1880 to 1940, three different currents of thought, or *ideologías de combate,* were dominant. These three intellectual currents deeply affected the processes through which immigrants were acculturated.

The first of these ideologies was laicism. From the very beginnings of the independent Argentine Republic, a major project of successive administrations was to capture administrative jurisdictions that previously had been in the hands of the clergy. The state took control of the registry of births, deaths, and marriages, and assumed ownership of cemeteries and schools. Although the Catholic Church initially had played a significant role in founding the Argentine state and a sense of Argentine nationality, it steadily lost ground to the state following independence, particularly during and after the presidency of Roca.

The prevailing anticlericalism in the political circles of the Argentine "Generations" of 1900 and 1910 was shared by atheists, agnostics, and lukewarm Catholics, who opposed sharing power with the Church, although they did not oppose Catholicism as the majority religion of Argentines. This laicism gained strength in the long and heated controversy over public education that resulted in the passage in 1884 of Law 1420, which mandated state-administered lay schools for all children.

Argentine laicism was not a civil religion in the sense that Rousseau and later Alberdi described, but rather reflected advocacy of a liberal state with full political control over the Church and a firm intention to achieve cultural unification of the diverse mass of immigrants. Thus the victory of laicism in education represented a loss of power for the Church, but the Catholic religion and its moral values were not threatened. The vast majority of the population continued to be Catholic.

With respect to the agenda of forming a culturally unified nation, laicism proved a powerful tool in the state effort to gain control over religious and private schooling. The Pedagogical Congress of 1882 was dedicated to the question of implementing lay power over education, even before passage of Law 1420. Eduardo Wilde, then Minister of Education and an outspoken laicist of the period, responded to a question from a Catholic deputy in the following terms:

> The State has no obligation to create Jews or to create Catholics, because to do so is in opposition to the goals of the State and to the liberty of religion that it proclaims. . . . If the Church says, "I can live in any State," then the State says, "I can live with any religion. . . . I am the State of Catholics, of Calvinists, of Lutherans, of the Jew and Muslim."[1]

A second major ideological influence was positivism. For the Generation of 1880, positivism offered a philosophical foundation for the idea of uninterrupted, evolutionary progress that dominated the Argentine ruling class. The fundamental tenets of positivism included biological evolution, a profound anticlericalism, rejection of the social consequences of Spanish colonial policies, and blind confidence in liberal democracy.

The attitude towards immigration held by such leading citizens of the time as J. Ramos Mejía, Jose Ingenieros, and Juan B. Justo serves to illustrate the positivist approach. Rationality was viewed as a guideline for introducing universal standards of conduct in order to undercut the hybrid character of the immigrant population, with its many languages, foreign mentalities, and exotic customs. Through its pretensions of applying Enlightenment ideals, positivism expected to overcome the main obstacles to progress, especially the traditional *criollo* way of thinking and the mentality of the heterogeneous immigrant population.

Positivist philosophy in Argentina, despite its constant invocation of universalistic rationalism and portrayal as being progressive and liberal, in practice developed into a distasteful xenophobia. The Socialist intellectual Jose Ingenieros proposed forming an "Argentine race." Domingo Sarmiento, in the Congreso Pedagogico Italiano of 1883, entered into heated discussion with those present in opposition to the idea of "educating a child in the

---

1. Consejo Nacional de Educatión, *Cincuentenario de la ley 1420,* Vol. I (Buenos Aires, 1934), 166.

Italian style." He opposed offering an English, Swedish, or any other type of foreign education as unnecessary and counterproductive in an age of universal scientific reason. For Sarmiento rationalism transcended national frontiers of thought, and his first priority was the victory of "civilization" over "barbarism."

The third ideological component of the time was cultural nationalism in the battle dress ideology of the *crisol de razas* (crucible of peoples), the Argentine equivalent of the melting pot ideology of the United States. Espousal of this doctrine permitted liberals, Catholics, anticlericals, nationalists, and even socialists to support the categorical assimilation of immigrants. The demand for assimilation was dressed in a variety of slogans opposing ethnic endogamy, opposing private schools, and supporting the inculcation of Spanish.

The theory of assimilation advanced by Argentine elites during the period of great immigration thus combined complementary rationales: the application of universalistic rationality as an antidote to prior nationality and ethnicity and the call for conformity to native Argentine language, culture, and nationality. State control over education was a primary vehicle for realizing this assimilation, along with other instruments of state power. These three mutually reinforcing ideological components shaped Argentine national culture until the transformations of the 1940s.

Jewish Identity and Argentine Culture in the Writings of Gerchunoff

The questions posed for the Jewish minority in the ideological context of Argentina during the period of immigration are clearly demonstrated in the life and work of Alberto Gerchunoff. Although Gerchunoff was not the only Jew integrated into Argentine intellectual life of his period, he was probably the first who throughout his life's work bore testimony to the tension and ambiguity that resulted from a dual cultural and national identity. For the gentiles who admired him he was the Jew of Argentine letters, and for his fellow Jews he was the Argentinian of letters of Jewish origin. His experience gives eloquent testimony to the asymmetries that governed the relationship between Jewish immigrants and Argentine national culture.

Jewish immigrants, to a greater extent than any other group, had to accept fully the rules of the *crisol de razas* ideology that governed Argentine national culture, simply because they were Jews living in a Catholic society governed by a constitutionally Catholic state. This religious asymmetry was buttressed by the rejection of ethnic and cultural pluralism by the native intelligentsia. Cultural assimilation and the dissolution of previous ethnic loyalties were basic tenets of the *crisol de razas* paradigm.

Gerchunoff was the first Jewish intellectual to understand fully and accept with resignation the tacit taboos of this context. From the very beginning of his career he managed to pass the test of national acculturation with flying colors. His 1910 book *Los Gauchos Judíos* was welcomed and honored by the readers of the Generation of 1890.[2] This volume legitimated the Jewish presence through its irreproachable cultural nationalism, expressed in the concept of *criollismo*. Bernardo Verbitsky, a second-generation Jewish writer, has rightly said that with the publication of *Los Gauchos Judíos,* Argentine Jews "acquired their citizenship papers."

By the 1920s Gerchunoff was a well-known writer whose pieces frequently appeared in the leading newspaper, *La Nación*. By this time Gerchunoff had abandoned the nativist *criollismo* style, which had developed into a literary subspecies dealing with immigration and acculturation. His newer work was treasured for its exquisitely pure Hispanicism, couched in the classical Castilian of the Golden Age of Spanish literature, a style few writers had adopted following the modernist movement in letters. By writing in the style of Cervantes, Gerchunoff appealed to the cultural nationalism of the 1920s, which was preoccupied with preserving the Hispanicism of preimmigration Argentina. The exaltation of the purity of the Spanish language was an important nationalist theme, conjuring up the specter of the invading immigrant masses, whose dialects would corrupt the linguistic heritage of the founding families of Argentina.

This approach served two important functions. First, of course, Gerchunoff's classical Hispanicism gained standing and legitimation in literary circles affected by Argentine nationalism. Second, it revindicated a Judeo-Spanish tradition as old as the influence of Yehuda Halevy, Augustín Rojas, and other medieval founders of the Spanish language. By stressing the Golden Age of the Hebraic–Hispanic past, Gerchunoff conferred respectability upon the Jewish community in terms of the Argentine context.[3]

This second function of Gerchunoff's style has been misinterpreted by some critics. Juan Carlos Ghiano, for example, argued that Gerchunoff disassociated himself from *porteño* (Buenos Aires) Judaism by writing "in the style of the ingenious nobleman of La Mancha."[4] But Gerchunoff's own words belie this interpretation:

2. Alberto Gerchunoff, *Los Gauchos Judíos,* rev. ed. (Buenos Aires: Gleizer, 1936).
3. These observations on ideology with reference to *criollismo* and the Hispanicist legitimation of Gerchunoff have been discussed in L. Senkman, *La identidad judía en la literatura argentina* (Buenos Aires: Editorial Pardes, 1983), chap. 2.
4. Juan Carlos Ghiano, "Gerchunoff, escritor," *La Nación,* 31 Dec. 1983, sec. 4, Letras, Artes, y Ciencias, Homenaje al Centenario del Nacimiento de Gerchunoff, 24.

> The Jew assimilated the Spanish language with extraordinary profundity. . . . He gave the Spanish spirit in the process of its culture, elements that characterized its genuine originality; he incorporated into his culture, in exchange, the expressive elements of language through which he realized himself from the start. It is not that the Jew easily adapts himself to the proper use of language. I would say that he does not adapt himself. What he does is to recover a language that already was his and represents to him a new promise.[5]

Like the early Lugones, much admired by Gerchunoff, he turned classical Spanish style into the didacticism of well-written Argentine expression. The great impact of his "Spanish" novel *La Jofaina Maravillosa* is reflected in the fact that Manuel Carlés, president of the Patriotic League that three years earlier had vandalized the Jewish ghetto of Buenos Aires during the tragic week of 1919, wrote an article of fervent praise for the book. Carlés did not hesitate to label this novel the "happy book of Argentine classicism" and to use it as a banner in the xenophobic crusade that the Patriotic League was waging against working class and immigrant intellectuals:

> The book by Gerchunoff is Argentine. It will not be understood by jackanapes, cabaret heroes, or youthful meddlers, intoxicated by Marx and Goldsmith, who will dismiss it by ridiculing the romanticism of noble deeds; but it will become the book of the rural soul, that understands the intrinsic value of the healthy and strong male, who rhymes to the strides of his horse . . . the verses that he will offer to his beloved at the next dance.[6]

No other Argentine writer of foreign origin managed to achieve this degree of legitimization. Gerchunoff's singular achievement offers a number of clues to a better understanding of the processes of Jewish acculturation in Argentina. His close friend and admirer, Manuel Mujica Lainez, writes that Gerchunoff "within himself channelled two distinct currents, the criollo and the Hebrew, and had the subtle gift of superimposing and alternating them."[7] This "alternation and superimposition" of Jewish and Argentine currents in Gerchunoff's work expressed the author's method of balancing two conflicting realities without achieving a stable merger between them.

Gerchunoff never deceived himself as to the personal nature of this conflict between Jew and Argentine, *gaucho-judío*. He fully realized that his successful personal integration in Argentine society, accomplished without renouncing his Jewish heritage, was not the type of integration that was

---

5. Alberto Gerchunoff, "Los judíos en la lengua castellana," in *El pino y la palmera* (1924; Buenos Aires: Sociedad Hebraica Argentina, 1952), 52.
6. Manuel Carlés, "La jofaina maravillosa. Agenda cervantina," *La Nación*, 12 Dec. 1922, 18.
7. Manuel Mujica Lainez, "Gerchunoff," *La Nación*, 31 Dec. 1983, 25.

hoped for by the Jewish community, despite the tributes paid to him by some intellectuals.

When in 1927 Gerchunoff became editor of the daily newspaper *El Mundo*, his achievement was celebrated by his Jewish friends. Salomón Resnick, coeditor of *Mundo Israelita*, on this occasion said:

> For us, the Jews of Argentina, Gerchunoff is the greatest evidence of our settlement in this country. Not forty years have passed since Jewish immigration began to flow to this land, and now for almost twenty years we have had a writer of Castilian who is one of the foremost exponents of Spanish-language literature.... Today we all recognize that Gerchunoff is the most eminent, most representative Jew of Argentina, the pride of us all. Yes, Gerchunoff has always shown himself to be generous to the Israelite collectivity, in spite of being so distinct from it and of not receiving from it the consideration that he deserves. He knew very well that the first generation would scarcely begin to understand him. For that we Jews of the second generation repay that debt of honor and gratitude.[8]

On the same occasion Leon Dujovne, the young philosopher, said that for his generation of young Jewish–Argentine intellectuals Gerchunoff was "more than a writer: he is our lay rabbi, our master."[9] Dujovne was not exaggerating. His circle of young colleagues—university students, academics, and intellectuals—had founded Sociedad Hebraica and had edited the magazines *Juventud* and *Nuestra Vida*. They had a real understanding of Gerchunoff's role. But notwithstanding Gerchunoff's success, the Jewish community at large, as in Resnick's accusation, saw a dangerous illusion in Gerchunoff's superimposing the *criollo* on the Jewish and preferred to live in the isolated world of the ghetto.

For the Jewish community the example of acculturation presented by Gerchunoff implied patterns of identification very different in style and conception from those that had been transplanted during the process of immigration: the Eastern European ghetto and the *shtetl*. It was also feared that the liberal Judeo-Argentine identity proposed by Gerchunoff would undermine the *Kehila*, or organized Jewish community, as the focal point of Jewish religion and nationhood. In consequence, Gerchunoff was viewed with fear and precaution by most leading figures in the Jewish community, despite his successes with the elite of Argentine culture.

Ultimately, however, the model proposed by Gerchunoff was to suc-

---

8. Speech by Salomón Resnick at an homage that was offered to Gerchunoff by a group of friends on the occasion of Gerchunoff's appointment as director of the newspaper *El Mundo*, as published in "La demostración de mundo israelita a A. Gerchunoff," *Mundo Israelita*, 3 Dec. 1927, 3.

9. "La demostración de mundo israelita."

ceed. It became institutionalized in the 1930s and 1940s as the second generation of Argentine Jews eagerly sought entry to the universities, the arts, and letters. This pattern of acculturation gave rise to the Sociedad Hebraica of Buenos Aires, one of the most significant institutions of Argentine Jewry. The impulse that led to the founding of the Sociedad Hebraica represented a middle course in the conflict between Argentine and Jewish identity. While some Jewish youths dealt with the ambiguity of their situation by denying everything Jewish, and others by choosing isolation in the *Kehila*, those who founded the Centro Juventud Israelita, later renamed the Sociedad Hebraica, chose a path leading towards Jewish integration in Argentine society.

In 1937 when laying the foundation stone for the new edifice of the Sociedad Hebraica, Gerchunoff reminded those present that this institution had helped to forge the way to Jewish integration by means of culture, "a means of approaching and making accessible the most typical and vernacular of the Hebrew spirit and at the same time placing the man who evinces this spirit in contact with the Argentine mentality, with the consciousness of a community that is his and in which he should play, without loss of his heritage, a cooperative role."[10]

In Gerchunoff's view, the Sociedad Hebraica should defend the acculturation and integration of Argentine Jewry; in his words, the mission of the Sociedad Hebraica was

> To affirm that in the environment in which we act and in the country with which we identify our will and desire to establish roots, deliberate hostility or faulty understanding will not be able to damage us; these will not diminish our capacity to contribute as Argentines, nor will we have to lose in this space, which should be of ample and cordial serenity, the most essential Jewish condition which is based in the vitality of the spirit.[11]

Gerchunoff's optimism remained even after the war, when the nature of the Holocaust became evident:

> In Europe they killed the Jews. Here the Jews continue their existence, with the bitterness and nightmares of brothers in mourning, without renouncing the necessity of linking themselves with the Argentine soul and their hereditary pleasure in doing so by means of thought, of beauty, of sociability. . . . The Argentine Sociedad Hebraica has this transcendental mission in Buenos Aires.[12]

---

10. Alberto Gerchunoff, "La sociedad hebraica argentina," in *El pino*, 125.
11. Gerchunoff, "La sociedad."
12. Gerchunoff, "Casa con su puerta abierta," in *El pino*.

This perspective was shared by a good number of Gerchunoff's intellectual contemporaries. Waldo Frank, the well-known American Jewish writer, visited Buenos Aires in 1942 and lectured at the Sociedad Hebraica on Latin American Jewry. He argued that the Jewish roots of Hispanic culture were such that even if the Jews coming to Latin America were not of Iberian origin, they participated in the same ethos that had formed the Hispanic tradition.[13] Frank, like the Argentine Jewish leader Dr. Moises Goldman, took the position that anti-Semitism was a foreign element with no authentic roots in Latin America to sustain it.

Jewish intellectuals visiting from Palestine also were willing to predict a great future for Jewish integration in the continent. In 1947, A. S. Juris spoke confidently of the "incubation of a new tribe of Israel in America." For him, intellectuals like Gerchunoff, Carlos Grunberg, and Saúl Gidekel were the first fruit of this new tribe. On the other hand, Juris warned of the possible conflicts between Jewish and Latin American identity:

> It is worth asking if the new Jewish intellectualism, creating in native language and in original form, will be equipped with the historical-religious baggage and the indispensable national and ethnic factors, as in the case of those Jewish bards and philosophers of the Iberian peninsula making possible the duality of being an integral part of the nation, and at the same time, an organic part of the universal Jewish people.[14]

Juris proposed to avoid the risks of isolation and complete assimilation by developing the dual loyalties resulting from Jewish integration into the larger society into a community project, rather than an individual project of a few intellectuals like Gerchunoff.

> The aspirations of the Israelite collectivity do not in any way contradict the Argentine national tradition and are impregnated with the highest sentiments of illustrious Argentine forefathers, such as San Martín, Alberdi, Moreno, and Sarmiento. The Jewish postulates are moderate complements of the Argentine ideal in contemporary history.... For the Argentine Jew there is only one premise: Argentine yes, Jewish yes. I am Argentine and I am a Jew, concepts that are inseparable and highly just. The love of Argentina is a natural love for the land of my birth, education, life, and custom. My love for the Jewish people is an organic part of the love that I profess for my parents, my blood, my people.[15]

---

13. Waldo Frank, *El judío en nuestro tiempo* (Buenos Aires: Ediciones Ela, 1945), 30.

14. A. S. Juris, "Un intermedio espiritual: La incubación de una neuva tribu," *Judaica*, Año XIV, Numero extraordinario en homenaje a la memoria de su fundador y director, Salomon Resnick (July 1947), 13–14.

15. Juris, "Un intermedio."

Unfortunately for the integrationist project advanced by intellectuals such as Gerchunoff, Frank, and Juris, the *crisol de raza* ideology of assimilation shared by Argentine liberals, Catholics, Freemasons, Socialists, nationalists, and Marxists opposed the idea that the integration of Jews as Argentine citizens could imply a continuing loyalty to Jewish ethnicity and community. The paradox of the Argentine experience is that immigrant groups continued to practice and persevere in such loyalties, despite the melting pot ideology that discouraged ethnic and cultural loyalties in favor of assimilation.

The Image of Jews in the Argentine Press

A defining characteristic of the Argentine newspapers' coverage of Jewish matters was its defensive attitude, particularly with respect to Jewish education and Jewish cemeteries. Thus far no systematic study of press coverage of such issues has taken place, although the material reported here, which emerged from a study of the reaction to Jewish immigration, may be considered characteristic.

The efforts of the Jewish Colonization Association to promote Jewish settlements in the provinces of Entre Ríos and Santa Fe were the subject of uninterrupted criticism in the two major Buenos Aires dailies, *La Prensa* and *La Nación,* until the end of the 1920s. The items that provoked the greatest hostility were the cultural and educational features of the new communities, which were viewed as constituting a betrayal of Argentine values.

The publication in 1909 of the book by Ricardo Rojas, *La Restauración Nacionalista,* attracted considerable press attention. Rojas stressed the dangers of private schools and called for the elimination of Jewish, Italian, and German education in Argentina. The press in the same year also devoted considerable editorial space to the reports of municipal education inspectors, emphasizing those hostile to private education, such as one by a man named Bavios that criticized Jewish education for a disregard of the national spirit while overlooking a report by an inspector Antequera that took a favorable view of Jewish schools.

On June 19, 1914, *La Nación* published an article by its correspondent in Santa Fe on Jewish settlement in that province under the title "Israel in the Promised Land." This piece attacked the Jewish character of the settlements as constituting a challenge to national institutions.

> One hundred twelve square kilometers of the north of this province constitute a veritable Hebrew country with its extreme peculiarities of spirit and

custom, its private laws generally observed, its religion, and the real autonomy that these social elements have been able to institute. The national offices . . . of this region have to fight constantly and interminably against this population's spirit of resistance against a regime that is not of their tradition and laws. To laugh at foreign laws is a program that one could believe obligatory of every Jewish colonist. . . . Our young, rich, free, and hospitable nation's power of assimilation is broken down by the jealously differentiated persistence of the characteristics of this spirit, of this historical position without social, moral, or ethnic variance, tirelessly and painstakingly preserved despite everything and everyone. . . . The Jews of our country are, will die, and will make their offspring as Jewish as in other parts of the world.[16]

The author of this editorial in *La Nación* took the position that this situation was practically a crime against Argentine magnanimity and placed the blame upon Jewish education in the following terms:

> The Israelites never send their children to public schools, but send them to the Israelite schools of the Jewish Colonization Association where they are instructed to obey the secular spirit of their race, building on the position continually reinforced in the home, that since the territory of these colonies was acquired with Hebrew capital, and populated and worked by Hebrews, those who are born in the colonies are Israelites and not Argentines, and that they should take as their own laws the Jewish laws.[17]

Twelve years later *La Prensa* took up the same line, arguing that Jewish schools did not promote nationalism. The lead editorial of February 29, 1926, criticized Italian and "Russo-Jewish" schools for "impeding the formation of an Argentine soul in students born on our soil and not forging in the children the civic character that will make them apt to fight for the establishment of democratic institutions, as well as not inspiring love of the national heritage and faith in the superior destiny of the fatherland."[18]

The following day the general manager of the Jewish Colonization Association sent a letter to the editor of *La Prensa* rebutting the editorial, which was not published. Instead, the newspaper repeated its charges under the heading "An Observation That We Will Not Retract," and claimed that a favorable report on Jewish schools prepared by the minister of government of Entre Ríos, Dr. J. Sagarna, merely reflected the fact that the schools had come under the control and direction of national authorities.[19]

In response to this statement *Mundo Israelita* published an editorial

---

16. "Israel en la tierra prometida," *La Nación*, 19 June 1914, 11.
17. "Israel en la tierra."
18. "Escuelas particulares que no fomentan el nacionalismo," *La Prensa*, 29 Jan. 1926, 14.
19. "Observación que no rectificamos," *La Prensa*, 30 Jan. 1926, 14.

by León Kilbrick, attempting to remind the public that Dr. Sagarna's inspection of the schools had taken place while they were still under private control, and that such schools had educated "all the cohort of Argentine citizens, industrialists and merchants of Jewish origin, who have contributed so much to our progress, who are so useful to the country, and who love it as much as those who flaunt an ebullient patriotism."[20]

The lumping together of Jewish and Italian schools in the attack by *La Prensa* was particularly unfair because at the time of this exchange the formerly Jewish schools had passed to the control of the state and offered the national curriculum, supplemented by complementary Jewish education, whereas the Italian schools offered a completely Italian curriculum. The *Mundo Israelita* editorial asked, "Jewish children attend the public schools; outside of them they receive a complementary education. What harm can come of this?"[21]

Thus although the Argentine press was willing to celebrate the achievements of individual Jews such as Gerchunoff, Jewish education for the Jewish community was viewed with fear and suspicion. In the words of *La Nación*'s correspondent from Santa Fe, the image propagated was that "Jewish intelligence and sagacity" were being used to "persevere in that quiet but stubborn resistance" against assimilation.

Jewish Identity and the Argentine Socialist Party

The Argentine image of Jewry in the period under discussion is particularly highlighted by the positions taken by leading politicians of the Argentine Socialist Party. This party had a strong following in the urban working class, which included a substantial Jewish element. Several Jews were prominent in party affairs, most notably Enrique Dickmann. Other leaders, such as Dr. Alfredo Palacios, were considered friendly towards Jews. Given the socially progressive character of this party and the nature of its appeal to the urban working classes in which Jews were a large element, the Socialist position on the Jewish question might have been expected to be more sensitive to the maintenance of Jewish identity than the attitudes expressed in the mainstream press. Such was not the case.

Probably the most important figure in the Socialist party was Juan B. Justo, the founder and editor of *La Vanguardia*. Justo, himself married to a Jew, was a strong anticlericalist and advocate of the assimilation of immigrants. In 1913, on the occasion of the Beilis trial, he issued a strong state-

---

20. "La Prensa y las escuelas judías," *Mundo Israelita*, vol. 3, no. 140 (1926): 1.
21. "La Prensa y las escuelas."

ment demanding the ending of state subsidies of the Catholic Church, the complete secularization of all education, and a ban on allowing foreign clergy into the country. This was coupled with an attack on all forms of religion as a drug of the people, including Judaism, which was denounced by Justo for the practice of circumcision, which he termed a "bloody and dirty rite."

Throughout his writings and speeches Justo advocated the naturalization of immigrants, attempting to persuade the immigrant working class of the importance of fully participating in Argentina's political life. When addressing himself to Spanish and Italian immigrants, Justo argued that taking up Argentine nationality did not imply disloyalty to Spain or Italy, but on the contrary would simply enable the immigrants to provide more efficient support to their country of origin, with which ethnic, sentimental, and moral links could be maintained.[22]

In contrast, when addressing Jewish immigrants, Justo's position was very different. In a famous article published in 1923 in the Jewish periodical *Vida Nuestra* entitled, "Why I Don't Like Writing for a Newspaper That Calls Itself Jewish," Justo articulated many of the themes that dominated Argentine thinking about Jewry.[23] One of these themes was rejection of Jewry as constituting a separate community combined with acceptance of individual Jews as human beings.

> Separately, or in the crowd of peoples, I admire some and appreciate many human beings who are labelled Jews. When the Jews are together, in contrast, they immediately seem suspicious and enigmatic to me. They offend my nationalist sentiments.

Justo then extolled the virtues of Argentina as a melting pot combining such elements as outstanding schools and newspapers, world-class nutrition and cuisine, English bulls, American agricultural machinery, and cosmopolitan commerce. He asked rhetorically, "In this atmosphere, what could be the importance of a group of people singling out and perpetuating themselves with the label of Israelites or Jews?"

---

22. Juan B. Justo, *Educación pública* (Buenos Aires: La Vanguardia, 1930), 32. With respect to Justo's views on Italian immigration, see *Obras Completas*, vol. 5, 116–121, and *Internacionalismo y patria* (Buenos Aires: La Vanguardia, 1933), 181–192, 201. A useful source is Jacinto Oddone, *Gremialismo proletario argentino* (Buenos Aires: La Vanguardia, 1949), 286–295.

23. Juan B. Justo, "Por qué no me gusta escribir en una hoja que se dice Israelita," *Nuestra Vida*, vol. 6, no. 9 (March 1923). All the following quotations are taken from this source.

Warming to this theme, Justo accused the Jewish community of separatist tendencies opposed to the direction taken by the rest of Argentine society:

> Little sympathy can be inspired in us, a people of mixed origins, by the fruitless effort of one of the smallest groups that has entered the country to maintain themselves as a race apart, when we absorb and allow ourselves to be absorbed by, in a general mixture, the great immigratory masses coming from countries of major current importance and grandiose historical traditions. Should we Balkanize the country, making the Republic into a mosaic of races, another Macedonia? Should we aspire to always have two races here, the Jewish race and one which is formed by the merging of all other races, a duality that some would consider more simple?

Justo then proceeded to condemn Jewish rites and customs, such as circumcision, the prohibition against eating pork, and kosher dietary practices. After criticizing the colonies in Argentina of the Jewish Colonization Association for being self-segregating, he attacked Jewish nationalism as being opposed to international socialism. Jewish settlement in Palestine was considered justifiable by Justo under two conditions, the first being that other peoples not be molested and the second being that the Zionist movement purge other nations of abnormal and unassimilable elements. Finally, Justo called upon Jews to abandon their "intellectual pride in calling attention to the Jewish character of the great philosophical and scientific geniuses of modern times," and other forms of "secret pride."

The same year the Socialist periodical *La Vanguardia* published an article by Marcos Wortman criticizing the work of the Jewish Colonization Association.[24] The author, a militant Socialist who formerly had been a farmer in one of its colonies, accused the association of assigning land titles to colonists in a manner that prevented land from falling into the hands of non-Jews, thus promoting "racial and ethnocentric sectarianism."

General Director Starkmet of the Association in Buenos Aires replied quickly to the charge of sectarianism in a letter of which portions appeared in *La Vanguardia*:

> It is probable that some of our colonists prefer to have some of their co-religionists as neighbors, due to affinities of race, of origin, of education; these colonists might regret that the lands of their colonies change hands. With respect to the Jewish Colonization Association, its only concern is that the lot belongs to the family that has acquired it after long years of work, so that the

---

24. This piece by Wortman was published in three parts in *La Vanguardia*, on November 12, 13, and 14, 1923.

agricultural tradition continues in the family and so that the family will always be in the category of productive workers.[25]

Juan B. Justo decided to intervene personally in the dispute between Wortman and Starkmet with a strong statement, also published in *La Vanguardia*, that attacked the Jewish Colonization Association:

> The Jewish colonists appear subject to a tutelege that takes away their liberty and their responsibility. As long as they stay in place and do not bring non-Jews to the farm, they can be as late as they want in meeting their payments, without being bothered by the Association. In fact the more delinquent they are, the more they are appreciated by company officials, because the less likely they are to obtain title to their land. Their production and sale of wheat doesn't matter as long as they produce Jews. . . . We affirm once again that this is a sectarian enterprise, managed by professional Jews who see in the Jewish character of this colonization their own reason for being.[26]

Another demonstration of Socialist antipathy toward Jewish community institutions was provided by the opposition of party leaders to the establishment of a Jewish cemetery. After twelve years of concerted effort, the Jevra Kedusha Azkenazi, or Jewish Burial Association, was given permission in 1910 to establish a Jewish cemetery in the Buenos Aires suburb of Liniers, despite a bitter controversy in the press and the opposition of Socialist city councilmen. In 1926 the Jevra Kedusha attempted to obtain permission to expand the cemetery, again in the face of strong Socialist (as well as Conservative) opposition.

On the occasion of consideration of this request by the city council, the well-known Socialist leader Americo Ghioldi applied once again the *Crisol de Razas* arguments to oppose granting approval to an expansion of the cemetery:

> Someone has said that the nationalist character of our party is due to its internationalist sentiment. Men of all races have mixed and blended, contributing to the generation of a new race, with a unique physical character and new mentality. All the work of the country is the expression of international solidarity among men of different races. . . .
>
> The only group of persons who constitute an isolated society that rejects biological and spiritual exchanges with men of other races and nationalities are precisely the Jews. . . . We cannot be accused of being antisemitic, but we cannot accept negative prejudices and traditions, any more than other factors that slow the development of society. . . . It seems ridiculous to

---

25. *La Vanguardia*, 22 Nov. 1923, 5. The full text of Starkmet's reply was published in *Mundo Israelita*, 29 Nov. 1923, 5.

26. *La Vanguardia*, 23 Nov. 1923, 5; this letter was also published in *Mundo Israelita*, 29 Nov. 1923, 5.

us that the Jews should have their own slaughterhouse and it seems equally ridiculous that the Jews should have a cemetery exclusively for their own use.[27]

A second councillor named Gimenez, who signed the Socialist declaration along with Ghioldi, had written a book analyzing the conflict between Church and State when the law establishing the Civil Registry Office was passed by Parliament. Gimenez objected to the Jewish cemetery for two reasons: because it would be "an example of intolerance" towards sons of non-Jewish mothers who would be denied Halakic burial and because it would establish a precedent for other non-Catholic communities, which might ask for separate cemeteries. Gimenez favored closing the Jewish cemetery and replacing it with a new large cemetery with an area reserved for Jews. His attitude was summed up by the comment that the only Jews he would accept for the sake of the nation's progress were those "like our two deputies of Jewish origin, fortunately redeemed Jews who honor the Argentine Parliament."

Conclusion

The treatment of Jews in the Argentine press and in the positions taken by prominent Argentine Socialists demonstrates the extent to which the ideologies of laicism, positivism, and the *crisol de razas* (melting pot) dominated Argentine attitudes during the formative period in which modern Argentine institutions took shape. Jewish identity and Jewish institutions were suspect and constantly portrayed as antithetical to Argentine identity and Argentine institutions.

Even Gerchunoff, whose literary achievements were rewarded with social acceptance, was unable to translate his personal achievements into the acceptance of Jewish culture by Argentines. He was viewed by non-Jews as an exception and treated with suspicion by many Jews. Although Gerchunoff's careful balancing of Jewish identity and Argentine nationality was to presage the adaptation made by later generations of Argentine Jews, the ideologies that have dominated the rise of modern Argentina remain influential among Argentines and problematic for Argentina's Jewry.

---

27. This discussion took place in the Sesión del Consejo Deliberante de la Ciudad de Buenos Aires on April 23, 1926. See *Versiones Taquigráficas del Consejo Deliberante Ciudad de Buenos Aires* [Typed transcript of the Deliberative Council of the City of Buenos Aires], vol. 34, Jan.–July 1926, 187–192, primer periodo de sesiones. All the following citations come from this source.

14
Informal Jewish Education in Argentina

Israel Even-Shoshan

Introduction

In 1977, against a background of intensifying socioeconomic crisis, the Jews of Argentina experienced both a fear of being overwhelmed and assimilated by a society increasingly dominated by nationalist and Catholic ideologues and a contrary fear of ideological conquest of Jewish youth by a radicalized and outlawed political left. They believed that, contrary to previous experience, the military authorities of the Argentine junta would not be content with destroying the Left, but that they would go on to mold an Argentine society that conformed to their own way of thinking.

What that way of thinking implied for Jews was illustrated by an article that appeared in the weekly newspaper *Carta Politica* in June 1977. In an article entitled "The Jews," journalist Mariano Grondona expressed disapproval of United States–style cultural pluralism as a model for Argentine society. European societies that have created monolithic nations are more suitable models for Argentina, he claimed; and if Argentines are to achieve this goal, they must strengthen Argentine national values. Primary among these is the tradition that Argentina is a Catholic state. Of all the national minorities living in Argentina, Grondona argued, the Jewish minority has kept its special character longer than any other. Hence, Jews present a challenge to Argentine society. Only when the Jewish minority is entirely assimilated will it be possible to create a monolithic society. Jews who value their Judaism more than they do their *argentinidad* and who consequently find it difficult to integrate into such a social structure have an alternative: They can develop their values freely in the State of Israel.

Grondona summarized the challenge to Jewish survival in Argentina. His close ties to ruling Catholic and military circles gave his ideas importance. His words thus provide the context for understanding the system of informal Jewish education that developed in response to a perceived threat. Although the union of Catholicism and nationalism is an old one in Argentina, never in the past had its adherents been so strong and so close to positions of power as they were in 1977.

The increasing tendency to define Argentine nationalism as specifically Catholic came at a time when Jewish identity was considerably attenuated. Third-generation Argentine Jews are substantially removed from the traditional Jewish values of the immigrant generation. Those immigrants, though mostly irreligious, nevertheless brought with them specifically Jewish experiences, which they expressed at a cultural level (language, customs, tradition, historical awareness) and at a social level (a network of institutions imported from their countries of origin).

As newer generations moved away from the immigrant experience, Jewish values founded on Old World experience became weaker. As integration into the new local society progressed, Jewish values became diluted by those of the non-Jewish bourgeois society that so wholeheartedly embraced European cultural standards. Faced by this reality, Jewish families resigned their task as Jewish educators and, rather than withstand the influence of their environment, joined it in creating their children's formative environment. The struggle to form a Jewish identity among young people was left almost exclusively to organized Jewish education, both formal and informal.

Research on Informal Education

The small amount of research that has been carried out on Jewish informal educational systems inspired this writer to investigate this area of Jewish life.[1] The present study reached 4357 young people aged 13–18 and residing in Buenos Aires and its suburbs, or 34.9% of the 12,480 persons of this age residing in the designated geographic area.[2] It therefore appears that approximately one-third of the young persons residing in the Buenos

---

1. The field study on which this chapter is based was carried out in April–September 1977; data and conclusions are contained in a seminar paper submitted to Professor Haim Avni of The Hebrew University.

2. According to calculations by U. O. Schmelz and Sergio DellaPergola, "Mivneh Yahadut America Latinit," *Machon Horowitz* (Tel Aviv) (1975), 40–57.

Aires area are involved in some form of informal Jewish education—a more optimistic picture than that usually presented.

The study surveyed all Jewish institutions in Greater Buenos Aires that included among their activities at least one youth group within an educational framework. Seventy-four were identified, of which 68 were carrying out educational activities at the time. Because 19 of these were not concerned with the age group under study, the findings for the remaining 49 institutions, based on visitations and interviews with significant personnel, are presented here.

In the group of institutions comprising the pioneering Zionist youth movements, there were 1155 young persons between the ages of 13 and 18 active in 22 different branches. In the group of 4 large social clubs—Hebraica, Maccabi, Club Atletico Sefaradi Argentino (CASA), and HaCoaj—there were 1295 persons of this age enrolled in educational programs. Beth El, the principal institution of the Conservative movement,[3] enrolled 812 youngsters of this age in its synagogue school. Agudat Israel youth movements, which are religious and non-Zionist, enrolled 90 young people, and two local institutions connected with the Jewish Agency—the Movement for Young Aliya and the Editti School for Counselors—enrolled 20 and 23 pupils, respectively. Finally, 962 young people were identified in independent youth organizations unconnected with any of these groups.

Following a preliminary survey to obtain basic data on the institutions and the youngsters attending them, 6 organizations were chosen as representative from the point of view of the type of organization, the type of youngster participating in it, and geographical dispersion. These 6 include 2 Zionist youth movements (Dror and HeHalutz LaMerhav), 3 large clubs (Hebraica, Maccabi, and CASA), and a synagogue (Beth El).

In order to examine their educational systems as these are seen by the people involved, the researcher surveyed students by means of a questionnaire, eliciting their views of the educational system and of their own Jewish identity. In addition, school administrators, psychologists, directors of communal organizations, and other experts were interviewed. Because the information developed revealed a substantial change in approach occurring about 1973, brief sketches of the persons interviewed and who played a role in carrying out those changes are given here.

> 1. David Fleischer. Past president of Hebraica; president of the Argentine Federation of Maccabean Community Centers (FACCMA). The chief person involved in the process of change.

3. In this context, *Conservative* refers to a religious movement that attempts to bridge religious Orthodoxy and liberal Reform. Particularly strong in the United States, it was introduced into Argentina by an American rabbi, Marshall Meyer.

2. Hector Shalom. Psychologist. Responsible for organizing the youth department of Hebraica and later the executive director of FACCMA. His persuasive personality helped launch a new kind of youth movement.
3. Alberto Senderey. Executive vice president of Hebraica, an interesting instance of importing a United States style of job to Argentina. Scion of a respected Argentine Jewish family, through his personality and views he became the central figure in the institution.
4. Emanuel Raz. Israeli emissary (*shaliah*) who worked within Hebraica for three years.
5. Mauricio Entenberg. Vice president of Maccabi at the time of the research, director of its education department, and the brains behind its educational activities.
6. Danny Yofe. Executive director of the education department of Maccabi.
7. Yossi Haiat. Israeli emissary who was at the center of educational activity at Maccabi.
8. Quito Weinstein. Israeli emissary to CASA, who as educational program director injected Israeli content into the club's activities.
9. Rabbi Marshall Meyer. A charismatic American who founded the Conservative movement in Argentina in 1959. A controversial figure, he is the person responsible for the movement's success.
10. Rabbi Mordechai Edrei. Moroccan-born and from an Orthodox background, he was chief assistant to Rabbi Meyer.
11. Pesah Fried. An Argentine who became the Israeli emissary to the Dror youth movement.
12. Aharon Steinhardt. An Argentine who became emissary to the HeHalutz LaMerhav youth movement.
13. Luis Karpf. Social psychologist, a gifted and effective person in his field. In charge of community center development and training of educator cadres for the informal educational system.
14. Abraham Golek. Israeli emissary. For five years he was principal of the Editti School for *madrichim* (counselors).

The survey revealed a single disturbing point of reference: Jewish identity is eroding among the youth, and assimilation is growing. Many young Jews seek their fortune in greener, non-Jewish pastures. Those who remain within the Jewish fold indicate that Judaism has a negative connotation for them: To be Jewish is to be different, but the meaning of this difference is vague and undefined. As Golek expressed the problem, the Editti School for Counselors is compelled to instruct future counselors in the subjects they are supposed to teach because they are for the most part ignorant of them. Not only has traditional Judaism been severely eroded, but changes that have taken place in the general society, and that impinge directly on Jewish educational needs, have not been adequately taken into account. "We act as though disciplines such as sociology, social psychology, etc., do not exist," said one educator.

Class, Identity, and Repression

The Jewish community itself has changed considerably over the generations. The traditional economic structure based on wage-earners and independent owners of small businesses was described in 1977 in the following way:

10% upper middle class
45% established middle class
35% lower middle class
10% impoverished[4]

As the Jewish population ascended the economic ladder it migrated from the old Jewish neighborhoods to higher class districts to the north of the city such as Belgrano, Barrio Norte, and Palermo. The migration has not been examined closely but it is generally thought that most of the younger generation of Buenos Aires Jews is concentrated in these neighborhoods. Educated mainly in government schools, they have come under the influence of a secular national culture, and were unprepared for the resurgence of ultramontanism. They inherited from their immigrant grandparents a feeling of being different, without knowing what constituted that difference.

In the absence of a Jewish religious alternative such as never existed in Argentina, and as traditional Jewish culture became more remote, a hesitant movement began toward identification with the Zionist parties that controlled the Jewish establishment.[5] Through these, Zionist education as well as pro-Israel attitudes developed. In a nation of immigrants, establishment of the State of Israel placed Argentine Jews on a level of equality with other immigrant groups.[6] But this rather hesitant pro-Israel attitude, combined with the remnants of Yiddish culture, did not suffice to ward off the strong ideological and social impulses that shook Jewish youth in Argentina in the

---

4. Joseph Bergio, "Juifs d'Argentine a la recherche d'une identité," *Les Nouveaux Cahiers* (Paris) 48 (Spring 1977), 38–52.

5. Arie Tartakower discusses the Jewish Zionist establishment in *Shivtei Israel* (Tel Aviv) 3 (1966), 49–53.

6. Moshe Davis analyzed the concept of *madre patria* as it applies to the Jewish attitude toward Israel in "Centers of Jewry in the Western Hemisphere: A Comparative Approach," *The Jewish Journal of Sociology*, 5 (June 1963): 4–26.

early 1970s. All the persons interviewed, without exception, considered the years 1972–1973 as the time when leftist influences reached such a peak that entire sections of the Jewish educational structure collapsed.

In the previous generation, the threat to Jewish life in Argentina had come from the ideas of the international Left. In the early 1970s, it was the national Left that swept the country and swept Jewish youth out of the Jewish community. Responding to the threat, informal education altered course in 1973.[7]

1973 was the year of the return to power of Juan Perón. In a short time, the regime brought the country to social chaos, economic crisis, political instability, and a state of civil war. Disappointment and political polarization proceeded hand in hand, causing many young people, including a good proportion of Jewish youth, to take up extreme positions, join underground organizations, and participate in armed revolt. Other Jewish youngsters, like people everywhere, responded with apathy and a feeling of helplessness. Matters came to a head when the armed forces renewed their control of the country in 1976.

Two factors compounded the problem of Argentine Jewish youth: alienation from Judaism and an accelerating rate of assimilation. The war against the left, which the military viewed as its main task, was conducted by right-wing military and paramilitary forces, which by definition in Argentina are militantly anti-Semitic. Young Jews were persecuted and physically annihilated as leftists even when they were only slightly inclined to the left. Apprehended as leftists, they often were made to suffer as Jews even though in many cases they did not personally identify as Jews.

As the crisis grew worse, it became clear that the economic policy of the government was aimed at destroying the broad middle class, which formed the basis of Argentina's democratic system and which supported the two major political parties, the Peronists and the Radicals. Striking a blow at the middle class obviously meant striking a blow at Argentine Jewry.[8] This created the atmosphere of alarm in which informal Jewish education developed. Against this general background, it is now appropriate to examine how representative educational organizations operated.

Institutions for Informal Jewish Education

Dror is a pioneering youth movement founded and developed within the Sholom Aleichem network of Jewish schools. Like the schools, Dror

---

7. Any conclusions written about now must be conditioned by the realization that the process was just four years old when studied, that development was continuing, and that the process was far from complete in 1977.

8. See Aaron Viñas, "Jewish Presence and Identity in Argentina," *Forum* 34 (1979), 101–119.

belongs to Poalei Zion Smol (Zionist Workers' Alliance/Left), which transmits a synthesis of Zionism and socialism. This synthesis was easier to achieve when young persons arrived at the school already sensitive to Judaism. However, the youngsters coming to the movement in the 1970s had been greatly influenced by their non-Jewish surroundings; their Jewish identity was weak, and it did not engage them emotionally. Roots in traditional Judaism were missing. Consequently, the leaders of Dror concluded that their first task must be to develop a feeling for Judaism, relying more on direct experience and less on ideology.

The chief aim of Dror is *aliya* (emigration to Israel), and specifically to kibbutz life. Zionism for this group is largely negation of the Diaspora. Without a Jewish background, the socialist–Zionist ideal that infuses members of this group tends to turn into objective analysis of alternatives in the face of latent or actual anti-Semitism.

Dror has not succeeded in penetrating the new Jewish neighborhoods, although many of its members actually live in Belgrano or Palermo. It lacks the resources to finance its own headquarters and has not found another institution to house its activities. Interviewees claimed that Zionism would be welcomed into the new neighborhoods only in a watered-down version.

The crisis of values that struck Argentina severely affected Dror. According to the testimony of those in positions of responsibility, the organization was brought to a grave qualitative crisis. Although Dror's young members, as determined from their responses to questionnaires, are searching for a Jewish way of life, the movement has educational deficiencies of which it is well aware. Yet it can claim some success in that Dror sponsored a cadre of immigrants to Israel each year in the period 1973–1983.

Another pioneering youth movement, HeHalutz LaMerhav, is linked to no ideological trend within the Zionist movement and affiliates with several kibbutzim in Israel. This movement is active in greater Buenos Aires and in Bahia Blanca and nearby Jewish agricultural settlements. Most of the young people in this movement come from lower income groups whose families cannot afford to send them to the large social clubs.

The primary objective of the movement, given the powerful trend toward assimilation, is to provide a foundation for Jewish identity. Only when Jewish identity is firmly founded can the task of Zionist education begin. Special emphasis is placed on group activities: It is in the framework of a group that young people come to Israel and possibly remain as a nucleus of permanent immigrants. All senior members of HaHalutz LaMerhav spend a year in Israel, and education for *aliya* is in fact the ultimate goal of the movement.

In difficult circumstances, with scarce resources, and in the face of a general identity crisis among Jewish youth, the Argentine Zionist youth movements contribute proportionally the most immigrants of any community in the world: Over 3% of all Argentine Jewish youth settle in Israel each year as members of kibbutzim.[9]

The late 1940s and 1950s witnessed the height of activity of the pioneering youth movements in Argentina. Anyone aware of their activities at that time who sought them out now would be greatly surprised to find that the closest thing to them is located in the youth department of the Hebraica Club.

Until recent years, the Hebraica—the largest Jewish club in Argentina and one that originally presented a bourgeois, assimilationist face to the nation—offers a mix of Jewish and Argentine culture. It stressed social and sporting activities equally, and was not Zionist in outlook. The general public considered it a Jewish middle-class organization. In 1973, when thousands of Jewish youth were swept into leftist political organizations, Jewish institutions were emptied of their young people. Simultaneously, the Yom Kippur War drastically altered the status of Israel in the Middle East. Following this event, the Hebraica renovated its program, accepting three basic principles.

1. Only a movement with a strong ideological component can attract young people who are highly politicized.
2. The defense of Israel required mobilization of all forces; any counselors not in agreement (the Communists) were expelled from Hebraica.
3. The centrality of Israel offers an alternative to Jewish youth whose idealism had led them to Argentine leftist movements.

The classic model of Hebraica as a liberal bourgeois institution did not suit the new realities, so a search was begun for a new framework. The model of a religious congregation was not regarded as suitable either, and at last the pioneering youth movement was seized on to provide the main elements, both in principles for action and in educational structure. Hebraica adopted Zionism: not a pioneering Zionism based on negation of the Argentine diaspora, but a Zionism founded on Judaism and the Jewish people's special relationship to Israel. Starting with a summer camp in December 1973 in which 15 people participated, the movement grew to encompass 600 young people between the ages of 13 and 18 in 1977—without doubt the largest Jewish youth movement in Argentina.

During this entire period, the relationship between the developing youth movement—growing ever more independent within the framework of the club—and the club itself remained problematic. Sectors of the club

---

9. Data from the Government of Israel, Department of Aliya.

membership viewed the new youth organization with apprehension; others held a more favorable attitude, led by the club president who supported the new body and granted it freedom of action. Even after four years of activity the possibility of conflict still existed, but an equilibrium was maintained between the ideological line of the youth department and the official orientation of the club.

The educational ideal of the youth department of Hebraica is the formation of a young person healthy in body and in mind, possessing both Jewish and Zionist awareness. A visit to Israel for a two-month seminar is a compulsory stage in the young person's educational development. There is education for *aliya*, but no obligation to implement it, as in the classic pioneering youth movements. In the words of the developer of the program, Hector Shalom: "The educational work is intended to encourage development on three levels: feeling, thinking, doing, so that the individual will reach the point of feeling he is part of his Jewish surroundings. Only on the foundation of this sense of belonging is it possible to build a Zionist conception as a coherent answer on all three levels." Zionism is perceived as recognition that Israel is part of modern Jewish reality and at the center of Jewish life, an open possibility for continuing one's own life. However, the alternative of living an Argentine life while being active and contributing to Jewish community life in Argentina also exists. As a result, Hebraica today is a pluralistic institution that is home simultaneously to a Zionist youth movement and to a country club catering to the wealthy Jewish middle class, which considers that its future lies in Argentina.[10]

The external situation, as we have seen, exerts strong pressure on Argentine Jewry. The answer provided by Hebraica rejects assimilation and rejects as well the negative attitude of Argentine society toward Jewish life. Either as a result of premeditation or of the harshness of reality (quite likely the second), Hebraica's response was to become Zionist. To reach this result, the institution traveled a long way from its original assimilationist, anti-Zionist stance.

Hebraica today is a Zionist institution within its own definition of the term. It believes in the existence of one Jewish people, of whom Argentine Jewry is a part and at the center of which is the State of Israel. The ideal is for every Jew to continue life in that center. However, so far, the majority of Jews in the world have chosen to remain in the diaspora. Where there is a center, there is a periphery. The strengthening of the periphery is an obliga-

---

10. 50 km from the capital, at Pilar, Hebraica has built a country club comprising some of the most expensive villas to be seen at the exclusive clubs frequented by wealthy Argentines. The Hebraica's youth department represents an antithesis of country club life among the rich bourgeoisie who are putting down roots in the country.

tion, because only in this way will it be possible to ensure the existence of Zionism and of immigration to Israel. *Aliya* is the highest ideal; the means of ensuring that is to strengthen Argentine Jewry.

Among the large clubs, the Maccabi occupies a special place. From its establishment, the club emphasized sports and self-defense. It differed from other, assimilationist clubs, in that it adhered to Zionism from the start. Maccabi belongs to the Argentine Zionist Federation (OSA) and the club's program consists of the realization of Zionism, that is, education for *aliya*. Leaders of Maccabi feel that the chief problem confronting Argentine Jewry today is assimilation—hence their emphasis on education for Jewish self-identity. Maccabi sends about 100 young people to Israel each year under various programs of the World Zionist Organization. Its aim is a Zionist education based on Jewish awareness and not on the exploitation of the hardships of life for Jews in Argentina.

Informal education within Maccabi developed greatly during the 1970s. Recruitment came almost entirely from among children of club members; 30% of these had attended a Jewish school up to the age of 13. This relatively stronger commitment to Jewish education also shows up in the *Cuerpo de Lideres,* or counselors' school, which Maccabi sponsors. Teaching Zionism with a view to *aliya,* the counselors frequently come into conflict with the parents of youngsters in their charge, who would prefer a more general Jewish orientation. This conflict came to a head when a group of counselors established a nucleus and settled in Israel in 1977. Eventually, Maccabi granted them full support, but organizational changes were made to permit closer supervision of the educational program. Because many younger members expressed stronger support for *aliya* (in the questionnaires) than did the club leaders, the possibility of future conflict continues to exist.

CASA differs from the other two clubs in that nearly 70% of its members are of Sephardic origin. The club was established after World War II, whereas the other two clubs were established before the war. CASA was set up as a Sunday recreation center and it observes Jewish tradition: Persons in mixed marriages are not accepted for membership, nor are their children; *kashrut* (dietary law) is observed; and there are no activities on Saturday.

The club integrates education and sport by requiring every young person who devotes seven hours to sporting activity at the club to devote an additional three hours to education. The teachers are not sports instructors. The club leadership permits complete freedom to the Israeli emissary, who acts as director of its department of culture.

Because CASA considers that its main task lies in general community work among the Sephardim of Argentina, much of its effort is directed toward material objectives, such as collecting funds and building a facility to serve as a center for educational and cultural activities. It also considers itself a Zionist institution and is linked to the Zionist establishment. In 1976, the educational department proposed a resolution to the effect that immigration to Israel is the highest aim of Zionist education at the club. This did not receive the full support of the leadership and consequently no public declaration was made. However, education was left in the hands of the education department, which was under the direction of an Israeli emissary. Consequently, the club's leaders support Israel and the Zionist movement at the educational and political levels; they do not support the idea of the negation of the diaspora or its eventual destruction.

When the Conservative movement first started in Argentina, its activities were obstructed by mainline Jewish institutions. The outlook of these institutions was secular, reflecting the orientation of their members, but religious affairs had been left in the hands of Orthodox rabbis who exercised veto power within that sphere. Within that context, the introduction of Conservatism to Argentina was viewed as heresy. The founding of Beth El Congregation and of a rabbinical seminary thus constitute an overwhelming achievement. It is difficult to find Argentine Jews today who are indifferent to the Conservative movement and its founder, Rabbi Marshall Meyer. There is sharp criticism on the one hand and enthusiastic support on the other; the only agreement is on its success in attracting congregants, particularly among the young.

Rabbi Meyer, who lived in Argentina from 1959 to 1984, states that the objective of the educational program of the movement is to instill awareness of Judaism and loyalty to the Jewish people and to the State of Israel. "We tell our young people that every one of them owes one year of his life to the State of Israel. We say that to live a full multidimensional life as Jews, Israel is the only solution. At the same time, anyone who does not settle in Israel should not feel that he is a second-class Jewish citizen or that he should give up Jewish life entirely. The contrary is true: It is possible to live a creative Jewish life in the diaspora also. We are not in favor of the negation of the diaspora."

Although Meyer and others regard the synagogue as the central institution of Judaism, this has never been the case in Argentina. According to Rabbi Edrei, the Orthodox synagogues were unable to meet the needs and the changing situation of Argentine Jews. Their lack of organizational skill also contributed to their lack of popularity.

When the Argentine political situation deteriorated after the military coup, Jewish youth who were disillusioned with their generally hostile surroundings and parents who feared for their children's lives if they became involved with the left flooded the rabbinical seminary with requests for informal educational activities that would engage young people's interest and bring them back to Judaism. In this way, the idea of establishing community centers struck root in Argentina. These centers are attached to a coordinated program originally designed to prepare counselors to attend the seminary. Most of their graduates visit Israel for a one-year course on completion of their program.

Modern pedagogical methods distinguish the Conservative educational programs. Classes meet for study on Friday and Saturday afternoons. Winter seminars and summer camps fashioned on the American model stimulate the youngsters both to study and to socialize within a Jewish circle. The aim is to promote the continued existence of the Jewish people. Life in Israel is described as the height of realization of Zionism, but Zionism must be strengthened by Jewish values, not by negation of the diaspora or the fear of anti-Semitism.

The Conservative movement in Argentina takes the position that secularism does not have the strength to combat assimilation. "The history of the Jews in the liberal western world," says Rabbi Edrei, "shows that there is no place for the secular Jew. The Jew who abandons traditional Jewish values ends up by assimilating. . . . From the sociological point of view, the image of the secular Jew in a liberal western society is not possible."

With respect to Zionism, the leaders of the Conservative movement do not believe in the necessity for political parties in the diaspora that mirror the politics of Israel. These parties, they claim, inhibit the development of Zionism. On this point, their position is close to that adopted by the social clubs, which likewise do not affiliate with Israeli political parties. The "nonpolitical" Zionism of the Conservative movement has nonetheless been effective in encouraging the *aliya* of individual congregants. Within Argentina, the Conservative movement has provided an alternative to the classic secular attitude that reigned in Argentina from the start. Expanding both at the expense of Orthodox synagogues and among independent youth, it has come to the forefront of informal education in Argentina.

Conclusions

Informal education in Argentina takes place within three sectors: the Zionist movement, the sports and social clubs, and the Conservative movement. The pioneering youth movements are characterized by their radical attitude toward the Zionist ideal. They preach Zionism with the sole meaning of *aliya*; there is no room in the movement for one who does not intend to put training into practice. Zionism is understood as the negation of the diaspora; there is no foundation in Jewish values. Members develop a rational–conceptual identity as Jews but completely lack an emotional attachment to Judaism. These youth movements gain declaratory support from the larger Jewish community but in fact are totally isolated. They themselves doubt whether they can recapture the leadership of the Zionist camp they exercised a decade ago.

The large sports and social clubs attract the largest numbers of Jewish youth to the field of informal Jewish education. This great change in orientation came about during the mid-1970s, not as the result of a coordinated plan but as a response to conditions imposed by the external environment. Efforts to coordinate their activities—such as formation of FACCMA—can be seen as an attempt to create a political force within the Jewish community capable of offering an alternative to the Zionist parties. But the clubs have no common ideological identity and are divided on the issue of Zionism, with younger members tending to take a more radical pro-Israel position than their elders.

The Conservative movement emerged during the 1970s as an important alternative for Jewish youth seeking to reorient their lives as Jews. Perhaps to a greater measure than the other institutions discussed here, its growth and expansion resulted from the general situation in the country. Alone among those institutions, it denies the possibility of survival in the long run for secular Judaism. Thus, it emphasizes traditional and historical values of the Jewish people, within a Zionist framework. *Aliya* is the summit of personal Jewish involvement, but not the only path for a Jew to follow.

The mid-1970s witnessed the expansion of the three principal ideological and institutional trends examined here. Each broadened its sphere of influence and brought a number of other organizations within its ranks. The trends observed to be taking place during a repressive military regime cannot be extrapolated beyond the ending of that regime in 1983. As Rabbi Meyer said in 1977, reacting to the article by Grondona cited at the beginning of this essay: "If this article ["The Jews"] reflects the views of those now in power and who will be in power in Argentina in the future, then there is no chance for Jewish culture to flourish in Argentina. If this is the Argentina of the next 30 or 40 years, we must move heaven and earth to achieve aliya.... Today I do not see any signs of pluralist possibilities."

In these postelection years, it is still unknown where the balance will settle for these institutions: whether they will focus on *aliya* or on maintaining Jewish identity in Argentina. Either way, they have opened new vistas for informal Jewish education in Argentina.

15
Culture, Identity, and Community

David Schers

Introduction

This study presents critical reflections on the experience of Jewish communities of the Southern Cone, particularly the largest of these communities, that of the Argentine Republic. The central thesis of the analysis is that the Jews of Latin America, with certain differences resulting from variations among countries, are the victims of contradictory pressures that place them in a situation of being subtly oppressed. Their situation is more serious than that of Jews in other areas of the world, and in some cases more complex and alienating than in those societies that show open hostility or take restrictive measures against their Jewish populations.

The effort that is invested by Latin American Jewry in maintaining Jewish identity, fighting against assimilation and anti-Semitism, and attracting youth are in large measure ineffective, because they are routinized and based on a superficial analysis of the factors that condition the situation in which Jews find themselves. In the few cases that more profound analyses are offered, as in the case of some academic works (for example, Elkin[1]), their impact has been limited and has served neither as a guide to political or institutional action nor as a critical instrument capable of aiding individual Jews in liberating themselves from the sophisticated oppression that they suffer.

1. Judith Laikin Elkin, *Jews of the Latin American Republics* (Chapel Hill: The University of North Carolina Press, 1980).

Only a critical analysis of the Jewish condition combined with action that addresses the issues of identity, culture, and the framework of social interaction will increase the chances of liberating Latin American Jewry from oppression and of contributing to the pluralization of the societies in which they live. A clear conceptual framework based on an analysis in depth is the decisive factor required, and therefore the development of such a framework is of practical importance. In contrast, pragmatism based on routinized opinions reflecting common sense or stereotyped ideology have been shown to be sterile and counterproductive.

Factors External to Jewish Communities

The characteristics of the larger society that have decisive influence on the Jewish community have been noted repeatedly in the literature.[2] In addition to the effects of historical development,[3] in each specific moment or period certain basic factors can be of importance. From the larger national society, the three decisive influences are those of the economic structure, the political culture (e.g., nationalism), and the political regime. From outside the national society, the two major influences are those of Israel and other Jewish communities, in particular the U.S. community. Although in theory the Jewish minority can also be viewed as influencing the larger society, in practice this reverse influence is very weak, and the Jewish minority finds itself in a situation of dependency vis-à-vis the larger society.

The course of political development in the Southern Cone of Latin America has created a situation in which instability, violence, and repression (not particularly oriented towards Jews, although marked by anti-Semitic elements) motivate Jews to fall back upon their own institutions and groups. This rapprochement does not reflect the attraction of Jewish institutions as much as the physical and psychological insecurity that results from being separated from them. It is clear that the growth in the number of participants creates greater possibilities of collective action and a sense of strength that serves as a psychological reinforcement. Professionals who find themselves without work due to layoffs, economic problems in the institutions in which they work, or political reasons find in Jewish institutions a place of employment for growing numbers of people.

This process, which was most evident in Argentina but also occurred in other countries to a lesser extent, serves to exemplify the dependent

---

2. David Schers and Hadassa Singer, "The Jewish Communities in Latin America: Internal and External Factors in Their Development," *Jewish Social Studies,* Summer 1977, 241–257.

3. Haim Avni, *Iahadut Argentina: Maamadá Hachevratí udemutá Hairgunit* (Jerusalem: The Hebrew University, 1972); Elkin, *Jews of the Latin American Republics.*

character of the Jewish community. This dependency is augmented by the lack of consciousness on the part of Jews with respect to external processes and influences. Their conceptual framework simply does not correspond to the complexity of the situation. Aspirations to maintain Jewish identity while actively participating in all aspects of national life (or integration) are confronted by the loss of Jewish identity (or assimilation) and by tendencies toward alienation that result from neither achieving full participation nor maintaining Jewish identity as a positive element of personality.

The factors exogenous to the national society, such as influences from Israel or the U.S. Jewish community, exercise a variable effect. Emigration from Latin America, especially in certain professional strata, has been one collective response. Unlike the United States, which was considered by many Jewish immigrants as a promised land, the Latin American countries were considered by many Jews as a temporary refuge for an indeterminate period. Emigration to Israel was considered by many Jews as a dream that would be realized if local conditions became sufficiently negative (the "push effect") or if conditions in Israel became sufficiently attractive (the "pull effect"). In periods of negative economic conditions or growing anti-Semitism, many Latin American Jews speak of emigration to Israel, some consider it as a practical possibility, and a certain percentage actually emigrate. A similar phenomenon occurs with respect to emigration to other countries in the Americas, particularly the United States, or to Europe.

A particularly alienating situation emerges when factors stemming from the local society are negative and exercise a push effect, but when the exogenous factors do not exercise a positive pull effect. During the Falklands/Malvinas War, for example, the image of Argentina as a peaceful nation was suddenly broken, following the earlier loss of the image of Argentina as a country without internal violence. The war with a world power in a country in which universal military service was established signified a concrete and tangible danger for Argentine Jews. A similar danger was posed in more diffuse form by the threat of a war with Chile, and had similar implications for Chilean Jewry.

The Falklands/Malvinas War developed at the same time as Israel's invasion of Lebanon. The attacks on Israel in the world and local press, the extreme divisions in Israeli public opinion, and, for the first time, the divisions in Jewish opinion outside Israel were all factors that had a major impact on Latin American Jewry and created a profound feeling of crisis. Yet, paradoxically, this crisis, which was fully justified in terms of reality, was for some Jews a catalyst that permitted them to realize the crisis that they had unconsciously been living under for years. Those who took this opportunity to clarify their situation were no longer forced to continue suffering a subtle and sophisticated oppression due to their Jewish condition.

The preponderant influence on the Jewish community of national and international factors also reflects the weakness of the community and its institutions, as well as the previously mentioned absence of a critical analysis of reality and a frame of reference to guide Jewish action. External circumstances therefore are dominant, and the reaction of community leadership to these circumstances can be considered "spasmodic." Thus moods of despair and depression are replaced by euphoria and quasi-mystical hope when circumstances change, as in the case of the return to democracy in Argentina. The unexpected democratic *apertura* dazzled everyone, and found many—perhaps even all—Jewish community leaders unprepared. Circumstances come, circumstances go, but the improvisational character of the Jewish response continues.

We should not fool ourselves by imagining that the nature of the Jewish response to external circumstances is merely a reflection of apathy or inactivity on the part of the leadership of the community. On the contrary, there are frequent outbursts of activity and institutional political conflict. Leaders arm themselves with the pen and battle acerbically against their rivals in the community. Some openly oppose anti-Semitism and fight against it with an eye to strengthening the community, although frequently for self-interested political purposes that, although legitimate, do not respond to the fundamental needs of the community. To state the point differently, when Jewish self-hate is common it is difficult to combat the anti-Semitism of others, which sometimes leads to an escapism that results only in participation in some demonstration of sentiment that does not lead to major changes in attitude or in long-term behavior. The Jewish "problem" in Latin America is not unique, but it appears to be more grave and complex than elsewhere, even if in some countries, such as Argentina, it has elements that are difficult to detect. A more complete perspective that would contribute to clarifying this problem could also have relevance to understanding the societies in Latin America in which Jews live and the problems of Jews in other, apparently disparate, societies. Indeed, such a model could throw light on the problems of non-Jewish ethnic minorities, as is implied in the proposal of Calvo Muños[4] for ethnic education for Indians and *mestizos*.

A Conceptual and Methodological Perspective

The model that is proposed here, for methodological and theoretical purposes, singles out fundamental factors that can be examined in terms of both analyzing data and practical applications. This model reflects the basic

---

4. Carlos Calvo Muños, "¿Educación indígena o etnoeducación?" *Educación de Adultos y Desarrollo,* Asociación Alemana para Educación de Adultos, Sept. 1983, no. 21:115–118.

questions that emerged from the research undertaken by the Horowitz Institute of the University of Tel Aviv, as given cohesion and clarity by their application in adult education and the education of community activists. The three basic factors considered are (1) identity, not only in emotional terms but also in the intellectual dimension of definitions of "who I am as a Jew" and what it means "to be Jewish" for oneself and for others; (2) Jewish culture, with its historical, religious, and artistic–aesthetic dimensions; and (3) the social structure of interaction, the framework within which Jews interact. The first dimension can be labeled social–psychological, the second sociocultural, and the third sociological.

Different social or historical theories place different emphasis on each of these three factors. We prefer in this discussion to employ the experience derived from adult education programs in which the participants—all with university education and varying degrees of community involvement, including some individuals alienated from the community until their involvement in the program—expressed their personal opinions and then their collective judgment about the relative importance of each of the factors.

Reflecting the tendencies that characterize the opinions of experts and laypersons, the participants in these discussions frequently chose the factor of identity as paramount. During the discussions the participants themselves noted the tautological trap posed by defining the Jew in terms of self-identification.[5] A more detailed analysis generally resulted in the conclusion that it is important to consider all three factors. The most effective analyses resulted from considering each of the three factors as if it were the only one, and then analyzing the results of this assumption.

Clearly unsatisfactory were statements such as "to feel good as a Jew," "to know what it means to be Jewish," or "to consider that Jews have every right to be Jewish even in societies that are not Jewish." One can not have an identity without *belonging*. Moreover, without the cultural values of the minority, only the values of the majority remain, leaving identity vacant and without positive attraction. To reduce the meaning of being Jewish to its psychological and intellectual elements is to run the risk of identifying Judaism with a sentimental nostalgia centered on gastronomic folklore or in emotive symbols bereft of real content.

On the other hand, the mere accumulation of knowledge about culture without a positive (emotional) identification leads to "cultural experts" in conflict with their own Judaism. In some cases such knowledge is used to express hatred of Jewishness. Such extreme cases clearly indicate the limited nature of the cognitive dimension and the ingenuous character of magical solutions that recommend "education" in the sense of the simple

---

5. Irving L. Horowitz, "Jewish Ethnicism and Latin-American Nationalism," *Midstream*, 1972, no. 9:22–28; Schers and Singer, "The Jewish Communities," 1–2.

accumulation of cultural facts and information. One of the participants in the discussion groups dealing with this issue clearly articulated the exaggerated importance that can be given to knowledge when other factors are given short shrift by stating, "Non-Jewish experts on the Talmud are not necessarily converted into members of the Jewish community because of their cultural knowledge."

The social ties of an ethnic group, product of the frequent interaction of its members and of the attitudes of the societal majority that have segregationist effects, are also not sufficient. Moreover, community activism and leadership that are not accompanied by elements of positive identification and Jewish culture are also insufficient, creating a problematic situation that makes the work of many Jewish institutions ineffective. A leader who is without cultural orientation and is incapable of expressing his identity positively will appear to be a hyperactive politician desirous of maintaining or advancing his position, motivated by personal desires that could equally find expression in non-Jewish institutions.

Resolving the leadership problem does not require idealized figures that cannot be found in human reality or pretense that leaders are mythical idols. It is, however, necessary to draw attention to the paradox of leaders and activists who try to maintain and spread a culture that they themselves do not know and to reinforce in others an identity that they themselves have not clarified and strengthened. The essential element of personal example vanishes, and the attraction of Jewish institutions in open societies is weakened.[6]

The issue is not merely one of the leaders and activists only, but also of Jewish institutions and all their members, particularly for the new generations for whom Judaism is not a natural, automatic, and unquestioned part of their life and personality. A Jewish institution with little or no Jewish cultural content is a self-segregating ghetto, although many persons cannot clearly articulate this consequence because of their own identity problems and the pressure of the larger society. If there is not a specific content to express what it means to be Jewish, then is being Jewish merely the avoidance of that which is gentile? Jews feel attracted to interaction with other Jews, but—because of the pressures of a larger society that does not legitimate Jewish culture and Jewish membership—do not take advantage of being together to express their own culture or to clarify the specific problems of their own identity. Instead the Jewish content of their institutions and informal groups is maintained at a very low level.

6. Paul Warszawski, "Los dilemas de la redemocratización: La comunidad judía de la Argentina frente al proceso de transición política," *Controversia de Ideas Sionistas,* Dec. 1983, 113–123.

There are exceptions to this situation. Some community organizations in which Jews are exclusively with other Jews have moved towards programs of Jewish cultural enrichment and have adopted a positive attitude towards the strengthening of Jewish identity. Others, taking off from the base of a strong Jewish identification, have developed activities designed to attract and retain members. Institutions of cultural transmission, such as the schools, have become more effective when they have expanded their activities to include parents of the students and have introduced cultural elements and Jewish identity into the curriculum. This integrative tendency appears in juxtaposition to the increasing specialization of the services offered by many modern Jewish institutions.

Returning to the theoretical framework, the integration of cultural elements, of identity, and of social interaction emerges as the fundamental requirement of the effort to maintain that which is Jewish. This integration can be attained by those individuals who discover the elements of identity in their history and personal life, study in a framework that offers cultural content or cultural activities, and who remain united to the formal and informal groups of the Jewish community. These individuals are, however, the exception. Social processes are generally conducive to the exercise of free will only by exceptional individuals. The creation of opportunities for integration is the product of institutions that adopt programs responsive to the individual and collective needs of Jews and of those exceptional individuals who by their personal example lead such institutions to adopt such programs. To be Jewish and to transmit Judaism in Latin American societies becomes a revolutionary act when the conception of being a Jew ceases to be an undesirable but tolerated destiny and becomes a means of being a human belonging to a people, a religion, a culture, and an ethnic group.

Identity, Culture, and Interaction: The Focus of the Problem

Following Gordon and Elkin,[7] we can affirm that the Jews of Latin America have faced a process of acculturation without structural assimilation. The process of acculturation has included adopting the national language and culture as well as the acceptance of values, beliefs, and attitudes of the so-called political culture of the larger society. The internalization of these values implies for many Jews that they consider their Judaism a prob-

---

7. Milton M. Gordon, *Assimilation in American Life* (New York: Oxford University Press, 1964); Elkin, *Jews of the Latin American Republics*.

lem or a negative feature to be overcome.[8] Faced by a lack of structural assimilation, Jews remain within their own interaction networks, but without their own cultural resources and above all without a positive identity. The small groups that completely isolate themselves, such as the Orthodox, are less acculturated and do not represent a model that can be followed by the majority of Jews.

In this situation, patterns of interaction with the larger society or with other Jews are devoid of Jewish content, leading to a culture that is adopted from the larger society, which in turn leads to an identity that is repressed and conflicted. Identity in this context is a dependent variable that is subject to outside influence and internal conflict of which there can be no resolution. Contradictory pressures block any open treatment of the problem, which is either ignored at the conscious level or reflected in an attitude of guilt and denial of self. The problem is centered in the fact that the culture mentioned here is that of the larger society, induced by an interaction that falls short of permitting full structural assimilation.

The Jew in such a context does not recognize the right to have his or her own social–cultural group, because that would constitute a form of separatism that conflicts with the cultural norms of the larger society. Although this situation is less marked in some countries of northern South America and of Central America, it remains a problem for younger Jews that is growing in importance.

Here the logic of the theoretical scheme gains force: Without a legitimized Jewish interaction, there exists no framework for creating and transmitting a specifically Jewish culture and no mechanisms that would allow individuals to develop and exercise a positive identity. This point has an importance that is difficult to express or to accept in societies in which universal humanism is accepted, nationalism is highly respected, but in which ethnic minorities, especially Jews, are viewed negatively. Liberating the Jew from the acceptance of this bind is a fundamental step, not easily taken. If Zionism proposes such an action, it is limited in its more popular expressions in Latin America to the realization of *aliya,* or migration to Israel, which transfers the framework of Jewish interaction to a society in which Jews are the majority. This solution applies only to a self-selected minority that is disposed towards a rapid and total change of behavior. The gradual nature of a process of liberation is impeded by the radicalism that is common in Latin America, postulating "all or nothing." Too radical conceptions of Zionism may impede the development of a gradual change of perspective.

The hopes of many "progressives" (who were not a few in the Jewish

---

8. Schers and Singer, "The Jewish Communities."

communities) that a just society without classes would solve the problem of Jews were dashed by events in the Soviet Union and other "popular democracies." Although it would seem that such societies should attach little importance to Judaism, in practice non-Jews have continued to attach importance to Jewish identity. Thus, as Sartre noted throughout much of his life, the Jew is defined by the non-Jew, generally by anti-Semites.

It follows from these observations that the trap of anti-Semitism in Argentina is especially sophisticated. The disguised anti-Semites pretend, under the mantle of universalistic humanism or equalizing nationalism, to love the Jew on the condition that he limits himself to being a person, a citizen, or a member of a movement. To kill the Jew without spilling his blood, or to kill his Jewishness by convincing him that it is negative, is an elegant, if frequently unconscious, anti-Semitism that is effective because it is internalized by the Jew himself. It appears less diabolic than Nazism, which allows no escape to the person considered Jewish and leads to physical extermination. But to achieve the spiritual suicide of the Jew as a Jew has implications that have not been sufficiently studied, certainly not in the version that was played out in the decade of the 1970s in Argentina as a tragic counterpart of the terrible "dirty war" carried out by the military regime.

The Oppression of Those Who Are "Well Off"

Is it possible to speak of the oppression of those who eat well, have attractive lives, and live in relative prosperity? The case of the Jews of Latin America demonstrates that it is indeed possible. Alienation, self-hate, and family conflict are not as tragically visible or dramatic as the poverty of the peasants of northeastern Brazil or of the slums surrounding the various cities of Latin America. The very invisibility of Jewish suffering, however, makes it more painful than might otherwise appear. The "conscientization" proposed by Paulo Freire[9] also can be effective in liberating people of the middle classes from the opprobrium and ethnic oppression that they suffer.

The oppression of classes is not any less unjust than the oppression of ethnic groups. But to argue that Jews (a minority neither as rich nor as powerful as is claimed) who suffer discrimination and persecution themselves persecute the oppressed social classes of Latin America is a fallacy. Nevertheless, this fallacy influences Jews themselves, particularly young Jews and those who have a negative self-image. Even when they join movements of social reform, they are aware of being Jews, and their costly efforts

9. Paulo Freire, *Pedagogy of the Oppressed* (New York: Herder and Herder, 1970).

to demonstrate that they are not leads them to become in many cases "more papist than the Pope" or to behave in ways that are abnormal. If they remain instead in the mold of their social class of origin, in more or less isolated Jewish groups, without placing importance on Judaism, their guilt damages them: They feel that they are segregating themselves from non-Jews. The testimony of Jewish university students and young Jewish parents is that "we do not wish to stay in the ghetto." Without a clear identity, their own culture, and a conceptual framework that justifies these, their interaction patterns and Jewish institutions are viewed as asphyxiating, enclosed, and ghettolike.

Applying a Theoretical Framework

What then is the road to escape from the trap and to liberate Latin American Jewry from its self-repression? Our first conclusion is that an excessive emphasis on formal education and on the transmission of knowledge is an expression of a disequilibrium among the three basic factors that have been described: identity, culture, and interaction. Another symptom is the exaggerated expectations placed on maintaining Jewish interaction through attractive institutions that do not have a "tiresome" emphasis on atavistic or sectarian ties to Judaism or to Israel. Finally, the overmanipulation of the concept of identity, unaccompanied by research and by an effort to repair the cultural poverty of most Latin American Jews in terms of their own Jewish culture, is another weakness that indicates a disequilibrium among the basic factors.

Education or organizational strategies, or the path taken by individuals or groups sensitive to the problem, may vary. What counts is not to ignore any of the three factors, and to achieve a high level of congruence among them by elevating those that are less developed. In the specific case of an awakening of Jewish identity—perhaps achieved by some personal crisis or as the result of external influences—the individual moves closer to his culture through reading or studying, and closer to a Jewish interaction context. The highest stage of equilibrium among the factors is achieved when cultural awareness and interaction patterns are in harmony with the sensitivities and interests of identity. The different factors can then be mutually reinforcing.

This theoretical scheme suggests various other possibilities as well. The study of Judaism, the reading of Jewish works, and contact with Jewish cultural events and other elements of the wealth of Jewish cultural inheritance that are discovered by an individual can lead him to increased interaction with other Jews, because through them he can better experience his new cultural acquisitions or because the new value he places on culture itself leads him to seek the company of those who are its bearers. Alternatively, a Jewish context of interaction, requiring the individual to respond to requirements in the areas of culture or identity, can carry the individual from interaction toward culture and identity. What is important is that the process result in an equilibrium among the factors at a higher level by elevating those that are inferior.

The experience that has been accumulated in working with Jewish study and action groups shows that such a process in fact exists and is significant. The experiences are of course limited and should be repeated and amplified both for methodological reasons and for the community purposes that they serve. What can be confirmed on the basis of existing experience is that the scheme we have outlined has a high educational value and that it clarifies the problems and the concrete possibilities for action of those who employ it. In this sense adult education—not as technical education or literacy training in Hebrew, but rather to "change perspectives"[10]— is of great potential to community institutions and to individuals who are searching for solutions to the Jewish problematic.

The use of Habermas's critical theory[11] to explore the underlying causes of the social phenomena that have been discussed, of analytical psychology to disclose the falsity of certain assumptions, and of participatory adult education programs all have great promise. These would not only benefit the Jewish community and individual Jews, but also the countries in which they live. The acceptance of a distinctive minority community can contribute to the strengthening of pluralism in societies that remain far from the pluralist ideal. This would apply not only to Jews. Indigenous minorities in both Latin America and North America also could benefit from the experience that has been accumulated at the theoretical level and in educational and organizational practice. Precisely the fact that the Jewish minority is not generally impoverished allows it to single out this cultural problem and the value of all aspects of identity and frameworks of interaction.

Community institutions can only fulfill their mission effectively if they comprehend that identity, culture, and interaction should be their central preoccupation. The dependent character of these minority communities means that their autonomy of action is limited, giving greater importance to

---

10. Jack Mezirow, "A Critical Theory of Adult Learning and Education," *Adult Education* 32(1) (Fall 1981).

11. R. Geuss, *The Idea of Critical Theory: Habermas and the Frankfurt School* (Cambridge, Mass: Cambridge University Press, 1981); *Habermas: Critical Debates.* J. B. Thompson and D. Held (eds.). (Cambridge, Mass: M.I.T. Press, 1982); T. McCarthy, *The Critical Theory of Jurgen Habermas* (Cambridge, Mass: M.I.T. Press, 1978).

what their community institutions can accomplish. It is fundamental that the role of these institutions be based on the analysis in depth of social reality and upon a clear conceptual framework. The basic premise that Jews have a right to an identity based on self-respect and integrity, to receive, re-create, and develop their culture, and to establish social contexts where these rights can be developed should be accompanied by clear explanations of their purpose. In societies such as those of Latin America, the right of a special relationship with Israel should be explained and defended. But such explanation and defense will not be meaningful, particularly in the face of the previously mentioned anti-Semitism, if the members of the Jewish community do not themselves understand why they are trapped in the premises of the local political culture. The challenges are great, but so are the possibilities for theory and practice and for the transfer of these accomplishments to other Jewish communities and to other oppressed minorities.

16
Latin American-Jewish Writers: Protecting the Hyphen*

Saúl Sosnowski

The hyphen is a useful commodity: It contributes to a unifying feature where none would be expected to exist. As we join terms such as *Latin American* and *Jewish* with a hyphen we are struck by its implications: They do not "normally" belong together. Both terms have a set of references that conform to different historical and political realities and, above all, to different *public* perceptions of what each *should* mean. Associations to the commonality of definitions of Latin America are just as inappropriate as the perceptions of the Jew that appear in all too many Western literary characterizations. Within the mainstream of Western discourse, and until very

*This reading is based on a number of studies that I have carried out on Latin American–Jewish writers; thus the absence of detailed notes to identify specific issues with given authors. For individual authors, the patient reader may wish to consult: "¿Quién es Edmund Ziller?" *La Semana de Bellas Artes* (Mexico), 8 (1977): 8–11 (re Pedro Orgambide); "Germán Rozenmacher: Tradiciones, rupturas y desencuentros," *Revista de Crítica Literaria Latinoamericana* (Lima) 3 (6) (1977): 93–110; "Gerardo Mario Goloboff: Hacia el décimo mes en la diáspora," *Escritura* (Caracas), 4 (1978): 255–282; "Los gauchos judíos y los gauchos no-judíos," *Nueva Presencia* (Buenos Aires), 5 (347) (24 Feb. 1984): 8–10 (re Alberto Gerchunoff); a study of Mario Szichman's work remains in manuscript. Two more general studies on the subject are S. Sosnowski, "Contemporary Jewish-Argentine Writers: Tradition and Politics," *Latin American Literary Review* (Pittsburgh), 6 (12) (1978): 1–14, and "Latin American Jewish Writers: A Bridge Toward History," *Prooftexts* (The Johns Hopkins University Press), 4 (1) (1984): 71–92 (with particular references to the Argentines Gerchunoff, Rozenmacher, Szichman, Goloboff, and Orgambide, the Venezuelan Isaac Chocrón, the Mexicans Margo Glantz and Esther Seligson, and the Peruvian Isaac Goldemberg). I have developed this topic further in my book *La orilla inminente (Escritores judíos-argentinos)*. (Buenos Aires: Legasa, 1987). From a thematic piont of view, Leonardo Senkman's *La identidad judía en la literatura argentina* (Buenos Aires: Editorial Pardés, 1983) has become mandatory reading.

recently, both *Jewish* and *Latin American* conveyed the notion of the outsider, of the troublesome presence that incommodated with his awkwardness, his resilience, and his tacit accusations against wrongdoers. With varying degrees, admittedly, these are images of refusal: refusal against odds of survival, against historical complacency, against peaceful acceptance of repression. Both are literary figures of marginality that, as such, establish the parameters of the reach that the dominant culture and dominant powers—the metropolis vis-à-vis Latin America and the Jew also *within* the majority's control—can have over them. In very different contexts and with very divergent historical, cultural, and linguistic developments, the hyphen unites elements that do not necessarily evoke from the reader urgent pleas for recognition. Apparently uncomfortable in their respective niches, they are protected by the hyphen from an assimilationist integration into the mainstreams of a majority cultural or geographical identification.

Comfort in itself is not, however, a determining factor of major works of literature. Their avowed aim is, precisely, to generate in the reader a disquieting sense that runs through the written page to the realities that literature founds on the uneasy edifice of words. Literary discomfort, in its highest and most positive sense, is at the very core of the text that probes into its very own existence and questions its capacity to convey with mere words the enormity of the universe (Borges dixit). Far from ratifying the resilience of the printed word, such a text challenges superficial understanding and confronts the complacent reader as it hurls reality toward the one who is willing and able to absorb the impact and launch a new search for meaning. Thus seen, a literary text will have to encompass, even in its transit through the descriptive charms of bucolic passages, the very sense of itself: the "reasoned" conglomerate of words that at every step looks back and asks about its past as it draws the configurations of the future. Not many pages will belong in this highest category, but even as an ideal—perhaps a poetic height that should be reached before a word meets its printer—the troubling essence of literature should be considered along with pleasure and imitative modes or escapist proposals in the ideological spectrum of critical readings.

Within this strict notion of literature, an extraliterary projection can be made towards the presence, or the view, of minority power in the numerical vastness of majority dominance. Until very recently, Latin American literature did not rank—and, according to many, did not belong—in the leading cultural centers of the West. This literature came to the forefront when historical events forced the world to look south and to recognize the existence and uniqueness of some independent states.

As part of political and historical recognition, the presence of Latin American literature and culture was accepted under the pretenses of the "new" and the "different." It may have been a new literature for those who had refused to see it; it was an integral component of national knowledge for those who did not await recognition from "above" to see their own literature and value it as such. The fortunes of an empire as the guiding light of its language and subsidiary artifacts are well known. Discovery by the masters assures public (the nonlocal public) acceptance. With it also comes the positive byproduct of dissemination of knowledge and the promotion of a literature worthy of world readership. But, and therein lies a disturbing feature, promotion itself is done on the basis of the element of surprise. The emergence of a literature of universal proportions has somehow run counter to expectations because, as certain faulty reasoning would have it, political subservience by the ruling elites compacts all national creativity. Some Latin American works belong to that disquieting realm that I have mentioned before, not only because of their radical proposals in literary theory and production—undeniable merits indeed—but also because of the world that they portray. This literature is built on another meaning of "the different," on the estrangement that the unsuspecting reader finds when the unknown or the unexpected are thrust upon accepted versions of reality.

When in addition to *Latin American* one adds the defining term *Jewish*, it is easy to recall astonished gazes and conflicting images of the accepted and simple cliches for both. This is oftentimes the reaction when writers, through the mediating effects of all literary language, have combined both components into one single text. The reaction—and the readership—will be different for those who, in spite of their biographical attributes as members of both the Latin and Jewish communities, have chosen to write only about one or to write of each independently of their interaction. The conflict that can arise from the confrontation of disparate categories spills over a series of questions on the nature of separate treatments. In the lack of integration lies another source of inquiries, because it is as powerful a literary and critical motif as the incorporation of two elements into a body that searches for a cohesive self.

Without engaging in endless definitions of national or ethnic literatures, it may prove useful to consider that in many cases it is the explicitness of literary motifs that render a text "Latin American" and/or "Jewish." Identifiable content, then, may serve to delineate the parameters around the hyphen. Perhaps it is a sign of the exigencies of time and pressing contemporaneity that particularly Jewish elements appear in sharp contrast to the "other." The emphatic presence of the "I" as a different and differentiating entity emerges in a series of contrasts and oppositions that can ill afford the subtleties of an aura that only other minority members will recognize as fitting their particular interests and character. Jewish components are defined as such in order to mark the entrance into a realm where a new set of literary and cultural conflicts will emerge beyond the seemingly flat surface of the page. The need to accentuate identity imposes itself upon the reader who from the outset is forced to recognize that "Latin American" in itself is not sufficient to place a text that challenges partial definitions. Molds are broken when elements considered extraneous to dominant cultural patterns are challenged. New perceptions are broadened when into the very strict definition of nationality caveats are made for the different; and even more when the different in itself, and not the common, becomes part of the norm for the national.

When we establish, then, the Latin American–Jewish (or vice versa) as members of a minority we take ourselves out of a vast identity to proclaim that it does not suffice to cover our being. Geography is not enough to provide a territorial belonging; it mandates the assumption of a historical past and the embodiment of traditions extraneous to the new land. Within literary parameters, cognizance of a double or triple (national/hemispheric/cultural–religious) allegiance—let alone one of class values—may, and in fact does, become a central issue for many of these writers. No issue can be taken with writers who, regardless of their Jewish origins, abandon ancestral traces in favor of an exclusive concentration on either their local or universalist readings of reality, nor can claims be laid unto writers whose exclusive concern is their historical origin. Both have found their milieu to the exclusion of literary zones of friction. It is, however, in the writers who (un)settle themselves in the uneasy gray areas of identity, of belonging, and of future allegiances, that other dramas begin to unfold. This does not mean addressing different issues—"Jewish subjects" and "non-Jewish subjects"—in different texts, because then the conflict is resolved in a separate but equal doctrine of inner peace. Conflictive elements emerge when coexistence of the Jewish with the non-Jewish national state are thrust upon each other and self-recognition is challenged by state doctrine or non-Jewish perception of the foreign elements in the national fabric. The Israeli writer is probably the only one for whom Jewish identity will not be posed in an initially adversary relationship to his or her state. Probably most others who *incorporate* and assimilate into their self-definition the majority, and often hostile, attitude toward the different will engage in the debate over what it is to be a citizen of a given land *and* a Jew in a land where being Jewish in many cases marks distances from the civil privileges given to all others.

Belonging always refers to space, to territory. It also refers to identity. The inhabited space that shrinks to the measure of man and expels people from the land of the living as a conscious decision to extirpate them has not only exercised a political and programmatic decision, it has also fulfilled a definition of cultural values. Whether murder or cultural suicide, negation asserts disappearance and perpetual silence. When space is expanded beyond the limits of the self to encompass a sense of community in the midst of an acquiescent or merely tolerant social construct, that conquered space becomes the territory upon which a new set of alliances will be established between the new inhabitants and their hosts. In the long historical journey of migratory movements, the dynamic relationship that will emerge from that original contact and the laws that govern expansion, growth, or ghettoizing restrictions will mark the oscillating lines between tolerance and integration—assimilation being the end of all conflicts.

Territory acquires a special meaning for Latin American–Jewish writers, not in the sense of appropriating a land—a central concern of the conspiracy-bound fascist mentality—but in the very limited sense of the descendant of immigrants who searches for space to rest the body and develop the soul. With that acquisition comes the embodiment of lofty ideals of liberty and religious tolerance absent in many of the countries of origin. For the newly arrived, Judaism constitutes an unquestionable set of values and a way of life in search of freedom to carry it out. But emergence from the *shtetl* and contact with the nonkosher world contaminates the past. New desires are readily accepted by many of the immigrants' descendants, by those who practice a new language and who find their own identity in the hyphenated call of the different. In the New World, clearly delineated options can be exercised: Either of the two components is given, and so are combinations of the two with *shifting* allegiances. It is those very shifts that mark the transit of generations who accept the land that is a birthright with the tradition of ancestors that is their other rightful obligation to consider, to integrate, or to dismiss. Boundaries also shift: Zion as the messianic ideal is Israel, but it can also be a land of liberty and plenty elsewhere; Judaism is faith and strict adherence to religious observance, and it is a set of cultural tenets and human values that extend beyond the confines of the immediate community. Judaism, moreover, can be a perception of the world, a mode of behavior of a nationality built on the lofty ideals of most civil constitutions, or the mere folkloric remembrance of culinary tastes. Judaism can offer the path to cultural or religious introspection, and also the means of emphasizing the heterodoxy of free thought where all discourse submits to obedience or irretrievable silence.

A global reading of Latin American–Jewish writers will afford a varied mosaic of attitudes vis-à-vis both components. The denial of a Judaic presence in some will be countenanced in others by the overriding folkloric dominance of Judaic motifs that bury Latin America under a cloak of acrobatic reminiscences of a misplaced exegesis. Serious and lofty analyses of Israeli–Arab relations and Zionist ideals will be confronted with folk behavior and sounds as definitions of Judaic character. Talmudic discourse will find its way alongside coarse Yiddish expressions as definitions of Jewish belonging.

Although Yiddish writers have made important contributions to an understanding of the newly arrived's contacts with the New World—notably in Argentina—it would be difficult to establish a direct linkage between them and the more recent generation of writers whose sources lie far from those whose language most are increasingly unable to understand. Their literary masters are not these writers but the same writers who have served Western minds. Moreover, many of them have drawn their Judaic motifs from family stories and literary glimpses at unknown worlds rather than from Yiddish authors. The issue forced upon us is, however, that regardless of the degree of knowledge of Judaism, a series of identifying motifs single out a number of authors as possessing a literary baggage that is different from the texts of their national counterparts. The question remains whether it is only content and allusions that make certain Latin American writers Jewish. The answer does not revolve around theological tenets on "who is a Jew?" but on what makes certain literary texts part of a developing body of literature that is *both* Latin American and Jewish. It is possible to discount awareness of Judaism, in any number of its facets and degrees of close allegiance to canon, as a sine qua non for such a textual recognition, regardless of the author's individual behavior. Perhaps the best proof of such criterion is the inclusion of Jewish motifs in writers who had not had any direct proximity to Judaism in previous works but in whom historical circumstances (exile chief among them) evoked mythical figures of the wandering Jew as an epitome of their own situation. The claim could rightly be made that the occasional appeal to Jewish motifs does not in itself incorporate a text into the Latin American–Jewish category. Or can it? If literature is accepted as a changing (mutating) exercise of perception and apprehension of a given reality, the appeal to any word and to any motif to reproduce any given literary moment is a legitimate exercise. When motifs heretofore unused are called for in a text that builds from any platform on a literary interpretation of reality, and when the motif called for is rooted in a Jewish tradition or in an interpretation of Jewish motifs, we can legitimately incorporate such a text into the global literary tradition that falls under this rubric. No quantification can justify inclusions or exclusions, nor can a single text justify definitions of its producer, but that precise text in itself is a *free-standing structure* that attests to the need to call forth Jewish elements as the only ones capable of responding to literary needs. If exile in Mexico from a repressive Argentine regime is understood through the eyes of the wandering Jew clad in the historical raiments of global persecutions and the exploitation of unprotected masses, that element constitutes an important contribution to the understanding of the Jewish impact on literature and to the incorporation of that text into our hyphenated categories. Further, this one incursion into literary lore may in itself serve to reexamine the meaning of the Jewish presence in any given country and to explore the immigratory past as a fundamental step in the historical changes of Latin America and in the individual and national transformation of the Jewish immigrant.

Bucolic images and endless pastoral bliss may provide the immediate gratification of the senses and respond to demands of aesthetic equilibrium. But the literature that concerns us—with exceptions appropriate to the initial stages of integration in the New World and the idealization of all promises—surges out of conflict. Complacency with the present and blind acceptance of the past is unacceptable, for both times are rooted in failed hopes and corrupted chronicles of deceit and betrayal. In this central aspect, Jewish writers join many others in denouncing the failures of liberalism, the advent of authoritarianism and its ensuing moral bankruptcy, and individual responsibility for being acquiescent, silent, an accomplice to decaying values. The time has long passed since streets were seen with the golden shades of wealth and rural scenes evoked songs of praise to the Almighty and to the benefactors of new republics. Colors have drastically changed and the acquisition of unrestricted wealth has taken its toll in unmitigated deaths and in the suspension of disbelief when graves reveal the seeds of gore. In this respect, to be Jewish and Latin American adds an experiential dimension that no other can evoke with equal force and, at the same time, with the fragile disdain of one who has experienced and survived human hell. The all too easily used words *genocide* and *holocaust* weigh heavily in the analogies to current facts and shed a historical perspective on the processes of the arrogance of power. To be Jewish and Latin American does not preclude alliances along class lines and along institutional affiliations. No uniformity there. When faced with real or apparent danger, ranks will not be closed along Jewish lines but along class lines: Property, the impoverished notion of a territory possessed that is one's own, digs trenches that are also graves.

In Latin American countries that have faced unparalleled repression, survival—perhaps *the* major motif of all Jewish literature—has also occupied a central role. For individuals, as such or as members of a persecuted minority (not the Jewish minority, but the broad-based spectrum of the opposition to a repressive regime), survival has become an everyday struggle that has filtered through literary explorations both inside the countries and in the new exile communities. And it has also been within these parameters that Jewish elements surfaced as means to interpret a reality to which centuries of persecution had already accustomed the Jew of the past. Judaism is then perceived as a bridge from history toward projections for the future. Far from heroic exploits, survival acquired the smallness of everyday life, the routine *kleinmenschlichkeit* of characters in search of a sign to rise from mediocrity as fundamental historical changes passed them by. Or it leaped toward the fantastic in search of hopeful responses to ceaseless misery.

To survive had the primary literal meaning of staying alive and the secondary attributes of maintaining human dignity and self-respect, identifiable traditions that ought not to be dismissed at the stroke of an armed pen. Survival is also finding the means to accommodate varying national sources of identity into a working definition of the human. Until a bridge is found across conflicting traditions, until sounds and habits juxtapose into a livable harmony, and until a common language is created to surmount contrasts as these are enunciated, lines will be drawn along conflicts and clashes of purpose and desire. Demands for strict allegiance to misunderstood national exigencies will in some cases produce a rejection of the different (i.e., the Jewish) side of the nationals with ensuing anti-Semitic outbursts. Only when to be "Jewish" and a "member of a nation" are understood by the politically conscious writer as compatible elements of a pluralistic society will the conflict deflect in another direction: the division of both the national fabric *and* the Jewish community into class lines. These, in turn, will serve to exacerbate for some that hated segment of the personality that still accentuates differences as it tries to deny them in integrationist proposals. For some, rejection of Judaism will come as a result of mistaken identifications with questioned middle-class values or petty bourgeois modes of behavior, as if Judaism itself were intrinsically and inherently embodied within a class structure. For others, it will come in a drastic demystification of Judaism until only a vague remnant of historical echoes will sound out of a scarcely recognizable past. In others still, it will be reduced—in both positive and negative terms—to the folkloric tints of Yiddish expressions, Jewish jokes, an appeal to identity through cliches and local garb and sound. What remains is oftentimes a pale memory of childhood or a secular version of wishful Judaic history and thought. But even then, these motifs may suffice to bring forth a literary dimension that is strikingly different from similar Latin American voices. An ironic mode, sarcastic self-deprecation, a moist remembrance of an old immigrant grandfather, a vulgar Yiddish expression, and the shape of Hebrew letters begin to mark the difference. And so does the excruciating need to recall the distant past and also the recent immigratory past, to rebuild history and thwart the crooked future from distorting hopes and repeating a sequence of persecutions and pogroms that were supposed to have died with the Old World.

Other Latin American writers have also centered their literary projects on a revision of history. Nevertheless, one is tempted to view historical introspection within definite geographical and linguistic parameters organized around the theme of survival as an identifiable motif of many Latin American–Jewish writers. Whether in highly developed urban centers or on the roads that lead from small towns to nowhere, whether through the reconstruction of a petty and immediate past or through the glorification of imaginary feats, the remaining sounds of another world attest to survival. Witnesses attest to it through children and grandchildren who speak another language and build new chapters of a continuing history. And building these new histories may perhaps constitute another definition of survival itself.

When Judaism cannot be affirmed solely on the basis of a national territory, and when religion is challenged within its own parameters in a refusal of formal observances or probing disbelief, Jewish identity in literature must per force acquire an aura of ethnicity as a defining feature. But it can also acquire, as it has, an exaltation of human values found in Judaism, an internal code of ethics that rises above history's latest atrocities. Ethnicity and heterodoxy are the signs of Judaism's lay incorporation into Latin American literature. Again, religious celebrations, concrete references to holidays, traditions, and "typical" Jewish subjects or characters, are not wholly absent in many authors. What is striking, however, is—in my opinion—that Jewish literature in Latin America is not built exclusively on the readily identifiable "Jewish" motifs, but on their relationship to developing realities where accepted tenets are questioned and challenged in modified social constructs. Jewish motifs might then be the loose threads that weave fantasies and family memoirs or the acerbic impact of institutional and class oriented critiques. At any rate, when restrictive and secure borders become elastic and allow into the midst of faith and innocent complacency the shadows of doubts that collapse the infallibility of a ruling center, Jewish motifs can once again be a backdrop to establish identity and probe its own definition. History and tradition are not necessarily denied, they are reworked, like all other fictive matter, to respond to patterns in constant flux.

One of these central concerns is precisely security, or the lack thereof, in societies where the survival of a minority must be justified. Not only concrete geography comes into question with the ensuing debates over immigration to Israel or Jewish assertiveness in any land of the diaspora, but also the logical and spiritual territory that amasses concepts of freedom of rational discourse and free expression. Families, communal institutions, and anti-Semitism are themes that open up the debate over identity and survival in hostile territory. Further, for some writers, repressive societies have made literary Judaism—quite distinct, but not necessarily opposite, from accepted norms and rabbinical definitions—a new area of inquiry. Far from marginal security, Jewish memories call forth migrations and exiles and the hopes for their end, and thus, within the mutations of circular history, they convey the trust that this too shall pass and the return to the home/homeland will recur. In this sense, the accepted referents to Israel and the diaspora have also changed: Their territorial place has shifted to accommodate any definition of homeland–exile in the dynamic correlation of peace–repression. In other words, this Jewish–Latin American literature flies over boundaries as it redefines its perceptions of nation, exile, communal ties, and the role that Judaism, in whatever personal definition, has achieved.

Jewish motifs can be found throughout Latin America's literary history, whether in the recreation of immigrants' experiences, in the processes of adaptation, or the less kind perspective of anti-Semitic fiction. Still, it is in recent years that a number of young authors have emerged as a notable global voice within the overall rise of Latin American literature. The assembled works of the writers who exist within the parameters here outlined do not satisfy a separate literary category; the analysis, even in the best of terms, still constitutes a thematic approach. These works will survive within their respective national literatures and *not* as a separate entity labeled "Jewish–Latin American literature." The critic's eye singles them out of their national literatures to assemble a new vast literary text that is garnished with a collective title. It is a legitimate practice provided each work is also seen as a direct result of hybrid elements in search of unity and of amalgamated voices. These texts are important, further, because they do address one of the significant components of a plural society by traversing the full gamut of the ideological debate and by forging tenets for renewing the dialogue along cultural and political lines. Jewish topics do not emerge now as a result of the nostalgia wave that has affected other circuits, but as expressions of conflictive relationships that find expression in the radicalization of historical processes.

Fiction stands, and rightly so, on the power of imagination and on the aesthetic relationship forged between the reader and the text. Jewish–Latin American fiction stands also on the strength of its documentary phase and on the emergence out of that phase of the references that underline that, given certain conditions, tradition and remembrance of things past are a flight to present-day conditions. If identity and survival can be considered fundamental motifs of Jewish literature in its many national versions, the debate over identity surges out of the threat to survival. Survival of Jews in Latin America, however, is not contingent only on memories of the Holocaust or on total integration in the state of Israel, but on a firm stand within Judaism in the new native lands. The response to this stand is a literature that bridges worlds, rescues filtered versions of Jewish traditions, and accommodates them to this hemisphere and to its languages. For Latin American–Jewish authors there is no question of a language that is their own. Spanish and Portuguese are not the languages of renewed exiles, but the languages of native affirmation that tolerate the reading of old–new debacles on the history of integration. As such they join Hebrew and the Jewish exile languages, Yiddish and Ladino, as languages to express the hopes, aspirations, and the reconstruction of all pasts that have been marked across the centuries.

Languages are transformed by the information they channel unto the conveyors of historical versions. Fiction works on a language of confrontation with the outside world. It achieves its inner coherence when that outside world is molded into the only possible version for its own singular fictive universe. Within a thematic approach of the Jew vis-à-vis Latin America, whether it be the case of a newly arrived immigrant, of the product of mixed marriages, or of the second- or third-generation "Latin-born Jew," we can address a Jewish sector of Latin American literature. Individually, each of the texts finds its own reading within a localized national environment nourished by readers who share either or both ethnic or national components or who approach the text with the illusion and care that all myths and fantasies require. Literature is not ethereal nor does it belong in idealist categories that preempt its correspondence to specific modes of production. To project a text beyond its origins and its concrete specificity is to create a new definition of diaspora, one that lies beyond all limits, detached from its producer, alien to the material reader that affords it its own right to exist through interpretation.

Language presupposes a dialogue with the other. Within Latin American–Jewish literature, the other is embodied in the dialectics of affirmation of these two components as they develop a mode of *co*existence that strives to affirm unified existence. Needless to say, no single text achieves peaceful unity. It is the search for that unity of purpose in drawing the design of Latin America from the perspective of a multicultural history that constitutes a major contribution to contemporary letters. Comparison to other, non-Jewish authors establishes modes of identification and marks the pace for the readers; it also stresses national belonging. To mention the Jewish component marks the entry to the exotic within Latin America—the foreign yet recognizable element that sheds light on the majority as it stares at itself with the fading belief in its uniform authority. Hyphens always produce unease. They signal the inability of language to produce a composite word and of beings to give birth to a gray, melted self; they also refer to the victory of the composites against assimilation. No single word can call into one that which belongs to many worlds. Latin American–Jewish writers and their texts stretch along millenary historical bridges as they walk firmly across the map of their new countries and their new letters.

17
The Evolution of the Latin American–Jewish Communities: Retrospect and Prospect

Judith Laikin Elkin

Introduction

Data on the Latin American Jewish communities are scattered, disparate, and lacking in chronological depth. It is difficult not only to see the trees for the forest, but even to locate the forest, let alone assess its health and its place in the ecosystem. This chapter attempts to identify trends in the life of these communities and to draw some inferences for the future.

The principal change that strikes the informed observer in reviewing the history of the Jewish presence in Latin America is in the manner in which Jews insert themselves into their host societies. Early Jewish immigrants saw themselves as inheritors of a civilization far superior to the one in which they now found themselves, which they perceived to be at a relatively lower social and cultural level. Arriving poor, they made their homes in the slums of port cities, on rural homesteads, or in the tiny commercial sectors of interior crossroad towns that had been systematically starved of social services by national legislatures. A literate people with a strong family structure and hygienic practices that controlled birth and death rates, they found themselves surrounded by people who were to a large extent illiterate, unaware of or unable to be concerned with personal hygiene, and tolerant of appalling rates of infant birth and infant mortality. Jewish immigrants found little in these settings that attracted them; their rejection of local culture was reinforced by its unremittingly Catholic nature, which imparted to Jewish immigrants the message that, in any event, they stood outside it.

Isolated Jewish individuals—itinerant peddlers of interior Peru, rubber planters of Amazonia, Alsatian bankers in Mexico City—did blend into the majority society, usually through intermarriage. But once mass immigration had compounded a base for organized Jewish community life, a more typical response was to withdraw into the Jewish group, seeking support there which was not forthcoming from the general society. The stronger the link to the Jewish community, the less need or inclination there was to establish fraternal ties with the majority society. Much effort went into sustaining and transmitting the cultural heritage the immigrants brought. Lacking a local history with which to identify, Jewish immigrants relied heavily on ties with their overseas communities of origin. In a manner contrary to the Jewish experience in the United States, these ties actually grew stronger over time, thus reinforcing the ethnic divisions among them. Memory became all-important: Latin American Jewish communities regularly observe the anniversaries of Krystallnacht and of the Warsaw Ghetto uprising, to the exclusion of events that are noteworthy in their own histories. Apparently no irony was intended when the Jewish community of Buenos Aires demonstrated on behalf of oppressed Soviet Jewry during the years of the Argentine repression. The tendency of Latin American Jewry to look to Jewish communities abroad for moral support is particularly pronounced with respect to Israel. Emotional reliance on the Jewish state becomes more pronounced when Jews are not fully accepted by their host societies.

A great deal has changed since the patterns of Jewish adaptation to Latin America were established. The social class structure of the host societies has been altered by increased industrialization and social mobilization as well as by improved transportation, communication, and educational systems—all developments in which the Jewish immigrants themselves played a role. In Argentina, Brazil, Chile, Uruguay, Mexico, and Venezuela most especially, but in all countries to a lesser degree, there now exist identifiable middle classes marked by relative affluence, high levels of education, and a modernized world outlook. It is now not only possible but also enjoyable and culturally rewarding to identify oneself as a communicant of these cultures. Native-born Latin American Jews are themselves members of the new middle sectors, attending school and university together with other middle-class sons and daughters and sharing similar concerns for the political, economic, and cultural future of their homelands. The life-style of these middle sectors—literate, urbane, emotionally attractive—is light-years removed from the poverty and stagnation of the cities and rural towns into which the immigrants came. It exercises a powerful seductive force over Jewish youth who prefer integration to continued marginalization. The vitality, creativity, and relevance of contemporary Latin American culture contrasts with the encysted traditionalism of the organized Jewish communities, which are locked into emotional postures derived from a distant past, whose relevance to modern life has scarcely been critically examined. Latin American–Jewish institutions have had difficulty being flexible in the face of changing times. Leaders of the older generation resist stepping aside for younger leaders, who might be more adept at tuning the community to contemporary needs. The celebrated gap separating generations of Jews is more than political; it represents a fundamental difference concerning the nature of Judaism: Does Jewish identity require only reflex adherence to ancient formulas, or has it the capacity to flex, to grow, and to open outward?

Religious Considerations

Despite certain exceptions, the early immigrants tended to be irreligious or antireligious in orientation; often, the formation of synagogues was incidental to the formation of institutions with more pragmatic tasks: cemeteries, schools, and mutual aid societies. When they did face the task of religious organization, these secular Jews established orthodox synagogues and imported orthodox rabbis, as though to ensure that the thing would be done correctly. They neither demanded nor did they receive from their rabbis moral and spiritual leadership. The Latin American–Jewish communities never produced their own rabbis or other religious functionaries, who continued to be imported from orthodox communities abroad. Latin American rabbinic decisions are not influential in other jurisdictions. The Latin American rabbinate has been outstanding only in its maintenance of an unreconstructed Judaism that rivals the inflexibility of the Catholic Church prior to Vatican II.

This lack of religious potency was matched by the failure of the transplanted rabbinate to exert moral leadership in secular matters. In the crisis that overtook Chile in 1973, the rabbis were among the first to leave the country. Ten years later, in the midst of Mexico's financial crisis, an Argentine rabbi occupying a pulpit in that country announced that Mexico was not a fit country for Jews and then departed for a job in San Diego, leaving his congregation to cope with the public criticism that followed.

The frozen postures and *shtetl* mentalities that characterized the Latin American rabbinate and that largely discredited Judaism in the eyes of younger people are only now beginning to thaw under influences proceeding from the North. The Reform movement (which began in Germany in the nineteenth century and has thrived in the pluralistic religious setting of the United States) as well as the American-born Conservative movement (which attempts to bridge Orthodoxy and Reform) are each having an impact in Latin America today. The two movements are not clearly distinguished from one another as they proceed through local adaptation and pragmatic arrangements from one congregation to another. Reform-minded congregations may be known variously as Conservative, Liberal, or Progressive; what they have in common is the desire to effect a Jewish *aggiornamiento,* blending elements of tradition and modernity according to local choices. The movement has taken its leaders from among rabbis trained in the United States, including such as Marshall Meyer of Comunidad Bet El (Buenos Aires), Henry Sobel of Congregação Israelita Paulista (São Paulo), and Roberto Graetz of Associação Religiosa Israelita (Rio de Janeiro). A Seminario Rabinico, founded in Buenos Aires in 1959 by Rabbi Meyer, is now training rabbis and teachers in the Conservative tradition, and its graduates are serving, officially and unofficially, in congregations around the continent. Hebrew Union College, the mother institution of the Reform movement in the United States, offers two-year assistantships in Latin America to its graduates. The drawing power of the modernized synagogues, and of others like them that are located in the principal cities of Argentina, Brazil, Panama, Mexico and Curaçao, far outweighs that of the older, unreformed synagogues, which continue to focus on the performance of ritual obligations at the expense of addressing moral and spiritual dilemmas.

Reform and Conservative synagogues utilize Spanish or Portuguese as well as Hebrew in their services, although they are not always able to overcome the ancient prejudice against mixed seating of women and men. They have introduced such innovations as youth groups, summer camps, and instruction in Judaism. Perhaps most important, they perform conversions to Judaism for non-Jews seeking to marry Jews, and have thus begun to reverse the tide that has carried off the intermarried and their children for the past century. These conversions, however, are not recognized by the orthodox rabbinate, creating the potential for a split within the Jewish people among those who regard themselves as real Jews and those considered not to be authentic.

It is among the Reform and Conservative rabbinate that Latin American Jews are beginning to find their leaders, confirming for these societies the novel impression that Jews are a religious group, not solely a "racial" one, as they have been traditionally regarded. Rabbis Meyer and Graetz revivified the concept of a living Jewish civilization by offering resistance to the Argentine military junta. By acting courageously on behalf of Jewish prisoners in a time of unprecedented stress, they forced a reconsideration of the meaning of Judaism. For the first time since Jewish religious life appeared on the South American continent, it stood forth as an ethical command rather than a ritual obligation. This revelation galvanized a sense of

Jewish identification in countless persons who had previously been immune to such feelings. Today, Argentine progressive congregations are filled with enthusiastic young Jews, presenting a lively contrast to the older orthodox congregations.

Ethnicity and Population Issues

In addition to this shift in religious sensibilities, another encouraging sign is the decrease of interethnic rivalry. Ethnic differences among Jews were preserved in Latin America far longer than in the United States because Jewish immigrants to the southern hemisphere were presented with so few opportunities for assimilation to national norms.[1] The lack of viable public secular education was particularly important, retarding the process of turning immigrant Jewish children into Argentines or Mexicans. Instead, immigrants turned inward on themselves, supplying their own educational needs and replicating the only educational systems they knew. Thus they recreated, not "Judaism," but specific national variants of it, such as *yiddishkeit* or *alepeño* culture. Without a national norm to which they could assimilate, ethnic norms persisted far longer than they did in the United States, where religious and ethnic differences were subordinated to patriotism through the agency of the public school.

Today, interethnic rivalry among Latin American Jews is diminishing along two axes, the generational and the geographical. Younger people, particularly those of the third or fourth generation, are far less interested in ethnic origins than their parents were. As the older generation passes, the ethnic clubs (*landsmenschaften*) that sustained them are dying out; recent years have seen the closing of the Hungarian club in Santiago and the German club in Mexico City. The sports clubs, which as modern inventions never lent themselves to ethnic separatism, have become the primary Jewish institutions, often attracting more communicants than the synagogues. But this development has not yet broken the hold the ethnically based clubs have over the central representative bodies. A facade of ethnicity is thus perpetuated, alienating younger Jews who might conceivably be interested in the politics of Jewish survival but who are put off by ethnic squabbling.

Along the geographic axis, interethnic rivalries tend to diminish at both ends of the scale: in towns with very small Jewish communities, such as Guadalajara or Paramaribo, where ethnic differences are deliberately

---

1. For a discussion of this issue, see Judith Laikin Elkin, *Jews of the Latin American Republics* (Chapel Hill: University of North Carolina Press, 1980), Chap. X.

downplayed in the interest of pooling limited resources, and in large metropolitan areas where there exist substantial urban middle sectors into which immigrant differences can be plunged and laundered. In the larger, more cosmopolitan societies, Jews are acculturating to Argentine, Chilean, or Brazilian urban society, leaving behind their parochial identities.

Ethnic subdivisions remain more or less intact in societies with a restricted definition of nationality. The centrality of race to the concept of *Mexicanidad* and the impossibility of Jews being included in *la raza* raise impassable barriers for Mexican Jews. These barriers are imitated within the community, which is still characterized by water-tight communal organizations for Jews of different ethnic origins. It seems that the greater the racial and cultural distance between Jews and their host societies, the more they are thrown on their own resources. This in turn reinforces traditional behavior patterns, which include the avoidance and deprecation of Jews who are unlike themselves. The entire question might be investigated in the light of Hoetink's theory of phenotypes.

Schmelz and DellaPergola inform us that the Jewish communities are shrinking at the rate of about 1% per year. The shrinkage in size of total population is paralleled by shrinkage in the number of communities that exist on the continent. In my earlier work, I noted the move out of the countryside and provincial towns to the big cities, spurred by the abandonment of farming and the lure of higher education. Now we must add the unstable political conditions in the countryside, which drive Jews, as others, out of rural areas and to the capital cities. A young woman reports that of nineteen classmates who graduated with her from the Jewish high school of Cali, just four remain in that city. Responding to many of the same factors that are causing Latin Americans generally to experience the highest rate of urbanization in the world, Jews are becoming more urbanized and more centralized than at any time in the past. Considering their overall small population and the erosion of communal institutions as they lose their membership, one can foresee a time when there will be very few Jews indeed in the interior of the continent.

Urbanization of Latin American–Jewish nuclei extends well beyond the region's boundaries. One-sixth of Latin American Jews now live either permanently or temporarily in Israel; comparable numbers probably reside in the United States, with other groups scattered throughout Europe, especially Spain and West Germany. The departure of Jews from Cuba under the spur of Castro's economic reorganization did not result in the relocation of Cuban Jews to some other Latin American country (though some few did resettle in Venezuela). For the most part, Cuban Jews settled in Florida, as other Cubans did. The exodus of Jews from Allende's Chile swelled the small Jewish community of West Germany. Radical Jewish exiles from Argentina went, like their compatriots, to Spain.

Economic Considerations

Substantial shifts in the economic structure of Jewish communities have been reported for some years. Early Jewish immigrants concentrated in petty trade, for which they possessed the advantages of literacy and previous commercial experience. The societies they entered exhibited gaps in the manufacture and distribution of consumer goods, providing points of entry into the economy as peddlers, kiosk salesmen, and handicraftsworkers. Additional advantages in these pursuits were that they could be started up with very little cash and that the immigrants, being self-employed, did not have either to combat prejudice on the part of employers or to submit to nonunionized working conditions.

Over time, Jewish craftsmen and traders moved into industry and large-scale trading, a process that by now has been well documented for Argentina and for the city of São Paulo, and reported anecdotally for every country of Jewish settlement.[2] Beginning about 1960, there was a detectable shift out of commerce and industry and into the liberal professions. A decade later, community leaders pointed to the growth of professional and service sectors, without necessarily bringing forward the data to substantiate their observations.

Jews are coming to maturity today in circumstances far different from those that enveloped their parents and grandparents. Raised in affluent circumstances, they are for the most part the product of advanced education. They feel themselves naturally to be Argentines or Brazilians as much or more than they are Jews; the effort to merge the two identities has given birth to a whole new literary genre. Whether the political orientation of any particular individual within Latin America's polarized societies will be toward the defense of property or toward rebellion against the maldistribu-

---

2. The best of the published literature on this subject includes Henrique Rattner, *Tradição e Mudança: A Comunidade Judaica em São Paulo* (São Paulo: Ática, 1977); Jacobo Schifter Sikora, Lowell Gudmundson, and Mario Solera Castro, *El judío en Costa Rica* (San José: Editorial Universidad Estatal a Distancia, 1979); Alfredo M. Seiferheld, *Inmigración y presencia judías en el Paraguay* (Asunción: Revista de la Universidad Católica "Nuestra Señora de la Asunción," 1981); and Eugene Sofer, *From Pale to Pampa: The Jewish Immigrant Experience in Buenos Aires* (New York: Holmes & Meier, 1982). For additional evidence, consult successive volumes of Comité Judío Americano, *Comunidades Judías de Latinoamerica* (Buenos Aires: 1966, 1968, 1970, 1971/1972, 1973/1975).

tion of wealth will be determined by a relationship to their local economies that is totally different from that experienced by their predecessors.

Political Considerations

Internal

The Latin American–Jewish *kehillot* derive from European models, which were driven by the need for unity in the face of external pressures. The *kehilla* was never a forum for the free interplay of opinion, let alone the representation of diverse ideological currents. To the contrary, diversity of opinion was feared because it could provide an opening through which the enemy might enter.

Transferred to the authoritarian societies of Latin America, which lack what has been called "the democratic mold," the *kehillot* failed to evolve in democratic directions. Instead, they retain their orientation to self-defense against a hostile world. In this posture, the most threatening action a Jew can take is to utter an opinion that does not conform to the community position. Although this may seem abhorrent to some, it may well be adaptive to the conditions in which the Latin American *kehillot* find themselves. One consequence, however, has been to alienate progressive elements among Jews. The organized Jewish communities, lacking political power, seek safety in identification with whatever regime is in power, even if that stance requires the abandonment of Jewish radicals or of the entire Jewish working class.

Jewish university youth of the 1960s and 1970s were thus confronted by a choice of opposed political styles: on the one hand, the conformist, go-along-to-get-along manner of the Jewish establishment; on the other, the confrontational reformist or revolutionary postures of the national left. It is not surprising that many chose to go with the latter, which they perceived to be more relevant to their own lives and to the life of the nation. Unfortunately, those who did so felt no impetus to carry reform inside the *kehilla*. To the contrary, they often cut their ties to the Jewish community and to their own families in the belief that being Jewish was irreconcilable with being radical. But this perception was a product of local circumstances. The rest of the world scarcely needs reminder of the radical Jewish tradition that started with Isaiah and that has been a moving force in European and U.S. political history.

The result of this political schizophrenia was an increasing number of dropouts from Latin American–Jewish life. The existing high rate of assimilation had been associated with men of working age who intermarried and dropped their association with the community. It is now increasingly common for Jewish youth of both sexes—urbanized, educated, and surrounded by the prerequisites for conducting life in the Jewish tradition—to cut their ties with the Jewish people, even if they marry other Jews. The Jewish educational systems of the region failed to achieve a synthesis of Jewish with Latin American culture that would satisify these conflicting needs.

External

Paradoxically, while some societies—notably the Argentine—were just coming through a dark passage of time in which anti-Semitism reached previously unknown depths, acceptance of Jews as members of their respective national societies was growing. This may be associated with the revival of Jewish religious values: Catholic societies have always accommodated Jews as a religious minority capable, it is thought, of testifying to the truth of the gospels. Sephardim long ago internalized this role, but it was a new one for the Ashkenazim who came to Latin American with a vision of themselves as secular participants in a dechurched society. It is possible that, with the revival of Judaism among Jews generally, Ashkenazim may reposition themselves as the Sephardim have done—as a tolerated religious group.

It may seem strange to raise the possibility so soon after the passage of Argentina through the religious hatred of the "dirty war" against subversion, in which thousands of innocent persons were killed or disappeared— among them, a disproportionate number of Jews; but a new period of tolerance for Latin American Jewry is not impossible. The defense of Jewish Argentines became notable as soon as controls on the press were relaxed by the military dictatorship. Raúl Alfonsín won the Argentine presidency despite being depicted as the candidate of the Jews. Once in office, he appointed Jews and friends of human rights to high government positions. Bernardo Greenspun had a predecessor as minister of finance in José Ber Gelbard, appointed by Perón to the same position. But Marcos Aguinis's appointment as subsecretary of culture was unprecedented and marked a departure from the previous policy of imposing a single standard of Catholic culture on the population. Numerous ministerial subsecretaries and university deans are Jews, and men with a commitment to cultural pluralism have been appointed to the Supreme Court and to the governing body of the Central Bank. Several Jews were elected to the Senate, including Adolfo Gass, who became chair of the Foreign Relations Committee. Six Jewish individuals were elected to the Chamber of Deputies, one of whom, César Jaroslawsky, was subsequently elected majority leader of that chamber.

Even in Mexico, where ten years ago participation by Jews in politics seemed unthinkable, there are now Jews occupying important appointive positions in government. Informed observers believe it is only a matter of time before Jews will have gained sufficient political experience to win acceptance by the apparachiks of PRI, the dominant political party.

At the core of anti-Semitism in Latin America lie the teachings of the unreconstructed church, which until now has declined to accept the declarations of Vatican II with respect to Jews and Judaism. The Latin American Bishops' Council (CELAM) on two occasions (at Medellín and again at Puebla) declined to go on record as removing the infamous teaching of contempt. True, some clerics—Monsignor Jorge Mejía of Argentina, Monsignor Ernesto Corripio Ahumada, archbishop of Mexico—took to heart the papal injunction to relieve the Jews of collective responsibility for the death of Jesus. In 1981, the National Conference of Brazilian Bishops created a National Commission for Jewish–Catholic Dialogue. With the approach of the twentieth anniversary of the declaration *Nostra Aetate,* an ecumenical impulse was at last activated in the body of the Latin American Catholic churches.

What has caused this increased awareness of the necessity to adjust the tenuous status of Jews and Judaism in Latin America? It would be too much to suppose that the Church was seeking allies in the small and politically powerless Jewish communities. One factor may be the perception of the consequences of unbridled anti-Semitism in Argentina. There can be little doubt that many decent citizens who had never examined their own latent anti-Semitism were forced to do so by the revelation of crimes committed by the military, who were only acting out the prejudices common to much of the population. The disgust voiced by international opinion and expressed in the world press would surely have an effect—as it had in Chile, where a somewhat cleverer junta stifled anti-Semitism from the start, in the interest of its image abroad.

An incipient decline in anti-Semitism may also be assisted by the entry of Jewish intellectuals into national cultural life via literature and the mass media. The appearance of talented novelists, poets, and filmmakers who are concerned with issues of Jewish identity offer to non-Jewish Latin Americans a point of entry into Jewish sensibilities, something that was lacking when the best Jewish literature was being produced in Yiddish. Identity—the issue of the "cosmic race"—has been a traditional theme in Latin American literature. Now its corollary, the conundrum of Jewish–Latin American identity, enables the non-Jewish reader to empathize with and begin to enter into the dilemmas of the Jewish condition. The acculturation of the Jews in itself becomes ground from which to combat anti-Semitism. Jews are no longer *polacos, rusos,* or *turcos*; they are making their debut as Argentines, Brazilians, and Mexicans.

Jews view anti-Semitism and assimilation as twin threats to continued

Jewish life on the continent. The question of Jewish survival invariably heads the agenda in any communal discussion of that area of the world. Although this debate consumes Jews worldwide, no corresponding debate has arisen among non-Jews, not excluding human rights activists and adherents of liberation theology. For the majority of Latin Americans, the survival of their Jewish communities is a negligible concern. A creative and bouyant Jewish presence within national society is not viewed (as it was earlier in Europe and in the United States) as a litmus test of that society's devotion to human rights, but as a failure of the national mystique.

Latin America's Jews and Israel

Over the years, Latin America's Jews contributed generously of their funds and personnel to the Zionist cause. They lobbied their governments in favor of pro-Israel positions. Much international exchange of persons takes place between community leaders and Israel. Israeli ambassadors to the several Latin American countries reap more adulation than should be the lot of any human being. Partly because of a semantic confusion between *israeli* (a citizen of Israel) and *israelita* (a genteel circumlocution for "judío") there exists a predisposition to confuse the two—a situation that is compounded by the mimetic character of the organized *kehillot*. These conduct their elections along Israeli party lines, which is to say that voters in communal elections in Buenos Aires and elsewhere face the same choice of parties, programs, and personalities as do voters in Tel Aviv or Haifa. What relationship these campaigns bear to local issues or to their resolution is unclear. But the cathexis is so complete that participants never even frame the question. The Zionist core of Jewish communal life has been helpful until now in maintaining the unity of the Jewish people.

Israel's own early relations with the Latin American governments were devoid of conflict. The Jewish Agency, and later the government of Israel, appeared in the southern hemisphere as petitioners, seeking support of the powerful Latin American bloc at the United Nations. Israeli and Latin diplomats found common ground in their Judeo-Christian heritage; as humanists, the latter lent their votes, their strategies, and their will to the achievement of recognition for the Jewish state. Relations between the two sides were personalistic and altruistic. As reported as late as 1982 by Natanel Lorch, one of the prinicipal actors of the period, "The truth is that none of the vital interests of Israel . . . is closely linked with Latin America; and vice versa, the major problems of Latin American countries . . . are basically unrelated to their contacts with Israel."[3]

3. Natanel Lorch, "Latin America and Israel," *Jerusalem Quarterly* 22 (Winter 1982): 70.

During the 1960s, Israel became a purveyor of technical assistance to almost every one of the republics, establishing such projects as an experimental seed farm in northeastern Brazil and an agricultural settlement in Choapa, Chile, advising the government of Ecuador on citriculture, and prospecting for water in Peru. In the process, Israeli experts generated a certain amount of goodwill toward the local Jewish communities as well as for themselves. A warning note was, however, sounded when in 1960 the Israeli intelligence forces abducted Adolph Eichmann from the streets of Buenos Aires and brought him to Jerusalem for trial. As much as persons around the world may have applauded his apprehension, the act aroused considerable anti-Semitism in Argentina, symbolized by an assault on a Jewish school girl and the carving of a swastika on her breast. Israel, in the view of many Argentines, had violated the country's sovereignty—just the sort of invasive action imperialist nations customarily engage in. Perceptions of Israel began to shift. Jewish communities became the target of " progressive" Third-World groups that identify Israel with the forces of imperialism and local Jews with Israel.

During the early 1970s, links were established between the PLO and various guerrilla groups in Latin America (the Sandinistas, for one); Fidel Castro led a retreat by Latin American governments from their earlier positions of support for Israel. Contributions to the United Jewish Appeal increased and *aliya* swelled. Local political crises contributed to this development. For example, some Chilean Jewish families sent their children to Israel in order to avoid their being tainted by the Allende government; among these, some returned to take positions under Pinochet. Conversely, other families sent sons and daughters out of the country in order to remove them from public life during military rule. Still others are simply relieved when authoritarian governments forbid all political activity. Brazilian parents expressed relief, during the height of the repression in that country, that when their children left for school, they were really going to class and not to some street demonstration where they might get killed.

By the late 1970s, commerce was playing a more important role in Israeli–Latin American relations. Bank Leumi and the Mizrahi Bank opened over thirty branches in principal cities of the continent. Israeli-owned agribusinesses started up in the Dominican Republic, prompted by films of Sosua, the refugee farm community that was established on that island during World War II. Commercial fish farming is being undertaken on some Caribbean islands by Israeli entrepreneurs, and Israeli firms have contracted to carry out parts of the U.S. Government's Caribbean Basin Initiative.

The most sensational development has been the entry of Israel into the Latin American arms market. This development stems, on the Israeli side, from increased specialization in the manufacture of armaments because of its exposed security position, and on the Latin American side from the demand for weapons that has been stimulated by both military regimes and insurgent movements. An additional factor is the de facto U.S.–Israeli alliance, which counsels Israeli cooperation with the United States in the western hemisphere in return for American support in the Middle East.

In 1979, the Stockholm International Peace Research Institute (SIPRI) identified Israel for the first time as a major weapons exporter. Ranked eighth that year, Israel had in fact sold just $155 million worth of arms, or 0.8% of the world total. Small arms made up most of these exports, led by the Uzi machine gun, which was being sold in sixty different countries.

By the following year, Israel was exporting the Gabriel ship-to-ship missile system, the Reshef fast patrol boat, and the Kfir C-2 fighter plane. Four years later, SIPRI reported Israeli sales of airplanes to Argentina, Brazil, Colombia and Ecuador, and the *Latin America Weekly Report* suggested additional sales to Honduras and Venezuela. There were reports in the press of substantial sales to the governments of El Salvador and Guatemala.

Israeli weapons sales increasingly tied the government of Israel to United States policy in the western hemisphere in support of conservative governments allegedly engaged in combating communist subversion. Most Israeli weapons contain U.S.-made components and cannot be sold without U.S. authorization. To a growing extent, Israel came to be viewed as cooperating with the American administration to circumvent efforts by the U.S. Congress to suspend or limit arms shipments to specific Latin American regimes.

The parallel interests that emerged between Israel and the United States in the Middle East, capped by the 1983 agreement for strategic cooperation, predisposed Israel to support U.S. foreign policy in the western hemisphere. Henry Kissinger's conclusion that the United States cannot afford to be diverted from its real security interests by a Soviet incursion into its own backyard (in reference to Nicaragua), whether reality-based or not, carried weight so far as Israel was concerned. Were the United States to determine that it faced a genuine threat in Central America, there would be considerably less energy directed toward combating the mutually perceived Soviet threat in the Middle East. Moreover, the association of Latin American guerrilla movements and political parties with armed proponents of the Arab cause created a natural alliance between Israel and the governments that were seeking to put down these rebellions—especially when the government of Israel was itself under the conservative administration of the Likud party. Thus Israel, itself accused of imperialist policies at home, now found itself allied with Latin American governments and parties that were tied to the principal imperial power of the western hemisphere.

The entry of Israel into western hemisphere wars had an impact on the

Latin American–Jewish communities. Jews, already so closely identified with Israel, are now closely identified with the United States as well, and stand in danger of inheriting all of the United States' enemies. Israeli arms sales reinforce the trend. This may ultimately have a stabilizing or a destabilizing effect on the communities, depending on local variables. In the Nicaraguan case, the long-range effect was to destabilize the Jewish community, which had to depart in the wake of the demolition of the Somoza regime, which Israel had supplied with arms.

In the case of Argentina, Israeli arms supply to the military junta appears to have been a stabilizing factor. At first blush, traffic between Israel and the junta appeared inexplicable in any but the crassest of commercial terms. Arguments in defense of Israeli sales, at a time when the junta was engaged in a war against its own civilian population, including Jews, focused on the need for Israel to break out of the Arab trade embargo, the need to keep Israeli armaments industry functioning at the outer edge of technological achievement, and the value-free nature of the market in international armaments. France, after all, had supplied the junta with the Exocet missile that sank the Sheffield, a vessel belonging to France's ally, Britain. But there was a deeper rationale: The supply of weapons to Argentina throughout the Falklands/Malvinas War placed Israel (and therefore *israelitas*) squarely within the patriotic camp. Israeli officials and industrialists gained access to Argentina's military rulers, the most reactionary sector of Argentine society and one that had been totally impenetrable by Jewish Argentines. As a result, the Israeli embassy was able to send consular officials into Argentine jails to extricate Jewish prisoners. The fact that Israel honored her contracts for arms deliveries during the war became a trade-off for the appointment of four Jewish chaplains to tend to the spiritual needs of Argentine Jewish soldiers. The appointment eased the apprehension of Jewish families at a time when draftees were being "disappeared" and also brought public attention to the fact that there were Jewish draftees serving in the army. Further, the appointment reversed the well-established Argentine tradition of refusing commissions to Jews.

The new Israeli role carries with it the danger of turning Latin American Jews into pawns in the power games being played. Ariel Sharon's widely quoted remark to the effect that he did not want to see Jewish boys fighting one another over the Falklands was enough to bring into question Jewish patriotism in Argentina, if not in England. The most troubling aspect of this situation is that Israeli foreign policy has impact on the Latin American Jewish communities without the latter having any input into its formulation. As a result, Latin American Jews have become pawns in a power struggle that owes nothing to their presence and is not concerned primarily with their interests.

Conclusions

It is a truism that the lives of immigrants are conditioned by two sets of variables, one internal, the other external. The traditions Jews brought with them to the New World were initially as determinative of their lives as were conditions in the societies into which they came. But these variables changed intrinsically and in relation to one another over time and historic space. Much of the immigrants' cultural heritage has now been left behind them—in the deserted agricultural colonies, in the unfrequented cemeteries and synagogues of provincial towns. Refreshing winds of change, blowing mostly from the north, bring intimations of a Judaism that goes beyond ancestor worship, a Judaism that can be a source of vitality and renewal.

As for the external factors, there has been change within change. Anti-Semitism remains embedded in the core institutions of society, but there may be increased realization that its free play on the political scene is hazardous not only for Jews but for society at large. As Jews enter the swelling socioeconomic middle sectors, they seek to enter more fully into the life of the nation, bringing with them their individual talent and enthusiasm, some of which springs from Jewish sources. The limits to their participation will be set by their host societies.

Now a third factor has been introduced, namely the foreign policy of the independent State of Israel. The events of the early 1980s demonstrated how quickly the Latin American Jewish communities could be reduced to colonial status by their fixation on the distant dream of Zion. It remains to be seen whether these communities will be able to extricate themselves from their dependency. One would not expect any diaspora to cut the link to Israel; certainly not the Latin American diasporas, which still lack strong roots in their own national societies. But the commitment to Israel may be balanced by a judicious concern for the wellbeing of the diaspora community itself, as well as for the nation to which it owes allegiance. The future of Latin American Jewry at this writing is far from clear; it will be determined by the interaction of these three sets of variables.

Notes on Contributors

Haim Avni is on the faculty of the Institute of Contemporary Jewry, the Hebrew University of Jerusalem. He is the author of *Argentina y la historia de la inmigración judía, 1810–1950, Argentina, The Promised Land: Baron de Hirsch's Colonization Project,* and *Emancipation and Jewish Education—A Century of Argentinian Jewry's Experience 1884–1984* (the last two in Hebrew).

Sergio DellaPergola is senior lecturer and associate director, Division of Jewish Demography and Statistics, Institute of Contemporary Jewry at the Hebrew University of Jerusalem. He is co-author of *The Demography of the Jews in Argentina and in Other Countries of Latin America* (Tel Aviv, 1974) (in Hebrew) and *World Jewish Education: Cross-Cultural Perspectives* (Jerusalem, 1987).

Judith Laikin Elkin is Research Associate to the Program in Judaic Studies at The University of Michigan and author of *Jews of the Latin American Republics* (University of North Carolina Press, 1980). She is founding president of the Latin American Jewish Studies Association (LAJSA) and editor of the *Latin American Jewish Studies Newsletter*.

Israel Even-Shoshan emigrated to Israel from Argentina in 1961. He teaches at the School for Overseas Students in Jerusalem and directs the Institute for Youth Leaders from Abroad, sponsored by the World Zionist Organization.

Notes on Contributors

Lowell Gudmundson is a member of the faculty of the History Department, University of Oklahoma. He is the co-author (with Jacobo Schifter Sikora and Mario Solera Castro) of *El judío en Costa Rica* (San José, 1979).

Robert M. Levine is professor and chair of the History Department, University of Miami at Coral Gables. He is the author of seven books on Latin American history and producer of the documentary film, "Hotel Cuba: The Pre-Castro Jewish Experience." He is vice-president of the Latin American Jewish Studies Association.

Daniel C. Levy is Associate Professor of Educational Administration and Policy Studies and of Latin American Studies at SUNY–Albany. His most recent book is *Higher Education and the State in Latin America: Private Challenges to Public Dominance* (University of Chicago, 1986).

Victor Mirelman is spiritual leader of Congregation B'nai Israel in Millburn, New Jersey, and a member of the LAJSA Board. His doctoral dissertation, "The Jews in Argentina: Assimilation and Particularism," Columbia University, 1973, was followed by numerous scholarly articles on the subject.

Gilbert W. Merkx is Professor of Sociology and Director of the Latin American Institute at the University of New Mexico. He has been editor of the *Latin American Research Review* since 1982 and has published extensively on social change in Latin America.

Anita Novinsky earned her Ph.D. in history at the University of São Paulo, where she is professor of history and the history of mentalities. A frequent lecturer abroad, Dr. Novinsky has published four books and many scholarly articles on the Jewish presence in Brazil during the colonial period.

Henrique Rattner*,* who is on the Faculty of Economics and Administration of the University of São Paulo, specializes in socioeconomic issues of the Third World. He is the author of *Tradição e Mudança: A Comunidade Judaica em São Paulo* (São Paulo 1977).

David Schers was born in Buenos Aires, received his Ph.D. in Political Science at the University of New Mexico, and currently teaches at the Tel Aviv University School of Education. He coordinated the research project on the Jewish communities of Latin America carried out by the David Horowitz Institute of Tel Aviv University.

Bernard Segal, Professor of Sociology, Dartmouth College, lived in Buenos Aires as an FAFP Fellow in 1966, and again as a Fulbright Scholar in 1972. A student of ethnic relations, he has worked on issues in American bilingualism, ethnic transformation in Peru, and the nation-ethnicity connection.

Leonardo Senkman is the author of *La identidad judía en la literatura argentina* (Buenos Aires, 1983). Argentine born, he is now on the faculty of Hebrew University in Jerusalem.

Saul Sosnowski is professor and chair of the Department of Spanish and Portuguese at the University of Maryland and editor of the literary journal *Hispamerica*. He has published several studies of Argentine-Jewish writers and, most recently, *Borges y la cábala* (Buenos Aires, 1986).

Carlos Waisman is Associate Professor of Sociology at the University of California, San Diego and author of *Modernization and the Working Class: The Politics of Legitimacy* (Austin: University of Texas Press, 1982) and *The Question of Revolution and the Reversal of Development in Argentina* (Princeton: Princeton University Press, forthcoming).

Index

Abejdid, Elias J., 13, 18
Abejdid, Isaac E., 13
Acculturation, 291–292
Action Française, 244, 245, 246
Age, of Jewish population in Argentina, 102–103, 110–112
Agriculture, 36, 49–50, 59–60
Aguinis, Marcos, 317
Ahaba Vehajaba, 30
Ahavat Sedek, 30
AIU schools, 18, 20–21
Aleppine Jews, 27, 28, 29
Alessandri, Arturo, 51
Alfonsín, Raúl, 317
Algeria, 13, 14, 15
Alienation, of Latin American Jews, 78–84, 293
Aliya (*see also* Israel, immigrants to): aspects of Latin American, 120–127, 292; country differentials, 120–124; crises in Latin America and, 319; youth movements and, 277–282
Allende, Salvador, 123, 164, 315
Alliance Israélite Universelle, 15–16
Alsatian Jews, 5, 7
American Jewish Committee (AJC), 80, 147, 148
Amram, David, 18n
Anglo-Argentines, 214

Anti-Christ, 245
Anticlericalism, Argentine, 255–257
Anti-Defamation League, 80
Anti-Semitism, 6, 9, 28, 62, 84, 305; in Argentina, 76–77, 166, 201, 204–212, 216, 240–245, 250–251, 288, 293, 317, 318, 320; in Brazil, 36–43; in Costa Rica, 220, 223–228, 231; Iberian, 43; in Latin America, 73, 121; in Nicarauga, 230
Anti-Zionism, 144, 146–148
Anzótegiu, Ignacio B., 236
Arabs, 150–151, 199, 242, 243, 301, 321–322
Aranha, Oswaldo, 62
Arendt, Hannah, 201
Argentina, 5, 8, 10, 20, 72, 82; anti-clericalism in, 255–257; anti-Israel policy in, 200; anti-Semitism in, 76–77, 166, 201, 204–212, 216, 240–245, 250–251, 288, 293, 317, 318, 320; arms sales to, 322–323; class conflict in, 208–216; culture in, and Jewish identity, 255–269, 286–288; demographic patterns of Jews in, 103, 107–110; emigration of Jews from, 100, 121–123; fascism in, 204–207; German Jewish refugees and, 50–52, 59–62, 65, 66; as homeland for Russian Jews, 137–140; Indian population in, 207–208, 288; informal Jewish education in, 271–

329

Argentina (*cont.*)
283; Jewish education in, 166–170, 174, 177, 263; Jewish population in, 86, 88, 100, 128–129, 132; Moroccan Jews in, 13–24; nationalism in, 204–208, 233–251, 272; Socialist Party in, 265–269; sociodemographic characteristics of Jews in, 110–112; Zionism in, 142–143, 145, 148–149, 273–275, 277–282
Argentine Zionist Federation (OSA), 307
Arms sales, 321–322
Ashkenazic Jews, 29, 71, 74, 78–79, 82, 84, 170, 182, 317
Assalam, 26
Assimilation, 84, 258–263; resistance to full, 73, 75–76, 215, 267, 271, 279, 318
Association des Anciens Elèves de l'Alliance à Tanger, 20
Austria, 58
Austrian Jews, 58, 60
Austri-Dan, Yeshayahy, 136
Auto-Emancipation, 138
Autonomy, in Jewish education: financial, 168–172; power holders, 172–176; school-state, 162–168
Avni, Haim, 4n, 136

Bahia, 36–37, 75
Balfour Declaration, 141–144, 151
Balkan wars, 27, 29
Bank Leumi, 320
Barylko, J., 170
Beagle Channel, 235
Begin, Menachim, 243
Beilis trial, 265–266
Bejarano, Margalit, 136
Bekmann, Manoel, 41n
Belém, 20, 141n
Belonging, identity and, 300–301
Benchetrit, Abraham, 19
Benchetrit (Benjetrit), Isaac, 16, 19
Benchetrit, J., 17
Benchimol, Isaac, 21
Benshimol, Jacob M., 18
Bensimon, Sultana, 17
Benmuyal, Solomón, 19, 20
Benyanes, David, 19
Benzaquén, Isaac, 18
Benzaquén, José, 17

Benzaquén, Moisés, 19
Benzaquén, Solomón, 18
Benzecti, José, 18
Bernal, Luis, 17
Bibas, Jacobo, 24
Bistritzky, Nathan, 136, 148
Black Africa, 21
Blis, David, 143
Bloch, B., 93
Blumenfeld, Kurt, 149
B'nai B'rith, 80
Bolivia, 53; emigration to Israel from, 121–123; German Jewish refugees and, 52–53
Bonacich, Edna, 210, 213, 214, 216
Boxer, Charles, 38
Brazil, 5, 8, 10, 15; anti-Israel policy in, 200; anti-Semitism in, 36–43; Dutch in, 37–39; emigration to Israel from, 121–123; German Jewish refugees and, 48–50, 52, 55–56, 60, 62–63, 65–66; gold rush, 40–41; Inquisition in, 34–44; Jewish education in, 167, 174–175, 177, 180; Jewish population in, 88, 101–103; Moroccan Jews in, 14–16, 20; poverty in, 188–189; racism in, 43; social mobility of Jews in, 187–200; Zionism in, 140–142, 144
Britain. *See* Great Britain
British Mandate, 151
Buenos Aires, 13, 45, 50, 74, 89, 93, 97, 107, 108; Moroccan Jews in, 16–24; Ottoman Jews in, 27–32; sociodemographic characteristics of Jews in, 112–119
Buenos Aires Herald, 25
Burial rites, 20, 23, 30, 268–269

Cabildo, 234, 244, 249, 251
Calderón Guardia, Rafael Angel, 224–226
Canada, French, 206
Capitalism, 9, 239–240, 245, 247
Caracas, 20
Cardenas, President, 64
Caribbean Basin Initiative, 320
Carlés, Manuel, 259
Carta Politica, 271
Carter, Jimmy, 241
Castillo, Alvaro de, 141
Castro, Fidel, 314, 319
Catholic church, 9, 18, 72, 77, 311; in Argentina, 204, 205, 206, 214, 237–238,

247, 250, 255–257, 266, 271–272; in Brazil, 35–37, 39, 42–44; in Costa Rica, 228
Catholic Nationalism (Argentina), 233–236, 243–251
Catholics, Maronite rite, 25–26
Cazes, David, 15, 21
Centro Macedonico, 143
Chaar Achamayim, 23
Chelminsky, Tzila, 172
Chile, 76, 241; emigration to Israel from, 121–123, 287, 315; German Jewish refugees and, 51–52; Jewish education in, 164–165, 166–167, 168, 169, 178; Jewish population in, 88, 101–103; Zionism in, 143–144
Christianity, 9, 24–27, 208–209, 215, 245; Jewish converts to, 33–44
Clothing manufacture, 222–223
Club Atletico Sefaradi Argentino (CASA), 273, 280–281
Cohen, Alberto, 17
Cohen, Samuel, 19
Cohim, Jose A., 76
Colombia: emigration to Israel from, 121–123; German Jewish refugees and, 53, 55; Jewish education in, 162–164, 169, 173, 175, 177, 181
A Columna-Ha'Amud, 141
Comite Hebreu-Brazilero Pro-Vitimas da Guerra, 147
Comité Nacional Judio, 144
Committee of Friends of the AIU, 19
Communism, 223, 238–239, 240, 241, 244–245, 321
Community, Jewish: activism, 290–291, 295; economic structure of, 315–316; evolution of Latin American-Jewish, 309–321; influences on Argentine, 286–288; politics and, 316–317; urbanization and, 314–315
Congregación Israelita, 17–19, 20
Congregación Israelita Latina, 19, 20, 23
Congregación Israelita de la Republica Aegentina (CIRA), 142–143
Conservatism (political): of Brazilian Jews, 197–198; of Latin American Jews, 76–77
Conservatism (religious), 281–283, 312–313
Converts to Christianity, Jewish, 33–44

Córdoba, 115
Corripio Ahumada, Ernesto, 318
Cortés, León, 224, 226
Costa Rican Jewry, 219–231; anti-Semitism and, 220, 223–228, 231; contemporary, 228–231; immigrant experience, 220–223
Coughlin, Charles, 206
Creativity, of Latin American Jews, 79–81
Criollismo, 258
Cuba, 55, 71–72, 73, 78, 247–248
Cuban Jews, 79–81; education, 165; emigration to Israel, 121–123, 314–315; and Zionism, 143, 144
Cuentanik group, 110
Culture, 7–10; Argentine, and Jewish identity, 255–269, 289–295
Curacao, 5
Curutchet, Ricardo, 235, 237

Damascene Jews, 27, 29
da Silva, D. Pedro, 39
d'Avigdor Goldsmid, Osmond, 57
de Goes, Damião, 38
de Hirsch, Maurice, 137–140
DellaPergola, Sergio, 158n, 314
Democracy, 8–9
Demographic patterns, of Latin American Jewry, 102–120
Demonstration effect, 9
Denmark, 61
de Paiva, Manuel, 41
De Rosas, Juan Manuel, 236
Dickmann, Enrique, 150, 265
Dominican Republic, 5, 78, 320; German Jewish refugees and, 55, 65–67
Dominican Republic Settlement Association (DORSA), 66
Don Pedro II, 35
Dourado, Antonio F., 41n
Dror, 273, 276–277
Duby, Georges, 33
Duhau, Luis P., 50
Dujovne, Leon, 260
Dulzin, Ayre (Leib), 154
Dutch, in Brazil, 37–39

Eastern Europe, 7, 23, 29, 93, 96, 169, 177, 260

Echandi, Mario, 227–228
Economic Commission for Latin America (ECLA), 193
Economies, Latin American (*see also* Industrialization; Poverty): 8, 10
Ecuador: emigration to Israel from, 121–123; German Jewish refugees and, 53–55, 60–61, 63–64, 65
Edrei, Mordechai, 274, 281
Education, Jewish, in Latin America: context, 157–162; emphasis on, 82, 110, 111; financial autonomy, 168–172; and group identity, 176–182; informal, in Argentina, 271–283; power holders, 172–176; state-school relations, 162–168
Effinger, Max, 224–225
Egypt, 242–243
Eichmann, Adolf, 58, 320
Elite(s): in Argentina, 210–211, 247, 257; Brazilian Jews as, 195–197, 199
Eljarrat, Abraham, 17
Eljarrat, Isaac, 17
Eljarrat, Lazaro, 17, 19
Elkin, Judith L., 72, 136, 177, 291
England. *See* Great Britain
Enlightenment, the, 42, 203, 256
Entenberg, Mauricio, 274
Entrepreneurship, 79–81, 190, 222–223
Esnaty, Marcos, 16
Ethnicity, 8, 74, 83, 213; in contemporary Latin America, 313–315; decline of, in Argentina, 202–208
Ets Ajaim, 23
Euro-America, 71; German Jewish refugees and, 49–52, 56
Europe, 6, 9, 14, 24, 67, 83, 84, 187, 250, 319
Experts Conference on Latin America and the Future of Its Jewish Communities, 3
Evian Conference, 58–59, 64, 66, 67

Falange (Spain), 244, 246
Falbel, Nachman, 136
Falkland Islands. *See* Malvinas/Falkland Islands
Fascism, in Argentina, 204–207; Catholic Nationalism and, 245–250
Federación Sionista, 144
Fernandes, Diogo, 36n

Ferreira, Jose H., 41
Fertility, of Argentine Jewish women, 108–110
Figueres, José, 226–227
Fischel, Max, 220n
Fleischer, David, 273
Ford, Henry, 241
France, 58, 246, 322
Franco, Francisco, 237, 247, 250
Frank, Anne, 242
Frank, Waldo, 262, 263
Freemasonry, 43, 240, 247
Freire, Paulo, 293
French Alliance Israelite Universelle, 140
Fried, Pesah, 274
Fuchs, Joao D., 76

Garazi, Ezra, 28
Garcia, Alejandro, 227
Gass, Adolfo, 317
Gastelau, A., 60
Los Gauchos Judios, 150, 258
Gelbard, José-Ber, 242, 249
Gemilut Hassadim, 30
Genta, Giordano Bruno, 237, 246, 251
Gerchunoff, Alberto, 150, 257–263, 269
Germani, Gino, 207
German Jews, 6, 7, 45–68, 79
Germany. *See* Nazi Germany
Ghettoization, 74–75
Ghiano, Juan Carlos, 258
Ghioldi, Americo, 268–269
Gibralter, 16
Gidekel, Saúl, 262
Goldman, Moises, 262
Goldsmid, Albert A., 137
Golek, Abraham, 274
Gomes, Dias, 42
Gordon, Milton M., 291
Graetz, Roberto, 312
Graiver, David, 240
Graiver, Manuel, 146
Graiver affair, 241, 249
Great Britain, 142, 151–152, 322–323
Greece, 27
Greenspun, Bernardo, 317
Grondona, Mariano, 271–272, 283
Grunberg, Carlos, 262
Gruson, Sidney, 227–228

Guami, Alberto, 51, 149
Guemilut Hasadim, 20
Gurany, Moshé, 230

Ha'am, Achad, 138
Habermas, Jurgen, 295
Haiat, Yossi, 274
Haiti, 28
Haleny, Yehuda, 258
Halphon, Samuel, 22
Handlin, Oscar, 82
Hantke, Arthur, 149
Hay, Eduardo, 64
Hebraica, 273, 278–280
Hebrew (language), 181–182, 307, 312
Hebrew University Institute of Contemporary Jewry, 87
HeHalutz LaMerhav, 273, 277
Hermandad, 27
Herzl, Theodor, 135, 138–140
Hes Hayim, 23
Hesed Shel Emeth (HSE), 30n
Hesed Ve'emet, 23, 30n
Hessed Laalafirm, 30
HIAS-ICA-Emigdirekt (HICEM), 45
High Commissioner for Refugees (Jewish and Others), 47
Himmelfarb, Harold S., 158n
Hispano-Argentines, 236
Hitler, Adolf, 45
Holland, 61
Holocaust era (*see also* Nazi Germany): German Jewish refugees in, 45–68; Zionism in, 146–150
Honduras, 54
Horowitz Institute of University of Tel Aviv, 289
Hyphen, use of, in Latin American–Jewish, 297–307

Ibarguren, Federico, 246
Identity, group: and Argentine culture, 255–265, 287, 291–295; and Argentine Socialist Party, 265–269; belonging and, 300–301; and Jewish education, 176–182; in literature, 304–307; and survival, 304–305; and youth movements, 273–282
Ideology: of Brazilian Jews, 196–199; of Catholic Nationalism, 233–236, 246–250; fascist, in Argentina, 204–207; positivist, in Argentina, 256–257, 269; Zionism as, 212
Immigrants: Costa Rican experience, 220–223; industrialization and, 190–191, 193, 202; Latin American-Jewish, evolution of, 309–310
Indo-America, 71; German Jewish refugees in, 52–55, 56
Industrialization: in Argentina, 248; immigrants and, 190–191, 193, 202
Informal Jewish education, in Argentina, 271–283; institutions for, 276–282; research on, 272–275
Ingenieros, Jose, 256
Inman, Samuel, 47
Inquisition, the, 34–43
Institute of Contemporary Jewry, 127
Institute of Jewish Affairs, 3
Integralista Party, 50
Intermarriage, 16, 75, 97, 107–108, 310
International Jews, The, 241
International Monetary Fund, 251
Irazusta brothers, 246
Iron Guard (Rumania), 244
Isolation, of Latin American Jews, 8, 77–78
Israel (*see also Aliya*), 4, 7, 8, 9, 18n, 32, 72, 76, 78, 84, 93, 100, 301; Argentine nationalists and, 242–243; arms sales, 321–322; educational aid to Latin American Jews, 170, 179; establishment of, 150–154, 275; immigrants to, 120–127, 132, 287; support for, 180–181, 229–230, 310
"Israel, the Promised Land," 263
Itaipu Dam, 236
Italy, 84

Jabotinsky, Zeev, 143
Jaffe, Leib, 145, 146, 149
Japan, 6
Jaroslawsky, César, 317
Jerusalem Post, 76
Jevra Kedusha, 268
Jewish Burial Association, 20, 268–269
Jewish Colonization Association (JCA), 20, 47, 57, 139–140, 263, 264, 267–268
"Jews, The," 271

Jews of the Latin American Republics, 136
Jiménez, Ricardo, 223, 226
La Jofaina Maravillosa, 259
Joint Distribution Committee (JDC), 47, 58, 66, 147
Joselevich, Moisés, 136
Joseph, Henry, 17–18
Der Judenstaat, 139
El judío en el misterio de la historia, 244
Juris, A. S., 262, 263
Justo, Juan B., 75, 201, 256, 265–268

Kaplan, Eliezer, 149
Karpf, Luis, 274
Kehilla, 74, 260, 316, 319
Kemerer, Jorge, 153
Keren Hayesod, 144–146, 149
Kisse Eliyahu, 30
Kissinger, Henry, 240, 321
Kovadloff, Jacobo, 170
Kristallnacht, 59, 310
Kubovi, Leon, 153
Kuznets, Simon, 195

Laicism, Argentine, 255–257, 269
Lainez, Manuel Mujica, 259
Laluche, 17
La Luz, 32
Landau, David, 76
Landsmanschaften, 31, 313
Language, 31, 181–182, 302, 307, 312
Laskier, Michael, 14, 15
Latin America (*see also individual countries of Latin America*): age structure of Jews in, 102–103; anti-Semitism in, 6, 9–10, 121, 318; anti-Zionism in, 144, 146–148; colonial, 5; conservatism in, 76–77; democracy in, 8–9; demographic trends of Jews in, 85–133; economies, 8; education in, 82; ethnicity in contemporary, 313–315; evolution of Jewish communities in, 7–9, 309–321; and German Jewish refugees, 45–68; ghettoization in, 74–75; hyphenation of Latin American–Jewish, 297–307; isolation of Jews in, 77–78; Judaism in contemporary, 311–313; literature, 298–300; marriage patterns of Jews in, 103–107; middle class in, 3, 8; nationalism in, 3, 4, 9–10; occupational alienation of Jews in, 78–82; outmigration, 78; overview of Jews in, 5–10; population projections for, 127–132; resistance of Jews to assimilation in, 75–76, 215, 267, 271, 279, 318; revolutions in, 3–4; Zionism in, 135–155
Latin American Bishops' Council (CELAM), 318
Latin American Jewish Studies Association (LAJSA), 4n
Latin American–Jewish population estimates, 85–102
Latin American Jewry: A Research Guide, 136
Latin American Weekly Report, 321
Law of Civil Marriage, 18
Law of Extermination, 35
League of Nations, 47, 150, 151
Lebanon, 6, 25, 84, 123, 287
Le Breton, Tomás A., 59–61
Lefebvre, Bishop, 238
Le Goff, Jacques, 33
Leibovici, Sarah, 15
Leitáo, Jeronimo, 37
Lesser, Harriet S., 74
Levine, Shemaryahu, 137
Levingston, Roberto M., 235
Levy, Abraham, 18, 19
Levy, Achille, 19
Levy, Haim (Jaime), 19
Levy, Salvador, 19, 20
Levy, Samuel, 17, 18
Levy, Samuel de, 18n, 21, 22
Levy, Tamar, 18
Lewis, Oscar, 83n
Liberalism, 239–240
Likud government (Israel), 200
Literature: Jewish identity in, 304–307, 318; Latin American, 298–300
Lobo, Helio, 60, 63
Lopez Pumarejo, Alfonso, 53
Lorch, Natanel, 320
Lovers of Zion, 135, 137–138
Löwenthal, Wilhelm, 139
Lugones, 259
Lustiger, Cardinal, 244

Maccabi, 273, 280
McDonald, James G., 47–58
Maduro, Moisés, 220n

Magdalena, Oscar, 240
Malamud, Samuel, 136, 147
Malvinas/Falkland Islands, 287, 322
Mamán, Jose E., 18
Mandrou, Robert, 33
Marmorek, Oscar, 140
Marrano, 34
Marx, Karl, 209, 216, 241, 245
Mayer, Marshall, 240
Meinvielle, Julio, 237, 244–246, 251
Mejía, J. Ramos, 256
Mejía, Jorge, 318
Mellah, 21
Mendes (Castelão), Ines, 37n
Mexico, 5, 10, 71, 76, 77, 317; anti-Israel policy in, 200; emigration from, 121–123; ethnic barriers in, 314; German Jewish refugees and, 55, 61, 64–66; Jewish education in, 164–168, 170, 173, 175, 178–179; Jewish population in, 88, 101–103; Zionism in, 146
Mexico City, Jewish population in, 116
Meyer, Marshall, 274, 281, 283, 312
Middle East, 6, 9, 21, 242, 278, 321
Middleman minorities, Jews as, 210–216
Mil Colores store, 220–222
Minas Gerais, 40
Minorities, 9–10; Jews as middleman, 210–216
Mirelman, Victor A., 136, 142
Mizrahi Bank, 320
Modena, Aquiles, 16, 17n
Mohliver, Shemuel, 138
Le Monde, 234
Monge, Luis Alberto, 230
Montoneros, 251
Morocco, 20
Moroccan Jews, 7, 13–24, 29–30, 32
El Mundo, 260
Mundo Israelita, 260, 264–265
Muños, Calvo, 288
Multinational corporations, 3, 4
Muslims, 24–25

La Nacíon, 258, 263–265
Nahon, Samuel, 18n
National Commission for Jewish-Catholic Dialogue, 318
National Conference of Brazilian Bishops, 318

Nationalism: in Latin America, 3, 4, 9–10; right-wing, in Argentina, 204–208, 233–251
Nazi Germany, 31, 43, 57–59, 83; Jewish refugees from, 45–68
Neighborhoods, Argentine Jewish, 117
New Christians, 33–44
New York Times, 227
Nicarauga, Sandinist, 54, 76, 165n; anti-Semitism in, 230
Nordau, Max, 141
North Africa, 21
Nunes, Guiomar, 42
Núñez, Benjamin, 230

Occupational structure: of Brazilian Jews, 189–196; changes in, among Argentine Jews, 110–112
Olim, characteristics of recent, 124–127
La Opinion, 241
Organization for Rehabilitation through Training (ORT), 170
Ortiz, Roberto M., 61
Osorio, Manoel O., 13
Ottoman Empire Jews, 24–32
Oungre, Louis, 48, 50
Outmigration, of Latin American Jews, 7, 78, 121–123

Pacelli, Cardinal, 48
Palacios, Alfredo, 265
Palestine, 47, 93, 137, 141, 151, 154, 267
Palestine Liberation Organization (PLO), 243, 319
Panama, 54; emigration to Israel from, 121–123
Paraguay, German Jewish refugees in, 52–53
Paraiba, 39
Paulista, Israelita, 312
Peddlers, 25–26, 28–29, 79, 81, 190, 222, 231, 310
Peel, Arthur, 142
Perez, David José, 141–142
Perlzweig, Maurice, 227
Peron, Isabel, 234
Peron, Juan, 121, 205–208, 247, 276, 317
Peronism, 205–208, 233, 247
Peru, 5, 14; emigration to Israel from, 121–

Peru (cont.)
  123; German Jewish refugees and, 53; Jewish education in, 165
Picado Michelski, Teodoro, 225–226
Pinochet, Augusto, 77, 319
Pinsker, Leo, 138
Pius XI (pope), 238, 244
Plaut, Juan, 80
Pluralism, 75, 83, 84, 204, 208, 257, 271
Poale Zedek, 20
Poalei Zion Smol, 277
Polish Jews, 59, 179, 242; in Costa Rica, 219–227
"Polish payments," 222
Politics: Jewish politicians, 5, 6, 80, 81; of Latin American Jews, 316–323; political attitudes of Brazilian Jews, 196–199
Population: of Latin American Jews, estimated, 85–102; projections, 127–132
Portugal, 13–14, 15, 20, 34, 35
Portuguese Jews, 5, 34, 38, 39–43
Positivism, 256–257, 269
Poverty, 14, 15
La Prensa, 263–265
Presencia, 234
Protestantism, 72, 214

Racism, 43, 62, 207–208, 210, 243, 244
Radical Party (Argentina), 247
Rauch, Eduardo, 183
Raz, Emanuel, 274
Recife, 16
Reform movement, 312–313
Reichsvertretung der Juden in Deutschland, 59
Religion, 7, 8, 15, 19, 23; in contemporary Latin America, 311–313
Research Conference on the Jewish Experience in Latin America, 4
Resnick, Salomón, 260
Retail sales, 223
Ribbi, Abraham, 18
Ricard, Robert, 15
Rio de Janeiro, 40, 50, 74; Jewish education in, 180; occupational structure in, 189–196; Zionism in, 141
Rio Grande de Norte, 39
Robles, Alfredo Sasso, 220n
Roca, President, 255
Rojas, Augustín, 258

Rojas, Ricardo, 263
Roosevelt, Franklin, 57, 58, 59, 61
Rose, Arnold, 210
Rosenswaike, I., 89, 96
Rothschild, M., 142
Rousseau, Jean Jacques, 255
Russian Jews, 20, 22, 25, 71
Russian Revolution, 241

Saavedra Lamas, Carlos, 61
Sable, Martin, 40
Sacheri, Carlos A., 237, 251
Sagarna, J., 264–265
Salvador, 54
Sammartino, Ernesto, 236
Sanches, Antonio N. R., 41
São Paulo, 82, 101; Jewish education in, 180; Jewish population in, 116; occupational structure of Jews in, 189–196
São Paulo University, 44
Sarmiento, Domingo, 256–257
Sartre, Jean Paul, 293
Schamun, Alejandro, 26
Schamun, Wadi, 26
Schers, David, 164n, 167, 170, 171, 175
Schiff, Jacob, 241
Schifter, Salomón, 226
Schmelz, U. O., 93, 127, 314
Schneider, Jacob, 142
Second Vatican Council, 250
Senderey, Alberto, 274
Sephardic Jews, 7, 13–32, 38, 71, 74, 78, 170, 179, 182, 217, 219, 226, 280, 317
Serfaty, León, 18, 20
Serido, 39
Shalom, Hector, 274, 279
Shamir, Yitzhak, 230
Sikora, David, 226
Silvert, Kalman, 207
Six-Day War, 123
Smith, John K., 162, 173, 181
Smyrna, 20, 21
Sneh, 180
Sobel, Henry, 312
Socialist Party (Argentina), 265–269
Social mobility, of Jews in Brazil, 187–200; context, 188–189; ideology and political attitudes, 196–199; occupational and social stratification, 189–196
Social status, 310–311; of Argentine Jews,

213–216, 275; of Brazilian Jews, 190–196; of Costa Rican Jews, 229–230; self-image and, 293–294
Sociedad Centro-Comercial de Beneficencia, 143
Sociedad Hebraica, 261–262
Sociedad de Proteción a los Immigrantes Israelites (SOPROTIMIS), 45
Sociodemographic characteristics: Argentine Jewry, 107–119; ecological correlates, 112–120; generational correlates, 110–112
Sofer, Eugene, 80, 81
Son, Henrique, 139
Sotto, Samuel, 17, 19, 20
Soviet Jews, 310
Soviet Union, 151, 321
Spain, 14, 15, 21, 34, 216; civil war in, 67, 247, 250
Spanish-Moroccan War, 14
Spotlight, 242
Steinhardt, Aharon, 274
Stockholm International Peace Research Institute (SIPRI), 321
Survival, group identity and, 304–305
Sweatshop, 74
Switzerland, 61
Syrian Jews: emigration, 26, 28; immigration, 25–26, 28–30
Szenkolewski, Silvia, 136
Szomstein, Cirile, 146
Szomstein, Samuel, 146

Tangier, 13–15, 20–23
Tétouan, 13–15, 20–23
Teubal, Ezra, 29
Teubal, Nissim, 29
"Theory of Middleman Minorities, A," 210
Third World, 7, 200
Tif'ereth Zion, 141
Time, 234
Timmerman, Jacobo, 76, 240
Toledo, Ricardo, 225
Trilling, Lionel, 84
Trotsky, Lev, 241
Trujillo Molina, Rafael L., 55, 66
Trujillo Molina, Virgilio, 65
Tuoff, Elio, 84
Turcos, 25n, 26
Turkey, 20, 26–29
Turkish Jews, 7

Ulate, Otilio, 226, 227, 228
Ullman, Luis, 18
Union *Israelita* en Chile, 143
United Jewish Appeal, 152, 319
United Nations, 151, 155
United States, 7, 8, 24, 241, 314; immigration to, 72–73, 78, 84, 93, 96, 287; intermarriage in, 108; –Israel policy, 321–322; Jewish education in, 158–159; power in Latin America, 3, 4; Syrian Jews in, 26, 28
Urbanization, 314–315
Uruguay, 5, 8; emigration to Israel from, 121–123; German Jewish refugees and, 51–52; Jewish population in, 88; Zionism in, 146

Vaad, 174
La Vanguardia, 265, 267–268
Vargas, Getulio, 49, 62
Velasco Ibarra, Jose M., 53
Venezuela, 5; emigration to Israel from, 121–123; Jewish education in, 179; Jewish population in, 88; Zionism in, 146–147
Vida Nuestra, 75, 266
Villa Michel, Primo, 61, 64–65

Waldman, Morris D., 148
Warburg, Jacob, 241
Warsaw, 221, 310
Weber, Max, 210
Weill, S., 89, 96
Weinstein, Quito, 274
Weiser, Benno, 152
Weizman, Jaim, 229
Wilde, Eduardo, 256
World Jewish Congress, 147, 227
World Jewry: population distribution, 87–88; population projections, 127–132
World War I, 15, 27, 29
World War II, 67, 81, 86, 89, 188, 247
World Zionist Organization, 135, 137, 139–140, 144, 154, 170, 176, 280
Wortman, Marcos, 267
Writers, Latin American–Jewish, 297–307, 318

Yagupsky, Maximo, 148
Yankelewitz, Doris, 230

Yankelewitz, Enrique, 220–221
Yarden, Rachel Sephardi, 150
Yiddish, 31, 181–182, 302, 307
Yofe, Danny, 274
Yom Kippur War, 242, 278
Young Turks, 27, 29
Youth movements, Zionist, 273–282
Yuris, A. S., 146

Zadoff, Efraim, 167, 173, 179
Zalazar Altamira, Guillermo, 51

Zangwill, Israel, 140
Zionism, 21, 32, 73, 76, 84, 292, 301; in Argentina, 142–143, 145, 148–149, 212, 247, 251, 273–282; in Brazil, 140–142, 145, 147; in Chile, 143–144; in Cuba, 143, 144; early years, 137–140; and establishment of Israel, 150–154; formative years, 144–145; in Holocaust era, 146–150; in Latin America, 135–155; in Venezuela, 146–147; and youth movements, 273–282

For Product Safety Concerns and Information please contact our EU representative GPSR@taylorandfrancis.com
Taylor & Francis Verlag GmbH, Kaufingerstraße 24, 80331 München, Germany

www.ingramcontent.com/pod-product-compliance
Lightning Source LLC
Chambersburg PA
CBHW071758300426
44116CB00009B/1132